ACTIONISM

HOW TO BECOME A RESPONSIBLE MAN

LENNART SVENSSON

Actionism: How to Become a Responsible Man
Lennart Svensson

© Manticore Press, 2017

All rights reserved, no section of this book may be utilized without permission, including electronic reproductions without the permission of the author and publisher. Published in Australia.

BIC Classification:
HPX (Popular Philosophy)

978-0-9945958-7-4

MANTICORE PRESS
WWW.HADEAN.BLACK

THE TEN BASIC TENETS OF ACTIONISM

1. C3 – *Calm, Cool and Collected.*
2. WTPOY – *Will To Power Over Yourself*
3. MMM – *Memento Mori Mindset*
4. ARYM – *Action Raising You Mentally*
5. MAASOM – *Movement As A State of Mind*
6. WAP – *Winning As Propensity*
7. RIA – *Rest In Action*
8. RIR – *Rest In Rest*
9. TIOHAN – *There Is Only Here And Now*
10. ESWY – *Everything Starts With You*

THE FIVE CENTRAL CONCEPTS OF ACTIONISM

1. I Am
2. Active Idealism
3. Responsible Man
4. Midsummer Century
5. Action as Being

Actionism is about summoning your Will to lead your Thought, merging the two to Will-Thought and affirming the Inner Light, a spark of the Divine Light. To all this, saying "I AM" is the performative confirmation.

TABLE OF CONTENTS

Introduction   8

PART I: THE MICROCOSM

1. *Fundamentals of Actionism*   13
2. *Mental Calm*   22
3. *Action as Being*   27
4. *Idealism versus Materialism*   38
5. *Active Idealism*   47
6. *Operational Esotericism*   52
7. *Metaphysical Action*   57
8. *Actionist Art*   61
9. *Eternal Values*   65
10. *Carlitos*   67
11. *d'Annunzio*   93
12. *Evolian Aspects*   109
13. *Lawrence*   128
14. *Operations 1*   134

15. Operations 2	*155*
16. Operations 3	*163*
17. Operations 4	*177*
18. Operations 5	*186*

PART II: THE MACROCOSM

19. Outline of History	*192*
20. Globalism versus Nationalism	*204*
21. Co-Nationalism	*208*
22. Declining War Trend	*213*
23. Frequency War	*220*
24. The Worst Is Behind Us	*224*
25. Politics of the Future	*230*
26. Nature of Decadence	*237*
27. Society of the Future	*243*
28. Antropolis	*251*
29. Actionist Diary	*266*

PART III: SAT YUGA SUGGESTIONS

30. The Coming Golden Age	*347*
31. Actionist Musings	*355*
32. Variations on a Theme by Poe	*362*
33. Will and Thought, Fire and Movement...	*371*
34. Deliberations	*382*
35. About God	*396*
36. The Dane	*407*

37. Der Pulverkopf	413
38. Spirit of Actionism	419
39. Actionist Poems	425
40. Hymn to the Active Life	436
41. Actionist Summary	447
42. Coda: Responsible Man	455
Disclaimer	457
Sources	458
About the Author	461
Index	462

INTRODUCTION

Actionism is a doctrine about everything, conceptualizing man's relationship to the world.

Actionism is optimism. Actionism is Fire and Movement, going Beyond the Beyond. The sky's no limit.

Actionism is a rebellion for Tradition, a meditation advocating action. Actionism is about idealism taking on the forces of materialism. Actionism is an active esotericism fighting the dead world of materialism, currently holding the world in its grip.

- - -

Actionism is many things: it's (1) an ethic footed in being (2) a system of tenets, condensed into acronyms (3) a comprehensive outlook on history (4) a system of beliefs encompassing all aspects of the contemporary world: politics, morals, arts, lifestyles – everything.

- - -

Actionism is a way of conceptualizing man's relationship to the world – both to the small world and the world at large, the micro- and macrocosm, man's personal Self and the world he lives in. "Conceptualize everything" is the motto, so to speak.

- - -

Actionism is a conceptual tool in a fight for freedom – freedom for you, freedom for the whole world.

- - -

Actionism is a doctrine and an attitude. It's an active esotericism. Actionism is about action and knowledge, Will and Thought, the pen and the sword.

- - -

In verse 3.5 of the Bhagavad-Gîtâ it says: you have to act. As a living, breathing individual you have to act. In order to sustain the body you can't abstain from acting. Every living creature has to act, even if it only means to breathe. This is the basis of Actionism.

Guiding people in how to act is called ethics. The discipline where you ponder over, elaborate upon and state how to act is called ethics. As for the ethical side of Actionism, it's an ethic of action, footed in ontology – in metaphysics, in essential reality. Most modern ethical theories forget that metaphysical part. This theory doesn't. This ethical system is based on the idea of reality being essentially spiritual (= non-material) in nature. Man has a soul, a divine element governing his physical body. The strictly ethical chapters of this book are to be found in Part I (Chapters 1 to 7).

Part I is the *microcosmic* part of the study, the one focusing on the individual. Part II focuses on the *macrocosmic* aspect of reality, like history (Chapter 19) and the politics of today: what's unfruitful, as well as options and ways ahead (Chapters 25-27). Part III deliberates further on themes already presented, generally tying up loose ends and aiming at a synthesis.

- - -

The book you're currently reading, *Actionism*, is a work of ethics – and ethics always have to be based in Being. This is the basis of the Perennial School of Thought, the doctrine expressed in the traditional creed of the East and the West, the perennial philosophy of Plato, Plotinus, Shankara, Goethe and Jünger. Actionism takes the gist of this philosophy and couples it to marginally different, more modern strains, such as the thought of Evola, Castaneda and Kierkegaard, making it all into a philosophy of action – and, as such, a hymn to the operational life, the active life, since we all have to act: even the forest recluse bent on meditating, because even a meditating quietist has to breathe, and to breathe is to act.

Actionism is a doctrine along these lines, a personal moral with the possibility to expand into a societal moral, a model for our whole human society at the beginning of the 21st century. The current politics are bent on materialism, degeneracy and irresponsibility. Actionism, on both the personal and societal level, stresses responsibility. This is sorely needed today.

- - -

In 2016, I published the book *Borderline – A Traditionalist Outlook for Modern Man*. It's a survey of the perennial thought of Western and Eastern tradition, the world-view saying that the material world is of a lower reality than the spiritual world. Invisible patterns and ideas govern the world; it can't be reduced to a serially working machine. *Wholes* govern both man and the cosmos. In delineating this, *Borderline* (1) summarized the ontology of Plotinus and his followers Goethe, Hugo Fischer and Ernst Jünger (2) criticized the reductionist strain in contemporary science and (3) gave a moral outline along the lines of holism, (man's soul as a mirror of God and the reality of Will as an elemental force). In this moral outlook, *Borderline* coined some acronyms that are used in this book, too (along with some specifically coined ones).

Overall, *Borderline* was a discussion and a metaphysical deliberation. *Actionism*, for its part, is a moral statement and a self-help guide. *Actionism* can be seen as the logical conclusion of *Borderline*. Both books mirror each other, both are based in perennial thought, both are founded in traditional philosophy as explained to contemporary man.

Man in the 21st century has to take responsibility for his being – both as a man of the world and as a spiritual being. He has to acknowledge his inner light; he has to assume responsibility for his soul and his place in society. Will fosters responsibility; Will is what modern man has to rediscover, Will is what's needed for modern man to become a Responsible Man.

Responsible Man is the man of the future. Responsible Man is the Actionist coda, end product and outcome.

Härnösand 26/7 2016

LENNART SVENSSON

PART I

The Microcosm

1. FUNDAMENTALS OF ACTIONISM

Actionism is a doctrine encompassing everything: from ethics to politics, from individual moral to global perspectives. In this and the next few chapters, the emphasis is on the individual sphere, on personal morality and conduct. It's about the ontological framework and the resultant creed, an ethic footed in Reality.

WHY ACTIONISM?

You might ask, "Why the label 'Actionism' to this creed? What makes *action* so special?" This, I'll now tell you.

The thing of it is, we all have to act. Even a forest recluse spending his days meditating must act. He must at least breathe. To breathe is to act. True, we can't volitionally stop breathing. But we can affect the way we breathe.

The very human condition is to act. This is expressed in two verses of the Bhagavad-Gîtâ, 3:5 a-b and 3:8 c-d:

> na hi kashcit kshanam api jâtu tishthaty akarma-krit (...)
> sharîra-yâtrâpi ca te na prasiddhyed akarmanah
> No one can, not even for an instant, remain wholly passive. (...)
> You can't sustain your body without working.

As human beings endowed with a physical body, we have to act in order to sustain our body. We have to breathe, we have to drink, we have to fetch food and eat it. This is action, this is Actionism.

More on action, per se, later in this chapter: the human way of acting, of *ethics* proper. First, some words on action having a cosmic character. You could say: Actionism is a *total concept*, encompassing both the microcosm and the macrocosm, man and the world. And in the beginning, the world = the universe, it was created by an act. "In the Beginning was the Deed," it reads in Goethe's *Faust*. "Im Anfang war die Tat!" Dr. Faust says in Chapter 6 of that play. Strictly speaking, there were other forces around than merely action, but to even speak of a "beginning," the start of a process, something has to happen. Like in the axiom: "time is measured movement;" something has to stir, to move, to change, in order for an event to even be called an event.

Thus, in the beginning was Action. With a founding in diverse sources, I propose the following Myth of Creation.

THE DEED

In the beginning was the Deed.

In the primordial abyss existed Will and Thought. And Will, according to its very nature, was the first to get going. It stirred; it willed itself to Will, to commit a Deed. In the beginning was the Deed.

Will got going; Will stirred in the primordial abyss. Will thus united itself with Thought. This dual entity, this Will-Thought, this Dyad of action and truth, now had to make a choice between the forces, Light and Dark. These two forces were also around in the beginning, in the same way as Will and Thought were primordially around. And, to make a long story short, Will-Thought chose to unite itself with Light.

Thus *God* came into existence, singing out I AM as a confirmation of the event. God had been realized, this radiant being of Light, a dyad of Will and Thought. As such, it immediately began to depolarize the Darkness.

Thus: in the beginning was the Deed = Action = Will. The

beginning saw Willpower willing itself to get going, to act. As intimated, Action is a fundamental of existence, for both cosmos and man. As human beings, we can't abstain from acting.

WILL AND THOUGHT

Will and Thought were primordially present. To think is a primordial activity, in line with the above, saying that primeval Will united itself with Thought. But Will has to take control of Thought, otherwise everything runs the risk of going off into weirdness – so in the divine realm, and so in the human.

Willpower controls the mind; mind controls the body. That is how Deeds are done. Individual Will wills itself to act, in order to ultimately join with the Light. Thus, there is no evil Will. Conversely, that which is drawn toward the Dark is lack of Will = desire = materialism.

Action is the fundamental of existence. Action is the uttering of Will wishing to join itself with Light. Thus, the history of man is the history of Action – of actions performed by men of action, leading us from the Dark to the Light. To act is to execute the endemic nature of Will to strive for the Light.

Action is the basis of existence, along with Thought. Sometimes you can discern Will from Thought, sometimes not. As intimated they merged in the beginning, together with Light making up God. Per se, Will-Thought can be seen as a unified concept, the two constituting elements having become one, a higher amalgam of being than they were as separate forces.

To all this, I have to add the concept of Compassion, because there was a phase even before Will willed itself to move. In the primordial abyss, before Will and Thought, Light and Dark, there existed what I will call *the nothingness now*: it was silence, sympathy, and compassion. This primordial Compassion will always exist, always be. Reportedly and mythically, it had the form of a glorified, golden egg. From this original egg was born the above intimated forces

ACTIONISM

of Will and Thought, Light and Dark. Thus God, when the above mentioned merger of Will-Thought-Light happened, became more than this. He became a composite force of Will, Thought, Light and Compassion, since this latter element is ever-present throughout the universe, being part of its immanent structure.

Above was intimated that this "Will-Truth-Compassion" pattern is based on various sources. Specifically, in esoteric theory, the idea of "the threefold flame" is established since way back, envisioning the triplet of Will, Compassion and Truth as the fundamental of existence. The idea is found in Gnosticism and Mithraic mysteries, and in some modern esoteric thought. For example, the idea of Will and Thought having a fundamental, ontological role is showcased in the document *Vandrer mod lyset*, Agerskov 1916.

ETERNAL VALUES

In other words, God came into being as a composite of Will, Thought and Compassion, embracing the Light. Then, what happened?

This: God, in his most sublime of heavens, in his causal sphere = the World of Ideas, next established the eternal values. From Will was derived duty, fidelity, courage and accountability. From Truth was derived honesty and justice. From Compassion was derived benevolence, enthusiasm, clemency, equanimity and magnanimity.

DYAD

God had come into existence and he became the source of the eternal values. Later, Man's soul was created from a spark of the Eternal Light of God. Thus, Man also became a composite creature: a dyad of Will and Thought placed between the Dark and the Light. But the divine patronage gave Man an inherent disposition to walk toward the Light.

Man was a dyad of Will and Thought, imbued with Compassion, as was God. Micro and macrocosm mirrored each other: as above, so below. And when the reflectively minded Men looked inwards, into the Light, they saw the eternal values: duty, fidelity, honesty, clemency etc. as intimated above.

HOW TO ACT

Thus the Myth of Creation being the fundamental of Actionism. Now for some ethical elaborations on this, on the basis of man being an eternal soul in a mortal body, of man being a creature endowed with Will, Thought and Compassion.

The science of ethics is to answer the question, "How shall I act?" As mentioned, the most basic human form of acting is breathing. So as an Actionist, you have to be able to control your breath, to calm down your way of breathing. This is done by Willpower, to will yourself to take a deep breath.

More on systematic relaxation in the next chapter. Here, the focus is on the more common forms of human action. How to act in order to be a more secure, harmonious human being.

A fundamental of Actionist ethics is MMM = the Memento Mori Mindset = to be aware that you're mortal. To be fully aware that the lifespan of your physical body has an end is a knowledge that in the long run is likely to assure you. It's true that the first phase of acknowledging this can be disconcerting but this is a transient phase. Willpower is the remedy: will yourself not to be so angst-ridden by this knowledge, one that every human being has to affirm. If you shy away from the Reality of Physical Death you'll become less than human, a frightened animal.

Don't be afraid of death. This will only strengthen it. Instead you must accept death, internalize it and live forever.

VOLITIONAL

These are the fundamentals of acting: (1) to calm down your breath and (2) to existentially calm down by acknowledging death.

ACTIONISM

"How shall I act?" – The above intimated forces of Will, Thought and Compassion can give an answer to that question, leading the way in formulating an Actionist ethic.

As for *Will*, it's a rather underrated force in human dynamics. But as a matter of fact, it's a central element of what makes us human. See above: in the beginning was Will. Will, united with Thought and merged with Light, is the fundamental of both the micro and macrocosm.

To Will is to Will the good. Therefore, there is no fundamental "dilemma of choosing" in ethics. Since the beginning, Will is united with Light, therefore to Will is to Will the Light. Contrariwise, the lack of Will leads to materialism and darkness.

Will is spiritual; lack of Will equals desire. Will is constructive; lack of Will is destructive. As it says in The Gospel of Philip, verse 64: "Will doesn't make them into sinners, but lack of will does".

WILL TO POWER

The Actionist, volitional life is about Will To Power Over Yourself, expressed in the acronym WTPOY. This is an Actionist interpretation of Nietzscheism, making the individual the focus of the volitional life.

Acknowledge your Will. Let faith in your personal power, directed toward positive, constructive goals, be the guiding light in your life. This is the victory of faith = the triumph of troth. Acknowledge the bright nature of Will – like the will to survive, the will to be a better, less indulgent person, the will to persevere through hard times – and triumph over darkness and despair.

Will is about taking responsibility, for yourself and others. Will is needed both for climbing a mountain and for calming down in meditation. Will is needed both for the *vita activa* and the *vita contemplativa*.

The volitional life is strong and active. This is formalized into the

Actionist acronym ASARIT = A Strong And Responsible Idealist, Taking charge. This means: the Actionist is a paragon of vigor and responsibility, embodying Norman Schwarzkopf's dictum: "*When placed in command, take charge.*" [quoted after Atkinson p 42].

THOUGHT

The second primal force of reality, a basic element of both Man and God, is *Thought*, equal to Truth. As we've seen, Will and Thought merged in the beginning and they can often be said to form the dyad "Will-Thought". It's sometimes hard to separate them. However, there is the case of "your thought wandering off," of Thought going off into less fruitful realms. Then Will has to step in and take charge, halting the straying Thought. When Will has command of every thought and every emotion, then you live a volitional, Actionist life. It's true that Thought has to be free, too, letting it roam constructively and creatively, but in the case of Thought leading you astray into angst and despair, Will has to go in and take control.

Thought equals Truth. To think is to seek truth. Acknowledge this and you're on the path to Actionist clarity.

COMPASSION

The third elemental force in this pattern is *Compassion*. As intimated, it's even older than the created universe; it's the primordial silence, the female nature of the void permeating everything, then and now, before, during and after the existence of the conditioned cosmos.

Compassion is akin to enthusiasm, benevolence, inspiration, the love you feel for your fellow human beings, for fish and fowl, the wonders of nature. Compassion is about the love of Self = "love your neighbor as thyself = everything starts in "self-love," in affirming and acknowledging that you're an individual, an ideo-ethical operation depending on the I AM-impulse to be embraced as a matter of course.

A DICTUM

Will, Truth and Compassion balance each other. Having them all present in your heart makes you into an integrated esotericist, an Actionist prepared for anything.

To integrate these impulses makes you into a whole being. As an Actionist you have to see wholes, the big picture. In Doing Stuff in the everyday world you of course have to analyze problems and separate them into their constituent parts, but an eye to The Whole has to always be present. To merely deconstruct leads nowhere.

I just mentioned "the I AM-impulse". If Actionism can be summarized into one, single formula, it's this: *I AM*. You could say: the I AM-dictum is the answer to "life, universe and everything." It's the phrase summarizing the holism of Will-Thought-Compassion, the dictum acknowledging man's divine nature; it's the saying affirming that we exist as conscious human beings.

The origin of the I AM-saying is found in the Bible, in The Gospel of John, with a certain desert prophet stating, on different occasions, "I am the true vine, I am the good shepherd, I am the door, I am the way, the truth, the life, I am the resurrection and the life, I am the light of the world, I am the bread of life". Also, In the Old Testament the God met by another desert prophet, the God saying "I Am That I Am," was an uttering of this same motto, (according to Rudolf Steiner). The Logos of Christian esotericism is this selfsame "I AM". Steiner meant: in the beginning was Logos, whose name is "I Am." And when in the Gospels we hear about "glorifying your name," this *name* also refers to "I AM". More on this in *Borderline*.

Thus, Actionism, in acknowledging this, is in line with the *esoteric* interpretation of Christianity. Actionism is a volitional creed stressing man's inner powers; no Christian priest or church is telling the Actionist what to think. But overall, the Actionist creed has some connection to the esoteric, primordial tradition, as regards

Christianity and other doctrines, like some aspects of Hindu thought found in the Bhagavad-Gîtâ (for instance, the latter document I quoted at the beginning of this chapter).

To say "I AM" is to affirm your inner, divine Light. To say "I AM" is to acknowledge that you exist as a conscious, reflecting, volitional human being. To say "I AM" is to be free and operational at the same time, the symbolic dictum of a Responsible Man living his life as an Actionist operation.

2. MENTAL CALM

To be tranquil is fundamental to the human existence. To act and yet remain calm, that's one of the goals of Actionism. To be Calm, Cool and Collected = C3 = is a basic element of Actionism. Actionism can be seen as a system of tenets where you don't need to know every one by heart. However, to be an Actionist you have to know the phenomenon of volitional mental calm.

WILL IS THE WEAPON

The enemy of calm is angst = anxiety. In our everyday, angst seems to be stalking us. Sudden attacks of anxiety can unnerve us. Thus, how not to succumb to these attacks?

Angst equals fear. Anxiety attacks give rise to fear-based thinking. This is counteracted by Willpower, by Will-governed Thought = Will-Thought.

Will is the sword, killing the dragon of angst. If you notice that you're under attack by angst, take a deep breath and assess the situation. In being assaulted in this way, assaulted by angst, ask yourself: are you thinking clearly? Are you reacting like a beast or a man?

If you're slipping away, if panic is starting to get hold of you, take a deep, gentle breath and say to yourself, "I will not succumb to fear, fear is the mind-killer". Then, having met angst in this way, you regain mental balance and can go on as before – with equanimity.

RELAXING

The central issue of equanimity is this: we have to have it in whatever we do, whether it's something nice or something trying. If you're excited about going to a party – calm down. If you're worrying about a visit to the dentist – calm down. This doesn't mean that "perfect apathy, perfect balance, perfect indifference" should prevail at every moment. Instead, you must be at least "51% positive", being slightly above the balance level.

And overall, you have to calm down. This is done by taking a deep breath. It can be done standing up, sitting down or lying down. Generally, it helps if you start by gently blowing out the air of your lungs. Then a deep breath follows automatically.

When relaxing standing up, stand with arms relaxed, hanging down, and with the weight distributed equally on both legs. The knees should be slightly bent. Then take a deep breath – gently, not forced. Next, you're allowed to take more than one such breath.

When relaxing sitting down, sit in a straight chair with support for the back. Your feet should both be firmly placed on the ground. Your hands can be folded. Then take that deep breath. And being settled in that gentle breathing mood, you can go on and breath meditatively.

When relaxing lying down, lie on your back, with legs outstretched (not one over the other). The hands can be folded or, with outstretched arms, rest just beside the body. Then take that deep breath.

WILLPOWER TAKING CHARGE

Calming down in this way is essentially an inner phenomenon. It's the workings of the Will. It's Willpower taking charge – over your thought, over your respiration.

It might help saying it out loud: "I am now upset, I want to calm down" or some such. This, of course, is done in private. But this kind of "mini-meditation" can also be done in public. Both the "relaxing standing up" and "relaxing sitting down" techniques sketched above can be done in public, *mutatis mutandum*.

INNER SILENCE

An important part of calming down is Inner Silence. When you've taken that mythological, gentle, calm breath, then the stage is set for quieting down your inner monologue. Stop thinking about everyday trifles and gain peace of mind. In Actionist lingo this is called, "reaching inner silence" = to willfully quiet down your internal monologue. For this you may use simple mantras like "I will now calm down" or "I will now empty my mind of useless thoughts".

C3

If you systematically muster Will in instances like these, if you calm down your breath and silence your inner, haphazard monologue, then you're on to something. If you, with time, and having practiced to calm down in this way, become equanimous before things that used to upset you, then you're C3. If you choose to avoid morning papers and mainstream media websites, things that used to interest you but then only tended to annoy you, then you're C3.

If you know how to avoid TV programs that bore you, disturb you or upset you, then you're C3.

If you stop seeing friends that drain you of energy, people that curb your enthusiasm and creativity, then you're C3.

If you go out in the kitchen about to make lunch and get the impulse to stand relaxed for a while, taking a deep breath – then you're C3.

If you're sitting down surfing on the net and get the urge to just halt the activity for a while, relaxing and breathing – then you're C3.

To become C3 = Calm, Cool and Collected, is hard for some, easier for others. It may take years before you reach that immanent, inherent calm. To reach it you need Willpower. It's done by mustering your Will, stating your ambition to become C3 in your everyday, and getting going.

You could say: the Actionist way of relaxing is about reaching inner silence = to willfully quiet down your inner monologue, your constant brooding. Inner Silence opens up for "mobilizing inner forces". With these inner forces, this mental energy, an overall state of C3 will be attainable.

INNER MONOLOGUE

For its part, "quieting down the inner monologue" is stressed in the Castaneda books. To reach mental calm you need to stop the mind from wandering, stop the endless internal discussion. Will has to take control over Thought. On top of this, taking a deep breath further calms you.

These things are simple but difficult. In your life, have you ever taken a deep, calm breath? Try it, you'll like it. To calm down the breath frees the mind.

We all have to act; we all have to breathe. To have some control over how you breathe is a fundamental part of living. It might be the beginning of a calmer, more efficient conduct of life. But you *have* to take that deep breath, it's got to be done IRL; this is no theoretical discussion.

This kind of "mini-meditation" can be done throughout the day. Example: you surf on the internet and a certain page takes some time to load. Instead of being stressed out over this, take this as an opportunity for a deep, calm breath.

The same goes for waiting in line, waiting for a TV program to start airing, waiting for the spaghetti to boil: instead of lamenting the fact that you have to wait, use the moment for a deep, calm breath. As intimated, such a breath should be gentle, not forced.

ACTIONISM

SELF-RESTRAINT

Self-restraint is a golden word. This is what you perform when into the phenomenon of volitional mental calm. You might be stressed out but you stop it by willpower.

You're a Man, not an animal. A thirsty animal rushes straight to the water bowl and drinks. An equally thirsty Man has the ability to restrain himself. Even if he has crossed a desert, is about to die of thirst and finally reaches a well, he can approach it in an orderly fashion. This is because he has Will prominent in his mindset. With Will he can raise himself to a higher plane, a plane of dignity.

RESTING

The Actionist way of seeking volitional calm is a glorified way of resting. For instance, if you lie down, calm your thoughts and then fall asleep, it's OK. However, in the more elaborate systems of *dhyâna yoga* ("ashtânga yoga" etc.), of "sitting down and meditating like a Buddha," to fall asleep is forbidden. But C3 is no system of *dhyâna yoga*; it's a basic, Actionist way of systematically calming down.

3. ACTION AS BEING

Actionism encompasses everything. We all have to act, we all have a Will. In order to sustain the body we all have to act, whatever we call ourselves. The Actionist, in knowing this, makes acting into an art. Turning necessity into a virtue, his life is a constant mission, a constant operation. He seeks peace in action = RIA = Rest In Action = to rest while doing something. It's the Tao of acting: "act as if you didn't act". Constantly relaxed and constantly on the go, the Actionist life is a state of total awareness and total dedication.

ACTIVE SIDE OF ACTIONISM

The "active" side of Actionism, this "constantly relaxed, constantly on the go" aspect may sound like a trying experience. However, an Actionist can also seek Rest In Rest = RIR. For instance, if you come home after a hard day's work you don't want to rest by climbing a mountain. Rather, you lie down, reach mental calm and do something ordinarily relaxing like reading, listening to music etc. Or you just lie down and think of nothing = you seek rest in rest, peace in peace and silence in silence.

Otherwise, the "more actively disposed" may be interested in Action as a way of life, acting as if not acting, seeking rest in action. In this way you can get embroiled in the action, like the artist being totally involved in his work. It's a kind of trance. If done correctly, it's enriching and in itself giving you energy. If not, then it's a case of stress, of being overwrought.

Being embroiled in your work in a positive way is expressed in the sentence, "You are the mission, the mission is you." This is the holistic, total mindset of an Actionist making himself identify with the operation he's currently performing – a glorified trance, possible to reach only by a person who has spent his whole life operating consciously.

Action in this way is to have contact with Being, with the cosmos. The seasoned Actionist performs his activities as if supra-conducted, transcending time and space. This is expressed in the concept of, "the operating self in the infinite here, the eternal now".

OPERATIONS

The Actionist conducts operations in order to be free. Besides "operating for the sake of operating," he operates to become wiser, he operates to gain knowledge. His life is a glorified Intelligence Operation. We come here to learn and the Actionist lives this wisdom in an operational way.

This can be rendered as, "conducting operations to attain knowledge". This is about making education into an intelligence operation. This is about the recon patrol as a symbol of getting smarter, getting a wider outlook, becoming more informed – about yourself and the world at large.

In this, you do like Napoleon: you get going in order to clarify the situation. This is NAMO = the Napoleonic Modus Operandi, expressed in his words as, "*on s'engage et puis on verra*" = "get going, then take a look around". This means: get going operationally in order to clarify the situation. Some situations can't be grasped by merely looking at the map, instead, you have to become tangibly engaged in them to fully fathom them.

I'll return to NAMO in this study, for example, in Chapter 14 where I deliberate on operational issues of the military kind.

CHALLENGES

The Actionist acts in order to gain knowledge, be wiser, and master his world conceptually. Like Napoleon he gets going in order to clarify the situation. War can be a simile to this operational attitude and the Actionist can be seen as a warrior. Thus Carlos Castaneda says:

> *"Only as a warrior can one withstand the path of knowledge. A warrior cannot complain or regret anything. His life is an endless challenge, and challenges cannot possibly be good or bad. Challenges are simply challenges."* [Castaneda 1974 p 108]

Castaneda, by way of his teacher Don Juan Matus, is rather 'in' for the warrior metaphor. Keep in mind that it's just a metaphor – so please, don't "dress your soul in camouflage" and go ballistic when hearing of "war as being". The gist of the warrior-as-a-man-of-knowledge is given thus:

> *"A man goes to knowledge as he goes to war, wide awake, with fear, with respect, and with absolute assurance. Going to knowledge or going to war in any other manner is a mistake, and whoever makes it might never live to regret it."* [Castaneda 1990 I p 52]

In Actionist terms this talk of being a warrior means: to be C3, to be totally concentrated and totally relaxed with a MMM = Memento Mori Mindset. It has got nothing to do with violence and destruction, those which "war" might also associate with.

Another fine Castaneda quote summarizing the warrior mindset in question is this:

ACTIONISM

"Only as a warrior can one withstand the path of knowledge. A warrior cannot complain or regret anything. His life is an endless challenge, and challenges cannot possibly be good or bad. Challenges are simply challenges." [Ibid 1974 p 108]

WINNING

An Actionist performs operations. An Actionist is always successful in this. This means: he posits attainable goals, constantly. An operation of this kind is, "to take a deep breath". Having successfully taken that deep, invigorating breath, the Actionist has conducted an operation. He has won; he experiences victory and triumph. This is what Actionism calls WAP = Winning As Propensity = learning to win = to constantly posit attainable goals in your personal operation and, having reached them, acknowledge them as the victories they are.

On winning, Don Juan (as "John Michael Abelar") says: *"[S]orcerers have only one path open to them: to succeed in whatever they do."* [Abelar p 207]

OPERATIONS

Castaneda by way of his teacher, Don Juan, has some insight into Action as Being. To have inspiration in your acting, to conduct operations as a form of leisure, to act as if not acting, to perform hard tasks while rising to the occasion, this is a very special state of mind and Don Juan describes it thus:

"I would say that the best of us always comes out when we are against the wall, when we feel the sword dangling overhead. Personally, I wouldn't have it any other way." [Castaneda 1974 p 146]

Again, this might seem like a hard life, a trying life. And it is, to the beginner. But the accomplished Actionist has this mindset engraved in him by years of practice. And, to be sure, Castaneda was trained to be a sorcerer and Actionism isn't sorcery: it's a science of the mind, a way to live your life in a more efficient way, having Will taking charge of the operation that is your life.

Don Juan knows MMM = the Memento Mori Mindset. This, every Actionist also has to know. A slight repetition, then, in Don Juan's words:

> *"Death is the only wise advisor that we have. Whenever you feel, as you always do, that everything is going wrong and you're about to be annihilated, turn to your death and ask if that is so. Your death will tell you that you're wrong; that nothing really matters outside its touch. Your death will tell you, 'I haven't touched you yet.'"* [Castaneda 1990 III p 51]

Life is a challenge, a constant operation. An Actionist acknowledges this; he affirms it by getting going in operational zest. Don Juan says this on the matter:

> *"A warrior, or any man for that matter, cannot possibly wish he were somewhere else; a warrior because he lives by challenge, an ordinary man because he doesn't know where his death is going to find him."* [Ibid 1974 p 114]

RAISING YOURSELF

Actionism is about raising yourself mentally. And this raising can be done by acting.

In acronym form this is ARYM = Action Raising You Mentally = get going and have your inner mind becoming more lucid, the action clarifying your thoughts *en passant*. ARYM is about "raising yourself mentally by living on the edge" = operational activity as an intelligence tool, clarifying and structuring your mind as you go. Along with MMM and C3 this is a central Actionist acronym.

ARYM is about "living on the edge as mental elevator". It's a phenomenon akin to NAMO (see above), the Napoleonic Modus Operandi of "getting going to have a look around". It's also akin to Cyril Falls' concept of "readiness to fight for information". Namely, some things aren't understood or realized unless you get going; you sound out your inner by being active, having the thoughts clarifying themselves by being engaged in any kind of action. It's also akin to Nietzsche's idea of, "*Only those thoughts that come by walking have any value*" that is, thoughts having clarified themselves while you were out walking.

Anchored in being, the Actionist performs actions. As an artist he operates as if in a trance, seeking rest in action and peace in performing. He learns by doing, seeking out all kinds of knowledge everywhere. In using the "warrior" simile for this, Don Juan says:

> "*The average man is hooked to his fellow men, while the warrior is hooked only to infinity.*" [Ibid p 7]

THE EDGE

The Actionist is raised mentally by acting. Again, this is ARYM = Action Raising You Mentally = getting going and having your inner mind becoming more lucid, the action clarifying your thoughts *en passant*.

In short, an Actionist raises himself mentally by living on the edge. He challenges himself constantly, constantly aiming higher. This doesn't mean doing stupid things like "hanging from a cliff". If he climbs a mountain, he plans the operation in an orderly fashion. And so, in performing the operation, he becomes mentally elevated, the act being a tangible experience of his thoughts clarifying, just as when climbing, the view of the surroundings gets evened out and finally, from the top of the mountain, the whole horizon is seen as an unbroken ring.

BEING

To act is to be; to be is to act. We all have to act. The difference between the common man and the Actionist is that the former acts unconsciously, the latter in a super-conscious, almost trance-like way. This, as it were, is "the beauty of the trance-like action".

The Actionist acts, he gets going while others sit and talk. This matches a certain Castaneda wisdom: "[A] *man of knowledge lives by acting, not by thinking about acting.*" [Castaneda 1990 II p 90]

An Actionist knows the power of the Will. He assumes responsibility for who he is and what he does. Again, he's ASARIT = A Strong And Responsible Idealist, Taking charge. The Actionist is a paragon of vigor and responsibility, embodying Schwarzkopf's dictum: "When placed in command, take charge."

CHALLENGES

Castaneda by way of Don Juan speaks a lot about challenges; see above. Another succinct quote in this vein is: "*The basic difference between an ordinary man and a warrior is that a warrior takes everything as a challenge while an ordinary man takes everything as a blessing or a curse.*" [Ibid 1974 p 109]

The Actionist concept of Action as Being is about becoming wiser by living your life as a series of Intelligence Operations. It's about summoning your strength, focusing on what you're good at = acknowledging your fortes. Life is not a problem to solve, it's an adventure to experience.

ACTIONISM

ASSUMING RESPONSIBILITY

Above I've delineated "Action as Being" rather exhaustively. Hereby some more notes on the subject.

You could say: Actionism is about Assuming Responsibility, objectively looking everyday reality in the eye and assessing what to do. In this "Evolian" way, knowing cause and effect, the Actionist needs no moral precepts. The Actionist acts by trial and error. An Actionist is a responsible Self in an eternally present Now, intuitively knowing what to do by having contact with his inner mind, his I Am-quality.

The Actionist is steeped in Tradition. Thus, he has some insight into the ontology of all times and all schools. But he doesn't reduce this knowledge of Being into rules of what *not* to do. As the figure, John Locke, said in the TV series *Lost*: "Don't tell me what I can't do,.

With his mind divinely-intuitively anchored, the Actionist does what has to be done, acting in accordance with Being. Thus Bhagavad-Gîtâ 2:38:

> *sukha-duhkhe same kritvâ lâbhâlabhau jayâjayau*
> *tato yuddhâya yujyasva nainam pâpam avâpsyasi*
> *Equal to luck and misfortune, gain and loss, victory and defeat*
> *He prepares for battle, not being entangled in materialism.*

This is acting with *samatva* = equanimity, letting the Inner Mind decide, "acting as if not acting" in the Taoist fashion. It's about acting "not on the thing, but on the soul of the thing".

This latter wisdom comes from Actionism formalized into the acronym: ANOTT-BOTSOTT = Act Not On The Thing, But On The Soul Of The Thing. The conceptual origin of this is Michel Random. In Actionist terms, this is a way to ennoble every act, turning away from its immediately material purpose and making action into *l'art-pour-l'art*. For example, when going shopping, act not with the single purpose of "buying proteins to keep your body alive"; act on the soul of going shopping and enjoy the ride as such, and say hello to people you meet, thereby embodying the archetype of The Good Neighbor.

SAMATVA

The just quoted Bhagavad-Gîtâ passage mentioned *samatva*, a glorified equanimity, rather similar to the Stoic concept of *apateia*. This, for its part, was no mere "apathy," it was about being anchored in Being while acting, letting the trifles of joy and sorrow run off you like water from a duck. Some further examples of this in Bhagavad-Gîtâ are these verses, 2:48 and 2:50, Action as Being in nuce:

yoga sthah kuru karmâni sangam tyaktvâ dhananjaya
siddhy-assiddhyoh samo bhûtvâ samatvam yoga ucyate
Abandoning bonds, act with an anchored mind, O Arjuna;
this indifference to success or failure is called yoga.

- - -

buddhi-yukto jahâtîha ubhe sukrita-dushkrite
tasmâd yogâya yujyasva yogah karmasu kaushalam

Having your mind anchored in reason means abandonment of both luck and misfortune. Therefore, engage in yoga which is proficiency in acting.

JOY

Action as Being is about acting in accordance with the elements, with Reality; to act intuitively, to act as if in a trance. The hiker Christopher McCandless (1968-1992) knew this way of life when he said, "There is no greater joy than to have an endlessly changing horizon, for each day to have a new and different sun." This was about hiking as the ultimate experience, to raise yourself mentally by going Beyond the Beyond. Again, remember ARYM = Action Raising You Mentally = use action as a mental elevator.

It's essentially not about "living on the edge," it's about *becoming* the edge. Remember the cartoon figure Aeon Flux: "You're skating the Edge – I *am* the edge."

The Actionist concept of Action as Being is to be an acting, performing self in an eternal now. The ninja Stephen Hays expresses it thus: "The present is our only opportunity for power. The passage of time controls and bends all things only when we believe in the passage of time. The future lived is merely another Now." [Hayes 1980 p 78]

C_3 = volitional mental calm, is a fundamental of the Actionist creed. And Hayes, for his part, says this about meeting onslaughts with calm:

"Do not fear them [your enemies] or become angry with them. Allow your heart to hold the emptiness of purity. Your receptive spirit will hear the sadness and rage of your attacker's intentions and your body will flow with the winds of their hatred. You will take them to the destruction they seek." [Hayes 1981 p 23]

ACT

Act and become wiser. Get going and raise yourself mentally. These are aspects of Action as Being, as shown in this Chapter. This isn't the only way of gaining knowledge; you also get it from calm, systematic study, pondering and mediation. But the Actionist way of acting is an ethical aspect mostly ignored by philosophy. True, we have the school of Existentialism which sometimes touched on the subject, as in "life and thought are inseparable".

I won't go into Existential thought per se in this study. However, the following is an illuminating quote from Richard Hillary (1919-1943), an RAF pilot killed in action, who had reflected on the connection between life and thought, action and mental elevation. As a Spitfire pilot he hailed the dogfight duel as the height of existence; here we find "the duel, the self-reliance, the utter responsibility for your own fate."

CODA

Again: we all must act. You all know this by now. If you need another concept to bring the message home, then it's this: "impossible to abstain from acting, we all must act" = even a meditating recluse must act, he must breathe = no one can totally abstain from acting = to act is the human condition. And the Actionist makes action into an art, a way of life.

4. IDEALISM VERSUS MATERIALISM

Hereby some further deliberations on the Actionist ethics. It's about idealism versus materialism and the possible value of "active nihilism". Also, I repeat some points already mentioned, like the I AM-impulse, willpower and freedom. The German philosopher Friedrich Nietzsche plays some role in this Chapter.

ACTIVE IDEALISM

Active Idealism, not Materialist Ignorance, is the Actionist way. Idealism is Light, materialism is Darkness. Darkness is the absence of Light, the absence of ideals. Conversely, Will-Thought-Compassion embracing Light, is the source of all ideals, all of the golden Eternal Values.

Actionism is idealism fighting materialism. In the form of concepts, this is expressed as the following:

1. Avoid materialism and defeatism, embrace tradition and self-reliance. This means: stop being an ironic dandy, start being an assertive agent, footed in Tradition.
2. Evade materialism and start building Antropolis. This refers to *Antropolis,* a novel I wrote, published in 2009 (in Swedish only). It's about the coming Golden Age of science and spirituality, denouncing the materialist ignorance of the previous era. So the concept – "Antropolis" – is already established, now we only have to start building it, making it

become real in our everyday. (More on *Antropolis* in Chapter 28.)
3. Fighting against materialist idiocy, for active esotericism = the struggle for realizing Sat Yuga in the current remnants of Kali Yuga.
4. In other words: materialism has a lesser reality than ideals = the immaterial side of being. Avoid materialist idiocy and build something that lasts; join me in building the virtual city of Antropolis, resplendent in the sun with its circular buildings and domes reflecting the sun.

RESPONSIBLE MAN

Actionism is an Active Idealism leading the way to a new era, an era of Responsible Men acknowledging their Inner Light, taking charge of their condition as thinking, reflecting beings.

The Actionist creed is an Active Idealism, going beyond the current nihilism. Nihilism, for its part, might have been the defining mentality of the 19th and 20th centuries. And it has to be stressed that nihilism isn't all bad. There is, for example, the "active nihilism" of Nietzsche – his stressing of self-reliance and skepticism, of not accepting the established truths of his day. Nietzsche pondered the essence of being free, noting for example that some people can't handle freedom. They gave away their "one valuable thing" when they threw off their yoke since they hadn't really reflected on what it meant to be free, that is, to assume responsibility for your Being. In the motto, *"wie man wird, was man ist"* = "how to become what you really are," Nietzsche touched upon the condition of the Responsible Man. The Actionist figure of the Responsible Man assumes responsibility for being the man he is, "doing what he can with what he has where he is". The condition of Responsible Man is summarized in the Coda of this study.

ACTIONISM

Active nihilism is better than passive nihilism = defeatism. As for this attitude, Ernst Jünger, for his part, in *Über die Linie* (1950) saw nihilism as a transitional phase from a misinterpreted, shallow idealism to a new life with the ideals anchored in your own being.

BE PROACTIVE

Nietzsche might have been an atheist and anti-esotericist but he had viable ideas nonetheless, ideas highlighting what Actionism is. For instance, he said "live dangerously". This is akin to the phenomenon sketched above in the form of ARYM = Action Raising You Mentally.

Also, Nietzsche spoke about "the Will to Power (over yourself)" which is a centerpiece of any existential creed. Within the Actionist framework "Will To Power Over Yourself," is shortened into acronym form: WTPOY. This is the Actionist interpretation of Nietzscheism, making the individual the focus of the volitional life. Along with MMM, C3 and ARYM, WTPOY is a central Actionist acronym.

Nietzsche can be needed as an impulse-giver, as a bringer of zest to attitudes bogged down in passive piety and quietism. It's true that Actionism respects the meditative recluse and the pious vineyard worker but to merely sit passive and receive the grace is not the royal road to spirituality. We all have to act, as humans we're active as a matter of course, and to say that passivity and meditation is the only way to enlightenment is dead wrong. We're all active and in formulating this as Active Idealism we underline the defining trait of the Actionist creed. We all act, we all make choices. Thus, be proactive and choose Light, Creativity and Awareness, shunning negativism, fear-mongering and sentimentality, syndromes that can threaten the realm of the passive mindset.

WILLPOWER

Again: willpower. Will must control the mind, mastering every stray thought and emotion.

Will rules the mind. And mind must control the body. You can't let yourself be guided by your impulses and carnal needs; this makes you into an animal. Instead, steer your life with the power of thought. Live life intuitively and reflectively. Create changes in your mind with the power of Will.

CAESAR

William Shakespeare (1564-1616) once wrote a play called *Julius Caesar*, about the last days and death of the legendary Roman statesman. The murder of Caesar in 44 BCE is the climax in the middle of the play; the civil war drama, ending with the murderers being defeated, plays out in Acts Four and Five.

Shakespeare's main source for the play was Caesar's biography by Plutarch (46-120 CE). But Shakespeare also adds something of his own, interpreting Caesar as a true Man of Action, a Responsible Man knowing his worth, an Actionist of his age. In summation, the Caesar of the play says: I am the brother of danger... I am like the Northern star... I am not afraid to tell grey-beards the truth...!

This is almost Nietzschean. And, reportedly, Nietzsche first thought about having Caesar as his mouthpiece for his "active nihilist" Zarathustra novel. Instead, as intimated, it became Zarathustra, the Persian seer.

Another aspect of the specificity of Caesar, of his unique style ushering in a new era, is that he wrote about himself in the third person. For this, see Caesar's works: *The Gallic Wars* and *The Civil War*. To portray yourself from the outside, from a "neutral" position, is a trait of a man knowing his worth, sure of his place in history.

Caesar is a historical figure embodying Actionism. Other such are Christopher McCandless, Richard Hillary, Carlos Castaneda (see

Chapter three and ten), Gabriele d'Annunzio (Chapter 11), Julius Evola (Chapter 12) and T. E. Lawrence (Chapter 13).

DRUNK

> *"I found them all drunk... for they are blind in their heart. When they have thrown off their wine, they will repent."*

Thus spoke Christ in the Gospel of Thomas. Today we see the same as Christ did: a confused humanity going round in circles. Dejected men, convinced that the end of the world is near. That's what you meet in the streets today.

The answer to this? The cure? Willpower. And, most fittingly, in another Gnostic gospel, it says, *"Will doesn't make them into sinners, but lack of will does."* That's the Gospel of Philip. Will is the answer. This was intimated in the first Chapter of this study. To repeat: in the beginning was the Deed. Willpower united itself with Thought and became a radiant being – God, coming into existence when Will-Thought merged with the Light.

God is a dyad of Will and Thought. Accordingly, an individual is also such a combo of Will and Thought. And Will must take command even in an individual's life. Will can create changes in the consciousness – by willing to think positively rather than negatively, for instance.

With Will taking control over Thought, mental energy is saved. It puts a stop to all the useless frittering and bickering of the inner mind. Instead, harmony is reached when every stray thought and emotion is reined in and controlled.

Let willpower guide your everyday. Don't be a plaything of The Powers That Be. You are the commander of the Ship That Is You, no one else. As Schwarzkopf said: "When placed in command, take charge," And you have the existence you have, the life you have, for a reason. You're not *geworfen* – "thrown out," as the nihilist Heidegger meant. You are who, what and where you are for karmic reasons. Acknowledge that, take charge of your life and assume responsibility for your being. That's the beginning of the Volitional Life, of the Will to Power over Yourself = WTPOY.

VICTORY

The Actionist aims for victory. How? By longing to be on the podium, cheered by millions? No! Instead he can do the quite opposite – saying "I'm finished, I'm done" – as a mental exercise, as a freeing of the mind. Having thus "reset the system" he can redefine what victory is, envisioning it in an ever attainable way. Like, "being able to take a fresh breath of air = victory". Then, he can be constantly victorious, basking in the glory of that victorious feeling forever.

Have you ever felt victorious? If not, it's about time you experience the feeling. In the coming Golden Age victory will be a common feeling, being victorious in the way Buddha was a victor – over himself, over desire. Again: *"[S]orcerers have only one path open to them: to succeed in whatever they do."* [Abelar p 207]

In the Actionist system of acronyms this is summarized as WAP = Winning As Propensity = learning to win = to constantly posit attainable goals in your personal operation and, having reached them, to acknowledge them as the victories they are.

WAR

Personally, I've studied war. And I've served in the army. I've worn the grey uniform of the cold war era Swedish Army.

A uniform is a symbol of service. Having worn the Swedish uniform, I've been prepared to defend my country with my lifeblood. I have served, I have studied war.

For its part, the time for prophesying impending war is over. In Chapter 22 of this book I advocate against these latter-day

Cassandras. Because we now live in the Sat Yuga of essential peace. Moreover, we have to realize Sat Yuga in our hearts. Therefore, to occupy yourself with prospects of a major war, of war breaking out and sweeping away the world in a storm of death and destruction, is totally misleading. However, it isn't forbidden to study the wars of the past as a historical and moral lesson, Actionist variety. This will be done in this book, and the following is what I philosophically have in mind.

For instance, battle can be seen as an inner experience, as a testing of your personal strength versus the elements. Combat thus becomes a mental elevation. In the face of death you have to mobilize your inner strength, making you act trance-like but fully conscious, in fact, being on a higher mental level. War thus becomes a trigger for heightened awareness. This has been covered by Ernst Jünger in *Battle as an Inner Experience* and by Carlos Castaneda, who wasn't a soldier like Jünger but Carlitos sure had his moments of heightened awareness, testing his strength against the elements.

"Raising yourself mentally in combat" is about being "enraptured in tranquility," as Edith Södergran said. It's about raising yourself mentally by living on the edge. As it were, you have to get going in order to get going: *on s'engage et puis on verra,* as Napoleon said, conceptualized by Actionism as NAMO (q.v. the preceding chapter).

In this vein, you can conduct operations in order to gain knowledge. It's akin to the phenomenon of "readiness to fight for information" that Cyril Falls spoke about.

"Combat as mental elevator" can be summarized in these three words: inebriation, inspiration, initiation. That's the Actionist Creed.

COMBAT SIMILE

The combat simile is a way to help the individual to act. The concepts of "war as being," and "war as a mental state" can show us the need for a spiritual, personal creed in order to survive the noisy confusion of life. As delineated in the *Metaphysics of War,* by Julius Evola, you can't go out in a war solely fighting for this and that political concept. You have to have contact with Being, with your inner reserves, with God, or how the ontology now shall be formulated in Evola's case, "Buddhist inspired magical idealist" as he was. You have to raise yourself mentally to sustain the hardships of any life, any situation: as a soldier and as a civilian.

You have to have a spiritual outlook on life, an ontology to base your moral on. I have sketched it above and will delineate it further below: the Actionist creed. Conversely, to discard spirituality and go living as an animal merely craving food, drink and sex, conceptually living in "the flesh, the subconscious, the impulses, the blood, the instincts, the elements" leads into chaos, desolation and, ultimately, banality. Instead, live your life reflecting on eternal values like Honor, Glory, Self-Restraint, Compassion and Accountability. Live anchored in *Sein*, not *die Seiendes*. Live anchored in Essential Reality, in the unchanging, eternal forms, not in the mindless, every day, ever-changing world called Maya of Illusion.

That's the Actionist creed.

OPERATIONS

I mentioned operations above, to conduct them in order to gain knowledge. Knowledge of what? Essentially, of your own being. It's about reaching calm while you operate, to have action as a form of super meditation. In the novel *Savrola* (1899), Winston Churchill, for his part, expressed this as "seeking rest in action"; that was how his hero lived, a man of action. It's the same mental disposition, the same ontological realm as the one visited by Ernst Jünger in *Battle as An Inner Experience*. This is the Tao of Acting = acting as if you didn't act. Indeed, you do act and you do it well but there's a sense of detachment in all this.

That's the Actionist creed.

FREE AGENT

A Man of Action, an Operational Man, an Actionist, is free but he can also engage in action. Conversely, a man who doesn't act is an absurdity; we all have to act, if only to breathe and sustain our bodily operations.

An Actionist is forever free, forever sovereign in the Realm That Is He. As a human agent he's in contact with Being. In acknowledging the I AM-impulse he's "God-Immediate" (= German, *Gottesunmittelbar*), a Responsible Man acting not on the thing, but on the soul of the thing. Thus, while engaged in Action he's essentially free and unbound, spiritually un-descended and remaining with his Self in higher realms – with God.

The Actionist is a free and responsible actor in harmony with the Universe. That's the Actionist Creed.

5. ACTIVE IDEALISM

As you know by now, the Actionist ethics are about affirming yourself positively. We're all created by God; we all have an Inner Divine Light. Affirming this is the Actionist way. But this is no passive idealism, having the person sitting around waiting for grace. Indeed, this attitude can be adorable, per se, but as humans we can't be wholly passive in developing ourselves morally. We can also act. The following delineates the Actionist ethics in this respect.

GOD

In the beginning God came into being as a force of Will and Thought, imbued with Compassion and Light. Eventually he took of his own Light and created man's soul.

Of this, I told you in Chapter 1. The Actionist world-view is divinely led and inspired. God is the ultimate reality; God is ever present: with his Will in the form of a conceivable gestalt, with his Thought in the form of an implicit presence. This, for its part, solves the ages old question of whether God is a person or an abstract ever-presence; he's both, depending on whether stressing his Will or his Thought aspect. This is elaborated upon in *Vandrer mod lyset*, available in English as *Toward the Light*.

The individual is a mirror of the godhead. As is God, the person is a composite of Will and Thought, imbued with Compassion and Light. Affirming this is a fundamental of Actionism.

ACTIONISM

The Actionist has Faith. This faith is realized both through contemplation and action. The actionist lives by *Faith In Action* = FIA. This means that faith, God-realization, never can be a theoretical exercise = it has to be integrated into your daily life = because we all have to act.

The god-realizing Actionist draws strength out of "the invisible" = the immanent ever-presence that God is exercising. This can be expressed as: "empowerment through strength out of the absolute" = drawing energy from higher, divine realms = this is what sustains you in the long run, not mere food and drink.

BRIDGEHEAD

We all have an Inner Light – so go on and realize it...! How hard can it be? Look yourself in the mirror, what do you see – a soulless robot or a living, breathing person with a spark in his eye?

A concept for summarizing the divine, inherent element in man is this: making your person into a bridgehead of the divine = realize the unity between your spirit and God = acknowledge your Inner Light.

God, in his invisible form, is ever present. In the Bible this is expressed as "The One We Move In, Exist Through And Live In" = a definition of the Logos, the Divine Word of "I Am" through which everything Is What It Is, as I explained in Chapter 1.

SELF-HELP

An old saying goes: "God helps the man who helps himself." This is akin to the Actionist creed: to acknowledge Higher Reality in the form of God by not waiting passively for everything, instead shaping your life positively while at the same time affirming that Inner Light.

As for this just mentioned "shaping", there is the Actionist acronym of SEP = Shaping Existence Positively = to make your life into a project, an artwork = affirmatively "doing what you can with what you have where you are".

"Be yourself". This may be a cliché but it's conceptually true. Also: "become someone different – yourself". In Actionist terms this is expressed as ABY = Affirmatively Being Yourself = choosing to be the one you are, realizing the limitless possibilities of your personal being.

G. B. Shaw was onto the same truth when he said, "Life isn't about finding yourself. Life is about creating yourself". This is a motto incorporating the Actionist attitude of esotericism (the truth is within, Greek *eso*), of using Will-Thought to sound out your inner, creative possibilities. It can also remind you of Nietzsche's dictum, "*wie man wird, was man ist*" = "how to become what you are".

SAVE ENERGY

Be yourself; affirm your personal being and the possibilities inherent in your being – and save energy. Stop hating yourself; this drains you of even more energy. Stop the eternal revolt against yourself = make peace with yourself = acknowledge that You Are You = "loving oneself is the beginning of a life-long love affair" (Oscar Wilde). As you can see it's akin to ABY = Affirmatively Being You, that I just spoke of.

SHAPING

I just mentioned SEP = Shaping Existence Positively. Summoning your Will entails acknowledging the Inner Light, having this along in creating a viable existence of your life. In Buddhist thought this can be conceptualized as, "see no evil, hear no evil, speak no evil". Namely, this is the Buddhist concept of letting Will govern your mind (speak no evil) and senses (hear no evil, see no evil). Indeed, "evil" has to be confronted, but to indignantly sit by and watch the ravages of evil leads nowhere; instead Will must lead you to greener pastures.

This is the Actionist creed; this is Active Idealism. Another example of this is: "summoning your strengths" = focusing on what you're good at = acknowledging your fortes.

Yet another is RAWALTAFA. This means: Rather Acting Wrongly And Learning Than Abstaining From Action = we all have to act. In other words, this is the trial and error of life, Actionism in a nutshell. – *Borderline*, page 139, says this in the instance of RAWALTAFA:

> *"I don't condemn people having gone astray on the mindless path. It's human to err. As individuals I forgive people sporting a defeatist attitude. Also, it's better to act wrongly and learn from the experience than not acting at all. I say it again: it's better to act wrongly and learn from it than not acting at all. This wisdom can be made into a motto: "Rather Acting Wrongly And Learning Than Abstaining From Action," with RAWALTAFA as an acronym. As you can see the action element is here, stressing the need to get out and get going, "tearing your nails bloody on the wall of existence" as Edith Södergran said. With this she meant that you have to live your life as a trial and error exercise. – It's said that "we come here to learn". In the samsâra of existence we live life after life, all the time getting better at it in the school of karma. Conversely, the worst conduct is to only live theoretically, trying to reach moral perfection merely by studying discourses on ethics, "dreaming of systems so perfect that no one will need to be good""* [T. S. Eliot, "Choruses from The Rock", 1934].

POSITIVE

Actionism is a positive approach to life, an Active Idealism. Conversely, to merely sit around waiting to be led by God, touched by God etc., this is "passive idealism". Now, I do note the idealist strain of this but I can't endorse the attitude of "only by grace, by faith alone man is saved," which has become a mainstay of Lutheranism. Personally, as I Swede I was born into the Lutheran *Svenska Kyrkan*, and I still formally belong to it – for I have no wish to join self-righteous atheists in making the act of "leaving church" into some statement.

That said, the passivity of today's Lutheran believers is not for me. Instead, I shape life positively = I help myself (and thus God may help me); I make my being into a bridgehead of the divine. To be is to act, to act is to be = we all have to act = thus, act positively, affirming your Inner Light and let it shine around you.

This is what I mean by Active Idealism.

As intimated Actionism can tolerate passive idealism, as a fellow idealist faith. And we can understand the "active nihilism" of Nietzsche, this attitude that I spoke of in the previous chapter. However, what Actionism can never tolerate in this pattern of "active / passive, idealist / nihilist," is the "passive nihilism" of defeatism. For example, this attitude is demonstrated in Harry Martinson's epic poem *Aniara* (1956). The gist of it is that we're all doomed; we're all going to die. The message is that as humans we're helpless, no willpower can take us anywhere, not even spiritually. Will-Thought is a dead letter in this world-view, as is Compassion, Light and the esoteric attitude in general. Waiting for doomsday is the only way.

Conceptually, this "passive nihilism" is the absolute opposite of Actionism.

6. OPERATIONAL ESOTERICISM

You're reading *Actionism*, a conceptualization of action. Everything is action, everything is an operation. I've touched on this previously, in Chapter 3, when I spoke about "Action as Being". Hereby some further operational deliberations:

INNER EXPERIENCE

We all act in order to sustain the body. But the Actionist does more than that. The Actionist action is an inner phenomenon, an inner experience.

Essentially, action is an inner, esoteric phenomenon. Acting isn't merely about planning the act, performing it and evaluating it. The Actionist action, performed in a glorified trance, is everything at once. It's the Napoleonic Modus Operandi (NAMO) as a constant process, that of "getting going to clarify the situation," of acting and perceiving, perceiving and acting, *ad infinitum*.

This is a subtle phenomenon which is only mastered after a life of operating. But it's a reality. When inspired, the Actionist is totally engrossed by the action. His holistic, total mindset makes him identify with the operation he's performing. This is expressed in the line, "you are the mission, the mission is you".

The Actionist *is* the mission, whose goal is itself. The path is the goal. With this I mean, of course you have a viable, everyday basis for most actions, but having that "an end in itself"-attitude, makes action into an art. "The reward is found in the work," as Bruce Lee said. This is the essence of operational esotericism.

STATE OF MIND

The agent *is* the mission; the goal of the operation is the operation itself. This is experienced in the phenomenon of Movement As A State Of Mind = MAASOM. If you have no outer point of reference you can't decide whether you're moving or standing still. This Einstein once stated.

For its part, MASOOM is one of the five central Actionist acronyms, along with MMM, C3, ARYM and WTPOY. They will recur frequently in this book. (To give you "an even ten," we'd say the following five are the other central acronyms of Actionism: WAP, Winning As Propensity, RIA, Rest In Action, RIR, Rest In Rest, TIOHAN, There Is Only Here And Now, and ESWY, Everything Starts With You. If they haven't been explained already they will be in due time.)

Conducting operations in this "inner," esoteric fashion enables you to seek rest in action. I've already mentioned this. It's formalized in RIA = Rest In Action. The operational pro can rest while he acts. To be sure, this should not be an obsession, like CEOs working 15 hours a day and spending hours off by discussing operational details. That borders on indulgence. In contrast, an Actionist also has the ability to seek RIR = rest in rest, peace in peace and silence in silence. This brings him into contact with the unconditioned, with inner, generative forces.

HOOKED TO INFINITY

The Actionist has contact with his Inner Light, with God, with the Absolute. To use the Don Juan simile, the Actionist is "hooked to infinity". The esoteric operation is about acting as if supra-conducted, transcending time and space. An Actionist is an operational self in an infinite here, an eternal now. This is formalized as: "the operating self in the infinite here, the eternal now".

The Actionist lives on the edge to raise himself, as I've already explained in a previous chapter (ARYM = Action Raising You Mentally). Action is an inner experience. In 1922 Ernst Jünger touched on this, in the study *Der Kampf als inneres Erlebnis* (*Battle as An Inner Experience*). It was about combat as a sort of super meditation, a glorified trance. To reach this subtle state you have to be C3, you have to conquer the fear of dying (= MMM). But, having done that, you have the basics for an operational life along the lines I've sketched in this chapter. You can start walking along the path of Actionism, living life as an adventure.

This is formalized as: "experience reality as a secret and life as a mission" = to live your life ontologically anchored, operationally set = there are secrets to experience in the everyday and adventures to be had in any situation.

TWO CONCEPTS

As for operational concepts, I've always cherished two that are used in the German army. The first is *Verantwortungsfreude* = "the joy of responsibility" = to assume responsibility gladly. It's a general clause permeating everything the army does operationally. The combat zone officer mustn't passively sit and wait for orders for everything. If he sees something that "has to be done" within the framework of the operation, he does it, like blowing up a bridge or mopping up a suspect copse.

This underlines the role of *responsibility*, which every Actionist already knows the importance of. An Actionist embodies the concept "Responsible Man". Again Schwarzkopf: "When placed in command, take charge."

The second German army concept of Actionist relevance is *Innere Führung* = inner leadership. This applies to the private soldier. In the same spirit of responsibility as the above concept, this is about every man, every ranker, becoming "his own chief," reasonably thinking ahead, like doing routine stuff that needs to be done, without being ordered to it all the time.

These two concepts may lack the subtlety of "action as an inner experience" and "operating in a glorified trance" that I intimated earlier in this chapter, but they are fundamentals of operating, like C3 and MMM, eventually leading to smooth operating on all levels.

PRESCIENT ACTION

Before some actions, you might have an internal image of how things at large are going to develop, or you have an inkling of how a certain operation is going to work out. This is a variety of "action as an inner experience". Here we'll exemplify this syndrome with Yeager and Patton, two American heroes.

What we may call "the Prescient Attitude" is an aspect of "battle as an inner experience". For its part, it isn't opposed to the Napoleonic approach to combat = NAMO. The Napoleonic approach is central to Actionism while the Yeagerian attitude is more of a peculiar aspect of the operational mindset.

The Yeager aspect of operating with an internal, intuitive footing is this. In 1947 aviation was on the verge of "breaking the sound barrier," in the process developing planes that could exceed the speed of sound. In dry air at 20° that speed is 1,236 km/h. In these attempts there had been crashes and accidents, the planes seemed to break up in midair when they approached the speed in question. Was there, in fact, a virtual barrier up there in the sky? The US Air Force pilot Charles Yeager (1923-) didn't think so. And with the rocket plane Bell X-1 he eventually broke the barrier. The plane was ingeniously constructed, and Yeager was no engineer, but he had the combined instinct and intuition that man could fly faster than the speed of sound. And on October 14, 1947 he "broke the sound barrier". Because, in essence, it had already been broken in his inner mind (q.v. Leo Janos and Charles Yeager, *Yeager: An Autobiography*).

Another example of this operational phenomenon, of "winning the battle in your inner mind," is this. In the summer of 1944, George S. Patton (1885-1945) made his famous "sweep through France," an armored, all-out onslaught to the east and the German border. The Allies, having finally broken out of Normandy, got their armored offensive going and swept everything before them. The interesting thing in this was that later, Patton's son found a map in his father's belongings, dated 1943, and outlining how an Allied armored sweep through France would look like, pretty much like it happened in real life in 1944. The source for this is Carlo d'Este, *Patton – A Genius for War*, 1996.

In other words, both Patton and Yeager held a more or less subconscious, prescient concept of how the operations in question would evolve.

- - -

This Chapter was about the Actionist attitude to operations. More on diverse forms of operations and their conceptualization in chapters 14 to 18.

7. METAPHYSICAL ACTION

As we've seen by now, Actionism is a doctrine footed in Essential Reality, in Being. It's an ethic based in ontology. Man is a microcosmic mirror of God. God symbolizes the macrocosmic level of complex, interacting forces; reality as a whole is an organism and man mirrors this. Conversely, man isn't a tool, nature isn't a machine. Planet earth is a living being and the whole cosmos vibrates with life and light. Bringing our heartbeats in sync with the rhythm of the cosmos is the Actionist way.

Actionism is an esoteric, soul-affirming doctrine, not a machine manual. It is axioms and general clauses that guide it, not rigid sets of rules. While it does have its "Ten Basic Tenets," "Five Basic Acronyms" and "Summary in 36 words" (see Chapter 41) they are merely overall helps, not prerequisites for being guided by Actionism.

INTUITION

Actionism is about intuition. To be guided by your glorified Inner Mind is the way not to be enmeshed by programs, formalities and rules. It's true that to master a specific skill you need to abide by the rules, but having learned the rules, having internalized them, made them into your second nature, you can conceptually step up a level and act more freely – with intuition. Otherwise you'll never advance beyond the basic level.

Intuition is about seeing wholes, the big picture. Again, programs and instructions might focus on details, but the Actionist has the ability to see the whole and the detail at the same time. This is formalized in the concept, "holism is the goal and the starting point" = the Actionist ontology is about seeing wholes = analysis and dissection are mere instruments to understand the holistically working micro and macrocosm.

HERE AND NOW

To see wholes is one fundamental of the Actionist creed. To be able to live in the Now is another. This is expressed in the acronym: TIOHAN = There Is Only Here And Now...!

Taking this wisdom to heart is worth a library of self-help guides. Constantly acting in the Here-And-Now saves you mental energy, spares you a lot of indulgence. Don't crave a gold medal for everything you've done, instead, act on what this experience means to you here and now. Again: ANOTT-BOTSOTT = Act Not On The Thing, But On The Soul Of The Thing. If the memory of the experience might enlighten it in the form of an anecdote, fine, but remember the ever-presence in all this. You're here, now: live it.

SUBTLE FORCES

The Actionist is in contact with the unconditioned, the Absolute, the Inner Light. Here his being is anchored. He lives in harmony with the universe. The subtle forces of the universe feed him. This can be done by seeking Rest in Rest = RIR. But he doesn't receive everything passively in this way. With Will-Thought he wills himself into an active state. Thus he, as an Active Idealist, sees another world than a passive nihilist sees.

The Actionist has an active eye. In Goethean fashion he's educated by the senses but he also educates them. The Actionist look is governed by his inner mind. This is formalized as: "as we are, so we see". The meaning of this is: truth is within, truth is an esoteric phenomenon. A sad person sees sadness around him; an energetic person sees energy around him.

ONTOLOGIC ACTION

To live is to act. To act reflectively is to have the I AM-impulse ingrained in you. Saying "I AM" makes you ready for everything. Saying "I AM" affirms your state as a man, divinely bred, esoterically led, idealistically fed. Saying "I AM" puts you in contact with your Inner Divine Nature.

CLARITY

The Actionist, God bless him, is no robot passively recording what he sees. He has an active eye. He sees the essence of things. This is formalized as, "clarity in things, clarity in yourself" = God is in everything and everyone = in the objects as ideas, in men as Inner Light. Observing the world gives the operational esotericist a sense of belonging.

The Actionist sees the ideas directly. He sees life in form, spirit in matter. This can be seen as a summary of the Actionist metaphysics, about seeing matter as formed by inherent ideas, which is otherwise known as Platonic idealism. As for this idealism it's elaborated upon in *Borderline*. On page 25, for instance, we read this about the Platonic idea:

> *"Plotinus meant that the idea is the 'beingness' of that which is, that which remains when the qualities have been removed. The eidos of an object is the force by which something is what it is."*

BEGINNING

In the beginning Will chose to merge with Thought. Next, Will-Thought chose Light instead of Darkness and became God resplendent. Then God created man's soul as a microcosmic mirror of this, man becoming a glorified mix of Will, Thought and Compassion, driven by the Inner Light.

This mythical-ontological base of Actionism engenders the whole doctrine. Seek and see this divine bond and you're ready for everything, stating "I AM" as God said when he came into being, when primordial Will-Thought merged with Light, the uttering becoming the *performative statement* of the event, the statement *being* the event. In the same way, to the individual, saying "I AM" becomes a virtually ontological act, a self-confirming statement inducting your being into a divinely led cosmos.

8. ACTIONIST ART

I've mentioned "art" in conjunction with the ethical deliberations above, like "living your life like a work of art" and "making action into a *l'art-pour-l'art*" (Chapters 3 and 5). In this, we have the meaning of this chapter's caption: "Actionist Art". It's about the way in which life and art intermingles, how an artistic attitude can give you perspectives on the holistic mindset that Actionism favors.

THREE ASPECTS

Three different aspects can help in giving you a clue of what Actionist Art is: vision, musicality and symbol.

As for *vision*, this is what an artist has. He sees something with his inner eye, then he realizes the vision to the public. Ideally, an artist is a pathfinder for man, a guide into future vistas. This is conceptualized as, "artistic vision is the avant garde of man" = art must go before everyday reality, as a glorified scouting patrol = art can envision things that "are not real" but, in time, may become real.

We should not worship artists as the sole source of vision. Philosophers, too, have a way of showing us the way ahead. For instance, the two most known authors from Greek antiquity, who are they? Probably, Plato the philosopher and Homer the poet. Both are needed to give a vision of the antique conceptualization of Reality. And today, both authors and philosophers are needed to show us the way ahead. We also need specific experts (engineers, lawyers, economists) but only in the conceptual framework of a vision.

MUSIC

A Muse is a Greek goddess of art, poetry, epics, dance and astronomy and then some. From Muse is derived *music* = "of or relating to the Muses". Musicality means to be able to play and sing but not only that. It's a whole attitude summing up the artistic mindset.

This attitude was present in Nietzsche, the philosopher who said: "Without music, life would be a mistake." And: "Those who were seen dancing were thought to be insane by those who could not hear the music." And: "I would believe only in a god who could dance."

In Actionism, this kind of musicality is a discreet ingredient. It's formalized into "mixing into your stringency a little musicality". This means that life can be fun, too = add some pizazz to your sagacity. Indeed, we have to be serious, but exclusive seriousness leads into sterility.

SYMBOL

We speak and think in symbols = metaphors. The visible form is there for the idea to be able to show itself to us. The objects of the tangible world – the outer forms of plants, animals, men, things – these all are perishable. But their essential ideas = souls live on. So what we see are mere approximations of their true nature. This was expressed by Goethe as, "*alles Vergängliche ist nur ein Gleichnis*" = "all things ephemeral are but a simile".

And the specific Actionist wisdom on this? It's that "symbolism always precedes actuality" = a concept has to be envisioned before it can be realized. This brings us back to the beginning, of the mentioning of the artist as a visionary. Essentially, the artist sees the *eidoi* of the things = their true nature = therefore he has an advantage over the common man who only sees the ephemeral and the subjective.

RUTHLESS

Art is a vast subject. However, it's a mistake to think that art is some leisurely activity, like "it's nice to write, nice to paint" etc. In a sense, the artist has to be ruthless.

A quote capturing this is: "the spirit of song is war," by courtesy of Edith Södergran. This is about acknowledging the "ruthless" character of the artist = he has to have a mindset like that expressed by the knight in Dürer's "The Knight, the Devil and Death," riding forth on his mission without caring about anything, not even "Devil or Death," nor about family, friends, critics or polite society. As intimated, art is musical = guided by the Muses, but along with this the true artist needs something of a ruthless mindset.

Put differently, artistic activities are in need of *willpower*, of summing up your gumption and getting going after you've perfected your original vision and concept. I here especially think of the performing arts, of standing on stage as an actor, a speaker or a musician. When doing this you have to grasp the nettle and rise to the occasion. Conversely, to merely think that people will be nice to you – to you, coming to them to sing etc. is a mistake. Meeting a reserved audience is trying indeed. Therefore, go for the "worst case scenario" = be prepared to deliver your act against the disbelief of the audience. You have to know your role, know why you're on stage.

Even if you have a friendly audience, as a performer you must get into character. By standing on stage you automatically take on a role – so cherish this and don't succumb to heartwarming disclaimers like "I'm no speaker" etc. Take responsibility for the act of taking the stage.

You might say: the privilege of the audience is to be skeptical, to be reserved versus whatever is presented on stage. In the same vein, the privilege of an actor / singer / speaker is to be skeptical about the audience he will meet. Don't count on it being friendly, instead, build up mental reserves to handle a skeptical audience.

Yet another attitude of the stage condition is this: passion, related to compassion. And an aspect of passion, according to an esoteric writer, is "a drop of joy plus courage". This formula equals passion. With such a daring mindset your odds at winning your audience increases. The keyword is courage, it takes some guts to go on stage and deliver. In comparison, to paint, to write, to tinker away in your solitary studio might also take willpower; however, it's not of the same nature as that which is needed by a performing artist. But if the stage artist realizes these fundamentals, he can bask in the glory of *audience response*, a special feeling indeed.

9. ETERNAL VALUES

As an Active Idealist I am fighting materialism. However, "idealism" mustn't solely mean resorting to bourgeois behavior like "reading classics, adoring beauty, advocating order". It's true that Actionism strives for a society espousing order and beauty, but nihilism per se can also be a necessary phase for reaching the source of existence. An Actionist reaches for higher ideals, but the way to learn about them may go through nihilism, as Jünger has shown us in *Über die Linie*. After only finding emptiness in an outdated, formally "idealist" tradition, the truth-seeker may become a nihilist. He's alone in the desert, alone with himself – and thus he has to see inward, look inside himself, and then he may be able to ponder the eternal truths, acknowledging his Will and Thought, the true source of the Eternal Values.

FOUNDATION

As mentioned in Chapter 1, man is a composite of Will and Thought, enveloped by Compassion. And these three fundamental elements can be seen as the foundation for the Eternal Values, the higher ideals guiding human existence.

Will, Thought and Compassion are the very elements in which man exists. Will, Thought and Compassion are eternal forces, there to be acknowledged as a matter of course. They aren't something you simply can choose to affirm or ignore.

If we begin with Will, from this source can be derived values such as courage, accountability, duty, vigilance, self-sacrifice, loyalty, self-reliance and determination.

Then we have Thought. From this we can derive truth, honesty, justice and impeccability.

From Compassion, finally, can be derived magnanimity, mercy, clemency and simplicity. From compassion also stems "passion" in all its varieties: love, artistry and curiosity.

EMBRACING

There you have it. Embracing Eternal Values isn't some haphazard collection of "stuff you like". It's a primordial condition. Conversely, to deny these eternal values is against nature, against essential reality.

10. CARLITOS

An author mentioned earlier in this study is Carlos Castaneda (1925-1998). Hereby a further look into his writings and what he has to say to the serious Actionist, bent on living life volitionally and holistically.

A sort of disclaimer is needed here: Actionism has nothing to do with sorcery and ritual magic, however, in the Castaneda books, some practices are openly spoken of as "sorcery". While I don't endorse sorcery I have, nonetheless, found rather many enlightening wisdoms in the Castaneda narratives. There's a place for Castaneda and Don Juan in the Actionist world, *mutatis mutandum*.

A diminutive of "Carlos" is "Carlitos," sometimes used in the Castaneda books. Hence the caption.

RESPONSIBILITY

Actionism stresses responsibility. You're responsible for what you think and what you do. However, this also makes you free. In this respect, just listen to what Robert Heinlein (1907-1987) says in his 1966 novel *The Moon Is a Harsh Mistress*: "*I am free because I know that I alone am morally responsible for everything I do.*"

From another American, Carlos Castaneda, we have a similar quote:

"When a man decides to do something, he must go all the way, (...) but he must take responsibility for what he does. No matter what he does, he must know first why he is doing it, and then he must proceed with his actions without having doubts or remorse about them." [Castaneda 1990 III p 56]

Both these quotes could make you think of Soren Kierkegaard (1813-1855), who said that realizing that you're human, a single soul part of the divine whole, you become free and responsible at the same time. (More on Kierkegaard in Chapter 36).

And the topical comment on this? This is the Actionist creed *in nuce*, living the responsible life, a life where you take charge of your personal operation. *You* decide what existentially to do, no one else. And this is the highest form of freedom. To control your every action, thought and emotion, this is to assume responsibility in your life, resulting in a strong, active and free life. It might sound like a stiff and inflexible way of being, devoid of spontaneity. But practice makes perfect and after a while, having put Will to the fore in your life, it becomes your natural way of being, a way of being both free and orderly.

In Castaneda's books there is a lot of wisdom mirroring the Actionist creed. This study, *Actionism*, has already proven that to you, mainly in Chapter 3. This chapter, Chapter 10, takes a more comprehensive look at the man, his thought and his work. It may mean some repetition – which, for its part, is a key feature of learning.

I choose to start by looking at Castaneda quotes dealing with two Actionist hobby-horses: Will and Holism. First, a holistic quote of the man, standing for itself: *"Life in itself is sufficient, self-explanatory and complete."* [Ibid 1974 p 59]

From the same book (*Tales of Power*), another poignant quote in the realm of existing holistically, a quote I indeed have highlighted before. This is rather reminiscent of the Actionist condition: *"The average man is hooked to his fellow men, while the warrior is hooked only to infinity."* [Ibid p 7]

LENNART SVENSSON

THE SPIRIT

Castaneda knew that the Operational Life is spiritual in nature. The spokesman in these quotes is Castaneda's teacher Don Juan and he never mentioned "God"; instead he said "the Spirit," as Native Americans sometimes do. As for Actionism, it has no problem with seeing the spirit as God; Actionism isn't "anti-God," it's divine. *"The average man acts only if there is a chance for profit. Warriors say they act not for profit but for the spirit."* [Ibid 1991 p 79]

To operate with feeling, having zest and flare in your actions, acknowledging that the Universe is alive, that the Earth is an organism you have to fathom holistically, is rather well captured in these quotes:

> "Look at every path closely and deliberately. Try it as many times as you think necessary. Then ask yourself alone, one question... Does this path have a heart? If it does, the path is good; if it doesn't it is of no use. (...) For me there is only the traveling on paths that have heart, on any path that may have heart, and the only worthwhile challenge is to traverse its full length – and there I travel looking, looking breathlessly." [1990 I p 106; p 182]

Next a quote in the same vein, about living your life as an adventure, acknowledging the wonder of living in an Omniverse of possibilities: *"We are men and our lot in life is to learn and to be hurled into inconceivable new worlds."* [1990 II p 160]

WILL

Now, as promised, for some Willpower related passages in Castaneda. Will is a mainstay of Actionism; this has to be underlined again and again. Every person needs Will to get going. And especially a soldier. To step up, take charge, chop-chop and on the double; that's the volitional life, military style.

ACTIONISM

Actionism isn't the first doctrine saying this. Already in the 20th century, a Mexican Indian formulated a variety of the Operational Lifestyle, the volitional creed. He summarized what it means to live a volitional life, determined to fathom the riddles of "life, the universe and everything," no matter what the cost. Specifically he, Don Juan, said:

> *"A man goes to knowledge as he goes to war, wide awake, with fear, with respect, and with absolute assurance. Going to knowledge or going to war in any other manner is a mistake, and whoever makes it might never live to regret it."* [Castaneda 1990 I p 52]

Castaneda, in the form of his guru, Don Juan, knew about operational willpower, of assuming the responsibility of living in the here-and-now: *"A warrior, or any man for that matter, cannot possibly wish he were somewhere else; a warrior because he lives by challenge, an ordinary man because he doesn't know where his death is going to find him."* [1974 p 114]

Finally this: summing up the art of living a volitional life in a complex, variegated, sometimes scary, but ultimately wonderful, world: *"The art of a warrior is to balance the terror of being alive with the wonder of being alive."* [1990 III p 202]

SERIES

Essentially, the Castaneda series consists of the following nine books:

1. *The Teachings of Don Juan – A Yaqui Way of Knowledge* (1968)
2. *A Separate Reality* (1971)
3. *Journey to Ixtlan* (1972)
4. *Tales of Power* (1974)
5. *The Second Ring of Power* (1977)

6. *The Eagle's Gift* (1981)
7. *The Fire from Within* (1984)
8. *The Power of Silence* (1987)
9. *The Art of Dreaming* (1993)

Books 1-4 portray Castaneda's journey from neophyte to magician. Then, in books 5-6, comes an ambiguous phase with Castaneda as the new magic ring leader without the presence of Don Juan, the low-key, yet charismatic, guru who had been the focus of the previous books. However, in books 7-9, Don Juan returns, with various retakes from the educational phase. In the rest of this chapter I'll take a look at some of these books, making an Actionist reading of them. I start in the middle, with the often neglected *The Second Ring of Power*.

BASIC ELEMENT

The basic thesis for an esotericist would be this: in its essence, reality is spiritual. The material has a lower reality than the spiritual. Castaneda's books fit like a glove in this world-view. Castaneda time and again depicts how he encounters "instances of non-ordinary reality" and, in the end, the trance becomes constant, the hyper-real becomes the real and the everyday world becomes a shadow, a mere emotion = Maya of Illusion.

However, the everyday is also portrayed. The narrator of the book at hand is Carlos Castaneda, operating in Mexico as the leader of a magic circle, a group of shamans. When *The Second Ring of Power* (1977) begins, he must take over the leadership of the circle; he's now the Nagual, the leader, having been groomed for this role by his teacher, Don Juan, for about ten years. Now Don Juan is gone and Castaneda must try it out alone; he has to take command, pointing the way ahead for his group. He has to learn the meaning of Schwarzkopf's dictum: "When placed in command – take charge."

Apart from the magical outings, this is a book about raising your mental awareness. The first level is everyday awareness = the first ring of power. The second level is a kind of trance = heightened awareness = the second ring of power, intimated in the title. This kind of heightened awareness, for instance, can be experienced by an author working in an inspired state. Things that have seemed difficult to solve become easy when in this state of mind, working in a sort of trance. Every true artist, be he an author, an actor or a singer – and even sportsmen and every kind of action man – can experience examples of this trance like phenomenon. It's called *flow*.

In order to reach heightened awareness you need Will, concentrated Thought = intuition governed by Will.

Later in this book, the Italian thinker Julius Evola will be treated (Chapter 12). And like Julius Evola's thought, the Castaneda creed (or Don Juan, by way of Castaneda) is somewhat adverse to Christianity. But the Castaneda books don't very much delve into this; this is no anti-Christian diatribe. An operational pro doesn't waste his time on what he doesn't teach. And having said that, there are traces of Eternal Light even in this doctrine. Like, for example: "*the world of the Nagual is the world of heaven*", it's said [Castaneda 1977 p 235]. And even Don Juan's shamans turn toward the sun to find power: "We are pieces of the sun" says La Gorda, "*That is why we are luminous beings.*" [Ibid p 137]

These luminous beings, for their part, refer to the human aura in detail in this and the following books. That we have an aura is a cornerstone of all esoteric theory; the physical body is surrounded by subtle bodies, this Western scholars have known since Plato, in short, we consist of body, soul and spirit. Here the system is described with some slight stylistic differences, but the theme song is that the body is material and less real than the subtler bodies. This unites Castaneda with the mainstream of Old World esotericism. As intimated, only the style and atmosphere is different, the style of a lightning illuminating the wilderness, crows at dusk and gold glitter from a butterfly's wings.

INTUITION

All esotericists emphasize the value of intuition, even Castaneda (as on page 261 in the 1977 book). The style of the book series in general is rather dry, but there are openings to art, poetry and the meaning of dreams. Dreaming in this context is fairly systematic, but it doesn't prevent the mood of Castaneda's world from being a great source of inspiration for filmmakers and writers, that is, for people who aren't directly mystics or esotericists. Castaneda has sold millions, so his ideas have been received to some extent; however, the materialist mainstream of today is against this Perennial Wisdom. But now the tables are turning; intuition and to seek within, willpower and meditation are becoming increasingly popular. The days are numbered for hedonistic liberalism and nihilist defeatism. And Castaneda has some part in this spiritual revival. He's a grey area figure but the essence of his books is about changing your life with willpower, becoming a spiritually guided operator and not a dejected, pleasure-seeking dandy.

POPULAR

Castaneda's books are serious fiction in popular form. Along with conceptual wisdom they are stories, narratives in reportage form with a tinge of atmosphere. So hereby some mundane quotes that convey, nonetheless, essential elements, those of tangibility and relatability. This is what makes Castaneda's books eminently readable. Many other spiritual books have page after page of esoteric ideas, but no scenes or details. It may become too much. Castaneda, however, has a balance between idea and form, between everyday and eternity.

> *"The next day I was by myself all morning. I worked on my notes. In the afternoon I used my car to help La Gorda and the little sisters transport the furniture from dona Soledad's house to their house."* [1977 p 217]

ACTIONISM

"She shook her head. Her teeth clattered but she could not say a word. Her fright seemed to be extreme. She pushed me to keep on walking. I could not help wondering why I was not scared out of my wits myself."[Ibid p 141]

"Pablito sat down to eat and among the four of us we finished a whole pot of food. Benigno washed the bowls and carefully put them back in the box and then all of us sat down comfortably around the table." [Ibid p 199]

INTRIGUE

Now on to *The Eagle's Gift* (1981), which is rather intriguing. Like the previous book in the series, *The Second Ring of Power*, it's about Castaneda asserting himself as a Nagual, as a leader of a group of shamans. Their previous leader, Don Juan Matus, was charismatic and seemingly all-knowing and without him they all seem destitute.

This is a group of magicians being conceptually lost. Now they have to remember anew various hidden knowledge they all possess, regaining it on their own, without the solid leadership that their former guru had always given them. With their new, immature, leader (Carlos Castaneda) in the lead, they gradually try to recall some lessons they received in different states of consciousness. The experiments lead them to abandon the house they have in a pastoral Mexican valley; the trip takes them to Mexico City and beyond, to the unseen countries and the unreal reality.

As in the previous book, *The Eagle's Gift* portrays the path of glorious knowledge, like how to dream, how to remember – and how to perform "not doing," in Taoist fashion, realizing the essence of the dictum: "Do nothing, and everything will be done." In this process Castaneda allows us to meet people like the Nagual Woman, Silvio Manuel, Vicente, Nestor and Pablito: clear-cut individuals all, rooted in the Mexican soil and refined by thousands of years of occult knowledge, a Tradition reportedly stemming from Atlantis and then further developed by Mexico's Indians in pre-Columbian and Columbian times.

SUNKEN LAND

Atlantis is said to be a sunken continent in the Atlantic Ocean – and this sea, for its part, takes its name from this particular land: Atlantis. This would be a case of cause and effect, a simple connection. What was first? Atlantis, the land with this name. The ancient Greeks didn't know any sea called "the Atlantic" but they knew of Atlantis.

The doctrine Castaneda utilizes reportedly originated on Atlantis and was then transferred, (12,000 years ago when the continent sank), to lands in the East and the West. To the East at the time was Egypt and Europe; to the West was North and South America. According to myth, such a figure as Aztlan, the man who gave the Aztecs their name, went to America with it. The doctrine took root and was further developed: it was formal magic and human and nature oriented mysteries. With the Spaniards' arrival, this esoteric movement had to go underground, but it didn't die out; the teachings were passed down from generation to generation, from guru to student in unbroken succession, and, according to the book in question, Castaneda was the last heir. Now the doctrine is passed on to us, we who are reading this. In our time, however, the formerly prevalent ritual and secrecy aren't needed anymore, there is no initiation or magic circle. Everything is public; everything is printed: just go to the books and check out titles such as *The Eagle's Gift* and others.

ACTIONISM

MOLD OF MAN

As intimated, in the Castaneda books Don Juan comes through as rather anti-Christian. I won't dwell on the reasons for that; he simply is. Castaneda himself, on the other hand, is more ambiguous in this respect. For instance, in *The Fire from Within* (1984) there's a glorified episode of "seeing God". That's how Castaneda interprets it. Per se, this divine rendering gives the otherwise obscure world of Castaneda some clarity, some common ground with Western mysticism. Castaneda's world is often conceptually unrelated to anything else – so when he speaks of "God" it becomes more relatable.

When Castaneda, in the current book, says that souls are created of some primordial light matter, then, it must be emphasized, it's in sync with Actionism. You might remember the passage in Chapter 1 of this book, *Actionism*, saying that man's soul was created from a spark of the Eternal Light of God.

Castaneda is into the same train of thought. For instance, *The Fire from Within* mentions that man is created in God's image. However, the guru Don Juan doesn't use the concept of God. He uses the term "the mold of man". But a qualified guess is that this, nevertheless, is the question of God as a model for man. For instance, the narrator Castaneda sees it in terms of God.

The central scene in *The Fire From Within* is literally rather far out: it shows us what happens in "heaven" when people's souls are created. First we see a primordial miasma of souls, still formless, "the soul matter," as it were. This is then shaped into human form through something called "the mold of man". It's like a glorified cookie-cutter: put in some mass, stamp it and voilà, we have a human soul, formed in God's image...!

It's described in an industrial and slightly irreverent manner. The disgracefulness is due to Don Juan, commenting on this magnificent scene with various pejoratives. Castaneda, however, is amazed and sees God.

Some quotes may illuminate the whole. It's from Chapter 6 of *The Fire From Within*, titled "The Mold of Man". It begins with Don Juan during a lesson out in the open having begun to talk to Carlos about "the mold of man". Don Juan gives an explanation of the mold of man...

> *"... in terms of a pattern of energy that serves to stamp the qualities of humanness on an amorphous blob of biological matter. At least, I understood it that way, especially after he further described the mold of man using a mechanical analogy. He said that it was like a gigantic die that stamps out human beings endlessly as if they were coming to it on a mass production conveyor belt. He vividly mimed the process by bringing the palms of his hands together with great force, as if the die molded a human being each time its two halves were clapped."* [Castaneda 1985 p 280-281]

Then Don Juan says that the mold shouldn't be seen as God. But this is just an interpretation. Here you could just as well agree with Castaneda (who personally objected to Don Juan's reasoning) that some might call it God. Don Juan, for his part, calls the casting a mindless process, "*a cast that groups together a particular bunch of fiber-like elements, which we call man*". [Ibid p 282] They argue over this. Castaneda then enters a deeper trance.

TRANCE

Castaneda is brought into a deeper trance. He feels a supernatural peace imbued with a hyper-real light:

> *"That light was a haven, an oasis in the blackness around me. From my subjective point of view, I saw that light for an immeasurable length of time. The splendor of the sight was beyond anything I can say, and yet I could not figure out what it was that made it so beautiful. Then the idea came to me that its beauty grew out of a sense of harmony, a sense of peace and rest, of having arrived, of being safe at long last. I felt myself inhaling and exhaling in*

quietude and relief. What a gorgeous sense of plenitude! I knew beyond a shadow of doubt that I had come face to face with God, the source of everything. And I knew that God loved me. God was love and forgiveness. The light bathed me, and I felt clean, delivered." [Ibid p 283]

But then the voice of Don Juan comes to him through the trance, saying that the stage of peace and tranquility you experience by the mold is only a stop on the way. The form itself is sterile and static. And then this:

"It was at the same time a flat reflected image and the mirror itself. And the image was man's image." [Ibid]

The last words are Don Juan's description, but still, this is Christian esotericism in a nutshell. In this tradition, it may read: "the primordial idea is both image and mirror image" = German, "*das Urbild is Bild und Spiegelbild*", as Jünger says in the novel *Eumeswil* (1977). So Don Juan's tendency to disparage it all into an industrial process seems to me rather wayward. And in the process, Castaneda objects to Don Juan's description. Then he thinks, well, it is what it is. And then he sees the glorified Being of Light:

[T]he light seemed to condense and I saw a man. A shiny man that exuded charisma, love, understanding, sincerity, truth. A man that was the sum total of all that is good. [Ibid p 284]

Next, Castaneda wants to kneel down and worship this God, but then he's taken out of the trance by his guru, the omnipotent Don Juan. What we see here are contradictory interpretations. Castaneda sees the mold in terms of God and so on. Don Juan sees it in terms of an industrial process. Maybe it's a matter of perspective. Don Juan teases Castaneda for his seeing God as a man, seeing the Being of Light in divine terms. But more than Castaneda have done this, such as Swedish mystic Göran Grip in his near-death experience (q.v. *Allting finns*, 1994)

LENNART SVENSSON

INTERPRETATIONS

This is a question of the immanent pre-understandings we all have. Castaneda personally has a certain Christian luggage. When, in the first book of the series, he encounters Mescalito, the peyote god, he falls on his knees before him and "confesses his sins". In some other places in the series some other Christian traits of Castaneda are uttered, although he's no Christian of the high-church kind. Don Juan, for his part, is completely non-Christian but he also admits that other members of the group see shamanism in Christian terms. So this is a matter of interpretation, nothing else – a question about how to express the things you see in a trance, not an objective description of the ontology itself.

Thus: the Mold can rather well be called God. If what Castaneda saw wasn't God, then what should we call it? This degenerates into a mere play of words.

BEING OF LIGHT

Chapter sixteen of *The Fire from Within* continues with various arguments. For instance, Castaneda recalls that he had seen the mold several times. It was unambiguously male, the Light Being encountered in a "near-death experience" by the above mentioned Göran Grip also was uniquely male. It's intimated by Don Juan that women see this god figure as female. This is in sync with Gnostic thought, wherein God is both male and female. Per se, Actionism also acknowledges this idea, although I use the pronoun "he" about God for simplicity's sake.

Castaneda then says that the shamans' approach to see the mold in an impersonal way gives you a more sober view. This is also in line with esotericism and Actionism at large: toning down the devotional attitude in favor of a, shall we say, operational mindset, even in the face of God. Then, in the chapter at hand, is reproduced a new trance-like, magnificent sight that Castaneda receives and, once again it's about obtaining divine warmth and piety. It's unconditional submission, service, love and quiet joy. Castaneda spontaneously feels this before "the mold," that is, God. He "receives the grace". Conversely, those trying to explain this away in reductionist fashion are blind and deaf.

RESEARCH

You could say: like Julius Evola, Don Juan in his creed is an unsentimental warrior type. So if this seasoned soldier isn't able to feel enthusiasm, be that as it may. But to see him, Don Juan, as the ideal man, the ideal of a guru, is difficult after this: his limiting, narrowing attitude to the divine.

However, this episode is very illustrative in general. On the essential points, it can't be more amazing than this. This is central to the metaphysics of Western and Eastern thought and Actionism. Who hasn't asked himself how souls are created, how this works with the "image of God" in reality? The above scene in *The Fire From Within* gives an answer as good as anything, the best answer I've personally seen yet, an illustration of the Actionist concept of "God creating souls out of his Light, shaping them in his image". In the beginning was Compassion and this is mirrored in the love Castaneda feels for the Being of Light. Also, to see the process partly in a sober way, seeing the process of the soul material being injected into a mold where it gets its human form, this is a substantial contribution to the question of how people's souls are created. The metaphysical research evolves. We need to express old truths with a new vocabulary. This is at the forefront of 21st century esotericism.

SILENCE

Castaneda's eighth book is called *The Power of Silence* (1987). Those who want anecdotes from the lives of the Mexican magicians will have a feast here. In order to highlight different ideas Castaneda's teacher, Don Juan tells stories about his own apprenticeship, about his guru Julian, and also Julian's guru Elias. Don Juan had the privilege to be instructed by both the stern Julian and the softer, older Elias.

Julian was a hard man, a man with a fiendish trait. It's true that even Don Juan, in his time, exposed Castaneda to tough trials, but Julian, for his part, seemed to outright enjoy testing Don Juan beyond the limits of safety. However, the goal was always a noble one: to increase the disciple's knowledge.

The stories that Castaneda reproduces in *The Power of Silence* have a specific purpose. They are said to be Don Juan's, his teacher's, way of illustrating how the Spirit (= God) can approach us. We are therefore given a series of stories with conceptual meaning, an essence called "abstract cores". In turn, these cores show how the Spirit approaches the agent, how the Spirit knocks on his closed world, how the agent is forced to respond and open and, lastly, to go out to meet the Knowledge of the great unknown. A general requirement for gaining knowledge in the Castaneda fashion is to silence your inner monologue. You must achieve Inner Silence to obtain Esoteric Knowledge. Having finally received this knowledge you can move trance-like in this world and the next.

In Actionism the importance of silencing of the inner mind is rather similar to the emphasis Castaneda puts on it. In Actionism the practice is called "reaching inner silence" = to willfully quiet down your internal monologue. This I mentioned in Chapter 2.

STORIES

The stories given in *The Power of Silence* sometimes tell us of how the wizards in the circle at hand met their vocations and became who they became. One interesting thing is that Julian, Don Juan's tough teacher, was a Spaniard. He had Spanish ancestry, like Castaneda. For his part, Don Juan was a Yaqui Indian. Elias, too, was a native, like most others in the magic circle as described here: Don Genaro, la Catalina, la Gorda, Nestor and Pablito and Silvio Manuel. However: some were Spaniards like Vicente and Florinda Grau (and Castaneda and Julian). Philosophically, this doesn't matter much in the books, but of course the ethnic factor occasionally rears its head. The Indians have a marginal advantage in that the sorcery described is Native American, having mostly been handed by Indians.

On the outset, *The Power of Silence* is a clearly structured book. We have the abstract cores; we have the stories of shamanism meant to illustrate how the Spirit knocks on the door. We meet Julian, Elias and the young Don Juan, and then we follow Don Juan and Castaneda on their contemporary hikes: in one scene, we are, for example, presented with their encounter with a puma in the desert, which is strange because pumas don't venture out into the open, boundless wilds. It's a crisp narrative giving the reader some leisure from the more abstract passages.

The Castaneda books aren't artistic; they aren't part of the more refined South American or North American literature per se. However, some bookshops and libraries do file them under *fiction*, not *esoterica*. And it's true that Don Juan likes poetry, he needs it to mirror the feelings he harbors of the sometimes arduous sorcerer path. One such poem is quoted in the book, a work by Juan Ramón Jiménez (Spanish Nobel Prize winner, 1881-1958). It says much about anticipating the ineffable, to intuitively fathom the invisible forces that are out there, instances of the astral world:

> *Is it I who walks tonight*
> *in my room or is it the beggar*
> *who was prowling in my garden*
> *at nightfall?*
>
> *I look around*
> *and find that everything*
> *is the same and it is not the same...*
> *Was the window open?*

Had I not already fallen asleep?

Was not the garden pale green?...
The sky was clear and blue...
And there are clouds
and it is windy
and the garden is dark and gloomy.

I think that my hair was black...
I was dressed in gray...
And my hair is gray
and I am wearing black...
Is this my gait?
Does this voice, which now resounds in me,
have the rhythms of the voice I used to have?
Am I myself or am I the beggar
who was prowling in my garden
at nightfall?

I look around...
There are clouds and it is windy...
The garden is dark and gloomy...

I come and go... Is it not true
that I had already fallen asleep?
My hair is gray... And everything
is the same and it is not the same...

YAQUI WAY

In the summer of 1960 anthropologist Carlos Castaneda met up with a Yaqui-Native American named Don Juan Matus. It was in Arizona, USA. Castaneda studied at UCLA in California. He sought out the Indian to receive information about psychotropic plants. After some hesitation Don Juan began to tell him of this. In 1961

Castaneda formally became Don Juan's disciple in Yaqui wisdom. The discipleship lasted until 1965, when Castaneda withdrew from it all. It was too arduous, too trying. In 1968 he published *The Teachings of Don Juan – A Yaqui Way of Knowledge*. And then, when he had the impulse to visit Don Juan and show him the book, the discipleship started anew. For instance, as for ideas conveyed, in the subsequent books *A Separate Reality, Journey to Ixtlan* and *Tales of Power*, Don Juan teaches Castaneda the importance of being a spiritual warrior, of being familiar with the idea of death. In Actionist terms this is equal to MMM = the Memento Mori Mindset. Of this I told in Chapter 1. And in Chapter 3 I discussed the Castaneda books on instances of Willpower and Holism, on challenges and how to win, how to act in accordance with Infinity.

So what's left to tell?

A fine episode is given in *Journey to Ixtlan*. As intimated at the beginning of this chapter, Actionism has nothing to do with magic in the formal sense. But in general spiritual terms, the vision quest that Castaneda performs in this book is of great interest. A vision quest is a rite of passage for the Native American disciple – it's the test, the big test that will determine whether you have the right stuff, if you can face the powers of nature on your own, meeting the elements and the invisible forces being out there.

This is classic. We've seen it before: in comics (the Buddy Longway graphic novel *The White Demon*) and even in comedies like *Family Guy* and *The Simpsons*: venture out in nature completely on your own, barefoot and without food, drink or camping equipment, and meet a coyote speaking with Johnny Cash's voice... These parodies don't denigrate the myth as such, its tempting and alluring qualities; instead, they contribute to the whole. And a serious example of the narrative in question is to be found in Castaneda's *Journey to Ixtlan* (1972) where the somewhat slow disciple Carlos finally must go out on his own vision quest. As usual, he's resisting the task, finding a thousand excuses, but Don Juan cuts him short:

"No more of that." [Castaneda 1990 III p 262]

This is a wonderful line to hear. This is the third book in the series and in all three the sluggishness of Castaneda-the-person annoys you. He doesn't understand the gist of Don Juan's world, doesn't understand the invisible, the unconditioned, the reality of the discreet forces governing Reality. Carlitos is stuck in an everyday, conditioned view of the world.

But the task at hand is exactly about this, to shatter this everyday image. He must stop the world, stop the usual flow of impressions. The mirror of objectivism must be smashed and an individual-centered approach must take its place. "Subjectivity is truth," as Kierkegaard said. It's about finding the truth within, of reaching inner mental calm in order to see more clearly.

Carlos has to go out into nature, alone, and he can't bring along food or a tent. He must venture out into the boundless desert, into Meister Eckart's "Stille Wüste". "All true prophets have come from the desert," as the saying goes. Specifically, Carlos has to meet up with his *totem animal*, the sacred symbolized in an animal. So he takes his car and drives away from Don Juan's cabin there in Sonora, Mexico; he drives a little haphazardly, stops the car and goes out. And sits down on a stone and calms down, fading into the spirit of the landscape.

COYOTE

After a while he sees a coyote, an American wild dog, sauntering out over the neighborhood. And it approaches. And soon it's only a few meters away; its brown eyes are friendly and clear.

Some sort of telepathic communication begins ("How are you, little coyote?" – "I'm all right, and you?"). And this makes Castaneda start. But then he calms himself down, and:

> "[The coyote] lay down on its stomach and tilted its head and asked, "Why are you afraid?" I sat down facing it and I carried on the weirdest conversation I had ever had. Finally it asked me

what I was doing there and I said I had come there to "stop the world". The coyote said, "Que bueno!" and then I realized that it was a bilingual coyote. (...) The coyote stood up and our eyes met. I stared fixedly into them. I felt they were pulling me and suddenly the animal became iridescent; it began to glow. (...) [T]he coyote was a fluid, liquid, luminous being. Its luminosity was dazzling. I wanted to cover my eyes with my hands to protect them, but I could not move. The luminous being touched me in some undefined part of myself and my body experienced such an exquisite indescribable warmth and well-being that it was as if the touch had made me explode. I became transfixed, I could not feel my feet, or my legs, or any part of my body, yet something was sustaining me erect. – I have no idea how long I stayed in that position. In the meantime, the luminous coyote and the hilltop where I stood melted away. I had no thoughts or feelings. Everything had been turned off and I was floating freely." [p 266]

In other words: Castaneda has stopped the world. Then he comes back to Don Juan and becomes his usual, doubting self again. However, step by step, he loses his old self and becomes ready for a new totality, "the totality of oneself". This is what Castaneda's books are about: going from reductionism to a systemic view à la *shamanique*, going from a fragmented everyday self to a whole Self, in harmony with the cosmos. This is also the case with Actionism, which is about holism and living the Big Picture, as I elaborated upon in Chapter 1. It's about becoming what you spiritually are, it's about *individuation*.

POETRY

Actionism is a phenomenon in the grey area between ethics, history, art and politics. As for art, the Castaneda books, as intimated, aren't expressly artistic but they have instances of musicality among all the esotericism. For instance, above was quoted a poem by Juan Rámon

Jiménez that Don Juan himself liked to hear, a poem illustrating the ambiguous character of the esotericist life.

Another Jiménez poem quoted in the series, in *The Fire From Within,* is "Hora Inmensa". This, too, highlights the indescribable character of Being, of living reflectively and consciously, of trying to do more in life than just indulging in materialist ignorance:

> *Only a bell and a bird break the stillness...*
> *It seems that the two talk with the setting sun.*
> *Golden colored silence, the afternoon is made of crystals.*
> *A roving purity sways the cool trees,*
> *and beyond all that,*
> *a transparent river dreams that trampling over pearls*
> *it breaks loose*
> *and flows into infinity.*

Surrealist poetry has become something of a cliché in our time, but the vaguely surreal payoff in this poem gives it that delicate touch. Just enough – just wonderful.

In Castaneda's books it's told that Don Juan likes to hear poetry, it speaks to something unspeakable in him, and Castaneda's books reproduce these kind of poems – central, essential lyrical poems, poems expressing that which only poems can express. It doesn't educate, it doesn't narrate, it simply – *is*.

Another such central lyricism is found in *Tales of Power*: a poem by César Vallejo called "*Black Stone on a White Stone*". Perhaps the poem has some didactic aspect – but then it's discreetly presented, in symbols, as in all art worthy of its name.

> *I will die in Paris while it rains,*
> *on a day which I already remember.*
> *I will die in Paris – and I do not run away –*
> *perhaps in the Autumn, on a Thursday, as it is today.*

ACTIONISM

It will be a Thursday, because today,
the Thursday that I write these lines,
my bones feel the turn,
and never so much as today, in all my road,
have I seen myself alone.

"A poem can do without everything except rhythm," someone said, and this we see an example of here. The text has rhythm, it's got flow, and then the matter of it being abstract or concrete is of lesser importance. Without rhythm, the whole thing would seem like prose, rather bland prose to that. Such is the language of magic.

Vallejo, by the way, was a Peruvian born in 1892, living for a while in Paris in his youth, hence the poem's theme. Indeed, he did in fact die in Paris, in 1938.

TALES OF POWER

In order to give an overview of all the central Castaneda books, some lines about *Tales of Power* (1974) should be delivered.

Tales of Power is a sort of summation of the discipleship of Castaneda; the student isn't so slow in this book, he's about to graduate – and he does. Don Juan is in excellent shape throughout the book, he delivers moral-metaphysical one-liners by the bag. As they say, this is "a great read". Also, it's an exposé of the weird and the occult, Mexican style, so this is no ordinary fantasy. However, a classic of esotericism, existentialism and Actionism, it is.

SIMILARITIES

Two thinkers anticipating the essence of Actionism were Carlos Castaneda (1925-1998) and Julius Evola (1898-1974). Despite all the superficial differences (one a New World shaman, the other an Old World esotericist) Castaneda and Evola are two of a kind, highlighting the active life as a way to mental development.

For instance, Castaneda spoke about the seer as a warrior, having the same attitude as a soldier going to war: the attitude was summarized above as "with fear, with respect, with apprehension and with total determination". Having "memento mori" ingrained in his being the seer is both meek and fierce: metaphysically meek, operationally fierce. This soldiery aspect was also present in Evola, who spoke about his "kshatriya bent". Like no one else, Evola stressed soldiery ideals in esotericism.

Overall, Castaneda and Evola shared these traits: a no-nonsense attitude toward life, indifference toward Christianity, an interest in magic and contempt for devotional religion and the *petit bourgeois* life.

As you know, Actionism has nothing to do with magic in the formal sense. And it's not hostile or indifferent toward Christianity at large. But otherwise, the Castaneda-Evola mindset of active esotericism, of stressing the volitional life and the need for a warrior-like approach, is a constant inspiration for Actionism.

Evola, as such, will be treated in a following chapter. As for the affinity between Castaneda's and Evola's thought, Evola's *The Yoga of Power* (1968) is a viable document to examine. For instance, Chapter 7, "The Virgin: Release From Bondage," delineates the basics of becoming a Tantric yogi, a *vira*. For example, Evola means that a vira disciple may use everyday delusions, hardships and failures as lessons toward yogic mastership, and in Castaneda's books we read of "the art of stalking" that uses everyday situations as ways of spiritual evolution.

Furthermore, a vira takes responsibility for all his actions and doesn't acknowledge "sin," of being impure and waiting to be "redeemed" as if by a court of law; this is a fundamental of Evola's ethics, and is much in the vein of what Don Juan teaches Castaneda. In the latter respect, it's conceptualized as *Assuming Responsibility*. In *The Yoga of Power* Evola goes on to say that a vira faces fear, he has a contempt for the bourgeois lifestyle and he has to purify his will, and this we also find in Castaneda's apprenticeship. Specifically, as for the anti-bourgeois element, Castaneda, when he had started out being a disciple, after a while found out that his friends back in LA were only materialistic whiners, whereas the world of Don Juan, hard and arduous as it was, was infinitely more variegated and wonderful. Being a disciple, purifying one's will, testing one's mental strength, was the thing to do, much like the vira ideal that Evola embraced.

The Evola Chapter in *Actionism* won't mention viras or *The Yoga of Power* per se – but you'll see some more aspects of the above strains there, like discussing the volitional life, the no-nonsense attitude and the interest in Eastern doctrines like Buddhism.

MYSTICISM

Returning to Castaneda proper, his doctrine is a bit unsystematic. It's holistic, for better or worse: for us, living now, the wisdom is gained by reading all of the nine basic books, following the narrative of Castaneda becoming a master esotericist, of stories Don Juan relates to highlight the argument and of stories of the other disciples of the ring. I'll give you none of this here, instead I'll mention some additional wisdoms of the Castaneda books that are enlightening.

Enlightening indeed, like speaking of *light*, of sunlight. In *The Fire from Within* it says that inner peace, plus looking at some shimmering or shining object or surface, like sunshine on a mountain, is a key that unlocks spiritual treasures. In the same book it says that earth is a living being, she has an aura like us; the same wisdom is repeated in *The Power of Silence* which mentions that the earth has a soul and that its consciousness can affect a man's consciousness. This book also speaks of the silent knowledge we all have within, it can be reached by meditation and contemplation.

In this manner the Castaneda books convey a lot of esoteric wisdom, more often than not, possible to relate to. True, there's a lot of "weirdness" and specific terminology in this series, but the fruitful aspects dominate. *Mutatis mutandum* Castaneda is worth listening to.

Now, finally, let me add a personal remark. Evola practiced yoga, Castaneda practiced magic and I don't endorse all of their respective doctrines. But overall, these two figures remain inspirations for Actionism. As for Castaneda, his books, above all, taught me *Memento Mori*. This was in the mid 1990s, the lesson was hard to learn but I did embrace it after a while. It took time. But it was worth it, worth the endured angst. Castaneda taught me to face death, sober up in view of this and to assume responsibility for who I am and what I do. For this I am eternally grateful.

Castaneda (often in the form of Don Juan) taught me to shape up and stop indulging in never ending ruminations. We come here to learn and there's a life to be lived. As for the Castaneda books at large, you may find more inspiration in the stories and the moods than the practices as such; when they "do magic," when Castaneda relates some incomprehensible instance it gets a bit esoteric. But he remains a commanding figure. He went far. Actionism might lean more toward Christ as a way and a portal – "I am the door" he said, being the Logos, the element of The Beginning whose name is "I AM". This, Steiner has showed us. Logos is inside us all; this is the defining feature of man. That said, Castaneda stands as a symbol of a man raising himself mentally, a man discovering the force of Will, a man becoming all that he could be. On the net can be found this verdict that makes him into a vanguard of esotericism, a portal figure for our age:

> "[T]he spirit of the times dictates that today we no longer need naguals or gurus to help us on the Warrior's path. [Carlos Castaneda] left an energetic door open for whoever can go through it." [source: "Florinda Grau Chronology, part XIII" http://sustainedaction.org/Chronologies/chronFlorindaXIII.htm]

This quote speaks about not needing a guru – but Castaneda had Don Juan as a guru...? True, but you can do a lot with your own Will-Thought. As for the just mentioned Evola, he also de-emphasized the guru aspect, the need for initiation. A clever Actionist, an Aristocrat of the Soul with a modicum of order inside, can develop himself spiritually by reading, meditating and creating systematically.

11. D'ANNUNZIO

Italian author Gabriele d'Annunzio might have been a controversial figure. I don't endorse everything he did. However, he had a vigorous outlook on life and art. d'Annunzio was something of an operational pro, a glorified Action Man. *Mutatis mutandum*, he incorporated Actionist traits such as artistry, Rest In Action and enthusiasm.

FLAME

Gabriele d'Annunzio (1863-1938) wrote several novels. The last one, *The Flame of Life* (*Il Fuoco*, 1900, English translation same year), was the epitome of them all. It's energetic, it radiates strength and inspiration, and yet the narrative pace is slow and deliberate. d'Annunzio wastes no time in depicting troubles or hardships; he isn't driven by indignation, he's driven by enthusiasm. And, at the same time, this novel isn't a monotonous song of praise. It explores art and life through the temperament of the protagonist, Stelio Effrena. The quotations from the book made below are translated from the Swedish edition from 1946: *Elden*, published by N&K.

The Flame of Life tells us about Stelio Effrena, a brilliant poet, composer and playwright, slightly more than 20 years old. The poet's last name is constructed to give this meaning: "no reins," from the Latin *ex frenis*. Stelio is a creative volcano, not curbed by the ideas of conventional morality. He lives his life creatively and amorously, shaping it positively and operationally. His accomplice is the 40 year-old actress, La Foscarina, modeled after Eleonora Duse (1858-1924) whom d'Annunzio was dating in real life. But there, IRL, the age difference was just four and a half years, to her possible disadvantage. However, d'Annunzio in *La Foscarina* enthusiastically portrays a mature woman. The passions run high although Foscarina isn't "drop dead gorgeous" in every inch. She has personality and charisma, as the actor she is.

The novel begins on an evening in Venice in September 1882, with Stelio and Foscarina riding a gondola over the roads. The woman worships her poet, she points to things in the environment that she figures would inspire him. Thus it goes on for about 30 pages: an energetic mood, yet quiet, with graphic depictions of the environment. The water of Venice is set afire in the annual fire festival that the city celebrates with fireworks. The fire is likened to creative fire and *the flame of life* itself, all the time balanced against the Venice channels, the lagoon and all. Like a painter, d'Annunzio conveys every nuance of the shifting waters.

As a side-note, this scene could remind you of the beginning of Werner Herzog's movie *Fitzcarraldo* (1982). The pair of Klaus Kinsky and Claudia Cardinale, in 19th century dress, going by a small boat to an opera, apart from the vaguely similar props, conveys the same spirit as in d'Annunzio's novel: a musical joy, steeped in the positive two-way flow of love. *The Flame of Life* also reminds you of a 1970 graphic novel by Hugo Pratt, *The Angel in the Eastern Window*, if only for superficial similarities, both being about adventurers in early 20th century Venice.

PALAZZO DUCALE

The gondola ride ends at the palace quay where the pair goes ashore, so that Stelio can make a speech in the Palazzo Ducale before an enthusiastic audience. In the speech, he expounds his philosophy of art, which consists of (1) the love for antique and subsequent forms of classical art (2) enjoying art as a means of mental development; it makes you intelligent (3) the artist is a magician who sees higher worlds by entering states of trance. Needless to say, this is in sync with the Actionist concept of art. As mentioned in Chapter 8, art has got to have some kind of spiritual sounding board; the artist is a visionary dealing with symbols, art is governed by the Muses. Conversely, art can never be reduced into conditioned instances.

During a subsequent dinner the company discusses Wagner, the German composer who then lived out his last days in the selfsame city. Stelio says he doesn't really like the German aesthetics of Wagner, to him Monteverdi and other Italian masters have more to say. But Stelio can't altogether free himself from the Wagnerian influence. To him German Culture is slightly barbaric, Latin culture is more advanced, but Wagner, in this context, comes to represent the genial artist. Stelio in Wagner sees a kindred spirit.

The novel has got a veritable sub-theme in the form of Wagner. For example, somewhat later in the plot, during the autumn of 1882, Wagner is spotted downtown, accompanied by Franz Liszt, the composer's colleague. At the end of the novel, in February, 1883, Stelio is told that Wagner has died. Stelio & co. then offer to carry the coffin off to the train station where it's loaded for its journey to Bavaria where it will be buried by the Villa Wahnfried in Bayreuth.

This all symbolizes the admiration that d'Annunzio still felt for Wagner. At this time there was a battle between Italian and German opera, between traditional *belcanto* and *espirito* versus Wagnerian gravity and dignity, but Wagner's work is something more than this. It's timeless art symbolized in the Tristan music, in the simple mysticism of *Parsifal* and in the *leitmotifs* of *Siegfried, sword, Rhine* and all the other captivating musical phrases of *Der Ring des Nibelungen*. This novel, *The Flame of Life,* covers this in several ways, as when the dinner guests sit and discuss Wagner, the Wagner character is seen downtown, and at the end with the carrying of his coffin, the Wagnerian spirit hovers over the story. Many artists are mentioned on its pages but Wagner, a historic artist actually living in Venice at the time, occupies a place of rank.

LA FOSCARINA

As intimated, the relationship with Foscarina is also a recurring theme of the novel. Stelio's and Foscarina's amorous meetings are portrayed in some detail. Back in the day this created some outrage; everyone knew that Eleonora Duse was the model for La Foscarina and she considered herself scandalized. But this is now a thing of the past, of the mere reception of the novel – because, as a text it still lives, it has an authentic, true character. Along with praising art, artistry and Venice *The Flame of Life* is a paean to womanhood. Later, the singer Donatella enters the plot; Foscarina has arranged for Stelio to amuse himself with this younger woman. But then Foscarina gets jealous anyway. This is an intricate psychological reality being caught in literary form.

Additionally, the relationship of Stelio and Foscarina symbolizes this: a man and a woman, both engaged in art, sharing their daily lives. The actress and the author in love seem like a sweet mix but it's also a difficult one. For example, you tend in cases like this to compete against one another, regarding how successful you are. But when career matters are put to the side, such a pair can live in sublime inspiration, seasoned with both physical and more sublime love. In real life, in this respect we have pairs like Ingmar Bergman – Käbi Laretei and Michelangelo Antonioni – Monica Vitti, love stories that had these ingredients. *The Flame of Life* captures the phenomenon in a fairly timeless shape, with Venetian interiors and backdrops.

Stelio and Foscarina eventually can't live together, this is almost a given, a part of the subtext. Yet they give each other inspiration whether they are together or apart. Stelio writes plays that she performs and at the end she can feel that he lives on in the magic of the plays, on stage she can continue to experience the electricity of their relationship, even if she's separated from Stelio himself. That was an original solution of the impossibility of an artist being together with another artist.

LENNART SVENSSON

STYLE

To give an example of the novel's style, you can quote a few things. First, let's take a look at when La Foscarina thinks about her lover, how he is. Stelio Effrena is something of d'Annunzio's alter ego, it's a self-portrait, and in the following lines d'Annunzio shamelessly can paint a perfect picture of himself, presented in the words of the heroine. Overall, this is a true characterization of a creative person:

> *She [= La Foscarina] knew from experience that he fully and unreservedly gave himself up to every budding feeling and that he was unable to pose and to lie. (...) She also well knew his clear and firm look which at times could become icy and sharp but never lurking. But she also knew the incredible speed with which his thoughts and feelings could change and that was the feature of his nature which made it impossible to keep him in place. There was always something surging and volatile about him, a force that made her think of fire and water at the same time. (...) Constantly he burned of a longing to live out his life fully and to make every moment the highest and best...* [p 225-226]

Here we again see the novel's theme of *fire and water*, as noted in the beginning. The creative life is one of fire and movement. In the novel this is symbolized by the Venice Lagoon and the fire festival celebrated in the introductory chapter. *The Flame of Life* is an incomparable picture of the city of Venice itself. Venice has been caught in many a painting through the centuries and this is how d'Annunzio's paints with words:

> *"Venice was resting on the water and shrouded in a veil of violet from which the marble campaniles arose, built by the hands of men to house the bronze bells that call to prayer. But the work of men and the prayers, the old city which rested there, tired after a long and eventful life, the crumbling marble and the frayed bronze, all these things burdened by memories and decay, they now became humble and small before the spectacle of the flaming Alps,*

tearing the sky apart with a thousand unbreakable laces – a huge and lonely city perhaps waiting to be populated by a generation of young Titans." [p 339]

Next, Stelio reflects over Venetian art, a symphony of light and shade with an undertone of autumn and decay, and concludes with an antique image:

"Thus appears to me the artistic production that's limited by the young Giorgione and the aging Tintoretto: it's purple, golden, florid and expressive as the earth's magnificent beauty in the sunset hours. When I meditate on the powerful creators of all this strong beauty, I see before me an image found in a Pindar fragment: when the centaurs had come to know the honey mild wine they would never again allow that the white milk was put on their table – and eagerly they began to drink wine out of silver horns ... No one in the world knew more than they how to enjoy the wine of life. It gives them a cheerful intoxication that fills their eloquence with a fertile energy, and in their most beautiful figures echo the violent pulsations through the centuries as the rhythm of the Venetian art. [p 57]

As hinted, a lot of art is discussed in the novel. Visual artists such as Tiepolo, Tintoretto, Veronese, Leonardo and Dürer are mentioned. For example, here is described the latter's "Melancholia," a woodcut of a neutral angel, neither good nor evil, neither a Deva nor an Asura, a resident neither in heaven nor in hell, virtually a figure "*Jenseits von Gut und Böse*". This makes him into an artistic angel, in the painting sitting, watching Life in all its ambiguous splendor, sitting there to plan a new work of art and not to rest. These words are put in the angel's mouth:

I know, that the harmony of the universe is created by noise, such as with the lyre and the bow. I know that I am and am not, and that the road is one and the same, both downward and upward. I feel the stench of putrefaction and the myriad pollutions which are united with the human nature. Nevertheless, from my knowledge I continue to complete my revealed or secret works. I see some go under, while I am still there, and I see others who seem to remain beautiful for eternity and impervious to all distress and misery, no more mine though born from my deepest accidents. I see how all things are transfigured before the fire as well as all the luck and all the virtues before the gold. One thing alone abideth: my courage. I sit down only to get up again." [p 344]

ITALY

If we were to say anything critical of the novel's attitude it would be this: Italy in the late 1800's was a somewhat stagnant culture, having an antiquarian passion for renaissance art and ancient art in general, and Stelio's artistic creed reflects this philosophy. It's a rather backward-looking art craze with a slightly academic touch. It's true that this attitude has a vital approach in the hands of d'Annunzio but you must also remember that spirits like Philippo Tommaso Marinetti (1876-1944) warned against this. Iconoclasm is nothing we want to celebrate per se, but Marinetti's modernist futurist passion was something of a kick in the butt on the stagnant Italian dreaming about bygone days, perhaps symbolized by Stelio Effrena's aesthetics.

That said, d'Annunzio himself didn't sit idle while Marinetti started his operations. d'Annunzio stopped writing when World War I broke out, he joined the Air Force and he also fought at sea and on land. Then he occupied Fiume and then he retired to private life, while Mussolini became the political leader of the country.

Another criticism that can be directed against *The Flame of Life* is the absence of esoteric depths. The ontology is ancient: when you die, you close your eyes and rest in the grave. There's nothing to gather here for the spiritually minded. But in d'Annunzio's defense it should be said that he, being an atheist, still wasn't blind to the aesthetics of Venetian churches. He doesn't hate the church as a place and a symbol, in the way that more negative atheists can do. As a traditionalist, he can appreciate the temples' beauty and this provides a silver lining to this story. The positive, affirmative spirit of *The Flame of Life* is demonstrated on every page, even when churches and church halls are depicted. d'Annunzio was inspired by Nietzsche, but he was beautifully free of revulsion against Christianity as a cultural phenomenon.

The Flame of Life is an example of that unique creation: a high-profile novel without anxiety, a resounding aesthetic painting of life, poetry and love, with Venice as a backdrop and with a Wagner-chord as *leitmotif*. d'Annunzio wrote more novels but in *The Flame of Life* he reached the furthest in terms of artistic width; it's not just a novel of manners, it's a timeless portrayal of the role of art and the condition of the artist. It has, for example, been compared with another aesthetically oriented novel, *A rebours* (1884) by Joris Karl Huysmans. Huysmans, for his part, may be an interesting conservative writer, however, between these two works, comparing the *Flame* hero Effrena and the *À rebours* hero Des Esseintes, the Frenchman comes across as a querulous, hypersensitive nerd who never gets satisfied in the attempt to create the ultimate, romantic interior in the form of a perfectly furnished apartment. Des Esseintes is an introverted indulger while Stelio Effrena is an outgoing Actionist positively shaping his life.

Therefore, d'Annunzio's novel is worth its salt: it vibrates with energy (but is told slowly), it doesn't complain, it doesn't whine, it just emphasizes what constitutes a life lived in constant inspiration. Stelio Effrena is, to quote Södergran, "enraptured in tranquility." I know of no other novel having drawn such a portrait, except possibly the narrator of Lars Gustafsson's *The Tennis Players* (1977), which had the same atmosphere of "vibrant inspiration." It also had a Wagnerian element, in the form of a Wagner staging playing some role in the plot.

If you should compare d'Annunzio to another radical conservative novelist, then Ernst Jünger (1895-1998) springs into mind. He shares d'Annunzio's lack of anxiety and a somewhat slow narrative style.

You could say that Jünger in *Heliopolis* (1949) wrote with something of a 19th century approach, like d'Annunzio in *The Flame of Life*, in the form of this implicit program: Tradition exists and it will never die.

Another voice of the radical right that d'Annunzio is reminiscent of is Yukio Mishima (1925-1970). Both were interested in depicting women, Mishima, for example, in *After the Banquet* (1960). Altogether, this shows that d'Annunzio isn't an oddball who will only interest traditionalists and conservatives.

D'ANNUNZIO HIMSELF

Gabriele d'Annunzio was something of a *larger than life character*. He was a person prompting the idea: "if he hadn't existed, you would have to invent him." He has been described as a fake superman, an operetta hero and a chauvinist. He wasn't free from fault and he had a histrionic strain to him but in all, like Stelio Effrena, he didn't pose.

Gabriele d'Annunzio was born 1863. The surname was originally Rapagnetta. The new surname seems to have something to do with *nuncio*, a Papal emissary. Already at age 15, d'Annunzio was an adroit poet who knew how to use the Italian language for vivid images and scenes. Novels, short stories and dramas followed. In a literary sense, d'Annunzio was a combination of Verner von Heidenstam (nationalist lyricist), Ernst Jünger (heroism) and Yukio Mishima (female portraits, drama).

d'Annunzio's first novels were *Il Piacere* (1889), *L'Innocente* (1892) and *Il Trionfo della Morte* (1894). These bourgeois novels of manners express atheism and emptiness in a sometimes fascinating landscape of emotions and sensations, an aestheticism à la Wilde, Baudelaire, Huysmans and Poe. Then d'Annunzio discovered Nietzsche and this is reflected in the novel from 1895, *Le Vergini delle rocce*. Here the Italians got to learn a new word: *superomismo*, the doctrine of the superman (= *il superuomo*).

Then we had the last novel, *The Flame of Life* from 1900. As intimated, it portrays the young poet, Stelio Effrena, and his women: the older Foscarina and the younger Donatella. d'Annunzio, as an author, is blind to mysticism and esotericism, to the vertical, invisible dimension of life; however, works of art, ancient myth, shadow and light in the Venice lagoon and the emotional play between humans, this he can capture. You could say that d'Annunzio expresses himself clearly, often with brilliance and evocative power, and always with calm and dignity. Again it has to be stressed that the novel's protagonist, Stelio Effrena, is an artist, a man touched by the Muses and free from anxiety, and such a figure isn't so common in the history of modern literature.

- - -

d'Annunzio for a while was occupied as a politician. His rhetorical, impulsive nature was reflected in rousing speeches and party changes. He was a non-confessional radical conservative with a passion for Italy's greatness during the Renaissance and antiquity.

In 1911, Italy launched its imperialist policies. The North African city of Tripolis was attacked and soon Italy had conquered the whole of Libya and Tunisia. This was the impetus for the 48-year-old d'Annunzio to change careers from both authorship and politics. He was thrilled by this revival of the Roman conquest policy, so he decided to become a warrior himself. Now, if not before, he trained to become a pilot.

But all wasn't rosy in this adventurer's life. A wasteful living, as befitted a Renaissance prince, forced d'Annunzio to flee the country. The period between the outbreak of the First World War in 1914 and Italy's entry into the war in 1915, d'Annunzio spent in France. There, he visited the front and he liked what he saw. According to Combüchen (1995), he saw the cathedral of Reims in flames after an air strike and this delighted him; he thought it was a beautiful sight. An aesthete's approach to war indeed.

After lengthy internal discussions and negotiations with the two belligerents, in May 1915 Italy decided to join the war on the side of the Western Allies. d'Annunzio was glad of this, having long been campaigning for an Italian war entry. On May 24, he celebrated the declaration of war at a tavern until dawn arrived. Then he said:

"Now, comrades, dawn is here. Time for goodbyes. So let's embrace and say goodbye. What's done is done. Now we have to go in separate directions – to rediscover each other. God will let us meet again, dead or alive, on fairer meadows."

In the First World War, d'Annunzio participated as a submarine sailor, an army soldier and a fighter pilot. Physically, he in no way lacked courage. As an aviator he performed a raid over Vienna. The goal was to drop propaganda leaflets. It happened in August 1918. Together with ten other planes, leaflets were dropped, written by d'Annunzio. They read:

"On this August morning, while the fourth year of your desperate convulsion comes to an end and luminously begins the year of our full power, suddenly there appears the three-color wing as an indication of the destiny that is turning. Destiny turns. It turns towards us with an iron certainty. The hour of that Germany that thrashes you, and humiliates you, and infects you is now forever passed. Your hour is passed. As our faith was the strongest, behold how our will prevails and will prevail until the end. The victorious combatants of Piave, the victorious combatants of Marna feel it, they know it, with an ecstasy that multiplies the impetus. But if the impetus were not enough, the number would be; and this is said for those that try fighting ten against one. The Atlantic is a path already closing, and it's an heroic path, as demonstrated by the new chasers who colored the Ourcq with German blood. On the wind of victory that rises from freedom's rivers, we didn't come except for the joy of the daring, we didn't come except to prove what we could venture and do whenever we want, in an hour of our choice. The rumble of the young Italian wing does not sound like the one

of the funereal bronze, in the morning sky. Nevertheless the joyful boldness suspends between Saint Stephen and the Graben an irrevocable sentence, o Viennese. Long live Italy!"

FIUME

At the end of the war in the autumn of 1918, d'Annunzio was disappointed. Italy was one of the victors, but the booty was less than expected. Italian nationalists had, among other things, wanted the Istrian town of Fiume incorporated into Italy; Fiume is now called Rijeka and belongs to Croatia. The city's population was predominantly Italian, but Italy's then prime minister was persuaded to allow the newly formed Yugoslavia to get it. It was placed under western allied control, with the garrison headed by an Italian general.

d'Annunzio was against this and he let the world know it. And after a year he went from sounds to things: he himself would conquer Fiume and submit the city to Italy.

- - -

The party did venture out, on September 11, 1919. d'Annunzio himself had a fever this day. But he got up anyway and left Venice by car. At Ronchi he met his core group of confidantes, his makeshift *Freikorps*. Then began the march eastward, toward Fiume.

After the first day's advancement the strength consisted of 600 men, Sardinian Grenadiers. During the night some additional 400 men are said to have joined, and perhaps it was a total of 1500-3000 that eventually drew eastward to occupy Fiume. On the way they seized vehicles and stole food and crops.

At dawn of Day 2, 9/12, the unit faced the border of the Free State Fiume. Here d'Annunzio was met by the Western Allies' appointee, the Italian city commandant, General Pittaluga. The following conversation took place, true or not:

The General: Poet! You'll be Italy's downfall if you undertake this.

d'Annunzio: General! It's you who are Italy's misfortune if you stand against fate and make yourself into an accomplice of a policy of infamy. I, Gabriele d'Annunzio, declare this town as Italian. Long live the Italian Fiume!

The General: I'm not here as an Italian but as an allied soldier.

d'Annunzio: In that case you have to open fire on my soldiers, soldiers who are your brothers. And if you must do it (opening tunic and showing a uniform breast graced with awards from all arms), you must first shoot on this.

The General (moved): Great poet! I don't want to be the cause of Italian blood being spilled. I'm honored for the first time to get to meet you. May your dream come true. May I soon get to cry out with you – long live the Italian Fiume!

d'Annunzio: Long live the Italian Fiume!

The soldiers: Long live the Italian Fiume!

The opposing parties embraced each other and went together into town.

- - -

Overall, taking power on Day One went easily. The Allied soldiers in the city retreated to their barracks. The Italian soldiers in the garrison fraternized with d'Annunzio's unit. A national and revolutionary frenzy prevailed. d'Annunzio still had a fever so he went to bed. Meanwhile d'Annunzio's brother in arms and pilot colleague, Guido Keller, saw to it that the City Council appointed d'Annunzio as Commandante, commander and head of state.

In the evening, d'Annunzio was feeling somewhat better. In the governor's palace he toasted to the honor of Italian Fiume. Then he wrote a letter to Mussolini:

ACTIONISM

"My dear friend! I have invested in the extreme. After giving up everything I intend to take it all. I am now the master of Fiume, over part of the armistice line, over the ships in the harbor, over the troops in the city. They only recognize me as its head. No one should dismiss me. I will keep Fiume as long as I live. Even though I only have the support of the shoddily armed troops the Fiume residents have received me. If only half of Italy were like these people, we Italians would be masters of the world. Fiume is but an isolated height of heroics telling of the glory of dying. I haven't slept for six nights and am tormented by fever. But still, I stand upright. Ask those who have seen me."

- - -

Also on 9/12, d'Annunzio gave a speech to the city's residents. It was six o'clock in the evening, the place was the square in front of the Governor's Palace. The poet stood on the balcony and the crowd below was encouraged to play along, as such, a style that Mussolini later copied. These d'Annunzio's speeches became a kind of conversation between the speaker and the audience, a "call and response" as among Baptist preachers. The events became attractions and drew tourists from Europe and the USA. It's testified that d'Annunzio could speak and he wrote his speeches himself. It was a form of seductive expressionism, a way of playing on the audience's emotional strings.

- - -

Toward the end of its existence, the Free State Fiume held a concert. The conductor Arturo Toscanini came to the city with a symphony orchestra, performing, among other numbers, Tchaikovsky's overture "1812". This was a work celebrating the defense against Napoleon's Russian campaign, illustrated in the score with cannon shots. Now this was heard, along with other weapons from the ragtag audience; guns and bayonets were wielded and there were casualties.

The scene with the visiting orchestra, the veterans in colorful uniforms, black shirts and ordinary people can be said to symbolize d'Annunzio: culture and brutality, celebration and folksyness, high and low, and all in one and one in all.

- - -

After the Fiume adventure, d'Annunzio retired into privacy. Passively, he watched how the fascists took power in Italy in 1922. Mussolini, for his part, named d'Annunzio Prince of Monteveneso. d'Annunzio's last home was the grand villa Il Vittoriala on Lake Garda. The rooms, still to be seen, are filled with souvenirs and art objects, reportedly rather much on the "kitsch" side. The house itself was shaped like a ship with a command bridge. On this bridge he had a cannon for the firing of salutes. Once, when he fired it, the gun smoke formed a ring. "Do you now understand that I'm a poet?" he said to the bystanders.

- - -

There's evidence that Mussolini copied much of d'Annunzio's style in Fiume. It wasn't just the way to hold a speech. Soldiers in black shirts, armed with daggers and saluting with outstretched right arms – these became typical fascist symbols and d'Annunzio's Fiume soldiers had all this. During the assemblies in Fiume, under the sky on the piazza, the people answered the proposals of the Commandante with an "Eja, Eja, Eja, Alalà," and even this was later adopted by the fascists.

In summarizing d'Annunzio's political character you can mention this, indicating that he wasn't so easy to pinpoint: he was against the German hegemony, he argued against antisemitism, he had an idea in Fiume to form an international community of imperially threatened states like Ireland, Egypt and Croatia, he wasn't uniformly right-wing but had syndicalist Alceste de Ambris as head of government (Ambris wrote Fiume's constitution, the Carnaro Act). Furthermore, d'Annunzio never joined Mussolini's Fascist Party. And to Fiume flocked not only nationalists, futurists and radical conservatives but also anarchists, syndicalists and socialists. After all, Fiume existed for over a year as a sort of anarchic republic, a modern, small-scale pirate state.

QUOTE

On the internet I serendipitously found the following d'Annunzio quote, *in nuce* giving us the Actionist attitude of life-as-a-work-of-art. It's also about willpower, about not indulging in complaint:

> *"I cannot understand why the poets of our day wax indignant at the vulgarity of their age and complain of having come into the world too early or too late. I believe that every man of intellect can create his own beautiful fable of life."*

12. EVOLIAN ASPECTS

An interesting 20th century philosopher is Italian, Julius Evola (1898-1974). Writing in the grey area between ethics, esotericism, history and politics, his attitudes and aspects have some bearing on Actionist thought. As with d'Annunzio and Castaneda, I don't support everything he did but in all, Evola's opus is rather impressive as regards erudition, outlook and relevance for 21st century man. *Mutatis mutandum*, Evola has something to say to the Actionist.

HAVING TO ACT

Of all the books Evola wrote, *Ride the Tiger* (1961), at least the first half of it, is the most relevant today. And the drift of it is this: today's Western world has run into a dead end, having become a miasma of defeatism, materialism and self-hate. But a radically conservative, esoterically gifted person facing this decadence shouldn't just withdraw from the world. Instead he should expose himself to it, riding the back of the tiger, riding it tired and then go in and take over. To totally turn away from the world and live in splendid isolation is not an option.

This harmonizes with the Actionist point of view, that of we all having to act, even a forest-living recluse. So much better then to act normally, being reasonably active in everyday society, however, without illusions as for its general ability to survive and thrive. We live in transitional times and in this context the "ride the tiger" option is viable.

PRAGMATIC ESOTERICISM

One forte of *Ride the Tiger* is the analysis of Nietzsche. Evola criticizes Nietzsche on esoteric grounds but at the same time saves him on these grounds. This is a unique Nietzsche interpretation, unique in the history of philosophy. Not even Heidegger – God bless him – managed to interpret Nietzsche in this way; he didn't see what Evola saw. Evola interpreted Nietzsche's creed as "active nihilism". A man, footed in essential reality, acts morally if he's intuitively set; no guidance in the form of moral programs or religious dogmas are needed: that's Evola's Nietzsche-inspired creed. I'll begin this chapter by focusing on the non-dogmatic, oriental-colored action ethics of *Ride the Tiger*, a reasonable application of Taosim and *samatva* for people today. In other words, this is an Actionist reading of the late-period Evolian thought.

One reservation should be made: Evola seldom or never spoke of such things as soul, transcendence, eternal etc. He was rather much influenced by Buddhism and used a terminology that more than often avoided these just mentioned "perennial" terms. But Actionism, being a divinely inspired perennialism, customarily uses concepts such as soul etc. Therefore the following is also to be seen as a Perennial reading of how Evola interpreted Nietzsche.

In *Ride the Tiger*, you can find lines on this:

- Pragmatic Esotericism (Taoism and Bhagavad-Gîtâ as ethics of action)
- Operational Ethics (indifference to success is not operational indifference)
- The Parable of Riding the Tiger's Back (quote from the beginning of *Ride the Tiger*)

LENNART SVENSSON

PARABLE

First, let's take a look at *Ride the Tiger's* symbol image, the image of riding the tiger's back. What does it mean? It means that a man in this era of desolation and decay shouldn't give way. Instead, you should be taking on the onslaught of materialism by letting the figurative tiger attack, whereby you must manage to get on top and *Ride the Tiger's* back. Evola always expressed himself in a transparent fashion, not – like, say, Nietzsche and Jünger – trying to obtain suggestive stylistic effects. But in these lines, still lucid and clear, Evola reached a stylistic zenith:

> *"The phrase chosen as the title of this book, "Ride the Tiger" (...) is a Far Eastern saying, expressing the idea that if one succeeds in riding the tiger, not only does one avoid having it leap on one, but if one can keep one's seat and not fall off, one may eventually get the better of it."* [Evola 1961 p 8]

And what this means for the current situation, with the materialism of Kali Yuga reigning but nearing its end, is this:

> *"When a cycle of civilization is reaching its end, it is difficult to achieve anything by resisting it and directly opposing the forces in motion. The current is too strong; one would be overwhelmed. The essential thing is not to let oneself be impressed by the omnipotence and the apparent triumph of the forces of the epoch. These forces, devoid of connection with any higher principle, are in fact on a short chain. One should not become fixated on the present and on the things at hand, but keep in view the conditions that may come about in the future. Thus the principle to follow could be that of letting the forces and processes of this epoch take their own course, while keeping oneself firm and ready to intervene when "the tiger, which cannot leap on the person riding it, is tired of running.""* [Ibid]

ACTIONISM

ANOTT-BOTSOTT

So what about another point on the list I've just made, "pragmatic esotericism"? Of this, I've already spoken in this study, *Actionism*. I made it in Chapter 3 and it was about avoiding rules saying "what not to do". Instead, you have to be equanimous and do what has to be done, like Bhagavad-Gîtâ 2:38 says (according to *Actionism*, Chapter 3): *"Equal to luck and misfortune, gain and loss, victory and defeat he prepares for battle, not being entangled in materialism."* This is acting with samatva = equanimity, letting the Inner Mind decide, "acting as if not acting" in the Taoist fashion. It's about acting "not on the thing, but on the soul of the thing".

This latter wisdom is formalized into the acronym, ANOTT-BOTSOTT = Act Not On The Thing, But On The Soul Of The Thing". The conceptual origin of this is Michel Random. In Actionist terms, this is a way to ennoble every act, turning away from its immediately material purpose and making action into a l'art-pour-l'art.

The gist of this we also find in *Ride the Tiger*, the attitude of basing action in ontology, in "do nothing, and everything shall be done" and the equanimity of Bhagavad-Gîtâ. However, as Evola himself has underlined, this doesn't mean that the Actionist is totally indifferent to the outcome of the action. With a calm mind he acts, and he acts well, but the immediate material results are equal to him:

> *"Hato vâ prâpsyasi svargam jitvâ vâ bhokshyase mahîm / tasmâd uttishta kaunteya yuddhâya krita-nishcayah"* (either you die and come to heaven or you win and will enjoy a kingdom; therefore stand up, Arjuna, prepared for battle.)[Bhagavad-Gîtâ 2:37]

In other words: the Actionist acts not on the thing but on the soul of the thing = ANOTT-BOTSOTT. Evola, for his part, expresses this way of acting intuitively, without detailed rules as such, in these lines:

> *"Such a line of conduct refers to the domain in which one's own nature is allowed to function, and to that which derives from the*

particular situation that one has actively assumed as an individual. This is the very context in which the maxims of 'acting without regard to the fruits' and of 'doing what needs to be done' apply. The content of such action is not what is given by initiatives that arise from the void of pure freedom; it is what is defined by one's own natural inner law." [Evola 1961 p 68f]

This chapter is an Actionist reading of *Ride the Tiger* and other relevant Evolian works. Actionism is a state of mind, not a rigid following of prescripts. And Evola, in stressing the role of intuition in acting, was on to this. He addressed his book to "the Aristocrats of the Soul," people who knew this kind of intuitive attitude, people having order inside them; this was a necessary prerequisite. Esotericists have some knowledge of intuition and how it works. Conversely, you can't teach Actionism to a negative nihilist interpreting everything in a reductionist manner.

RECONQUISTA

Actionism is a concept with both personal and societal relevance, and so was the case Evola's *Ride the Tiger*. As intimated, Evola wrote this book with an overall view on society and man, how an Aristocrat of the Soul should act in a time of decay, a time of defeatist materialism eradicating all Tradition, learning, honor and glory.

In his early work, *Revolt Against the Modern World* (1934), Evola rather much focused on formal, outer factors in the process of reforming society at large. He didn't sufficiently put the individual in focus (per se, he preferred the term the "person" but let's not obsess). The role of the individual is a moot point. Actionism argues that it can't be ignored. Contrariwise; the role of the individual has to be stressed. For, in fighting passive nihilism there has to be a "personal reconquista" as a basis for the larger, full-scale reconquista. And having written *Men Among the Ruins* (1953), Evola, for his part, seems to have realized that we can't recreate antiquity and its perfect, traditional society in a formal, political, macrocosmic fashion. We have to begin with the person, the microcosm. And this is what Evola's last major work, *Ride the Tiger,* advocates, rather fruitfully so.

JUGGERNAUT OF MODERNISM

Ride the Tiger is *not* to be seen as a curious epilogue, as a belated retreat from most of what Evola believed and advocated during his lifetime. Rather, Evola here said something critical to us contemporary men of the Western world. He gave a direction to the postwar, Cold War-and-beyond generation, to people who wanted something more than to live in consumer liberalism and hedonism. He gave the building blocks to a forward-looking traditionalism.

In *Ride the Tiger* it's recognized that the juggernaut of modernism has wiped out most of Tradition. The titanic world of the Jüngerian "Worker" (q.v. *Der Arbeiter,* of which I wrote in my 2014 Jünger bio) has transformed the earth into an industrial landscape. Evola doesn't think we should regret this: on the contrary, we should embrace it all, venturing out into modern life and in judo-style, meet and receive its onslaughts – and, in this, repel the force of the attack on the attacker. Like few other traditionally minded thinkers, Evola dared to take the bull by the horns. Literally, he dared to *Ride the Tiger*. It may be a bit extreme, this, as *Ride the Tiger* advocates, to engage in pure, crude materialism to enrich yourself spiritually. But this attitude is partly rooted in the Buddhist Tantra that Evola had embraced already in the interwar period.

It's rather difficult to live as a world-defying hermit today, like entering a monastery or "banging on the Hare Krishna tambourine". That is, kudos to current students of the Bhagavad-Gîtâ, Prabhupâda, Christian esotericism and so on, but existentially a customary quietism is not the king's road to enlightenment today. Better to live esoterically-spiritually free in the midst of society, taking part of what is offered and not sparing yourself any experience. This is more in the Western spirit, this affirmative approach to life, spirituality,

Tradition and everything, than to live as a reactionary saying *no* to everything.

Indeed, you can live like a hermit and spiritual explorer even in our time. But to completely renounce the world is nigh impossible. Everything today is politics. You can't be neutral to the materialist regime ruling the world today. You have to philosophically accept this and, to a reasonable extent, engage in politics, economics and world events. You may return to your hermitage in between – meditation, art and reading may be the mainstream of a thinking man's life – but the mere presence of the outside world is different today than in ancient times. *Ride the Tiger* to me seems to integrate this fundamental lesson and formulate an alternative, affirmative radical esotericism, designed to transcend the materialism and passive nihilism, the irony and dandyism that in the culture of today is seen as the normal stance.

ENRAPTURED IN TRANQUILITY

Like few other thinkers, Evola combines esotericism with traditionalism, Nietzscheism and passion. This is no inflexible rigorism, no blind vitalism, no one-eyed worship of action and power per se. It's about having power over oneself, "enraptured in tranquility" steering through the maelstrom of latter-day modern society with all its consumerism, desolation and debility. Evola is recognizing the state of things; he affirms the situation in the spirit of a combat officer and outlines a plan of action for these bizarre times.

This Action Plan, as a starting point, in the late-period Evola's and my mind, is focused on the individual, not society. The bourgeois society with its conventional religion, as well as its modern religion in the form of hedonism and sentimental materialism, may go to the dogs. The individual is the starting point.

- - -

ACTIONISM

The battlefield is yourself. Being able to achieve a moment of tranquility in the storm; this is decisive. Mental peace and calm is won through esotericism, by willpower and meditation. You have to go inside, if only for a few seconds.

Evola may have had some Nietzschean influences but unlike this old *Pulverkopf*, he had an esotericist outlook on reality. Evola found the reality in the invisible, not in the Western world's embracing of the outside world. Being well rooted in the esoteric and the traditional cultural heritage, you could then go out into the world and meet and turn the power of its attack.

This, to Actionism, seems to be the creed of the late-period Evola. He was influenced by Buddhism, Nietzsche and a lot more; he wasn't exactly the kind of esotericist that Actionism favors, but his overall creed can, as you've seen, highlight some aspects of Actionism. If Actionism is summarized in acronyms such as MMM, ARYM, ANOTT-BOTSOTT, WAP and C3, and concepts such as Operational Esotericism, Holism and Here-and-Now, this would not have been alien to the venerable Julius Evola. As I show you below in this chapter, Evola's thought had a more or less Actionist flavor to it.

REVOLT

As previously mentioned, Evola published *Revolt Against the Modern World* in 1934. This study both underlined the eternal values embraced by traditional civilizations, such as the Roman and the Brahmanic Indian cultures, as well as it sketched how these values were discarded over time in favor of a passive-nihilist materialism.

Revolt Against the Modern World is something of Evola's magnum opus. Like Spengler in *The Decline of the West* (1922) , Evola in this work outlines the decline of civilization, but overall there is more depth to the Italian's outlook than the German's, since Evola is more spiritually gifted. *Revolt* is about the degeneration of a primordial order of meaning and harmony into materialism and desolation. To him, the Aryan Bronze Age and early Iron Age societies made up the World of Tradition, a world totally opposite from that of the Modern World. In this respect, Evola seems to mean that there is actually no decline, as in Spengler's view on history, but a question of two separate categories of civilization, of a *duality* of life-forms. You either have a society anchored in the eternal values or you don't. For its part, this is a somewhat rigid attitude, not shared by Actionism. Evola, because of his not being a spiritual perennialist, rather he is a "magical idealist" inspired by Buddhist ontological nihilism, had to posit "the World of Tradition" as a separate aspect of reality in order to have a firm foothold to criticize modern society from. Actionism, for its part, doesn't need a made up concept of Tradition as an alternative to nihilist materialism. Instead, it has the idealism of Plotinus and the spiritualism of the I AM saying as the eternal antidote to materialist ignorance.

Evola's *Revolt Against the Modern World* may give the reader a pointer or two as to what a more traditional, spiritual society means. However, on the whole, *Revolt* with its rigid concept of Tradition and its focus on a supposed northern, virile and solar culture as opposed to a southern, female, lunar culture, the latter for example embodied by Christianity, reads wrong. Because, Christianity isn't lunar, it's solar. Because JC said, "I am the Light of the World". Christ was a solar deva incarnated in human form (more about this in *Borderline*).

As for the "Actionist interpretation" of *Revolt*, it can also be said that Actionism isn't so overall negative to the tangible and conceptual participation of women in shaping a future society. Actionism is a creed for both men and women. All told, an Actionist doesn't sit and long for a bygone era of admitted spiritual glory; Ancient Rome and Brahmanic India were great societies but they won't come back as overall concepts. We need "more spirituality" but it won't happen by taking whole societal models of the past and reinstate them. Instead, it's more fruitful to see what Evola's *Ride the Tiger* depicts as a conceptual way ahead for the world.

ACTIONISM

TIGER

The late period Evola had no hopes about a traditional society coming about by political means. Instead, he focused on esoterically minded individuals, the *differentiated persons* having order within themselves, the aristocrats of the soul; to these the late Evola turned when he wrote *Ride the Tiger*, teaching them that the world has gone astray but that this shouldn't let you down. Instead, as an aristocrat of the soul you could gain strength exactly by living in such a desolate era, figuratively *riding the back of the tiger* until it's run itself tired. When all is over, you and other spiritual noblemen can go in and take over, rebuilding society on the shards of the bygone civilization – you, the ones having order inside, having the ability to project order around you, Responsible Men taking charge.

In other words, as an aristocrat of the soul you can be stimulated by this age of decay. You shouldn't love decay for its own sake; however, here you might think of Oscar Wilde: "Romantic surroundings are the worst surroundings possible for a romantic writer." So inspiration-wise, the creative esotericist wishing to build a new, spiritual world, should only be stimulated by things today being so comically plebeian, materialistic and decadent.

That's the gist of Evola's thought, captured for the Actionist mind. Below I'll give some insight into other Evola writings of topical interest, such as *Meditations on the Peaks, Essays on Magical Idealism* and *Abstract Art*. In this, there will be some guidance from H. T. Hansen and Evola's own *The Path of Cinnabar*.

MEDITATIONS ON THE PEAKS

Meditations on the Peaks was issued after Evola's death, collecting his writings on the spiritual meaning of mountain climbing. In *The Path of Cinnabar*, page 183, Evola briefly mentions that he used to pursue mountain climbing at dangerous altitudes as a means of putting himself to the test, of raising himself mentally and spiritually.

Fatally, the same wish to live dangerously made him walk the streets of Vienna during the final stages of World War II, even during bomb raids. During one such Soviet raid he was injured and hospitalized, leaving him paralyzed from the waist down for the rest of his life. He lived on though, going on to write a string of enlightening books even after WWII.

The full title of the book at hand is: *Meditations on the Peaks: Mountain Climbing as Metaphor for the Spiritual Quest*. Many have found the mountain environment spiritually uplifting. Like Nietzsche, one of Evola's gurus. When living in Switzerland and hiking in the alps Nietzsche for instance could say: *"Many meters above sea level – but how many more above ordinary men!"*

This, being quoted several times in Evola's book, is the gist of *Meditations on the Peaks*.

- - -

According to Evola, mountaineering combines heroic action with that of reflection and contemplation. Among others, he cites what Indian Buddhists have written about living on the heights and meditating. The book also delves into mythology (as in the mountain as an abode of the gods, and the hero who has to climb up the mountain to perform his deed). Even ontologically, mountains are important in that they are higher than the everyday world, being "closer to heaven". Although this analogy is a bit dated, it still has its bearing.

Evola lastly mentions the Russian artist, Nicholas Roerich, who painted strikingly simple, but not simplistic, pictures of mountains and hermits. The colors purple, white and gold were prominent in his paintings, the most spiritual of colors.

- - -

In the foreword Evola sums up the topic of climbing as a way to raise yourself spiritually:

ACTIONISM

"Feeling left with only one's own resources, without help in a hopeless situation, clothed only in one's strength or weakness, with no one to rely upon other than one's self; to climb from rock to rock, from hold to hold, inexorably, for hours and hours; with the feeling of the height and of imminent danger all around; and finally, after the harsh test of calling upon all one's self-discipline, the feeling of an indescribable liberation, of a solar solitude and of silence; the end of the struggle, the subjugation of fears, and the revelation of a limitless horizon, for miles and miles, while everything else lies down below – in all of this one can truly find the real possibility of purification, of awakening, of the rebirth of something transcendent." [Evola 1998 p 6]

- - -

A choice quote from *Meditations on the Peaks* is this, from East Asia. The Buddhist Milarepa praises Being after having survived on a wintry mountain, thanks to the power of meditation. This is from Chapter 4, "A Mystic in the Tibetan Mountains". The feeling in these lines is, you could say, Nietzschean:

"Is my spirit really awake? When I look up to the blue sky, the emptiness of what exists is clearly evident to me and I do not fear the doctrine of the reality of things. When I look at the sun and the moon, enlightenment arises in a distinct manner within my consciousness and I do not fear spiritual dullness and torpor. When I look to the mountain peaks, the immutable object of contemplation is clearly perceived by my consciousness and I do not fear the unceasing changes of mere theories. When I look down to the river below, the idea of continuity clearly arises in my consciousness, thus I do not fear unforeseeable events. When I see the rainbow, the emptiness of phenomena is experienced in the most central part of my inner being and I fear neither that which endures, nor that which passes away. When I see the image of the

moon reflected by the water, self-liberation, freed from all concerns, clearly appears to my consciousness and I do not fear stupidity and frivolity." [Ibid p 28-29]

- - -

Meditations on the Peaks also talks about the inner victory. Everything is decided within; this every esotericist knows. But your inner world can also have dangers in store for you. So you have to govern your thoughts and feelings with willpower. This is the inner victory, to defeat your inner demons. The spirit triumphs over itself, transforming itself in the process. That's why both the heroes and initiates of antiquity were surrounded by an aura of sacredness. To be a hero was to have a touch of immortality.

You have to fathom spirituality, live it and incorporate it. Having done this (1) the spirit lives with a natural sense of superiority (2) somatically this is expressed in a noble appearance. True nobility carries with it a sense of elevation, of lightness, of other-worldliness.

MAGICAL IDEALISM

In his autobiography, *The Path of Cinnabar*, Evola partitions his spiritual development into this: first an artistic phase (ending in 1921), then a philosophical phase (1921-1927), this in turn followed by an esoteric-traditionalist phase. Finally, from 1934 to 1953, you could say that Evola's thought was in a political phase, this parallel to his traditionalist outlook.

Evola was no academic philosopher. And in *The Path of Cinnabar* [p 26] he says that his philosophical interest was blended *"with an interest in what is supra-rational and transcendent."* Even as a boy he had read novels by Dmitri Merezhkovsky (1865-1941), a Gnostic symbolist. Also, after WWI he had encountered Buddhism and other eastern traditions. After that he was somewhat influenced by

Theosophy (Blavatsky) and Anthroposophy (Steiner). So even in his philosophical phase and its writings, Evola had some clear esoteric traits, like sporting the word "magic" in the title of his first book of this era: *Saggi sull'idealismo magico* (this book hasn't as far as this author knows been translated into English; the title means *Essays on Magical Idealism*). It was published in 1925.

Evola was a new-baked esotericist scholar, using as starting points new age philosophies he would later disown. But as he says in *The Path of Cinnabar*, you have to start somewhere, as long as you eventually delve into a study of the original sources of the traditions in question.

Magical Idealism was, for example, influenced by Nietzsche. Moreover, it was somewhat colored by the anti-rational, intuitive holism of Lao Tzu's thought, called Taoism. And Taoism, being anti-rational, had some affinities with the Dadaist art movement that Evola had been a part of after WWI. As for Taoism, he wrote a book about it in 1923 and then another in 1972, *Il Taoismo*. In 1993 there was an English translation of this with the title: *Taoism: The Magic, the Mysticism*.

In his memoir Evola says that he didn't get everything right about Taoism in the 1920s, for example, he had read Western idealistic strains into it. But he liked the sober style of Taoism, "*the calm and clearness of a thought untainted by sentiment*" [Evola 2009 p 29]. This, Evola thought, could act as a model for a doctrine "*for the superior and self-fulfilled individual*". [ibid] This seems to indicate the *Absolute Individual* that Evola later sketched as an esoterically founded Superman. Nietzsche, for his part, had discarded all metaphysics, but Evola, influenced by Tao, "being versus non-being" and emptiness, made his Absolute Individual into something more esoterically feasible. This is refreshing in a time where Nietzsche's labeling of all metaphysics as irrelevant is the *default mode* of the Western philosophical outlook.

Evola seems to have striven for a non-idealist system of philosophy. Personally, I don't think all forms of idealism should be thrown out. But the academic idealism of those days, the early 1900s, in some aspects was sclerotic and over-ripe. The tradition of Kant, Fichte and Hegel in those days seems to have meant that everything was well in a cosmos ruled by God. Happiness was guaranteed in a deterministic fashion. The role of the individual was irrelevant and there was no such thing as "free will".

20th century academic idealism can in some ways be described as "philosophy professors' professor philosophy" (a saying by Schopenhauer). And if Evola could challenge that with a Buddhist-Taoist inspired Absolute Individual, the better. Overall, it seems that Evola's starting point was that of the individual. With his willpower, applied in meditation and systematic contemplation, with the goal of overcoming the cravings of the ego, the individual could reach the supra-personal realm, The Absolute, the ultimate reality. Exactly how Evola perceived this Absolute is irrelevant from the view of the Perennialism that Actionism espouses. To Actionism, the Perennial God concept is the Absolute.

I AM

As intimated, Evola was no esotericist of the "soulful," divinely led, strictly Perennial kind. He seemingly didn't acknowledge the existence of an eternal soul. However, on page 31 in *Men Among the Ruins*, Evola says "I am the way, the truth and the life" etc. in sketching the mindset of an aristocratic ruler, an absolute individual taking charge of society.

We see the same ambiguous trait on page 71 in Path of Cinnabar, in some lines about *immanentism* in Tantra, of "becoming a god," which is seen as blasphemous in the West. However, in the East we have the idea of identity of the personal soul with the all-soul, âtman and brahman, I am brahman = *aham brahmâsmi*. Ignorance – avidyâ – is for man to perceive himself as merely human. "[S]*uch notions arose in an Eastern context devoid of any sinister and titanic overtones.*" [Evola 2009 p 71] In instances such as these, Evola frees Nietzscheism of its sterile traits, the gist of the passage being implicitly aimed at the inherent weakness of Nietzsche's thought in lacking a spiritual footing.

NO GURU

The life and thought of Julius Evola is interesting from many aspects: philosophy, esotericism, art and politics. Evola, *mutatis mutandum*, is a compelling example of a man unifying the role of the artist, the philosopher and the esotericist. He wasn't content with making abstract gestures and statements; he lived his creed.

I'll end this Chapter with some reflections of Evola's life and thought that I find especially interesting from the point of view of Actionism. The first is found in the Introduction to his memoir *Path of Cinnabar.* Throughout his life, Evola stressed the meaning of Tradition, of ancient, established schools of thought like the Platonic and the Indian (Buddhism, Tantra, some aspects of Vedânta). However, from a social point of view, it was a dead tradition the young Evola met. He had to approach Tradition virtually alone, without a guru:

> "[T]*o a large extent, I was forced to pave my own way. I have never benefited from the invaluable help which, at a different time and in a different milieu, was granted to those who, being in touch with a living tradition, wished to accomplish tasks similar to my own. Like a lost soldier, I have sought to join a departed army by my own means, often crossing dangerous, treacherous terrain, and only managed to establish a positive connection at a later date."* [Evola 2009 pp 3-4]

Positively, this can be interpreted as: to be initiated and taught by a guru isn't needed anymore. In our time you can get pretty far as an esotericist through systematic reading, led by Will and Thought. To sit at the feet of a guru, receiving secret wisdom and being initiated with some ceremony – this isn't necessary today. Certainly, you should pay tribute to the tradition that is still alive in this respect, as in the Sanâtana Dharma (Hindu, Vedic) guru system, but as for the mere "way of knowledge" (Jnâna Mârga as opposed to the meditation of Dhyâna Mârga), today there virtually are no secrets anymore. Everything is printed in books and the one who can read can also become an accomplished esotericist. Just look at Evola.

Evola's specific development as a thinker is to be found in his philosophical memoir, *Path of Cinnabar*. The meaning of the title, this red path, is supposed to be the road of royalty and of spiritual perfection. A comment on the Swedish think-tank Motpol in the summer of 2014, when I blogged about Evola, gave clues to the "cinnabar" element, to the use of the red color pigment resulting in the distillation of the cinnabar mineral – uses such as Roman victors having their faces covered with red vermilion powder, and how the color red was reserved for the Emperor, like him wearing a red toga. And in the Byzantine Empire official letters were written in vermilion ink, made with cinnabar. Furthermore cinnabar / cinnober, distilled and refined by alchemists, might symbolize immortality – hence the path of cinnabar is the path of immortality. The latter, Evola hinted at in *The Hermetic Tradition* (1931).

ART

In his youth, up and until 1921, Evola was active as a painter, as an abstract artist. He's not a major figure of this art movement (that of Kandinsky, Klee, Balla, Picabia) but he was indeed a part of it, making some notable contributions. My personal favorite Evola paintings are "Paesaggio interiore, apertura del diaframma," "La libra s'infiamma e le piramidi" and "Five o'clock tea" – abstract yet decorative and vibrant images. Evola meant that "art is egoism and freedom," a spiritual way of expressing yourself, a way of going into a trance and transcending the limitations of the individual.

ACTIONISM

POLITICS

A fine overview of Evola's thought is given in Evola's work on politics and philosophy, *Men Among the Ruins*. Specifically, we here find H. T. Hansen's foreword, about 100 pages critically examining the anatomy of Evola's creed in every aspect.

I will here only focus on one aspect, a fundamental of politics: how to base politics in the person. Evola namely meant that a conscious, self-reflecting person is the starting point for all politics. He talked about "Absolute Man," steeped in "Magical Idealism". Such a person has some rapport with the Absolute; not with "God" per se, Evola avoided this particular term and strain, but it wasn't far from it, since Evola also acknowledged the I AM-saying and the concept of Brahman, as we've seen above. Hansen sketches the Evola-style individual in this respect as a conscious, will-driven person, anchored in the Self beyond everyday trifles, beyond Maya of Illusion.

So how to move from these philosophical demesnes to the political? Hansen gives us this gesture, saying that according to Evola "*on the political plane one replaces the Self in its freedom and power with the State, which rules the people as the Self rules the body.*" [Hansen 2002 p 32] Although the late period Evola shunned politics per se (his was a stance of *apoliteia*, to use a fine word) this highlighting of the state element is something for the current, libertarian-influenced debate to consider. That is, to simply remove the state can't be the answer to the politics of the future, no matter how evil the state of today even may be. A state of some kind is needed to govern a nation for the common good, as a means to transform the needed priorities into political action. And in this pattern the basics of politics has to be the reflected Self, as Evola meant, and as I further develop the idea in Chapter 25 of *Actionism*. A just society has to be based on just individuals, persons having some internal conception of justice.

Finally, Hansen [ibid p 30] points to a viable distinction made by Evola, the one between *power* and *force* in politics. Evola got the idea from Tantra and Taoism. "Power" in this respect must be something of a sublime thing, self-evident by its very nature. On the other hand, if it resorts to material means, that is, "force," power loses its essential nature. Power must be like Aristotle's god: "the unmoved mover".

In short, all these aspects on the Evolian thought are more or less in sync with the Actionist creed.

13. LAWRENCE

A historical figure, embodying some Actionist traits, is T. E. Lawrence. Hereby a look into his life, with some focus on the 1962 film by David Lean. Some notes on the historical, "real" Lawrence are also included.

BIO

The Middle East has been an area of conflict for a long time. In the early 1900s, it was because of the Ottoman Empire collapsing and the British supporting the Arabs in their struggle for independence. However, this chapter will not go into MENA politics per se. The study intends to focus on the human drama portrayed by the legendary Lawrence of Arabia.

Who, then, was the historical Lawrence of Arabia? His name was Thomas Edward Lawrence and he lived 1888-1935. Even as a history student at Oxford, he was adventurous. For example, in 1909, he spent three months in visiting the ruins of Crusader castles in Syria. He also did national service, becoming an Army officer in the reserve. In 1910, he took his university degree, leading to a job in archaeological excavations in Syria. When WWI broke out in 1914, Lawrence continued with archaeology as a cover for espionage activities. Later that year, he was formally employed by the Army as an officer at the headquarters in Cairo; Egypt by then was a British dominion. And then came to pass what David Lean's movie is about, how Lawrence becomes a liaison officer among, and inspiration for, the Arab revolt against the Turks.

When the war ended, Lawrence had reached the rank of Colonel. His remaining life path until his death in 1935 isn't specifically depicted in the film (only his death in a motorcycle accident, dramatically opening the film). But his postwar career was, in its own way remarkable too, however not as heroic as his exploits during the war. For example, in 1922 he joined the Royal Air Force as a private, under an assumed name. A very bizarre career move for an Army Colonel, you might think. As an airman, he accomplished nothing of note. But he did devote these years to writing books, like the memoirs *Seven Pillars of Wisdom*.

Conversely, Lawrence accomplished a lot during WWI. In the David Lean film he's portrayed as a civilian who suddenly finds himself in a war, a civilian who then becomes an enthusiastic warrior. In reality, he had training as an army officer but of course, he wasn't a career officer. He was first and foremost an adventurer, with a free and fluid nature. This is rewarding to make a film about. And David Lean did this in 1962. He took to the big canvas and the broad brushes (the movie is 3 and a half hours long) but he didn't, for that matter, neglect the detail work.

ADVENTURER

The captivating theme of the film is this: how an adventurer and Reserve Captain is embroiled into a conflict he has some knowledge of, and how he, like a sleepwalker, led by a Higher Destiny, assumes the role of Commander and Chief of Staff of the Arab struggle against the Turks. Lawrence knew Arabic and he was well versed in Arab customs and way of life – but that this gentle archaeologist could draw up the strategy and inspire whole campaigns, this no one believed from the beginning. Step by step, he assumed the role of glorified liaison-cum-commander. However, he wasn't mentally prepared for all the extremes and hardships. This, too, is shown in the film. Willpower and self-restraint is needed for any man, especially the soldier, and Lawrence, maybe, didn't always know how to muster them. He learned more about Will than any ordinary man, however.

Lawrence (played by Peter O'Toole) was an officer but he was at heart a kind of amateur soldier. He's contrasted as such both by Colonel Brighton (played by Anthony Quayle), whom he meets in the field in the camp of the Arabs, and partly by General Allenby in his Cairo HQ. Lawrence doesn't have the same military education and stature as they have but he can see opportunities where a Sandhurst-trained officer only sees obstacles. This you can't do, this hasn't been done before...! Over time, there's a fruitful division of labor between Brighton and Lawrence where the former is assisting the Arabs with heavy support and military expertise, while the latter assists in laying out the broader strategy and being a symbol of inspiration, like some latter day Joan of Arc.

The film *Lawrence of Arabia* has many memorable scenes. Hereby some highlights from the first half of the drama.

October 1916. Lawrence is an odd, easy-going Captain serving in the Imperial HQ in Cairo. Then he's asked to go and probe the British ally, Prince Feisal, in his ongoing revolt against the Turks. The Turks were allied with the Germans with whom the British were at war in Europe, since August 1914.

Lawrence heads to Arabia, riding his camel with an Arab guide. By a well the guide is killed by another Arab, Sherif Ali (played by Omar Sharif). The Arabs were at loggerheads among themselves, with different tribes fighting for hegemony, and the killed guide would have needed permission to drink from the well in question. Lawrence, however, may live. Once in Feisal's camp, Lawrence meets Colonel Brighton, who asks him to keep a low profile. But Lawrence politely ignores it and, in the process, becomes Feisal's trustee. Feisal is played by Alec Guinness.

In the ongoing battle, Brighton believes that the Arabs should retreat. But Lawrence proposes an attack on Aqaba. Aqaba (today belonging to Jordan) is located at the Gulf of Aqaba, the northeastern tip of the Red Sea. If this port city is taken, the Arabs could be better supplied with British Army supplies. The city is strongly defended on the seaward side but weakly defended on the land side. Lawrence suggests an attack conducted by fifty camel riders. He gets them along, led by Sherif Ali, plus two servants in the form of the teenage boys, Daud and Farraj.

To reach Aqaba, they have to cross the Nefud desert. Not even Bedouins believed that it could be crossed. But Lawrence did it. Once on the road, a Bedouin named Gasim suffers of fatigue; he falls off his camel during a nightly ride. The rest of the unit has by then almost reached an oasis but Lawrence turns around to save Gasim. He finds him and returns with him on the camel's back. This heroic deed makes Sherif Ali finally gain confidence in Lawrence. He gives him a Bedouin outfit (with the kaftan and shawl on head), symbolically burning his British Army uniform.

ATTACK

To attack Aqaba, the unit needs the support of another tribe, Howeitat, led by Auda abu Tayi, played by Anthony Quinn. Lawrence's plan is crossed by one of Sherif Ali's men killing one of Auda's men due to a blood feud. The Howeitat tribe is now entitled to take revenge by killing the perpetrator, but then the alliance in attacking Aqaba will burst. The solution is that Lawrence, at his own suggestion, executes the perpetrator; Lawrence stands outside these tribal feuds, he's a neutral party. Then he learns that it's Gasim who is the perpetrator. But he gathers himself, takes out his revolver and executes him anyway. The alliance between Sherif Ali and Auda can thus continue, and the next day they attack the Turkish garrison in Aqaba. The city is taken and a brilliant victory is won.

Lawrence now must inform General Allenby in Cairo about the victory. During the crossing of the Sinai desert, Daud dies in an area of quicksand. But Lawrence and Farraj finally reach the Suez Canal and Cairo. After the HQ has learned about the success, Lawrence is promoted to Major. The aid to the Arabs is extended. During a conversation with Allenby, Lawrence says that he personally is concerned, the experiences were tough on him, especially that some part of him actually enjoyed executing Gasim. Again: self-restraint is needed in a solider in order to not become bloodthirsty, not to become a necrophiliac singing "Vive la morte".

THE FEMALE ELEMENT

There you have, then, the first half of the film. Everything is full of intricate, human and heroic aspects, with the desert landscape as a constantly present reference. The events of the film are condensed, simplified and romanticized but the main characters are all historical and overall the story is correct. A significant thing about this film is that it has no female roles, barely even a woman in a supporting role. This can be interpreted as you want, but as a drama it all works brilliantly. For the woman's role in it is played, you might say, by war itself. Lawrence becomes enamored by war, he "marries" it. At the beginning of the film Lawrence is on the edge of war (Cairo), he has rudimentary officer training. He gets a mission to Arabia to revive the rebellion, he does it and he suddenly finds itself to be a full-fledged warrior. He notices that he likes the warrior life. He agonizes over it but then again, what marriage is completely free of tension...?

After the first phase of the war, with the capture of Aqaba as the culmination, Lawrence is entering a period of uncertainty. Is he done with the war or will he go out there again...? Then Allenby lets him know that his destiny is to fulfill his legendary path. Damascus should be taken, this is both Allenby's and Feisal's dream. For the film's protagonist, this means: Lawrence and war belong together, they have a bond, they are married, as it were. You could say that the war is Lawrence's *anima*, a concept coined by Carl Jung. The anima is the individual's symbol of the opposite sex; a man has a feminine anima and a woman a male anima. You're connected with it in a formal-ritual way, as the captain to his ship. The old custom of the captain having to go down with his ship has been interpreted like this: that he's married to the ship, the ship is his anima. That's why ships usually have female names.

Lawrence is married to war and he embarks on his last campaign. The ecstasy and rapture in the scene with the troops on horseback and camel, marching off toward Damascus, has some mental elevation; this is the trance of inspired action that has been sketched earlier in this study. The culmination will be an assault on a Turkish column, which ends with a massacre. Lawrence has lost control of himself, again not having that self-restraint. But in love and war anything can happen, and the scene and the whole film illustrate these kinds of mental challenges well.

Then the war has its dubious epilogue in the capture of Damascus, with the political confusion, the eventual Arab retreat and Lawrence's resignation and self-repatriation. Once home, bereft of the challenge of war, he loses his lodestar in life. He, therefore, enlisted as a private in the RAF. This would have meant the new challenge, the new trance-like adventure, a new all-absorbing operation raising you mentally = ARYM in Actionist terms, "Action Raising You Mentally" = raising yourself mentally by living on the edge, with a looming life as an airman being the ultimate symbol for this. Then he has the fatal motorcycle accident: his hobby was driving fast with the bike.

Thus you can see Lawrence's heroic saga: formally devoid of women, but not essentially. Adventure was his mistress and war his wife.

14. OPERATIONS 1

Under the caption of "Operations", the study will, in the following chapters, look at different types of operations. The intent is to show operational moods, attitudes and aspects useful for the individual in his every day. It's about moral and ethical pointers, leading contemporary man to a more efficient, smarter life. The chapters will look at, respectively, operations in the realms of military, catering, travels, writing and vehicles. This is Actionist wisdom, conveyed operationally.

MEMENTO MORI

In this study I have talked about Will, Memento Mori and Assuming Responsibility. And taking the reasoning to the realm of the military, you immediately have use for these concepts. The military way of life is centered on Responsibility, Willpower and Memento Mori.

Not that you find "Will" or "Memento Mori" mentioned in today's military handbooks. But they were to be found in the handbooks of old, like the Japanese bushido manual *Hagakure*. There we explicitly read that "the way of the warrior is the way of death". The samurai has to have "memento mori" ingrained in him.

Why? Because, *Hagakure* continues, awareness of death, of the reality of the limited life of the physical body, brings sobriety to all of your mindset. This sobriety automatically engenders samurai qualities like self-sacrifice, self-restraint, accountability, loyalty, equanimity and magnanimity. Knowing that your lifespan is limited, you leave behind unnecessary traits like angst, greed, pettiness and envy. Awareness of your death makes you see that life is too short for such trifles.

The samurai, warrior and solider has a healthy relation to death. Death makes him focus on the necessary, namely: to live life to the full and to assume responsibility for his situation.

INNER LEADERSHIP

The key word of the military life is *responsibility*. I already intimated it in "accountability" above. Now, every organization depends on responsibility, on every person being in charge of a defined sector, but it all gets more clear-cut in the military. Every military operation, everything done in the military, has an appointed chief, be he a nominal or a formal one. The ranks (corporal etc.) and titles (squad leader etc.) are there to clarify who's in charge, who's to blame if something goes wrong. Accountability is thus assured as a matter of course.

The military system is one of strict responsibilities. Whatever you do you're responsible for it, even as a private soldier. Every soldier has to take charge of his being in the line of duty, of being a cog in the service wheel. In the German *Bundeswehr* it's called "Innere Führung" = Inner Leadership. If you, as a ranker, have time to spare, you shouldn't wait for orders, you should at least get going with some routine duty that sooner or later must be done.

I mentioned this in Chapter 6. There, I also mentioned another German army concept, that of "Verantwortungsfreude" = "the Joy of Responsibility". This is an ideal taught to officers, that of operationally doing everything possible within the framework of the mission at hand. This means, within reasonable limits, that you should go and check up on, and solve, things that bother you, intrigue you etc., if the solution of the task in question helps the unit to solve the greater task at hand. Leave nothing to chance and credulity.

ACTIONISM

JOY OF RESPONSIBILITY

The Joy of Responsibility: if this is at hand, then, of course, things run smoothly. Things are done, problems are solved, and the unit is one step ahead constantly. Then, conversely, if you're in a sloppy unit, if things aren't done, who's to blame? The unit leader, of course. And he has responsibility for his sub-unit leaders taking their responsibility. In this case, you have to focus on basics, such as what a squad leader should do, what a platoon leader should do etc. Is the man leading squad X showing his men the way, is he doing everything to keep them battle ready, does he know every man's strength and weakness? If not, displace him and have another guy take his place.

Someone has always to be in charge. Like, if you are the squad leader, you must also appoint a deputy. Even if it's in a peacetime exercise, you might break your leg and be sent off to hospital. Then it's got to be clear who's next in charge.

Being responsible also means to distrust your subordinates. That's right, distrust! In the sense of: don't get carried away by what your men openly say, don't be fooled by lip service. This, for its part, is akin to the concept of, "the wise man underestimates himself, the fool overestimates himself". The wise man underestimates himself and overestimates others. In this context, this means that you, if you're the leader = "the wise man," shall not think that every man immediately understands things the way you do. They may have a hard time learning. Therefore, you must check up on their really understanding what you say. Because, as the leader, you're responsible for what your men do.

Trust: of course you have to trust your men on a fundamental, existential level. You're the guru, the leader and the prospective father figure of your men. But do make sure that they really learn and follow your example. Otherwise, they will fail at the field test and the one responsible for this isn't them, it's you = the leader. The leader is responsible for what his men do. That's the very nature of leadership. To him the praise and / or the blame.

As for the issue of "distrust," it should commonly be seen as "realism, skepticism". Be skeptical about your men's actual performance so that you really make sure that they learn. Also, be skeptical = critical about what your neighboring units have responsibility for. This is akin to Clausewitz' dictum of, "errors which proceed from a spirit of benevolence are the worst". Among other things, this means: credulity must never guide the combat leader's mindset. Instead, he must act according to "worst case scenarios" since the survival of his unit depends on it.

Example: Company A and B defend a line. In the border between the two units is a copse. At one moment, the commander of Company A hears gunfire, possibly hostile, from this copse. A credulous commander of Company A thinks that Company B has it covered. A crisis-conscious commander of Company A sends a squad to the place to check it out.

Hal Moore (1922-, US Army, Lieutenant Colonel, Ret.) said: "There's always one more thing you can do to increase your odds of success." This is the essence of "the Joy of Responsibility".

ACTIONIST APPLICATION

To make some Actionist conclusion of this, some everyday useful wisdom, it would be: we all have responsibility. Contrariwise: in the professional life, if your post / assignment / employment has vague limits of responsibility, demand of your boss to know what they are. And if it's impossible to get such a brief, then try to formulate it yourself. In your work as X, what are your responsibilities?

This clarifies matters, professionally and morally. It may 'evolve' you to know what you're actually expected to do in your workplace.

And if you know what your responsibilities are, then, to a reasonable extent, try some of that "Joy of Responsibility" and see what other things to do there are in your workplace, things not included in your brief, but that need to be done anyway. It's true that this is a grey area of limitless tasks and wild-goose chases, like, you shouldn't start "cleaning out the basement" of your workplace in some brisk eruption of doing good to the boss. If you're too good at doing such extra chores, you might end up washing your boss' car and get nothing for it. But my point is, if you have reasonable talent and a way of spotting opportunities, then look at things in your workplace that might need to be done; you can, in the right circumstances, evolve personally in the process. You have, at least, learned of the spirit of responsibility, the joy of it.

This kind of ambition also includes learning more, and learning tasks related to your assignment, whether you do this in your spare time or in the service proper.

We all must act; we all conduct operations. Realize this and approach your job operationally. Like staking out responsibilities and stepping up in the responsibility ladder. And specifically, if you learn about everything about your workplace, getting an insight into every task and in this way learning to perform every task, you might become indispensable = impossible to fire.

EXISTENTIAL RESPONSIBILITY

Even outside of the workplace we have responsibility. As sons, fathers, daughters, mothers, sisters, brothers, friends etc. Ask yourself: as a son (daughter etc.), what do I have to do? Where are the limits of responsibility? What am I not required to do? There are no textbook answers to this, but to reflect on them might be useful.

Having kids is the ultimate responsibility. You're responsible for them being fed, clothed and given a home. But when they have left the paternal home to live the adult life, then, for better or worse, your immediate responsibility ends. You're still there as an existential constant, as a mainstay and a helping hand, but the responsibility isn't as acute anymore. The same goes for the son versus his parents. To take an extreme example: if the son chooses to become an Esotericist Monk (Hindu, Buddhist, Catholic etc.) then he renounces his role as a son to his parents. He doesn't need to take care of them; conversely, he has no claims on a possible inheritance. He's a man of God now. Is this responsible? Not formally – but still, he now serves God, he's now responsible for the perfection of his soul, making it ready to receive God in a total way. He's not responsible for his parents' weal or woe. He's no longer his parents' son. He's assuming responsibility in a wider fashion, as a soul-endowed, reflecting human being, prepared to live his life for, and with, God on every plane.

As for legalities, I don't know if these different kinds of monks (Hindu etc.) really are or aren't legally freed from being their parents' sons but, generally, this could be the case. To renounce the world is to renounce being your parents' son, transforming the issue of responsibility from a filial to an existential level.

WILL

I mentioned Will at the beginning of the chapter. As I showed in Chapter 1, Will is hardly a quality or a value, it's an elemental force. The divine Will is mirrored in the human Will; they're of the same substance, namely, Light.

Beyond that, Will, in the military framework, is what drives the soldier: will to learn his weapons, to persevere in battle, to sustain hunger, hardships, fatigue. It's the Triumph of the Will. It's the Will To Power Over Yourself = WTPOY, in Actionist lingo. The soldier's life is an example of the will-driven, volitional life par preference.

Also, in the world of the soldier and even the everyday person, Will can be applied to get used to the reality of death. At the beginning, becoming familiar with this notion, that your physical lifespan is limited, you might become dejected. Everything might lose its color, food might lose its taste, the mere sense of living may be gone. Then willpower is needed to keep on living.

But with willpower ever present in your mindset, as well as Memento Mori and the concept of Assuming Responsibility – responsibility for whom you are as a man, as an employee, everything; having integrated WTPOY and MMM in your being, then you might be impossible to beat. And in order to have a heart in all this, to not become a human robot, remember to have an "at least 51% positive disposition". This intimates the idealist strain present in every true Actionist, and this leads to the acronym ASARIT = A Strong And Responsible Idealist, Taking charge. That is, the Actionist is a paragon of vigor and responsibility, embodying the dictum of Norman Schwarzkopf: "When placed in command, take charge."

KEYWORDS

There is more to say about military operations. Hereby some additional deliberations on the subject, be they of general or personal use.

A personal remark: I once did my national service in the Swedish army. Specifically, it was at I21 Regiment, Sollefteå, 1984-1985. I served in the infantry, posted as squad leader. I led my squad, I saw other units and how they were led, and I gathered the one and the other operational wisdoms in the process. For instance, the pattern of giving orders said a lot about what constitutes an operation. If an order contains the following, after the Swedish army pattern, then we have *operational credibility*.

To give the order, the leader of a unit has his men (his subordinate leaders) gathered. Then the leader starts giving his order. First, there's got to be an *orientation* saying what the enemy is up to and what the mission is. This, enemy presence, is the constant point of reference for any military activity in the field: where's the enemy, what's he doing, how shall we counter this? The orientation element says "what to do," and the following elements of the order say "how to do it": how to divide the unit, where to group the subunits, what their specific tasks are. Then the order moves on to how *command* is performed during the operation, like the unit leader saying where his command post will be. Further, *communications* give info on this, like what radio channel is used, how cell phones can be used or in what fashion strikers shall be employed.

Then we have *support*, stating if there's heavy support around, like artillery, attack helicopters or the like. Then we have *logistics*, stating how the supply of ammunition, the evacuation of wounded and such are effected.

Apart from the "order" element, this is an image of how a military unit operates. It's applicable to squads, platoons and companies. Further up in the organization the orders become more elaborate, but this pattern is followed even there, that of "what do to and how to do it," that of enemy activity and mission, division of the unit and specific tasks, command, communication, support and logistics. Especially *support* is what gives an operation some credibility, some level of seriousness. To merely have men equipped with assault rifles chasing the enemy around, leads nowhere; some kind of heavy support is needed. Also, in the general sense, in an operation you have to have some back-up. Contrariwise, remember the TV series *Miami Vice* where Crockett often exclaimed about some operation, having "no back-up and no support". The team in question was left out in the cold.

HIGHER LEVELS

On the higher levels, how do military units operate? One formal element standing out is the presence of considerable *staffs*, substantial *HQs*, of personnel not fighting but planning, assessing supplies and handling intelligence.

The commander of a division, an army, an army group etc. is the leader, the one making the decisions. Helping him in making the decisions are a handful of different chiefs, handlers of, respectively, operations, support, logistics and intelligence. In other words, the leader has an advisor for the actual fighting (= operations), he has another guy advising on heavy support, he has a "steady workman" as logistics chief aiding with ammo supply, medevac and food, and he has a shamanic figure advising on intelligence matters, specifically, on the whereabouts of the enemy.

This staff is, in turn, headed by a chief of staff. This system of extended staff developed in mid-19th century Germany, before and during its wars of unification, a system of "substantial aid to the commander in making decisions". Before this, the staff was smaller, not as elaborate. The new kind of staff left nothing to chance. In the specific area of operations, the staff saw to it that the roads to travel were examined, the whole terrain was mapped, the whereabouts of the enemy was pinpointed, the supply was organized one step ahead. This had, of course, been done in combat even before, but with a larger staff element there were more people around dedicated to plan and execute all this. That was why Moltke won his wars from 1866 through 1871.

PECULIAR

The relation between the commander and the chief of staff can be peculiar. In Germany the system evolved to these two (the commander and his chief of staff) being rather equal, like in a happy marriage: you don't know who's actually in charge, there's an invisible division of responsibility in making the strategic decisions that makes the whole (the division, the corps, the army) function smoothly.

A way to show the comparatively elevated position of the Chief of Staff, is this: before Paris, in the autumn of 1914, the German assault operations had stalled. A certain conference of army Chiefs of Staff was gathered, having these figures, formally being under the leadership of the separate *Armee* commanders, to decide what to do to break the stalemate. The decision was to retreat and consolidate for defense. This might mostly illustrate that the current army heads were mere figureheads, like princes and such, but overall, the army, divisional etc. Chief of Staff had a peculiar position in the German army, up and until 1945.

LENNART SVENSSON

LEADERSHIP

The staff is there to help the leader lead. In Robert Heinlein stories like *The Man Who Sold the Moon* (1950) and *Sixth Column* (1949) we see a recurrent pattern, that of "a leader being deluged with trifles, then an advisor tells him to create a substantial staff so that he can concentrate on the big picture". In *Sixth Column* we, indeed, see Heinlein praising the German general staff for pioneering this high-level leading element. We first get the image of "Napoleon as the last general," the last commander having all the threads in his hand, symbolized by being able to lead the battle from a hill where all is laid out before him. Subsequent wars got more complicated; they got more bureaucratic and structured into office work on the higher levels. This was due, this was needed; the glorified staff work is office work, both in the field and in peacetime.

To the subject of staff work also belongs the element of "staff officers having no responsibility, the one taking the blows is always the frontline officers". This might also be true. Be that as it may, now back to more hands-on operational issues of the military kind – to the frontline, the combat zone.

So what is there to say about this? Some heartwarming operational wisdom from the cold war exercise field? One such wisdom of possibly general interest is this: it's easier to advance in column than in line abreast. Having a ten men squad, it's easier to lead it by going in a file, with the leader taking point and the rest merely following. Conversely, in line abreast there's always the risk of the flank guys lagging, possibly being left behind. This is a clear risk in wooded terrain. In the mid-1980s, only platoon leaders and up had radio. In modern armies, the ideal is that of each soldier having some kind of radio link-up and this is sorely needed to keep a squad gathered in the difficult to overview combat zone. The hardest unit to lead, in this respect, is the platoon, the leader having some implicit difficulty in projecting his commanding presence over all the men, about 20-30 men. This might be true, even if all the men have radio communication. Because, in comparison, the *squad leader* can clearly be seen and heard by every man, the squad's ten men force normally extending over a surface more than 50x50 meters, but a platoon might be stretched out over 150 meters and more, and that's harder to survey by one single leader.

FIRE AND MOVEMENT

The specificity of being a front line leader is the theme of my novella *Eld och rörelse* (2007, in Swedish only, the title means "Fire and Movement"). It's about reaching out with your presence as a leader to the spread out a platoon in the field, it's about the drama and the terror, the worry and belligerence; it's about *situational awareness*, a holistic phenomenon of combative apprehension. The unit in question is engaged in a sneak attack and approaching its first target, the story's "he" being a certain Sergeant F.:

> *"Throwing all reservations aside he finds the neutral and runs on intuition. All orders are given, the crew is hand-picked and the whole situation is so implausible that it all just has to succeed. He knows that the woods right now are full of forest rangers like themselves, being the division's vanguard, along paths and roads like this they're seeping into the enemy grouping. He looks at the watch, the artificial moonlight almost allows him to discern the face but now he hides it to see the luminous dots appear. 0515, fifteen minutes until H Hour. The last of the soldiers of the other half of the squad disappear in the darkness on the other side of the road, the Sergeant gets up and makes the sign for skirmish line, glancing at both sides to see if everyone is coming along, and after five meters traveled, most appear to be in place – and if someone is lost now it's no matter, he thinks, the main thing is that the support weapons are along. Side by side the soldiers advance with weapons in firm grips, staring under the helmet edges; every step taken with caution, a broken branch can bring the whole enemy strongpoint on alert – from his location in the middle the platoon leader*

spies ahead through the trees, he thinks he can see an opening in the front, he signs "down," and in turn crouching, crawling and shuffling the dozen men approach the starting position for the attack." [Svensson 2007 p 105]

KNOW YOURSELF

As a leader in the field, you must exert *spiritual remote effect*, projecting your aura on (1) your closest men (2) the unit as a whole, even though not all men are in your immediate vicinity. The best way to generate this remote effect would be to teach everyone Memento Mori since this generates apprehension like nothing else.

Sun Tzu said: know yourself and the enemy, then you're invincible. And starting with yourself, what do you know? Do you know that you're mortal, that your physical lifespan on this plane is limited? Do your men know it? A military leader in the combat zone has to impart Memento Mori on his men. This is the *gnôthi seavtón* of combat leadership.

Again, a leader in the field has got to have *situational awareness*. He has to be there, in the zone, with his five tangible senses and also his sixth sense, his combined instinct and intuition. And nothing engenders such a mode like Memento Mori, knowing that your next breath could be your last. In the combat zone, death is stalking you 24/7. To acknowledge this truth is rather essential for a soldier.

Again, this is the gist of *Hagakure*. This is the warrior ethic, founded on ontology – an amalgam of Reality and Action, of Life and Thought. *Mutatis mutandum*, it applies to every human being, this doctrine of Memento Mori and all that goes with it. The soldier's being, the life in the combat zone, only makes it more acute and poignant. As such, the simile of being a warrior is of use to the everyday man. Here, might be inserted the usual disclaimer, that of "don't be totally absorbed in the soldier's mindset, don't become 'emotionally dressed in camo' and go out in the street as if you're in the combat zone".

Don't take it too far. Actionism is a peaceful, lawful doctrine. Again, this chapter is about what today's peaceful individual may gain mentally from certain military concepts and attitudes. Being a soldier is about mental elevation, about the very existence in the combat zone forcing you to acknowledge your spiritual dimension. "There are no atheists in foxholes" as the Rev. William T. Cummings said.

Even pacifists acknowledge this state of things. Once, it was spoken about "the moral equivalent of war," something challenging and inspiring to lift fighters for peace to the zest and dare of soldiers in combat. The same goes for Actionism: in so far as it uses combat, soldiery and warlike similes, it's because they are a form of condensed ethics, a concentrated wisdom of life, an illustration of Will-Thought in motion, a synthesis of moral and ontology.

COMBAT CONCEPTS

As mentioned above, my 2007 war novella is titled *Fire and Movement*. Fire and movement are two of the basic principles of combat; the other two are *morale* and *discipline*. The enemy target is defeated by a combination of fire and movement, like a rifle squad advancing in bounds with half of the unit giving fire, thus supporting while the other unit forges ahead. Then the advancing unit halts and gives support while the other moves ahead.

Fire and movement is also symbolized by the tank: fire by the cannon, movement by the engine and tracks. To this, it has *protection* in the form of its armor, protection being a third basic element, mentioned along with fire and movement. For instance, the rifle squad just mentioned advances from protection to protection.

As for morale and discipline, a military unit both needs some elevated goal to fight for and some controlling, ordering measure. Morale makes the unit go forward; discipline stops it from dissolving in case of retreat.

Talking about tactical key concepts, the Swedish army, for its part, used to emphasize the following four: main effort, surprise, freedom of action and local superiority. In an attack operation, "main effort" means to amass force in one point, not squander it away with equal pressure along the whole line. "Surprise" means to think outside the box, not doing what the enemy expects you to do. "Freedom of action" is something you can fight to attain in a defensive operation, stop being caught up in the rhythm of the enemy. This can make you think of Miyamoto Musashi, who maintained that in a duel you either move by your own rhythm or that of the enemy; thus, make sure that you impose *your* rhythm on the duel. The final Swedish concept, "local superiority," is what an inferior combatant can try to achieve in a certain sector, amassing force so that he can gain a tactical victory even though the strategic situation is dire.

This summary of tactical concepts may be compared to a similar shortlist maintained by Montgomery of Alamein, a list of "concentration, surprise, cooperation, leadership, simplicity, speed and initiative". It's a list of simple concepts, however, not simplistic as such. As for cooperation, an infantry commander in an area must seek out support from other units, such as artillery, engineers and aviation. As for leadership, this has always to be stressed: the willful individual taking charge can change the outcome of a battle. As for simplicity, plans and orders must have a modicum of simplicity. Clausewitz, for instance, meant that, "everything in war is very simple, but the simplest thing is difficult". To merely keep things simple isn't easy but it has to be an operational ideal, an ideal of transparency avoiding misunderstandings and mistakes.

Montgomery also had "speed" as a tactical ideal. Napoleon, for his part, said: "vitesse, vitesse, de l'activité," stressing that in combat some opportunities come and go very fast. Monty also had "initiative" on his list, like the Swedish army and Musashi, highlighting that you have to impose your own rhythm on the fight at hand.

ACTIONISM

NAPOLEON

In Chapter 3 I talked about NAMO, the Napoleonic Modus Operandi, summed up by Napoleon's dictum, "on s'engage et puis on verra" = "get going and then take a look around". In that context I focused on the intelligence side of this kind of operation, that of getting a clearer view of the situation by engaging in the fray.

In a wider context, this is a general way to operate: you get going and then keep on going. This is symbolized in another, just mentioned, Napoleonic dictum: "Vitesse, vitesse, de l'activité" = "speed, speed, activity". Having gotten going, you've received a clearer view of the situation and so you know where to strike. Thus, force is applied to the point in question and, at best, the enemy is disrupted and routed. Napoleon won his best battles like this, like Austerlitz. Rommel also employed this "speed, speed, activity" approach in his North Africa battles, like the battle of El Agheila in 1941, and the battle of Gazala in 1942.

They say that Rommel was a bit too engaged in the battle, that he was everywhere and nowhere. It was a bit like Charles XII, Gustavus Adolphus, Alexander and, to some extent, Caesar, who all shared the tendency of top commanders for getting embroiled in the action, of participating in the fighting itself, instead of being in a focal point where they could have overview, exert command and easily be reached by strikers. Generally, apart from tactical sensibility, this other leadership style of "being engaged" has some Actionist aspects to it. It could be described as identifying yourself with the action, becoming action: I Am the Action. You are the mission, the mission is you. It also makes you think of RIA = Rest In Action = to have action as propensity, having to stage a battle to relax. This might sound frivolous but it's a psychological fact.

In this mental force field there is also the concept of "raising yourself mentally by living on the edge". You get going in order to raise yourself mentally, again useful for the mere intelligence situation, but also for your mind as a whole. This is what combat does to an individual, it's Action Raising You Mentally = ARYM.

It's about getting going as if in a trance, performing MAASOM = Movement As A State Of Mind = in the case of combat, meaning a perpetual state of fire and movement.

METAPHYSICS OF WAR

In Chapter 12 I looked at the philosophy of Julius Evola, which has some bearing on Actionism. Specifically, his collection *Metaphysics of War* has several instances of Actionist philosophy. This is a collection of essays Evola wrote from the 1930s and on. His was an aristocratic radicalism, a person-centered way of acknowledging Tradition by meditation, mental striving and intellectual development. It was a case of ESWY = Everything Starts With You. He rejected the collectivism of Fascism and Nazism.

In this respect, war and being a warrior was the ultimate acid-test for Evola. A warrior going to war must have an esoteric, inner guidance pattern, Evola said. The soldier can't rely on the slogans of the state given to him, simplistic mottos like "fight for democracy / the king / the Leader". These will leave him morally destitute if things go wrong, if the war is lost. And, even if he's part of a victorious army, the solider must have an esoteric creed leading him on in good times as well as bad. Otherwise the backlash will come, the existential sense of loss. The same goes for the civilian, the common man. He can't be morally guided by the form of governance of the state he lives in. He has to have an esoteric, idealist, everlasting creed to guide him.

An ethic, based in ontology, like Actionism (and Gnosticism, Vedânta, Buddhism, Christianity etc. etc.) is what you need to persevere through thick and thin, not a simplistic creed like believing in "democracy" or some other ideology proclaimed by the Empire. While a political system having a popular element capable of feedback is desirable as such, you can't set up your life led by a political ideology. You must go to the ontological sources, "ad fontes," to get something more durable.

ACTIONISM

Actionism is a system both for the individual and the political system. As for Evola, in his later years he tended to be apolitical, only focusing on the mental striving of the person. This should be remembered. Actionism, for its part, takes in the whole picture, having the reflected individual as basis for a just society. In a sense this is Platonic, like having a just (Greek, *dikaios*) person as the building block for a society based on justice (*dike*). The reflective, self-conscious individual has to be "disposed for justice" = *dikaiosyne*; only with such individuals can you build a just society. The part mirrors the whole, the whole mirrors the part; this is holism par preference. More on the Actionist societal concept in Chapter 25.

ARISTOCRATIC

In *Metaphysics of War* Evola discusses the warrior role tangibly, not as a mere simile which is otherwise the rule in moral contexts. The traditional way of the warrior in India and Rome was a viable way of reaching enlightenment, Evola meant. Today, and from the viewpoint of Actionism, it's not about going to war, since the wars fought are led by the Empire, upholding the regimen of fear and materialism. Instead, the ideal warrior role does become something of a simile and metaphor, as such, however having the role of a moral-ontological ideal and not just explained away in quietist goody-good posturing. Evola, for instance, quotes Bhagavad-Gîtâ on its warlike instances, like 2:38:

sukha-duhkhe same kritvâ lâbhâlâbhau jayâjayau
tato yuddhâya yujuasva naivam pâpam avâpsyasi

Having become equal to luck and misfortune, gain and loss, victory and defeat, get ready for the battle, thus you won't acquire sin.

Today, in the Actionist interpretation, this is a symbol of equanimity while acting, of doing what has to be done, of acting intuitively and thus reaching a higher mental state. You're led by something esoteric, something "inner," by God. This is how a warrior ethic like the one taught in Bhagavad-Gîtâ can be a guidance to the common man, the latter-day civilian, even though the context when the wisdom was given was a war, the battle between the Kauravas and their cousins as given in *Mahâbhârata*.

Again, Evola doesn't "reduce" the Bhagavad-Gîtâ wisdom to be applied to the civilian realm but he doesn't either speak against this, so in this respect *Metaphysics of War* becomes both a "field manual for the spiritually gifted warrior" and a philosophical dissertation of the higher meaning of war and warriors.

KEY CONCEPTS

For an Actionist, *Metaphysics of War* is about ARYM = Action Raising You Mentally. War, to go out and risk your life on the battlefield, becomes the ultimate symbol of life as a man, of challenges you can meet and overcome. And should you "fail" by being killed, this is no loss since Bhagavad-Gîtâ 2:37 says: "Either you are killed and you reach heaven, or you win and will enjoy the world. Therefore rise, Arjuna, and fight with determination."

It's a win-win situation. And it's a hard doctrine, a Zen-style moral of embracing death. Actionism, as we all know, is about peacefully striving to "become what you are" , but war as a simile is a viable aspect of the whole, taught in the best way by Evola in the current book. This is a Western *Hagakure*, a mirror of the above mentioned Japanese 18th century doctrine saying that "the way of the warrior is the way of death". *Hagakure* had some civilian applications to the warrior way too, like warning against "the perfectionist fallacy" (a *striving* for perfection is needed, however, you don't have to be perfect in exactly everything you do; see otherwise Chapter 5 of this study).

Evola is relatable to the common man, too. For instance, he deliberates on 20th century attitudes to war, like those seen in

Remarque's *All Quiet on the Western Front* (1929). The German WWI soldiers depicted in that book had no inner reserves, they were victims of defeatism and dejection when the euphoria of 1914 was gone. Therefore a soldier, and every man facing life in all its variety, must have a creed based in ontology – like Actionism, stressing willpower anchored in the divine Will, stressing the need for meditation in the form of C3, stressing the need to Assume Responsibility for who you are, what you do and what you think, 24/7 all year round, even when "the going is tough and the general euphoria is gone". Conversely, you can't rely on imperialist-materialist slogans anchored in the current type of governance. A creed worthy of its name is based in ontology, as both Evola and Actionism teaches.

WARRIOR MODE

Leaving Evola and returning to the elemental nature of being a warrior, you could say that the Warrior's Way is a kind of initiation. Like the adept entering a religious order, the soldier disciple has to "die" symbolically, leave his past behind and start a new life. In this new life of combat he lives in a kind of ecstasy, a kind of inebriation, by meeting and adapting to the hardships of the combat zone. The constant threat of being killed raises the soldier to a new level, a state of heightened awareness, a case of inspiration and inebriation, as it were. It's about constantly living at storming distance, raising yourself spiritually by living on the edge.

This is a hard life but it's a psychological reality per se. This is a trying, tough life but also rewarding if you can channel the energies involved. An old soldier wisdom says, "walking through Hell with open eyes only makes it half as hot." War is hell and by conceiving yourself in a combat situation, you make your soul into a battlefield for the forces of Light and Dark. This is similar to how things are in general too: in ordinary life any man's soul is the battlefield between Dark and Light. The combat situation only makes it more poignant.

So stay calm and assess the situation, find cover and live to fight on – or get carried away by the commotion, lose your mind and lose your life.

Thus the fight can elevate man morally. But fighting isn't everything. To be a complete warrior isn't everything. "Fighting is easy, living is hard." Many an accomplished warrior has found it hard to re-adapt to civilian life. Think of Rambo in the self-titled movie (1982) who complained that in Vietnam he could drive a tank, in civilian life he couldn't even park a car.

INFANTRY WISDOM

Earlier in this chapter I spoke about the wisdom gained from being an army soldier, an infantry man, a squad leader. For what it's worth, hereby a summation of this, with or without application to the civilian life:

- Assume responsibility even if you're a private, for even a private must be prepared to take over leadership of the squad if the leader falls. And the squad leader must be prepared to take over leadership of the platoon if the platoon leader falls etc., all the way up.
- Expect of your men what you know you yourself can manage. If you've put life behind you and are ready to die, then your men should manage the same thing. Leading men in the combat zone means imparting this wisdom, the MMM = Memento Mori Mindset. In guru-style, shape and change the mindset of your unit.
- Project your Will on the unit, making it act in your spirit.
- Every man should be trained to be his own leader; *Verantwortungsfreude* on all levels.
- Practice intuitive leadership: "I am the battle, I move with the battle".

- Be "enraptured in tranquility," realizing the paradox of the combat mindset: 100% concentrated and 100% relaxed at the same time.
- You can endure twice as much as you think, and four times as much as your mother / wife / girlfriend thinks.
- Never take the same route twice while on patrol; in this respect, act like a predator, like a wolf or lion, which never takes the same route twice.

NAPOLEON

There have been some references to Napoleon in this chapter: "On s'engage et puis on verra" and "vitesse, vitesse, de l'activité" are quotes of his I've deliberated upon. I'll end with a third quote by this rather impressive figure, this too with an Actionist application. It's about having a combination of Will and Faith, of acting in an operational trance protecting you from ordinary pitfalls.

In 1799, when Napoleon was about to leave Africa and sail home, he spotted an English corvette on the horizon. Some in his company were worried, however, Napoleon just said: "Bah! We'll get there, luck has never abandoned us, we shall get there, despite the English."

15. OPERATIONS 2

The subject of this chapter is *catering operations*. Personally, I once worked as a kitchen apprentice. I graduated as a chef in 1988. Since then I've worked in kitchens here and there and I've also written a cookbook, *Den musiske matlagaren* (2007, in Swedish only). Catering is an excellent area of operational deliberations. Any chef worthy of his name must know how to operate, along with being able to cook delicious food.

BASICS

If you go to restaurant school you learn to cook: you learn about foodstuffs, recipes, the ways of the handicraft per se. Next, you have to meet reality in the form of a real restaurant and then it all gets operational: on top of all your cooking skills, you now have to make it work in an actual restaurant situation.

Let's say you're hired as a subordinate chef. The head chef writes the menu and keeps the overall control. Now, if you're such a newly graduated rookie beginning to work in a real restaurant, you will most certainly hear: pick up the pace, work faster! For, in restaurant school, you learned to be meticulous. Now you have to be meticulous *and* work fast. That's the charm of the restaurant situation.

Me, I never went to a formal catering school. I learned on the job, working as an apprentice chef. Routine work (peeling onions, cooking rice, etc.) was interspersed with being allowed at the stove to start making actual dishes, food being served to paying customers.

ACTIONISM

I was shown ways of doing this and that, I was advised to take notes, and I got one (1) book to read (Karl Blunck, *Gastronomisk handbok*), a gastronomical handbook of 300 pages with condensed recipes, an overview of types of garnishes and a word-list of French kitchen terms and names of dishes. After about a year, I took a test by cooking a three-course dinner, I also took a theoretical test and then some. And after I passed; I was a chef.

There you have, *in nuce*, the specificity of the chef profession. Even though the theoretical part has increased lately the catering operation is still mainly hands-on, it's not about having to read a lot. Also, it's a profession rather non-computerized; the first day at work you get to peel onions, you don't go online. 99% of what a chef has to know is done by seeing and learning, about craftsmanship. You can surf the net for info and ideas, but this is a marginal aspect of becoming a chef. It's about being in the somewhat harsh environment of tile and stainless steel and cooking for your life.

Now I exaggerated a little. It's a creative work, it's alchemical: to transform raw materials into something else, an edible dish making people exclaim "delicious". Enthusiasm and musicality are key ingredients. Specifically, in every kitchen I've worked in, there has been music, in the form of stereos and radios and the staff itself singing, with or without hitting every note.

CONCEPTS

What key concepts rule the catering operation? Two of them were mentioned in the previous chapter, treating military operations: willpower and responsibility. The same goes for the catering operation, where Will is needed to sum up your sense of responsibility. Obviously, you choose to become a cook; so assume responsibility for this, even though you're an apprentice or a subordinate cook.

Willpower means *drive*: you can always learn more. Being a basic-level, examined, OK'd chef, you can and must improve your skills by working in several successive restaurants. You always learn something – by listening to colleagues, keeping your eyes open. Catering is a glorified "learning by doing" activity and not anywhere near "learning by reading about it in a book". Then you can go abroad and learn even more, become a head chef etc. etc.

Having said that, being a subordinate chef is OK too, he also has his responsibilities and his specificity.

As intimated at the beginning of the chapter: cooking skills are one factor, operational skills another. The rest of this chapter is dedicated to how to operate in a restaurant kitchen; no mention is made of recipes and delicious food per se, this is taken for granted. The following is a discussion of the catering *modus operandi*, equally applicable to lunch restaurants and gourmet restaurants. It's true that gourmet cooking very much relies on cooking each dish separately, so that the customer gets it fresh out of the pan, but even in highly prized restaurants, the chef has to think operationally. He can't just frivolously pick and choose to cook what he wants.

Thus, there always has to be a menu. To compose a menu isn't just about adding a number of "delicious courses". It's about what raw materials are in for the season, it's about having ingredients being applicable to more than one dish and it's about what's operationally feasible to cook. For instance, a soufflé might be nice to serve, but is it really practical to have it along with the other dishes offered? The amateur writing a menu only thinks of what looks and tastes nice, he doesn't have the whole operational process included in the equation.

The cook of a busy restaurant is an intuitive-instinctive operational pro. He has to be. He has to have operational prowess. For example, even though it's stressful, he shouldn't *run* in the kitchen; to walk is enough, if it's walking efficiently. Like, standing at his working station with its "tactical storage of items," cooking his ordered dishes and making a mental note of an item about to run out, successively adding up items on the list of "what to fetch" and then finally going to the fridge when he absolutely has to, in the process taking along several items at once. This saves time.

ACTIONISM

The kitchen of a moderately sized restaurant is divided into *stations* of first courses, fish, meat and desserts respectively, each with its own *chef de station* and subordinate chefs. However, the most operationally important work duty in the kitchen is not the cooking, but the *leading* of the cooking. This is done by the head chef standing at the bay = a gap in the wall or a certain desk, there to receive the bills with orders. Then the head chef makes a disposition of it, ordering what dishes to make and getting the order repeated by the chef in question. Then the dishes are made and the head chef calls for the service, the whole process assuring that all the guests at a table get all their dishes simultaneously. That's the mark of a top-notch restaurant, all the assembly of a table getting their dishes at the same time.

WHAT TO DO

Any kitchen worker must be an operational pro. Even the dishwasher. Because, you have to have a system when working in the dish bay too, putting every item in its proper place. Else the space will get crammed = the service can't clean the tables = guests are lining up, waiting for tables. Thus, the dishwasher has to prepare his workplace for a worst case scenario. The word is maximum efficiency, effectuated by the washing machine being up and running constantly, constantly served with washing baskets, the particular plastic frames into which dirty dishes, glasses etc. are put.

The cook in his station, whatever that station is, also has to have a system. Before the restaurant opens, things have to be prepared, "put in place" (= French, *mise en place*). Then again, you can't prepare too much. Like, slicing a tomato for garnish should be done just in time = à la minute, because having sliced tomatoes ready is not advisable, they quickly lose their freshness. However, minced onion can be prepared and stored in a container, ready to use. These kinds of deliberations are the heart and soul of catering: what to prepare, and what to do just in time. The rule of thumb is to prepare as much as possible in advance. This is good to know when cooking major orders, like serving a company of 100 people eating the same food. For instance, a cold first course can be done in advance; then, in the particular case, what first course is the optimal one to be offered? Again, the professional cook knows not only what's good, he also knows what's practical to cook in different circumstances.

Everything done in a kitchen has to be systematic. Even simple things like doing the dishes and peeling onions must be assessed. In the onion case, it's questions like, where to do it, where to put the sack, where the peeled onions go, where to toss the waste? These hands-on situations engrave operational thinking onto the bone of every kitchen worker.

WORKING

Working in a busy restaurant, say, on a Saturday, with a steady flow of guests, with yourself standing up and walking around for hours, cooking virtually non-stop, can move you into an Actionist trance, that of MAASOM = Movement As A State Of Mind.

This trance allows you to actually rest while working. It's the Actionist concept of RIA = Rest In Action = to rest while doing something. It's the Tao of acting: "act as if you didn't act". This is Zen-style relaxing-while-acting, being 100% concentrated and 100% at peace. To work this way in catering is a mentally uplifting experience. It's about being able to take short breaks, without even sitting down, mobilizing inner reserves in mini-meditation fashion, being able to take a deep breath now and then.

This all can lead into ARYM = Action Raising You Mentally. Having worked ten hours and then feeling that you can do more, that you can mobilize willpower to get through, this experience itself elevates you to a higher mental level. Because, "you can endure twice as much as you think and four times as much as your mother thinks," as the Swedish comic book *Buster* once said.

Action raises you mentally. While being concentrated on his work, the trained Actionist can think of other things simultaneously. The mere fact of getting up and going may clear the mind, putting your being into a more lucid state, even though you're formally active in hands-on duties like cooking.

Working in a restaurant is a fine way to experience the hands-on, tangible, operational aspects of Actionism.

STATIONS

As previously mentioned, work in a big restaurant is partitioned into stations: meat, fish, desserts etc. There's also the element of "changing of the guards," of the lunch watch handing over the kitchen to the dinner watch. Details aside, the system of doing this responsibly was introduced in the latter half of the 19th century by the Frenchman, Charles Auguste Escoffier (1846-1935). Escoffier is a kind of Helmuth von Moltke for the kitchen realm; cooks worldwide praise him for his operational skills, his structuring of *haute cuisine* cooking at large, along with his specific cunning in composing delightful dishes. Escoffier, for his part, also curbed the worst excesses of staff behavior, like drinking and smoking while on duty. However, he didn't succeed in stopping *swearing*; this remains a main feature of kitchen work, alas.

As for the station element, that of having separate workbenches / kitchen areas for fish dishes, meat dishes etc. this is the way of the bigger restaurants. However, throughout the Western world I'd say that the small kitchen, that of the "bodega / bistro / little restaurant on the corner" is the most common workplace, places typically having one head chef, one chef, possibly an apprentice chef (and then dishwasher, waitresses etc.). That was the style for my own alma mater in this respect, a restaurant in Uppsala now closed down: Sir Francis Drake. The usual way of working was the head chef taking care of receiving orders, structuring how to effectuate them and standing by the stove doing the main courses, while I would do first courses and desserts and apply garnish to warm dishes about to be carried out.

This way of working was operational prowess squared. The head chef gave the orders, but you also had to anticipate, having the preparedness to do things without ordered. In other words, you had to have *Innere Führung* and *Verantwortungsfreude*.

At calmer times, I could take care of the kitchen myself, effectuating orders on my own. Then, as an example: a waiter would come with an order, how to work it? If it's a poached salmon and a *tournedos Moskowitch* I'd start by cutting a three to four centimeter thick part of the *coeur de filet* and put it in a frying pan with the right, not-too-hot, temperature. This is done first because the meat in question takes the longest time to cook. Then I'd start poaching the salmon filet. Then I'd put some rice on heating.

The tournedos shall be flipped; this I do. It will also need garnish in the form of fried chanterelles. This I prepare. After some additional minutes (it depends not on the clock, per se, but on the actual foodstuffs being cooked à point) I can prepare the lay-up on plates. The *tournedos* gets its chanterelles and some black caviar plus *sauce béarnaise*; the fish gets some other, proper sauce plus some vegetable garnish. The meat dish gets an already made *gratin de pommes* to go with it; the fish dish gets the rice.

This is just an example. The idea is that all the plates for the same table should be ready at the same time. The cook has to structure his cooking around this, knowing how long each different dish takes to prepare. These are the kinds of operational basics that every cook gets ingrained in his mindset, his very being.

AVOIDING THE HOTPLATE

I've abstained from specifics in this chapter. True, above I mentioned the case of "poached salmon and *filet de boeuf*" but that was just an operational example, not a 101 on how to do it. But I'll close this chapter by giving you one (1) specific, tangible advice on "how to do it," gleaned from my restaurant career. It's a fundamental instance concerning coffee.

If we take the usual, brewed kind of coffee, the one made in a pot standing on a hotplate, my advice is to not let the pot remain on the plate. For, in this way, the brew after some 15-30 minutes gets sour, it's the release of what I call "tannic acid," bottom line = undrinkable. Instead, the newly brewed coffee should be poured into a thermos, preferably a so-called airpot, a thermos with a push-button pumping system. Thus the customer gets nice, hot coffee without the off-flavor it acquires when left on the hotplate.

It might be that you like this hotplate coffee as a symbol, this ordinary restaurant coffee maker of a metal frame using ground coffee in measured packs, just pour it into the filter and brew, the pot on the plate giving you "that truck stop feeling" or whatever. But in all fairness, this only works when you serve many people at once. For all other occasions, the airpot is the solution to this not unimportant detail.

16. OPERATIONS 3

It's rather nice to go traveling, to Paris, London and Rome. You see the sights, you meet new people, you're enriched spiritually. Even more so, when traveling into the wilds by foot or by bike, you're challenging yourself and your whole being, raising yourself mentally. This chapter is about such travel operations.

NAMO

There has to be an element of adventure to every travel experience. Thus, it's no use sitting at home planning everything you're going to do. An explorer can't delineate everything he will explore; he can only sketch the route at large.

That's the Actionist way of traveling: to use NAMO = Napoleonic Modus Operandi = not being stuck on the planning phase per se, instead do some basic planning and get the basic stores and then up and away. "On s'engage et puis on verra".

It's about shoestring preparations, shoestring planning. Again, I have to quote Christopher McCandless (1968-1992). An Actionist essence is caught in his saying: "There is no greater joy than to have an endlessly changing horizon, for each day to have a new and different sun." [this and other McCandless sayings are quoted after https://en.wikipedia.org/wiki/Christopher_McCandless] It's about hiking as the ultimate experience, to raise yourself mentally by going

Beyond the Beyond. Again, this is an illustration of ARYM = Action Raising You Mentally.

In his way of traveling, you could say that McCandless sought RIA = Rest In Action. You have to get out of your comfort zone, let yourself be imbued with impressions, sights and views, and in this mode find relaxation on a higher level, of a higher quality. McCandless said: "If you want to get more out of life, you must lose your inclination for monotonous security and adopt a helter-skelter style of life that will at first appear to you to be crazy. But once you become accustomed to such a life you will see its full meaning and its incredible beauty."

Also, remember the acronym ASARIT = A Strong And Responsible Idealist, Taking charge. That's the Actionist way of life, to feel strong, and McCandless has this to say on the subject:

> "The sea's only gifts are harsh blows, and occasionally the chance to feel strong. Now I don't know much about the sea, but I do know that that's the way it is here. And I also know how important it is in life not necessarily to be strong but to feel strong. To measure yourself at least once. To find yourself at least once in the most ancient of human conditions. Facing the blind death stone alone, with nothing to help you but your hands and your own head."

NO MAP

At this stage, I have to come up with some reservations. McCandless was young and reckless. See, for instance, the intimations of "a helter-skelter style of life" above. He took "minimal planning" too far. He put himself on the edge in an ostentatious way – not in the way of showing off, but in having to live on the edge at almost any price – even that of his life. He did, in fact, starve to death in Alaska. Partly, this was because of not having planned his wilderness outing enough. We're not judging the man, he remains an inspiration, as, for example, he's seen in Sean Penn's movie *Into the Wild,* 2007. But a criticism of the real, non-fictional McCandless is this: he hadn't enough reconnoitered the area he went into, the place he died in. He had misjudged the water volume of a certain river, due to melting snow rising significantly in the early summer; this hemmed him in, he couldn't cross it and get back to civilization. This mistake has been attributed to McCandless tendency to "do away with the map, then you're in the wilds". For indeed, the area he died in wasn't unmapped. But the man was a bit reckless and just ventured out.

So in all fairness, a cautionary advice in travel planning: in Actionist terms, NAMO mustn't become an *idée fixe*, an overriding principle in every instance. NAMO, for its part, is essentially about having to get going in order to clarify the situation. But if you're planning a hike, a bike tour or whatever in some reasonably remote terrain, don't leave all to chance. Whatever the purpose of the trip (vacation, science), take your time in planning.

Having said that, there always comes a time when you have to get going. A fine advice for the budding hiker is to start with a short outing, going off just some kilometers, raise your tent, make some coffee on a kerosene stove, sleep – and wake and praise the magic of the morning in "the wilds". I personally live in northern Sweden and we everywhere have rather wild terrain close by, woodlands without that much disturbing habitation in the form of villages etc. So in this country we can do these kinds of outings pretty easy as regards places to go, having the whole outback next door. The point was, to make a short, one-night outing first to test the equipment and yourself, see if you can handle this way of life of sleeping in a tent etc. Then you can plan longer trips.

BIKE TRIP

As for myself, in the summer of 1983 I made a major bike tour with two friends, in toto about 400 km, comprising one night in a tent, and one night in a summer cottage. The route taken was Örnsköldsvik-

Bjurholm-Fredrika-Åsele-Örnsköldsvik. All meals were cooked on a kerosene stove, water had to be fetched from houses along the way in a dunk; we had a tent and sleeping bags. In all, it was an enriching experience, to test your strength and raise yourself mentally in the process. I won't go into details about this trip except for this one, highlighting the Actionist concept of MAASOM.

It was day two, the stage from Bjurholm to Fredrika and eventually Åsele. It was an overcast day. At one particular time we rode along a fairly broad inland way, an asphalt strait, one being employed as forward air base by the Air Force if need be, one of the famed Highway Bases of the Swedish cold war defense, as such inspired by Nazi Germany which had tactical air bases on the Autobahn at the end of the war. There we went, cycling in line abreast, very leisurely, but still we made good time; it was a strait lined with coniferous woods, there was practically no traffic, this was in August and vacation times, but the Norrland inland doesn't have that much traffic even then.

There we went, playing UB40 on a cassette player, getting the feeling of movement as a state, of moving in a trance, moving as if supra-conducted. That the day was overcast underlined the timeless character of it all: midday – on a never-ending highway.

Timeless, time-bound: on a clear day the eye is drawn toward the horizon, to vistas Beyond the Beyond, to the realm where "space becomes time," as Spengler meant. Conversely, on a cloudy day the eye is somewhat drawn inward, you become "mental," you live in a more timeless mode. That was the spirit of that phase of the trip, going toward a clearly stated goal but still feeling rather timeless, being outside of space and time, experiencing Movement As A State Of Mind = MAASOM.

LENINGRAD

As intimated at the beginning of this chapter, it's nice to travel to cities, you just pay the price and go, you get your hotel and then you can venture out and be an urban explorer of the modest kind, see the city, see the world = the world as a city. The rest of this chapter will be about a trip I made to the Russian city of Leningrad in 1987. It's called St. Petersburg now, I , however, will always know it as "Leningrad," with or without totalitarian connotations. The element of "seeing decadent Bolshevism just before it fell" plays along with the theme of this book, that of envisioning a better future for us all, a future beyond any forms of imperial materialism, be it Bolshevik, Cultural Bolshevik, Liberal Decadent or just ordinary, default mode idiocy.

As for specific Actionist concepts, in a general way the Leningrad story is an example of the following Actionist concepts:

- A free operational spirit in a time of decay = I went to Leningrad as an operational esotericist, taking charge of this condition as a willful human being in a time of chaos and confusion.
- Conducting operations to acquire knowledge (COTAK) = making education into an intelligence operation. The recon patrol can be seen as a symbol of getting smarter, getting a wider outlook and becoming more informed, and the Leningrad trip was a glorified recon patrol in this matter. I got around, I saw the sights and when coming home, I brushed up my knowledge of the city and its history.
- Evade materialism and start building Antropolis = *Antropolis* is a novel I wrote and published in 2009, about the coming Golden Age of science and spirituality, denouncing the materialist ignorance of the previous era. And the Soviet regime, having its beginning in the Leningrad I visited, was the very symbol of mindless materialism, of 20th century non-spiritual, non-volitional, non-thinking insanity.

Now on to the travel story proper, the tale of my Eastern journey of about 30 years ago.

ACTIONISM

ALL INCLUSIVE

I visited Leningrad in 1987. Today, the name of the city is Saint Petersburg. I can understand that the Russians don't want to have their second largest city named after Lenin the dictator. But for me, the city will always be "Leningrad". And in this flashback it's historically proper to use the name "Leningrad" since that was what the placed was called back then.

I visited Leningrad in 1987. There were packages to buy, a four days' stay with everything included. The group I traveled with flew from Stockholm, Arlanda with Finnair; we had a stopover in Helsinki. Once at the destination, we were accommodated at Hotel Pulkovskaja, in the city's southern periphery. The hotel was modern and newly constructed but lacked a certain charm. It was meant to accommodate western tourists, as such, rather high-end within Soviet Russian standards.

- - -

A funny thing with some Metro stations was this: the platforms were completely separated from the tracks. The track was shut off by a wall, interspersed with automatic doors. These doors corresponded to the train doors. When a train had arrived and stopped, at the same time the station doors and the train doors were opened, the passengers thus being safely channeled into and out of the carriage. In other words, this prevented suicide candidates from jumping out in front of trains. But if this was such a good arrangement, why didn't all the stations have this contraption...?

- - -

Leningrad, as I remember it, was grand, an impression rendered by the wide main streets. The architecture was also rather beautiful and stately. From my visit, I remember classicist pieces like the Winter Palace, the Smolny Convent and the Russian Museum. And the Isaac and the Kazan Cathedral, heartwarming columns and fronts, and the sight of the Church on the Blood with its National Romanticism. The Palace Square in the evening light had its charm. But there were also slum-like environments abounding, even in the town center proper. Nevsky Prospekt was, in 1987, something of a "Potemkin backdrop," a street of fine fronts and façades, but behind them, dilapidation and neglect ruled.

However, it's also true that the run-down and neglected have their charm. In this respect, a tram ride on the Vasily Island was fascinating. This island, in the Neva River, was originally supposed to be the city center but this was not to be, the center ended up on the mainland to the south. In any event, during my expedition on this island I saw unkempt lawns, ugly buildings and gigantic buildings, arcade houses and some fancier houses of the "British row of terraces" type. The ugly and neglected, not completely rundown, but also "not suited for tourist postcards" – such views are what I, as a traveler, want. I felt the same when I was in Italy in 1978 with my mom and dad. Strolling in Riccione center with everyday apartment buildings, movie theaters, and a square with a sepia colored tram parked in the background, held more interest for me than to see the Ducal Palace of Venice. Well, the one doesn't exclude the other. , as an explorer I want more than palaces and churches.

Vasily: I got on a tram at the Neva quay. For its part, the payment was very simple, just putting a coin in a box, from a roll turning up your ticket and tearing it; done. There weren't any conductors. Otherwise, of course, Soviet Russia tended to overstaffing in such businesses like, "go to the counter with the goods, then go to a separate cashier and pay, then go back to the desk and show the receipt."

I went by tram in Leningrad, how fascinating to venture out alone, being rid of the group I traveled with. The vehicle passed dirty, run-down environments, straight out of Tarkovsky. And at the terminal station I got off. I was merely out to take a look around, a glorified drifter. For instance, at this station I saw a mega complex in the setting sun, a white mastodon of a house of ordinary Soviet proportions, cast into gold in the evening light. You could see those big structures here and there, like a certain palace I saw in the center during a bus trip: a large square, a Lenin statue in the center and in the backdrop this "Stalinist Gothic" construction. It can make you think of Ernst Jünger's stay in Russia, during his spying trip in 1942, when he would probe the morale and the revolt tendency of the officers of Army Group South. In Vorosjilovsk, November 24, 1942, he wrote:

> *"I live in the GPU building which has huge dimensions, like everything else belonging to the realm of police and prisons. Here I got a small room with a table, a chair, a bed, and above all complete windows. I also found a shard of a mirror that I can use when shaving. After the past few days' experience I recognize the value that these things have".*

- - -

I had full board, all inclusive. A dinner at the hotel could consist of things like boiled beef tongue and Pepsi Cola with a Russian label. If in the evening you wanted a snack, the hotel had a hole in the wall serving coffee, tea and meager sandwiches. A baloney sandwich I bought had more lard than meat.

- - -

Sometime during my stay in this city, I was out walking. It was downtown. It was a sunny afternoon. And once during this walk, I saw the police handle a drunkard. People looked on as they led him into the jeep – a Russian military green jeep. Strictly speaking, it wasn't "the police" for they didn't have that in the Soviet Bloc, they had "militia". That is, keeping the order, externally and internally, was all handled by the military. In France they also have strains of this system, like the possibility of doing national service as a *gendarme*, an official with both policing and military duties.

A backdrop for this scene of the militia handling the drunkard was a cistern shaped building, a subway station with an ornamented frieze. There were also some deciduous trees, abundant greenery; all these things don't mean a thing, however, I do remember it and as a tourist you want some authenticity and specificity, not just being herded around to "great vistas" where you say *ooh* and *aah* at everything.

WAR MEMORY

Just outside my hotel was a monument to the war, the WWII 900-day siege (the place is called Ploshchad Pobedy = "Victory Square"). The hotel was sitting by a large roundabout, and in the middle of this was a stone flat and an obelisk of red granite on which was inscribed, "1941-45". In connection to this were elongated pedestals on which statues of workers and soldiers, sailors and civilians, were placed. These bronze figures were truly heroic; they were timeless in their archetypal shine. They were heroes; they were, in the best sense, ideal men.

To see these bronze figures, illuminated by the setting sun, was a supernatural experience. It went beyond war and peace; it was something more than that: something archeo-futuristic, something elevating, something indescribable.

The monument also had a museum. It was intricately arranged: in the northern focal point of the structure was a round depression you could reach via a staircase. There, on the one hand, there was the museum. But it was closed when I was there. Well, it was a worthy monument. Actually there are no ugly war memorials, none that I've seen anyway. With tanks, soldiers, bronze, carved stone and more – how can you go wrong...?

- - -

ACTIONISM

I remember standing in line at Moskovskaja Prospect to buy an ice cream. The line was long, but since they only had one (1) type of ice cream to sell, it went quickly. The type was vanilla with wafer, very good and creamy.

- - -

Leningrad has its war history and I cursorily encountered it. Like buying Shostakovich's *Leningrad Symphony* at Dom Knigi. It was a massive double album recording of the Seventh symphony, the heroic musical reflection of World War II. First it's a bit chaotic, this is the retreat. Then a discreet military drum enters; this is the halting of the retreat, this is the resistance put up. Then comes the theme, which is growing. This is the heat of battle. Then comes a dramatic exclamation – and this is the front breakthrough, the lifting of the siege. Then comes the crescendo, again with somewhat chaotic aspects. This is the liberation of the motherland. Although I don't support Communism and Stalinism, as a work of art, the *Leningrad Symphony* commands respect, a deathless opus existing beyond the concepts of ideologies. The content received its impetus from the war but the shape is timeless. And that's what art is all about: to elaborate on something concrete or every day and give it a timeless feel.

My martial Leningrad – what did I see? I saw a BTR-60 parked at Kronverk, an outwork to the Peter and Paul Fortress. I don't know what this modern, still-in-use, eight-wheeled vehicle did there. Well, they had their military units in the city and this was proof of that. Otherwise, you hardly saw any soldiers in the street space. But in the Peter and Paul Church, the city's first church, built in the 1700s, I saw a captured Swedish banner, probably from Poltava. There is nothing to say about this, per se, it's a spoil of war, and we Swedes also have captured Russian banners in Stockholm; previously, they used to hang in Riddarholmskyrkan, the burial church of the Swedish monarchs. In the 20th century, the flags were transferred to the Army Museum.

And so it is: dubiously acquired spoils of war you can be forced to return, but never banners captured in battle. These have been paid for in blood, soldiers have ventured their lives when taking them. Lawyers and bureaucrats shouldn't afterward come and haggle about them.

COMMUNISM

In 1987, Russia was a communist land, the seat of evil, of godless Communism. Soviet Communism killed 62 million of its inhabitants: pure murder in gulags and prisons, war deaths not included. The figure is given in Staffan Skott's *Det nya Ryssland och arvet efter Sovjet* (2009) and is based on internationally acknowledged research.

But these deaths occurred from Lenin through Stalin. After that, it became a land among others, you might say. Then I say: no, it didn't. The fear remained ingrained in the system. Soviet Communism was one of the most murderous regimes the world has ever seen. It was nihilist materialism, anti-tradition, anti-life, anti-everything that's worth living for.

Personally, I was an anti-communist even then, in the 80s. In Sweden, by this time, there was a propaganda war in the media, dominated by left-wingers being against the idea of a viable national defense. I, however, vindicated the idea of national sovereignty opposing godless Communism. I served in the Swedish Army during my national service in 1984-85. The Soviet Union was aggressive back then, it took Afghanistan in 1979 and in the following years harassed Sweden with spying activities and submarine approaches (like Hårsfjärden, October 1981) and a major amphibious landing exercise earlier that autumn, ZAPAD 81. If you didn't oppose this, tangibly and metapolitically, you must have been mad.

I opposed Communism and Sovietism and my journey to the land proper in 1987 was instructive as a recon trip, a general look around. There were still signs of Communism being in charge, like a banner on an overpass saying, "Long live the Russian people building Communism". There was also the possibility to buy communist souvenirs in the Beriozka store. I bought a Lenin plaque made of cast iron, small, fitting inside the palm, silvery profile on a dark ground. Lenin was a murderous tyrant but he was and is also *history* and, as such, of value for a researcher like me.

I also bought two of his books, *Que faire* and *Un pas en avant, deux pas en arrière*.

I visited this seat of evil in 1987 and two and a half years later Communism was gone. Russia could restore its society on traditional grounds. It didn't become a paradise but it was a move for the better. The Soviet system was nihilist materialism squared.

CATHEDRAL

As intimated I visited the Peter and Paul Church. In it, there was a bust of Peter the Great. Fresh flowers adorned it. Indeed, but he was a tyrant...? Compared to Stalin, Peter was a mere village smith, to mention A. J. P. Taylor's characterization of him; however, per se, a much worse tyrant than our Charles XII. Examples of Peter's brutality: after the execution of a mistress (the lady in waiting, Marija Hamilton, who committed various crimes), he picked up the severed head and lectured the throng on the anatomical parts they saw in the cut interface (source Troyat, *Peter the Great*). Charles would never do such a thing. Maybe he practiced his sword arm to cut the heads off of calves but explicitly brutal, in the sense of Peter, he was not.

As for churches, I didn't visit any more than the one mentioned above. I can regret this now but I wasn't so much into churches then, in 1987. I was, however, once standing on the Nevsky Prospekt and looking at the Kazan Cathedral. It was, and is, grand with a semicircular colonnade in front of the actual church, a rather unique arrangement. This structure then had the infamous words: "Museum of the History of Religion and Atheism". What a sacrilege.

But of course, this is, again, a temple now and nothing else. The services here were resumed in 1992, I have been told.

The Soviet era humiliation of the Kazan Cathedral illustrates the way that Christianity was put on a starvation diet back then. However, the Soviet Union didn't completely prohibit religion, like Albania did. The Russian Orthodox Church survived. They had church services in some small churches. And during the war in 1941, the Communists noted that units fought better if they had priests along. "There were no atheists in the trenches" as they say.

The church survived, even under Stalin. Marxism-Leninism was openly atheistic, the program was to fight all that Christianity stood for, but it didn't manage to completely wipe out religion. And, as an organization and an administration, the Russian Church lived on through the Soviet era by donations from abroad, from private individuals. Sometimes it was even the case of investments: exile Russians bought Churches from the Soviet state. How often this occurred I don't know, but I have one example. In *Panzer Commander* Hans von Luck says that when he, as a conqueror, came to Smolensk in the summer of 1941, he was surprised to see its cathedral well maintained. The Germans took the city, it was partially destroyed by air strikes, but amid the ruins the cathedral rose to the sky, mostly undamaged. Going inside the church von Luck was impressed by its beauty. And when he asked how the cathedral could be in such a fine condition, the priest said that, after the 1917 revolution, Russian exiles in the USA bought the church from the Soviet Regime because the Soviets were in dire need of dollars. Thus, the Smolensk cathedral was American property.

- - -

Here ends my story about Leningrad. It was almost thirty years ago, I was there, and there still lingers in my mind the sight of Leningrad in the evening light, the Winter Palace, the curved arcades of the Kazan cathedral, the fronts, colonnades and the golden dome of the Isaac Cathedral, the Ploshchad Pobedy bronze figures – they all reside in the evening light, all being cast to gold in the flat angled evening light of the north, eternal symbols of a city sometime, somewhere, an immortal symbol of human existence.

17. OPERATIONS 4

There's no mystery to the art of writing. You just do it. "Try, fail, try again, fail better" as Beckett said. Personally, I've been writing for many years and the following are some informal notes on the writing operation.

THREE RULES

I'll structure my musings on writing along a short list of three rules, three central concepts. They are:

1. Finish your projects.
2. Time as co-creator.
3. Know your subject.

In a general sense these three rules are central to writing – any writing, although they apply best to more advanced projects, from essays and stories to books and major efforts.

As for Rule 1, "finish your projects," this is a self-evident idea that nonetheless needs to be highlighted. It's one of the rules Robert A. Heinlein (1907-1988) once delineated in his rules for writing. While it's true that most projects benefit from maturing with time, from being laid aside for a while (see Rule 2, more on this later), there comes a time when a project has to be completed or thrown away.

A completed project is easier to relate to and store, it's a living thing, while a half-done project is merely a promising draft. And, at a later stage, several completed smaller items can be combined into larger structures = books.

TIME

That a separate article may be combined with others into a greater whole may show only with time. This brings me to Rule 2, that of "time being a co-creator". Thus, time can help you to gain clarity, like seeing that several separate articles can be combined into a greater whole.

Time can be a co-creator in a different way. It may be that you're ordered to write an article on subject X, to be completed before a deadline. Then you don't have the luxury to let the project lie half-finished and mature with time. But in a general sense, if the subject you're writing about is something moderately profound and complex, then time, already from the perspective of writing a single article, has to be a co-creator in what you will write. Because, to really get to know, say, an artist, a band or an author may take years. Thus, a great essay on such a subject summarizes what you've realized through the ages, not just what you've read on the net or in a book you just picked up.

The time element is a glorious co-creator. For instance, let's say you have a day job other than writing. Then you get the idea of "writing a book on your holiday". Most likely, you will end up being stressed out by such a goal. And you should, of course, not turn a pleasure into a torment. Such a plan doesn't allow for time as a co-creator. Instead, plan this writing venture over, say, three subsequent holidays. Or start having writing as a hobby with generous criteria, such as not having to make it pay, instead allowing creativity to flow. This is the Actionist concept of WAP = Winning As Propensity. In this case it means: putting the criterion for "successful writing" into something attainable, like "having read through last day's pensum," "having blogged about my cat" and the like.

LENNART SVENSSON

KNOWING

Then, what about Rule 3, "knowing your subject"? I've already touched upon this in the example of, "getting to know a certain artist or author you'll write about". You might say: if you just give it time, then you'll end up as an expert. It's true. To have listened to the ten essential albums and having read at least one (1) book-length biography of a band or music artist, this makes you into a kind of expert. But it may take years to attain this, since you might have other interests. Again, time is a co-creator of the project.

A note on structure. If you know your subject, then you won't have to deliberate too much on how to structure your text. The structure will be evident based on your expertise, knowing what's important and not.

As for "knowing your subject," this can also be of a more abstract nature. Author Lisa Tuttle (1952-) once gave the advice that even in fiction you have to know what you're writing about. For instance, the event of approaching the site of some supernatural horror may not be something you've experienced, per se, but you might have known fear. Thus, this can make you tell about this make-believe with some kind of authority: you know the feeling. Even though you may not have known "the presence of cosmic horror" from personal experience you know what the scene in question *represents*.

PERSONAL

The best advice I personally got in writing fiction was the Heinlein advice of "finish your stories". Along with the allowance of "time being a co-creator" (which I discovered intuitively) this Heinlein rule makes you get up and go, getting things done. As I said, it's easier to relate to a finished text than a mere draft. An example: you might stumble upon a file in your hard drive with only drafts, fragments and shadows of stories to be. Finally there comes the time when you have to decide what to do with it, since the very existence of this file annoys you, it sucks energy. Then you might feel like joining these diverse fragments into a whole by adding some interconnecting passages, or you erase most of it except for fragment X which did show some promise.

Sometimes you have to be the gardener rooting out bad seeds, sometimes a painful act, per se, but in the end it cleans up your mind, it takes off the load of having "useless file Y that I need to get to grips with". You weed out in order to have it grow better.

INFORMAL

At the beginning of this chapter I said that these were "informal notes" on writing. This concept as such, "informal notes," is a discreet inroad to any subject. Conversely, if you plan on writing "the definitive article" (essay, book) on any subject then you're making it harder than it has to be. It will be like Casanova (1725-1798) who, according to Jünger, stumbled on the task of writing a book on cheese; I figure that it was to be an exhaustive study, summing up virtually everything there was to know about all sorts of cheese. But the subject was too big, there were too many cheese varieties even in his day. His mistake, as I see it, was that he applied a perfectionist approach. Instead, while acknowledging that cheese is a wide subject, he should have written an essay stating that this is merely "some informal notes" on the subject, being what the author has gathered in the matter throughout the years. This would have been the optimal way of structuring his knowledge, which undeniably was vast although not all-comprehensive. But who has such knowledge? It might be possible to get such an exhaustive study on cheese today, but sometimes "some informal notes" by a passionate amateur is more enlightening and enjoyable, the reader in this way being led by an inspired personality.

Even if you're a pro, even if you know most of what's needed to know on a subject, the caption of "some informal notes" can be mentally liberating. It's a headline saying "this is what I have to say on the subject now, this is no doctoral dissertation". Even in the academic world these kinds of "informal notes" are rather common. In German "some informal notes" we have the headline element of "Beiträge zur" (= "contributions to") this and that subject, serving the same purpose: that of honesty, of saying that this is not necessarily an exhaustive study. Then again, it might be, you just give the reader the benefit of doubt; you're not bound to amaze the world by having a too bold headline. The way of captioning a study with this modest line (*informal notes, Beiträge zur,* also, *toward an understanding of*) frees the mind and makes it easier to get going.

TO WRITE

So then, "how to write"? How to portray environments, depict human faces, create atmosphere...? This you might learn with trial and error, if ever. I've personally never attended any course or lecture teaching me "how to write". Instead, I've just done it. You have to have written a novel in order to know what it's like, even if that novel just remains a private tutorial or a qualifying piece. The budding writer sitting around talking about what he's going to write is not a promising writer in my eyes. He has to prove himself, if only by "having done it" as I just sketched.

It's like developing a new aircraft. No matter how meticulous the engineering, there comes a time when a test pilot has to fly the thing. The actual maiden flight gives information that no ground test can equal. This is an illustration of the Actionist concept of COTAK = Conducting Operations To Acquire Knowledge. There's no way of getting to know how the ship will fly except by taking it up in the air. It's risky and you may lose your life. The same goes for writing a novel – you might not lose your life, but you do have to cut loose from the everyday, you have to let yourself come into a trance. Not everyone wants that, not even professionals. After writing an X number of books they might think that they've got it, that they know the formula for producing a masterpiece. But it's different every time, each work has its own logic, its own power – a power the author, being the creator of it, is also enmeshed by.

I won't give any advice on how to write fiction, on how to create art. I'm the author of *Antropolis* (q.v. Chapter 28), I've written short stories published here and there, also, I've published a short story collection (q.v. Chapter 14) but to give advice on style is useless. "*L'homme et la style c'est la même*" as Flaubert said = "*the man and his style is one and the same*". You, the reader, are "NN" and I can't teach you how to write "NN stories". Only you can figure that out. The only things you need to know are to let time be a co-creator, know your subject and finish what you start.

The rest, how to shape a particular scene etc. etc. only you can decide. It's true that there are handbooks teaching how to do this. I've personally never read one. But in all fairness, you might even learn something from them. Just don't get hooked on formulas and "dont's" (like "don't use second person narrative, don't start a chapter with a lecture, don't use long sentences"). You have to break every rule. Then again, simply "breaking rules" won't make you into a literary genius. I'm merely saying that creativity is a hard thing to capture. So then, to let it flow and flourish, give it time. As a writer you first have to create a working environment, an everyday structure within which you can be free. This might mean to live alone, to have a day job to pay for expenses etc. etc.

ART

Actionism can't teach you how to become an artist. However, Actionism has some things to say on the subject of art, of music, literature and painting, of the activities inspired by the Muses. I've already done it in Chapter 8; now for some repetition and elaboration. For instance, one Actionist concept in this respect is, "artistic vision is the avant-garde of man". This means: art must go before everyday reality, as a glorified scouting patrol. Art can envision things that "are not real" but in time may become real.

A similar wisdom is, "symbolism always precedes actuality". This means: a concept has to be envisioned before it can be realized. The artist goes into a trance, being elevated to the Beyond, the Astral World and eventually the Causal Sphere, seeing the Eternal Ideas. Then he returns from his trance and can recreate what he saw Beyond, in the process putting something of his own nature into the ensuing artwork.

I just mentioned the Muses. To be "musical" in this sense is an Actionist fundamental, even for people not specifically creating art. It's expressed as, "mixing into your stringency a little musicality" = life can be fun too = add some pizazz to your sagacity.

Finally, there might by a trait of ruthlessness to the artistic endeavor. To be morally perfect is an ideal but an artist often moves in different lands, not expressly cruel but conversely, an artist can't structure his artworks into being simply morally justifiable. This is expressed as, "the spirit of song is war" = in the vein of Edith Södergran, to acknowledge the "ruthless" character of the artist. You could say, he has to have a mindset like that expressed by the knight in Dürer's "The Knight, the Devil and Death," riding forth on his mission without caring about anything, not even "Devil or Death," nor about family, friends, critics or polite society.

Again, art is musical = guided by the Muses, but along with this, the true artist might need something of a ruthless mindset. To be precise: as for "not caring about family and friends," this doesn't mean that an artist, by definition, has to break with every social bond. It only means: if your friends etc. say that you should not write about subject X, this is forbidden – then you must ignore them. That's what's meant with artistic freedom, artistic ruthlessness, the idea of the "artist as a warrior," vindicating the idea of "the Spirit of Song is War".

INTELLIGENCE OPERATIONS

ACTIONISM

I'm operational. I'm an operational esotericist, an operational scout. For as long as I can remember I've conducted operations in order to gain knowledge.

You could say: I've always been an agent in the realm of information, occupied with conducting intelligence operations. To write articles, essays and novels is a kind of intelligence operation. This I've done for a long time; professionally since 1997, when I sold my first article ("Kamikaze" to *Flygrevyn*, a Swedish aviation magazine) and existentially since the mid-1980s, when I first decided to become a writer.

To write articles, essays and novels is a glorified intelligence operation. For instance, it's a fine illustration of the Actionist core concept NAMO = Napoleonic Modus Operandi = get going in order to clarify the situation. For, there comes a time when your preparatory work for the text has to cease and you have to get going, actually writing the text. In the realm of book-length manuscripts, this is even clearer. I never write a synopsis before writing up the actual text. You can, of course, write a short synopsis, like an explorer largely mapping the route he will take, but you can't plan everything in advance. The general plan has to have room for whims and intuitions, for going off on fruitful sidetracks.

To plan the outline for a novel or a book-length essay is about *creating a structure within which you can be free*. That's what a synopsis should be for. Conversely, composing a synopsis mustn't serve as an excuse for not writing the actual piece. Personally, I only write a synopsis when the work is done, putting it in the beginning of the file to ease the decoding of the manuscript by the prospective editor.

KNOWING

"Knowing is the way to operate". A field commander has to have scouts, reconnaissance aircraft and intelligence staff working for him – so that he knows where the enemy is, so that he knows how to plan his operations.

Similarly, any human being has to have intelligence to work along. He has to know what the world is like. He has to ask the glorified scouts of mankind, the philosophers and pundits, what lies ahead and how to interpret what we see.

Knowing is the way to operate. I know my operation. Does anyone else need to know? I share my knowledge freely in this book. Otherwise, you might happen to work in operations on a "need to know" basis. Need to know anything? Or are you shut out? Or do you gain your information advantage by other means? These are operational deliberations of the intelligence kind.

Knowing is the way to operate. An Actionist conducts operations to acquire knowledge (COTAK, see above). Even by reading for pleasure you can learn a lot, like "the ways of a chief mate" by reading MacLean's *The Golden Rendezvous* (1962), "how a WWII battalion operates in the field" by reading Linna's *The Unknown Soldier* (1957) or diverse operational aspects of Cold War counter-espionage by reading Wright's *Spy Catcher* (1987).

18. OPERATIONS 5

To drive a vehicle is an operation attainable to many of us. But how many take this seriously? Vehicle operations are the subject of this chapter, delineating the Actionist way to drive.

SIX HORSES

In Goethe's *Faust* we read: "If I can pay for six strong horses, do I not own their power? (...) As an individual, I am lame, but money procures me 24 legs." This captures *in nuce* the spirit of the West, the forward moving restlessness of operational striving. It's about the very spirit named after this play, the "Faustian" spirit that, for instance, Oswald Spengler (1880-1936) saw as the *sine qua non* of the West, its defining mentality factor.

Riding a horse, driving a team of six horses, driving a car: it's the same spirit of dominance and submission, of an ordered, but triumphing, Will in action. Then, you might ask, does the random car driver have Will on-board? You might answer, not always. For instance, many people drive vaguely, not knowing where they're heading. Instead, as a driver you must take charge of the driver role, that of being the master and commander of the car.

Primarily, you have to drive safely. You go slow at first. Then, out on the road, you have to (1) follow the traffic rhythm and (2) show clearly where you're heading. The two are somewhat interrelated, such as, you can't go too slowly. As for clearly showing your purpose of your driving operation, this, for instance, means to choose the appropriate lane. Choose either, don't stray in between.

To take it from the beginning: you choose to drive. Your Will decides. The car is not a living thing, it's not intelligent, it doesn't know how to tangibly go a certain way. It may these days have a navigation system suggesting what road to take getting from point A to point B but in essence, you're in charge. When placed in the driver's seat, take charge.

And if you think a certain traffic situation is difficult, disengage. You might not be able to directly head for the roadside, and you can't always go slowly, but essentially, you always have the option of slowing down and disengaging from the traffic flow proper. You decide, you're in charge – *your* hands are on the wheel, not the person next to you or in the backseat. Heard about the "backseat driver"? Show him who's in command. When in command, take charge!

MILITARY

In the military of today there are a lot of vehicles. Some armies stopped using horses by the end of the 1930s (US, UK). In the postwar period, the rest followed. The 1980s Swedish Army I served in had no horses but it had many vehicles.

In a military unit, the Unit Commander is in charge. But in a vehicle the driver is Vehicle Commander. Operationally, in obeying and executing orders, the driver has to use his own discernment too. This might be true for all orders (= you don't have to execute an illegal order, like one ordering you to attack a hospital) but the vehicular situation makes this extra clear.

When driving in the military, the system of driver and co-driver is important. You often have to read the map. That, when traveling, is the task of the co-driver. A fine example of such cooperation I personally experienced in my military service in 1985: during the major exercise *Västgräns*, a comrade and I once were out in a Bv 206 all-terrain vehicle, functioning as a glorified taxi service, going to this place and that, picking up VIP's and taking them to this and that destination. The driving, as such, wasn't so hard, it was by ordinary roads, but Pettersson, the driver, indeed was glad that I was along reading the map; he himself lacked orientation skills, he said. And I was glad to be of help, the orientation wasn't overly difficult, but we all have different gifts in life.

ACTIONISM

And the payoff of the story is that previously, when starting this exercise, we had to unload the *bandvagns* from the railroad wagons they had been shipped by; it was freezing cold and we had to ask ourselves how to start the vehicles, having been out in the cold for 24 hours. But the selfsame Pettersson had his way with them, and managed to use the contraption for "start gas cartridges," not a wonder in itself, but in this it was the same as with reading the map: not a major task in itself but to actually do it, to make it work in field situation X? I, for one, could never have gotten my *bandvagn* off that railroad wagon, so it was good to have a helping hand from Pettersson, just as I could help him with the orientation business later.

THREE PRINCIPLES

Three principles for military vehicular operations are these, as I learned them when doing my national service.

First: when having grouped, the driver must leave the keys in the ignition lock. While this might seem frivolous and invite "the enemy to steal the vehicles," the rationale for this practice was this: if, while in camp, the driver gets injured and shipped off to hospital and he has the vehicle keys in his pocket, the unit will be stranded; better leave the keys in the ignition lock.

Second: a military vehicle has to be camouflaged, unable to be detected either by ground forces or aerial reconnaissance; therefore, some combination of poles, branches and camouflage netting has to cover the vehicle when bivouacking. Also, when grouping in the field, vehicles must be dispersed, they shouldn't be parked together, thus they can't all be knocked out by one (1) hostile burst of fire.

Third: when driving in column, the driver must check the connection backward, he has to have connection with the vehicles coming after. If the vehicle behind him stops, he must also stop. Thus connection is maintained in a military column of vehicles.

MAASOM

A central Actionist concept is MASOOM = Movement As A State Of Mind. Applied to driving in general, it's a peculiar feeling when you're out on the road, driving and traveling, and suddenly you don't feel the presence of time anymore, it's as if you're moving supra conducted. You don't feel hunger, tediousness, inconvenience – you just drive, you just go, you're experiencing movement as a state. The same can be experienced when biking (q.v. Chapter 16) and riding a train, even when walking. It's the fundamental state of Actionist traveling, of Actionist living: you move, but you don't have the sense of moving, not in the physical way. It's movement in a different quality, it's movement as a mental state.

OPERATIONAL SECURITY

This is the last chapter on operations proper. I'll end it with a note on online security. This subject could have required a chapter of its own but it will be attached to this "vehicular" chapter instead.

Very generally, from the view of "a common computer user," when you post stuff on social media, see to it that you have *operational security* included in everything that you do. This means some "don'ts," like not saying that you're going away for some days, not saying that you've helped a friend install a Bruno Liljefors painting in his house, not saying where you have your vintage car collection. Full security can't always be maintained, but by this kind of self-censorship on social media you make things more difficult for people with bad intentions, like burglars.

As for being silent about your near and dear on social media, this is a moot point. However, to be on the safe side, post as little information (and pictures) of them as possible, thereby minimizing any kind of hazard they might be exposed to. Not all people out there act in good faith. Having "operational security" ingrained in your online behavior, you then can post "almost whatever you want," you can post rather freely. There's a wealth of things to post that will not unnecessarily jeopardize your operation, this operation called "life".

PART II

The Macrocosm

19. OUTLINE OF HISTORY

Part I of this book, *Actionism*, focused on the individual, the microcosm. This part of the book focuses on the macrocosm = the society, the world at large. The following chapters take a look at the societal and historical Big Picture, all with an ethical slant. First, an outline of history is given. So then, what is the very moral leitmotif of history? The leitmotif of history is the struggle between idealism and materialism, light and dark. Reportedly, this battle has raged since the beginning of time. Hereby some aspects of the planetary development from the Beginning, until today, giving you an Actionist conception of history, a moral history of mankind, as it were.

LEITMOTIF

In Chapter 1 I proposed a theory by which God, in the beginning, came into existence as a being of Will, Thought and Compassion, united with the Light. God, being omnipotent, immediately started to depolarize the Dark. And with time he, as a *macrocosmic* being, created Man as a corresponding, *microcosmic* being, his soul becoming a unification of Will, Thought and Compassion.

As an embodied soul, man came to be a composite of Light and Dark. According to esoteric theory (like Gnosticism), God had two generations of sons and daughters: the Elder and the Younger. Here they will be called Asuras and Devas respectively. Asuras somatically created man, but God later adopted him, giving him a soul by taking a spark from his Eternal Light. The corporeal, material element in man has Asurean origin. Man thus is a mixture of Dark and Light. His Inner Divine Light makes him strive for perfection, shaping himself and the world into a better place. However, his material nature draws him to the dark, to lust, greed and wrath.

This struggle of man, choosing either Dark or Light, is the leitmotif of history. It's a struggle of Devas and Asuras leading man this or that way, to an existence of creating things and concepts positively, or to climes of dominance, submission and ignorance. The overall, divine meaning was for man to evolve spiritually, to realize his Inner Light and project it to the world.

To relate this whole human drama, this planetary, moral history of man, is a daunting task. As intimated, the following will give the strategic aspects of the development. It gives a background to the issues man faces today, the current struggle of idealism against defeatism, of Eternal Values against materialist ignorance.

LIGHT

Man has a long history on earth, according to esoteric theory at least 200,000 years. But we won't go into the oldest history here. We'll spare you the Hyperborea-Lemuria-Atlantis stuff. Suffice to say that man, having been created and having started to live on Earth was conceptually led along by Devas. These angels of Light incarnated among men and taught them constructive practices like speech, song, writing, philosophy, farming, husbandry and handicraft. With time Asuras also incarnated and led man astray with witchcraft, materialism and passive nihilism.

Man's soul was made of Light, therefore man instinctively walked toward the Light. But the power of the Dark was strong and the Deva-Asura battle over man's soul was fierce. Would man's Will persistently lead him to the Light or would the inability of mustering Will lead him astray, to debauchery and debility?

We all know that man, indeed, has evolved. Today, we don't live in an earthy paradise, but it could be worse. Truth and justice are still cherished, the Eternal Values of honor, responsibility, courage, modesty, clemency and faith still live on, despite this also being a world of sham, lechery and indulgence. The forces of the Light have managed to lead man into a state of freedom coupled with responsibility. Devas have taught man astronomy, architecture, poetry and sculpture and, by way of incarnated masters such as Orpheus, Zoroaster, Lao-Tse, Plato, Buddha and Krishna, taught him about his Inner Light.

Jesus Christ was also such an incarnated Deva. His mission was to teach man about the I AM-impulse, to affirm his Inner Light this way. And overall, his mission was successful. Organized Christianity, as it came to be, may have distorted some of Jesus's teachings, but, jointly led by the doctrine of Christ, Buddha, Krishna etc., man continued to walk toward the Light.

EGYPT

But I'm getting ahead. An intriguing look at man's development from 6,000 BCE to the birth of Christ is given in *The Ancient Secret of the Flower of Life, Part 1* (1998). It's an esoteric outing by Drunvalo Melchizedek (1941-). I don't support all the claims he makes. But he treads the same territory as other authors mentioned in this study, like Julius Evola, who also believed that Atlantis has existed.

As promised above, no mention will here be made of Atlantis and other lost worlds. Instead, I go directly to ancient Egypt. After the alleged fall of Atlantis, mankind was in shatters, mentally and spiritually. Just before the fall, some highly developed beings, like Thoth, supposedly left the sinking island and headed for Egypt and Mesopotamia where civilization was started anew around 4,000 BCE. Thoth's report on this can be read in *The Emerald Tablets of Thoth*. "Long time dwelt I in the land of Khem" it, for example, reads in Tablet 1, Khem being Egypt. Thoth and friends can be seen as Devas, "demigods," spirits of Light, in this instance incarnated in human form to help man forward in his development. They gave impulses to man to develop writing (= Thoth's specialty, being the god of writing), math and astronomy, as well as more basic things like pottery and the building of houses.

Thoth was part of the alleged Brotherhood of Tat. In ancient Egypt, polytheism flourished, but this Brotherhood taught that there in essence was only one God. This doctrine was obscured by other groups, but it again came to the surface and triumphed for 17 and a half years during the 18th dynasty, 1500 BCE, in the form of Pharaoh Akhenaten's teachings.

Akhenaten taught about one God – one God, elevated above the rest. He didn't, for that matter, deny the existence of the established Egyptian pantheon. The elevated God concept was illustrated by referring to the sun, so that contemporary people would understand. Akhenaten taught about the sun as the giver of life, the bestower of the omnipresent *Prâna*, the same as "the etheric body" giving life to the physical body, the vital energy in man also known as Chi, Qi and Od. In Akhenaten's art, Prâna was symbolized iconographically with the sun beams exuding small *ankh* crosses. This is the epitome of eternal life received from the sun.

Akhenaten taught "the common priesthood" (God is within you, priests aren't needed). This was a challenge to the previously ruling Egyptian priests. This led to Pharaoh Seti I soon taking over and deleting Akhenaten's effort, much like the work of Christ was thwarted in his time. And like Akhenaten, Christ taught the doctrine that, metaphysically, there is one God and that God is within you. Melchizedek's conclusion about Akhenaten's teaching is this: man spontaneously wants to return to God, it's encoded in his DNA. And Akhenaten performed his missionary life work (belief in one God) exactly because of this, to get it all coded into the Akashic Records, the Book of Life, and thus encoded in our DNA. As such, his mission was successful, even though his immediate achievements came to be formally wiped out by Seti I.

PYTHAGORAS

When the Egyptian civilization had blossomed and lost its vigor, Thoth conveyed his knowledge to Pythagoras (circa 570-495 BCE) so that he could start the Greek civilization. Pythagoras himself said, regardless of this modern narrative of Melchizedek, that he was led by Thoth to a hall under the Great Pyramid where he was taught geometry and ontology. Thoth became the formal origin of many religions; through various successions of disciples he also instructed men like Plato and Zoroaster. This is the theory of the "Prisca Theologia," that all religions have the same conceptual core (Lat. *priscus*, cf. *primus*; ancient, old, archaic).

Pythagoras, Plato and Zoroaster can also be seen as incarnated Devas, beings of Light embodied as humans in order to lead man forward. Buddha, Krishna, Lao-Tse and Orpheus were other such incarnates. This March of the Light is the theme of Actionist history; conversely, the fixation of Julius Evola on how the times degenerate, his stressing of "the regression of the castes" (first rule the priests, then warriors, then burghers and workers, leading to a successive increase in materialism and a decrease of idealism) isn't at the forefront of the Actionist doctrine, not in the categorical way Evola taught. (For instance, Evola had a somewhat perfectionist outlook, a dualist approach, that of societies either being fully spiritual and traditional or not being it at all; Actionism isn't so "binary programmed". More of this in Chapter twelve.) While it's formally true that nihilist materialism seems to rule the world today there have been counter-forces to this since the beginning of time. Since 6,000 BCE Enlightened Masters in the form of Thoth, Christ, Buddha, Orpheus etc. etc. have been around teaching the Perennial Philosophy of Light.

CHRIST

Christ, for his part, taught of the existence of one God, like the Pharaoh Akhenaten. A connection between the two is this: during his 17.5 year regime, Akhenaten created a mystery school with 300 members, 300 immortals allied with the Brotherhood of Tat. After a suitable wait of 850 years, until 500 BCE, they went to Masada in Israel and created the Essene Brotherhood. The 300 formed the inner circle. Then there was an outer circle with hang-arounds. Mary was an inner member; Joseph was a hang-around. [Melchizedek p 144]

Christ was eventually born and taught of the Light, of man's affinity with God, of man's soul mirroring God: "*You are in me and I am in you*" (Gospel of John, 17:21). Christ taught of Will: "*Will doesn't make them into sinners, but lack of Will does.*" (The Gospel of Philip, 64). Christ also taught of the I AM impulse. In the Gospel of John this "I Am" occurs seven times (as in I Am the door, I Am the Light of the World and I Am the Way, the Truth, the Life). According to Rudolf Steiner (1861-1925) "I Am" is the Logos which was in the beginning. "The Name of Christ" so often and obscurely mentioned in the Gospels is this "I Am". In the beginning was Logos whose name is "I Am". (More on this in *Borderline*.)

When Moses met God in the form of the burning bush, God said: "I Am That I Am." (Exodus 3:14). According to Steiner, this is the Logos speaking, the one eventually incarnated as Jesus Christ. The same spirit was reportedly present in the Persian solar deva Ahura Mazda and the Hindu god Vishvakarman. This I AM-impulse was embodied as a man in Christ. And as already intimated, the mission of Christ was successful, all things considered. Man's solidifying into a materialist moron was stopped. Man, led by the doctrine of Christ, Buddha, Krishna etc., continued to walk toward the Light.

20TH CENTURY

From the beginning of time, the forces of Light and Dark in the form of Devas and Asuras have been active among men. Devas have taught men of God, of philosophy and science. This has been countered by the forces of the Dark, dragging man down into materialism and defeatism. Bloodlines of dark influences have allegedly formed, carrying the idea of materialism further into Europe and the New World by way of secret doings. Atheist and anti-tradition, the forces of darkness have been active into our times. Now they reportedly run the world.

To stage conflicts and panics, to orchestrate stock market crashes, famines and catastrophes, to throw the world into wars upon wars – this, allegedly, is what the chaos faction does. But there have been forces of the Light around also. This I've shown you when mentioning figures like Thoth, Christ, Buddha etc.

As for the outline of the modern era, a lot could be said of its secret history. In this case, I refer the reader to Neal Wilgus's *The Illuminoids*. As for the spirit of history in general and especially Western history, I can recommend Oswald Spengler's *Decline of the West,* even though he was too much of a pessimist to fit into Actionism proper. The first half of Evola's *Ride the Tiger* might have something to say the latter-day idealist, waiting for materialist ignorance to end and to take over as one of the Aristocrats of the Soul. More about that book and Evola's thought in Chapter 12.

As intimated, Actionism has an optimistic view of history at large.

A key event in the history of the West, and the world, was the discovery of the New World. The vision to create the United States was a positive one, inspired by the Light. It was carried forth by the idealism of Roger Bacon in the 1200s (*Opus Majus*), Christopher Columbus in 1492 and Sir Francis Bacon (*The New Atlantis*, 1627).

The colonization of America had distinct aspects of idealism. As was often the case throughout history, the project was then co-opted by negative forces. However, embodied in Saint Germain's presence at the Declaration of Independence in 1776, you can say that the Light persevered in America's national life.

The US had its freedom tradition, its popular religiosity and its optimism. But the negative forces reportedly gradually took control, especially after the Civil War. Lincoln wanted to create interest-free money, but this attempt was quelled by elite club forces.

- - -

An American President in the early 1900s, Theodore Roosevelt, sensed the elite club presence in the corridors of power:

"Behind the visible government there is an invisible government upon the throne that owes the people no loyalty and recognizes no responsibility. To destroy this invisible government, to undo the ungodly union between corrupt business and corrupt politics is the task of a statesman." This Roosevelt said during his presidential campaign in 1912 when he was a 3rd party candidate for "The Bull Moose Party," his unsuccessful attempt to create a non-corrupt alternative to the elite controlled Democratic and Republican parties.

Roosevelt was succeeded by Woodrow Wilson. Like Roosevelt, Wilson sensed the presence of the Hidden Hand of the elite club: "... there is a power so organized, so subtle, so complete, so pervasive, that they had better not speak above their breath when they speak in condemnation of it."

Another President sensing that something was wrong with the governance of the USA was John F. Kennedy.

JFK

John F. Kennedy wasn't a saint, but still, his path was rich in meaning for the struggle between Dark and Light. According to esoteric theory, John F. Kennedy, US President from 1961-63, after a while in office discovered that the country was run by a shadow government. And there is tangible evidence that Kennedy realized he was on to something. For instance, he held a speech in 1963 in which he warned of the conspiratorial feature of American politics. The speech was delivered at the American Press Club ANPA on April 27, 1961. Kennedy, for example, said:

> [W]e are opposed around the world by a monolithic and ruthless conspiracy that relies primarily on covert means for expanding its sphere of influence—on infiltration instead of invasion, on

subversion instead of elections, on intimidation instead of free choice, on guerrillas by night instead of armies by day.

Kennedy said more in this vein. Ten days before his death on November 22, 1963, he, for instance, said, before an audience at Columbia University in New York: "The high office of the president has been used to foment a plot to destroy America's freedom and before I leave this office, I must inform the citizens of their plight."

Even in the economic field, Kennedy challenged the globalist network. He wanted to abolish the federal, in fact privately owned, Federal Reserve Bank. Perhaps he was inspired by President Lincoln's attempts in the same direction: Lincoln's launching of the "greenback dollars". This was interest- and debt-free money issued by the state, not by private banks as is the case with the Federal Reserve System.

It came to pass on June 4, 1963 that Kennedy signed Executive Order 11110, in itself an addition to President Truman's Executive Order 10289 of 19/9 1951. Kennedy's new orders gave him the right to create a state-issued currency backed by silver. It would thus be interest- and debt-free money. The new "United States Notes" were silver-backed paper money, issued by the US Treasury Department. Federal Reserve dollars, for their part, were associated with the payment of interest to the Federal Reserve, which consists of twelve private banks controlled by elite families. Federal Reserve money is debt-based currency, issued by the private banking cartel which is behind the Federal Reserve.

Kennedy began by issuing four billion in cash in the form of one-, two-, five- and ten dollar notes. But the system couldn't really get started; Kennedy was notoriously assassinated in Dallas on November 22, 1963. Kennedy's new "United States Notes" were withdrawn from circulation immediately, one day after the murder. Many have suspected that the reason for the murder was the same that was behind the assassination of Lincoln in 1865. Lincoln also had wanted to issue interest and debt-free dollars.

In order to fully create debt-free money issued by the US Congress, Kennedy had to suspend the Federal Reserve Act of 1913. But now none of this came to be. All redemptions of the new banknotes for silver dollars were stopped in March 1964. The strange Federal Reserve System continued.

However, to end this on a positive note, and to telescope the development from 1963 through to the present day, now this has happened as regards the Federal Reserve: it has now changed its homepage from .org to .gov, indicating that it's now part of the government. The Fed (as it is called), is no longer a private bank, as it was from its inauguration in 1913. This might indicate a victory for the forces of Light and a defeat for the Dark, not just on a symbolic plane, but essentially and tangibly. If the info given in this case is correct, then the Fed is now a truly *federal* institution and not a private enterprise, as was the idea when creating the Fed in 1913.

LUX AETERNA

This outline of Actionist history has only sketched the contours of the development. Overall, the message is clear: throughout all of prehistory and history, the Forces of Light have never been defeated. But the battle is still raging. While the Light currently seems to be gaining ground, this means nothing if not every positively disposed human being joins in the struggle.

Join us in the Light: this is the rallying cry. Every individual can do his part in helping Light win against Dark. Every individual must affirm his Inner Light, his essential affinity with God and *Lux Aeterna*.

This isn't about "being perfect, being a saint". It's about being at least 51% positively disposed. You have to be predominantly "service to others" oriented, to use lingo employed in *The Book of One* series. Conversely, if you're mainly "service to self" oriented then you're veering off toward the Dark.

Light is the goal and Darkness is the enemy. So, in joining in the struggle: how to do it? You can do a lot – like meditating on your I AM, reading uplifting books like the Bhagavad-Gîtâ, the Bible, *Borderline,* the Evola and Castaneda books highlighted in this study, as well as books by Walsch and Kierkegaard, to name but a few. You can look at artistic masterworks, read novels by Ernst Jünger and C. S. Lewis, poems by T. S. Eliot, Ezra Pound and Goethe etc. etc. The bottom line is, it matters what you do and think. Even what you feel. This is a "frequency war," to use a term by David Wilcock (1973-); what we feel, and how we conceive of both the private and global situation, counts. With willpower embracing Light a higher frequency is gained; by shutting off the TV and browsing positive, constructive websites, we steer clear of the attempts of The Powers That Be to lower our spiritual frequencies. More on this frequency phenomenon in Chapter 23.

Join me in the Light and be a fighter for freedom and peace. This struggle is real. It's happening now.

CHRIST CONSCIOUSNESS

The keyword to the significance of history, to what the above outline means, that of the Creation, the emergence of Dark and Light, the battle between the two with man as battlefield and the appearance of Elevated Masters leading man to a better future – the keyword to all this is Christ Consciousness. For those so disposed, it can also be called Buddha or Krishna Consciousness. It's about the evolution in man of a mindset affirming his Inner Light, a mindset finding peace and quiet in That Which Is, a mindset governed by Will-Thought choosing Light, turning away from mindless materialism. It's about man's soul realizing its divine nature.

This is Christ Consciousness. And this is what discreetly characterizes our times. This is the emerging zeitgeist. Today, sufficiently many human beings have, with their free Will, chosen Light instead of Dark. This is "the return of Christ" – man as a collective, evolving into will-driven-and-reflective beings affirming their Inner Light. Christ won't return in the flesh. The intimated return is a virtual return – in our hearts. The one making this interpretation is David Wilcock and in this, I support him fully.

Mankind has reached Christ / Buddha / Krishna consciousness. Man has risen from the miasma of materialism he dwelt in before the alleged Dawn of History 6,000 years ago. But to stay on this level and maintain the victorious momentum, we all have to affirm and acknowledge the Light, 24/7, every day.

We have to be at least 51% positively disposed. We have to tap into the divine source. We have to turn on the Light and let it shine.

20. GLOBALISM VERSUS NATIONALISM

In politics, we often think in terms of Right and Left. In a general sense these labels may still be viable. But today, these terms have begun to become somewhat irrelevant. The superior dividing line today is between globalism and nationalism. Globalism is the camp of materialist madness; nationalism is the camp of idealism and freedom.

RIGHT AND LEFT

The concepts "Right" and "Left" may, of course, still be used. Very simplified, with a summary of developments since the French Revolution, you could say: Right stands for tradition, the Left stands for modernism. But when you go into the current political issues, *Left* and *Right* are too blunt, as concepts, to analyze the situation.

It used to be simple. In the 20th century, the social struggle was about workers against capitalists; workers were Left, capitalists Right. But today's Left is essentially connected with capitalism in a materialistic, globalist, unholy alliance. The old map is no longer valid in this respect. Virtually all Western political parties seem to stand for decadent liberalism and depletion, all in order to secure that sacred, economic growth. In that perspective, I think that *nationalism versus globalism* gives a clearer picture of what's happening in today. And this goes equally for understanding Sweden locally, the Western world and the world at large.

The front line in today's political struggle, both in Sweden and in the rest of the world, to me seems to go between globalism and nationalism. Globalism's ultimate goal is to form an empire, a world government bent on conquering and destroying all the countries and states and replacing them with a streamlined nightmare. For example, globalism can be seen as the real power factor behind Political Correctness (PC). Today, PC is the prevailing ideology in the West. It depicts some selected groups, such as immigrants, LGBT people and women as victims of the white man's traditional society. If this society is abolished eternal happiness is implemented as a matter of course.

PC

This is PC, the political *Leitkultur* of today. This is the meta-political, ideological pattern that governs today's politicians. But this is just an ideological superstructure, a rhetorical façade. For under the surface is a practical policy not in the least caring about anyone's welfare, neither women, immigrants or LGBT people. Behind the happy façade of tolerance and diversity is a policy called globalism. In that case PC, is metapolitics; globalism is practical politics. The former is the means, the latter is the end.

How, then, does globalism manifest itself tangibly? Here you might come to think of the Bilderberger meeting in Copenhagen in May-June 2014. The Bilderberger Group, this international "elite group," advocates globalism. And thus, it's opposed to all forms of nationalism. For instance, during the 2014 meeting it was discussed, under Paragraph 3 of the published agenda, how nationalism is on the rise in Europe, demonstrated in the European Union elections, and how this puts a spoke in the wheel of the introduction of globalism. Under the title "Rise of Nationalist Moods in Europe" it was formulated it this way: "Populist eurosceptic parties are winning the hearts of Europeans from the UK to Greece to Hungary, dealing a blow to the EU's unity. A nationally driven and divided Europe would be reluctant to take globalization for granted."

NATIONALISM

It was noted how nationalism surged in Europe during the 2014 European elections. Marine Le Pen's *Front National* and UKIP in England scored record-breaking results. In virtually the entire European Union, parties with an anti-globalist, national agenda went forward. This worried the Bilderberg elite. This put a spanner in the works of the agenda to eradicate national characteristics of any kind (social, cultural, economic, ethnic), dismantle the welfare state and prepare the world for a world government.

This is the pattern. It may be argued that even nationalism may have its downside (as it can be misused to chauvinism and other excesses). And in very general terms, a planetary perspective and "transnational cooperation" can be beneficial (as opposed to strife, dominance and submission), but the globalism we see today seems to me anything but benevolent. It's pure imperialism. It is the Soviet state with a new face.

As regards the Bilderberger group's aversion to nationalism, it has a long history. Already during the meeting held in 1966 it was stated: "Nationalism is dangerous." At the time, the meetings weren't covered by the media, but a note of the cited text has been secured for posterity. The Swedish news site Fria Tider had graphical and textual evidence in its article "Bilderbergergruppens mötesprotokoll har läckt," 7/6 2012. Their source, in turn, was the site Infowars (www.infowars.com).

FRONTLINE

Again: the frontline today runs between globalism and nationalism. There the planet's future is determined, not on questions of Right and Left, per se. Capitalism and Communism have today joined forces in a materialistic alliance, and against them are nationalists, traditionalists, freedom fighters and people with some kind of spiritual ideals. "Be good, be legal, tell the truth" can be said to be written on the freedom fighters' banner. The fight is still going on. Resistance is made. And this pays off. It has a big marginal effect.

The global elite still aims for total submission of the planet. And the slightest resistance becomes a spanner in the works. It's like the *Asterix* comic series by Uderzo and Goscinny, about some ancient Gauls (Frenchmen) refusing to be subjects of the Roman Empire. The presentation of the series went like this: "It's the year 0 and the whole of Europe is under the Roman Empire's dominion. All of Europe...? No! In northern Gaul, one village is still putting up resistance..." Asterix the Gaul gave the Roman Empire legions a hard time and today nationalists and freedom fighters all over the world still offer resistance to globalism.

21. CO-NATIONALISM

As intimated in the previous chapter, nationalism is a viable feeling and a central element of human existence. To love your own people and your own country is natural. Stripped of its aggressive connotations, nationalism can be a part of 21st century reality – in the form of *co-nationalism*.

ENGDAHL

The term "co-nationalism" was coined by Swedish right-winger Per Engdahl (1909-1994). He meant that nationalism wasn't solely a way to protect your own; it also means respect for other peoples' right to the same feeling. "True nationalism is co-nationalism" was the catchphrase. Specifically, Engdahl meant this in a European context, but nothing stops the concept from being applied to the whole world.

The concept of co-nationalism is sorely needed today – today, when we always hear that nationalism equals chauvinism, marching in line and imperialism. However, for starters, few Swedish nationalists would like to conquer other countries. Personally, as a nationalist, I only have the ambition to live free in my country of origin, Sweden. And I give all others peoples the same right: to thrive in their home countries. Conversely, concerning the current regime to subdue the Swedes with forced migration, *that* is imperialism and chauvinism.

Co-nationalism is alive. It's akin to the concept of *Human Biodiversity* (= HBD), the idea that there's a value in letting separate peoples survive, not having them all forcibly out-bred and eradicated into a multicultural mass. Ethno-pluralism, HBD and co-nationalism can give nationalism a better foothold in the current debate. You can say: there are Turks, Somalis, Thais and Chinese – and Swedes, Frenchmen etc. And, as well, if Turks, Somalis, Thais and Chinese have the right to arrange their countries as they want, without the requirement that mass immigration will improve and "enrich" them, therefore Frenchmen in France and Swedes in Sweden must have the same right. Swedes and all peoples who want to say 'No' to mass immigration have to get their voices heard in the debate. The labeling of "racism" on perfectly sound national feelings must stop.

PC

In the current, overheated debate climate I figure that this key attitude, co-nationalism, can be highlighted and inserted into the Swedish and Western world debate to open the lock that surrounds ideas of Swedish uniqueness. Co-nationalism allows Swedish and other nationalisms to prosper. Co-nationalism is an idea for a global co-existence, aimed at equal rights and self-determination, not supremacy and ethnocracy.

Co-nationalism is a weapon against the Politically Correct (= PC) faction's tendency to smear nationalists. The co-nationalist concept allows for every people to thrive in its place of origin.

CONTEXT

Co-nationalism puts things into context. From The Powers That be we always hear "what is a Swede, define a Swede" etc. This argument is countered with saying: in the world today we acknowledge the

Chinese people, the Japanese, the Persians, the Arabs etc. Then, why is it so hard to acknowledge people such as Italians, Germans and Swedes?

This is about *customary concepts*, not about some rigid "Platonic" ideas. Thus, a Swede is what traditionally is meant by a Swede. Further, Swedes have a customary right to Sweden, as do other peoples to their countries of origin.

This conceptualization, to widen the topical scope into the realm of practice and custom (everyone knows what a Chinese, a Turk, etc. is), is fruitful. Then you won't end up in a tricky attempt to define Swedishness etc. in detail, per se. This could otherwise be hard in a live debate when you have to deliver a quick response. We're up against a compact, sentiment called PC. PC questions the entire existence of Caucasian peoples. All other people are fine and good, but Caucasian people are considered 'fascists' or even non-existent: the object of slow extermination by mass immigration. In this hostile climate of debate, co-nationalism is an efficient antidote.

EDGE

Co-nationalism can take the edge off of Swedish hostile commentators who say, "Indeed, you're Swedish, do you think this makes you superior to other people?" Then you can say, "Do you think that, say, a Somali nationalist claims that he is superior to the Chinese? Co-nationalism is about every people having the right to live peacefully in their place of origin." To this the PC-ist usually has no response.

TREATIES

As intimated above, this is about customary concepts = a Swede is what is commonly known as a Swede etc. As such, it belongs to the realm of common law as opposed to statute law. However, as for a viable nationalism for the 21st century, there are also international treaties in action, statutes and codices stating that everyone has the right to a nationality, and that racism and genocide must be prevented. And these are treaties we need to revisit today when we face low-intensity genocide by mass immigration of people to Caucasian countries.

Thus, we have to highlight such a document as the Universal Declaration of Human Rights from 1948, stating that every person has the right to a nationality (Article 15). This means: the right to belong to a people; the word *Nation* is from Latin *natio*, "I was born". Further, we have the UN Racism Convention, ICERD of 1965. ICERD = "International Convention on the Elimination of All Forms of Racial Discrimination". It says that "racism" means any form of exclusion or restriction made on the basis of race, color and descent, intended to discriminate and oppress. Therefore, to denigrate Caucasian people because of their race is an international crime.

We also have the UN Genocide Convention of 1948 = CPPCG = "Convention on the Prevention and Punishment of the Crime of Genocide". It says that measures preventing births of a certain people are considered to be genocide. The mass immigration and the anti-white propaganda that the Western world regimes and their mass media have spread since 1945 might fall under this convention. To be anti-Caucasian is illegal.

POSITIVE SHAPING

The current Western world is anti-white in outlook and intent. But in the face of rising self-determination, this policy has run its course. In this context, the above sketched concept of co-nationalism has a lot speaking for it. It can remove the mental block persisting in nationalist debate; it can free white people of constantly feeling subordinate to other peoples ("white guilt" etc.). We truly live in "one world" but this must not lead to forcible colonization of Europe by distant, foreign people. The Europeans have the right to Europe as well as the Asians have the right to Asia and Africans to Africa.

Ethno-pluralism and co-nationalism are both positive ideas. They are not based on negative ideas about different people. On the contrary, it's all about recognizing your own identity while affirming that other peoples have their culture and customs, within the framework of all peoples being assured security in their respective places of origin. Conceived thus, co-nationalism is a win-win situation.

SPIRITUAL MEANING

The concept of nations, and nation states with clearly defined borders, is still viable. It's even hinted at in the Biblical story of the Tower of Babel. Wasn't it so – as someone pointed out – that the separate nations arose in order to crush the international tyranny of the Empire, symbolized by the Tower of Babel, this God-defying venture of "disobedience and pride"?

Separate nations shall prevail while the Empire must perish. A nation is a sort of safeguard against the Empire of Anti-Christ, a safeguard until "Christ returns" – that is, until Christ consciousness is reached by mankind. And this is now the case, man is spiritually elevated into a Christlike glory, a sufficient number of people now willfully having their being anchored in the I AM.

Conversely, to abolish the national borders invites chaos and confusion. Seen thus, God gave the peoples borders within which to seek him. God is a nationalist.

22. DECLINING WAR TREND

At the time of writing this, "there is war and rumors of war". And still there are nuclear weapons around to "obliterate" us. But is there really a risk of major world in the world today? No, we'd say, not in the least. The war trend is going down. The zeitgeist is essentially peaceful. Thus, the war-mongering, even by seemingly sane commentators, has to stop.

TPTB

There is war and rumors of war. The Powers That Be indeed seem bent on starting the Third World War. But the current zeitgeist is against a major war breaking out. Also, the US-EU-Russia-China deal with Iran, 14 July, 2015, was a way toward a calming down of the global situation. For instance, in this treaty, Iran promises not to acquire nuclear arms – and these arms they gave up trying to build already in 2003, according to a National Intelligence Estimate from 2007 ("Iran, Nuclear Intentions and Capabilities").

So peace will prevail. All the internet pundits prophesying "war this, war that" are way out of line. Also, in the long perspective, the level and intensity of wars has gone down since 1945. The late 1990s saw another turn for the better. The war situation deteriorated a bit in the 2010s; that's true. The Ukraine and Syria conflicts have had many deaths. But the war situation of today is not anywhere near that of the 1970s and 1980s.

FIGURES

Hereby some figures to back up these claims. For instance, in 2013 two (2) significant civil wars were ongoing: Syria and Congo. I call that, overall, a peaceful world. My opinion is supported by a report from the peace researcher, Peter Wallensteen, published in July 2012. Our reading of Wallensteen is based on a *Dagens Nyheter* article by Anders Bolling from 6/9 2012. Bolling's article may be somewhat biased. The headline is, on the basis of the big picture given in the article, misleading. The title is "Minskande krigstrend bröts" = "Declining War Trend Broken".

That statement might be true in itself. But this was only about the development for 2010-2011. Looking at the period after 1950, the wars have both become less frequent and less bloody. In all, this declining war trend continues.

Bolling's article focuses on the negative aspects of the report, blowing them up. It's true that the number of armed conflicts increased in 2011. "The Arab Spring" with the focal point in Libya was behind the increase. But generally, Bolling writes, the trend is pointing downward. In the long term, it's obvious that we live in a more peaceful world after the Cold War ended: "In recent decades, the number of armed conflicts in the world has shown a clearly declining tendency." [Bolling, translated by the author]

This is worth remembering. In 2010-2011 Wallensteen and his researchers at the Uppsala Conflict Data Program UCDP could note an increase. Wallensteen thinks that this is a trend, that the trend of peace processes and agreements "may be threatened." I disagree. Of course, Wallensteen doesn't say that we're going back to the Cold War. And this is what we have to remember: the Cold War isn't coming back. This is an important factor when taking a look at the world of today.

I mean it like this: in my crystal ball, I can't see that the great powers would suddenly begin to openly threaten each other with nuclear arms again. And overall, the armed forces of the world are too small for a new cold war. The conflicts that used to rage over the whole world, they occurred more or less in the context of this former great power conflict. They were incited by the United States and the Soviet Union in order to sell arms to the contestants. This large-scale arms trafficking and "assistance in the form of weapons" doesn't exist anymore, at least, nowhere near the same levels as in the 1980s. Having this in mind, among other things, you have to be an optimist.

WALLENSTEEN OPTIMIST

In the topical article, Bolling also says that Wallensteen, overall, is an optimist: "At the same time he emphasizes that the level is still far below the darkest years of the early 1990s, when almost 53 armed conflicts raged." You should also remember that Wallensteen mathematically counts the number of conflicts, all of which have at least 1,000 dead. But there's another criterion available in making these trend estimates: the number of dead in battle in each of the conflicts. And this, in studying the global war situation, is a number which has plummeted dramatically. This, according to Bolling, researchers in Canada have stated. They say the number of dead in battle by conflict decreased by 90% between the 1950s and the 2000s.

This is a staggering figure. And a compelling figure. This must be considered when discussing our world and its supposed bellicosity. You must see the big picture. To believe in a return to a warlike world à la the 1950s, with bloody conflicts in Korea, the Middle East and Africa, or believing that we'll get back to conflicts such as the Vietnam War, Afghanistan 1979-89, the war in Iran at the same time or that Central America would become a war scene as it was in the 80s – this is totally irrelevant. It's a pessimism that's somewhat silly.

ACTIONISM

NO NUKES

Indeed, silly? But what about nuclear arms then? They are still around. They may be used. And a single atomic bomb going off could trigger a nuclear deluge because of misunderstanding. To this I say: nonsense. This is defeatist nihilism, advocated by people having chaos inside.

Since 1945 the so-called nuclear threshold is insurmountable. There won't be a nuclear war.

But then the war-mongering Cassandra might say this about the scenario of these times being so peaceful, as I claim: Before the First World War, the world was also peaceful, the wars were few and far between and distant. Then all hell broke loose between 1914 and 1918, getting an even more bloody reprise in 1939-1945. True, I say to this, but the zeitgeist is totally different now. Since after 11/11 2011 we reportedly live in the Sat Yuga of peace, harmony and spirituality. The preceding era was Kali Yuga where wars, so to speak, went with the territory.

SAT YUGA

You might ask: Sat Yuga is here, indeed? But overall, like domestically, we still see strife and violence. True that, I say, The Powers That Be currently use every means of instigating Chaos. Like mass-immigration to white countries. But overall I think we do live in the Sat Yuga – an era realized, an era essentially coming true, by each one of us acknowledging the Inner Light of our beings. That is, we must still fight the NWO. We must 24/7 advocate the ideals of co-nationalism, self-reliance and self-determination, the right of every people to exist in its place of origin. We must fight. But "when fighting demons, beware that you don't become a demon yourself" as Nietzsche said. Spiritually, Sat Yuga won't be realized until we, each one of us, affirm our Inner Light.

Sat Yuga is here and it will be an overall reality when we acknowledge our beings as Responsible Men. When we stop regurgitating the war propaganda of the NWO.

How can I be so sure about this, then? Am I some last court of appeal for the metaphysical truth of the world situation? No. I'm merely making an estimate in the gray area between contemporary events, pol-sci studies and my impression of the look and feel of it all – the zeitgeist.

THE DAWNING OF A NEW ERA

The old-school era of wars is over. It's safe to say that *hyper war*, the kind of war where two states attack each other with everything they have – that form of war is history. Vietnam was such a war, Korea another. And in the 1980s such a war raged between Iran and Iraq. Later, in 1990-91, the UN Alliance in Kuwait staged a war against Iraq in a similar hyper-war scenario. A few such wars have occurred since then (Iraq 2.0, Georgia). But now it's probably over. Until about 2007, the US threatened to attack Iran. And, true, some Americans continued to talk about it after that. But the current, autumn 2015, talk of "attacking Iran," is absolute nonsense. It will never come about. The window of opportunity for this and any hyper war, big league-attack-scenario anywhere in the world, is closed forever. Libya 2011 was the last show of this kind. Then Sat Yuga dawned. Essentially, we're not on "timeline war" any more.

The US defense forces have been cut in half by the current president. Russia (and China) may have more troops available than the US, but the sentiment that allowed hyper war simply doesn't exist anymore. Overall it's a peaceful world and the civil wars that are raging are manageable. The current battles in the Middle East are not equal to the Battle of Stalingrad. A tank knocked out by an ISIS rebel is not a major battle of the Kursk type. But this you are led to believe by mainstream media. And pundits and media players, even those of the dissenting, critical kind, should stop repeating these

NWO war memes. They should stop scaring people with saying that World War III is looming.

LAYMAN OUTLOOK

Personally, I can be said to be a layman in this area of conflict estimate. This doesn't mean that I'm a frivolous observer. I was born in 1965. Since at least 1980, I've observed the world and reflected on the wars being waged. Earlier than that, I had some knowledge of the US war in Vietnam. I never saw it on TV, true, but I do remember television images of the abandoned capital of neighboring Cambodia, Phnom Penh, in 1975, which was a conflict in the same context. China's attack on Vietnam in 1979 and the Soviet foray into Afghanistan in the same year, are "in my memory yet green," as well as the media reporting of 1983 from the Falkland Islands and Grenada. Not to speak of Desert Storm in 1991 and what, before and after, has occurred in the Middle East. And in 1984-85 I served in the Swedish Army as an NCO, seeing the Cold War from ringside.

So I would argue that I, for being a layman in this subject – peace and conflict research, strategic outlooks, foreign and security policy – have a specific, non-professional but unmistakable background. Thereto, I hold a BA in Indology, I'm a freelance writer and author of the novels *Antropolis* and *Camouflage* as well as bios on Jünger and Wagner. I've been published in innumerable magazines and anthologies. And what I overall see, with the main support of Wallensteen's study and the esoteric theory of Sat Yuga having begun, is that we now live in an essentially peaceful world, about to become a wholly peaceful and prosperous world in every sense. We're not there yet, but for the future we have to acknowledge our personal beings of light as part of the situation. There are no "random observers" anymore. Everything that we do, every sentiment, every thought, every word, counts in building Sat Yuga, the coming Golden Age.

Addenda: a list, given by *Dagens Nyheter* (ibid), on "the average number of deaths on the battlefield by conflict and years":

1950-1959: 9,800

1960-1969: 6,000

1970-1979: 7,000

1980-1989: 5,200

1990-1999: 2,200

2000-2007: 1,100

23. FREQUENCY WAR

Author David Wilcock (1973-) sometimes uses the concept *Frequency War*. This is something subtler than a mere shooting war, harmful as that may be. The Frequency War is a term covering elements such as propaganda war, brainwashing, media tricks, all kinds of strategic shenanigans in print media, TV and on the net. They're all deliberately done, there's a system behind it. It's about The Powers That Be holding back the development of man, keeping him enslaved in fear.

FEAR IS THE KEY

Blogger Steve Beckow has coined "Beckow's Law". It says: when fear and stress rise, the level of consciousness goes down. To exemplify: when a person reads "10 dead in Syria" he thinks woe is me, the end is nigh. He becomes stressed out, fear rules him. Conversely, a person beginning the day meditating and then doing "constructive stuff" remains C3 = Calm, Cool and Collected. The person browsing MSM (as the Mainstream Media is called) is exposed to blown-up, angled, agenda-driven news, bent on destroying his mind, to lower his mental frequency.

That's the battlefield of the Frequency War: your mind.

The remedy against this "mindfuck" simply means to stop reading MSM. Doing this along with performing C3, summoning Will and shaping your life positively is the way to mental health.

The Powers That Be rule us by fear. "Fear is the Key," as in the MacLean novel title. We live in "The Empire of Fear," to use another title (a Fritz Lang film). Now, however, we liberate ourselves from this Regime of Fear, partly by finding peace and strength in our own spiritual beings, partly by going online and IRL (which stands for In Real Life) recovering the world and the freedom that was ours which was stolen from us by The Powers That Be. We already have freedom, as soul-endowed, civilized beings; no one can take that from us. Now we have to affirm this fact by saying, "I AM a person driven by Will-Thought affirming the Light; the Dark harassing me with fear will never win."

ENERGY THEFT

The Powers That Be steal people's mental energy, according to David Wilcock. On the Art Bell Network there's a show called "Fade to Black"; in this show, on May 7, 2014, Jimmy Church interviewed Wilcock on matters of freedom and spirituality, and there Wilcock said that key world events can be seen as some kind of enormous sacrificial ceremony. "They steal energy through sacrifice." In this context 9/11 and the Kennedy murder are other examples of such theft, aiming at making people upset and afraid. And when the stress level goes up the level of consciousness goes down (Beckow's Law, remember).

This can be seen as an illustration of the Frequency War, it's the same strategy of lowering peoples' mental levels, killing thought, eradicating consciousness. The battlefield is you. Willpower, personally summing up your Will and positive thought, your Good Will and optimism, envisioning the Victory of the Light, is the defense against it.

ACTIONISM

PREVIOUSLY

Chapter 19 of this study outlined the moral history of the world. In some concluding remarks I said this, on the role of the individual and what he can do to write history:

> "The bottom line is, it matters what you do and think. Even what you feel. This is a "frequency war," to use a term by David Wilcock; what we feel and how we conceive of both the private and global situation, counts. With willpower embracing Light a higher frequency is gained; by shutting off the TV and browsing positive, constructive websites, we steer clear of the attempts of The Powers That Be to lower our spiritual frequencies."

This is simple, but the simple is difficult. I can only say: don't succumb to artificially machinated fear. See through the MSM shenanigans of trying to make you sad and afraid. Practice C3 and go victoriously into the virtual battlefields of today.

EKERWALD

Swedish author Carl-Göran Ekerwald once mentioned a woman who supposedly killed herself due to "the world situation". She was somatically healthy and lived in peaceful Sweden, however reading in the news of "constant war" somewhere, anywhere, made her depressed, with a fatal outcome.

Thus, she became a victim of the Frequency War. Media affected her mindset so deeply, that she decided to take her own life. This is serious. And so unnecessary. If the info divulged isn't needed for your daily operation, then stop reading media if it only makes you dejected. It's true that we live in the world and "need info about it" but conversely, negativity and suffering have no function and this is what the Frequency Warring MSM is all about: negativity and a lowering of our mental activity, blotting out our consciousness with fear and stress.

Don't be a victim of the Frequency War. And don't be a collaborator in it. Don't forward all the sad and irrelevant news you hear about. While it's true that "we need contrasts to see wholes" it isn't sound, as a private citizen, to dwell on every piece of MSM information of the sad, dejecting, mind-killing kind. "Fear is the mind-killer" as Frank Herbert said. In his novel *Dune* (1965), the mentally apt operators sometimes recite a mantra or a litany, "the litany of fear". They do it when they feel that they're about to be overcome by fear. So here it is, a golden wisdom useful to us all, a counterforce to the mental down-pull of MSM news:

> *I must not fear.*
> *Fear is the mind-killer.*
> *Fear is the little-death that brings total obliteration.*
> *I will face my fear.*
> *I will permit it to pass over me and through me.*
> *And when it has gone past I will turn the inner eye to see its path.*
> *Where the fear has gone there will be nothing.*
> *Only I will remain.*

24. THE WORST IS BEHIND US

The ice age is coming - punk band The Clash sang in the 1980s. This might have been justified, then. For example, the years 1996-2003 reportedly were the Biblical "seven years of famine". This Chapter discusses an interpretation of Biblical prophecy with the gist that now "the worst is behind us". All Biblical quotes are from "The New King James" edition.

REVELATIONS

This attempt at prophetic interpretation focuses on the Book of Revelations, the Revelation of John. Parenthetically, the title should probably be "the Revelation of Jesus Christ" because the first line reads: "The Revelation of Jesus Christ".

Throughout history, people have tried to interpret this text. And there have been more or less good interpretations, more or less plausible. Here I'll try to present some by focusing on modern times. Note, to say that this or that figure is Caesar or Napoleon, to me, seems pointless in this context. I see the text as depicting the era from the First World War onward.

And the First World War is said to be predicted here, in Chapter 8, verse 7:

> *"The first angel sounded: And hail and fire followed, mingled with blood, and they were thrown to the earth. And a third of the trees were burned up, and all green grass was burned up."*

Then, in verses 8 and 9, follows the Second World War:

> *"Then the second angel sounded: And something like a great mountain burning with fire was thrown into the sea, and a third of the sea became blood. And a third of the living creatures in the sea died, and a third of the ships were destroyed."*

WWII, really? Indeed, for this "burning mountain" in verse 8 has been interpreted as the atomic bomb over Hiroshima. Why not: WWI in the first verse, WWII in the second. And the post-war period? It's symbolized by the Chernobyl nuclear accident. Chernobyl, for its part, is Russian for "wormwood" which we find in verses 10 and 11:

> *"Then the third angel sounded: And a great star fell from heaven, burning like a torch, and it fell on a third of the rivers and on the springs of water. The name of the star is Wormwood. A third of the waters became wormwood, and many men died from the water, because it was made bitter."*

GULF WAR

Now quickly over to another quote that is current, 11: 6: *"These have power to shut heaven, so that no rain falls in the days of their prophecy..."*

This control of the heavens has been interpreted as HAARP, "High Altitude Auroral Research Program," an atmospheric research program whose forest of antennas reportedly greets the visitor at Gakona, Alaska. But the circumstantial evidence is weak here; the current chapter speaks of "God's two witnesses," two olive trees, two candlesticks standing before the Lord. These are the ones being able to prophesy, as intimated above, and they have been interpreted by others as something completely different from HAARP. So who knows what you should interpret this passage as.

Chapter 9 talks about visitations by a kind of bizarre locust and armored horses. In a particular YouTube Movie, this has been interpreted as combat helicopters and tanks in the Gulf War of 1991... Battle helicopters do have some similarity to those locusts, specifically the rotor hum: "... and the sound of their wings was like the sound of chariots with many horses running into battle." [9:9]

As for other signs of the Gulf War, in this conflict it can be noted how the sky was darkened by all the oil fires. In the just preceding 8:12, where the fourth angel blows his trumpet, it's said:

> "Then the fourth angel sounded: And a third of the sun was struck, a third of the moon, and a third of the stars, so that a third of them were darkened. A third of the day did not shine, and likewise the night."

BUY OR SELL

Now for a central section, Chapter 13, with its famous Beast and 666. And the Mark of the Beast, delineated in verses 16 and 17:

> "He causes all, both small and great, rich and poor, free and slave, to receive a mark on their right hand or on their foreheads, and that no one may buy or sell except one who has the mark or the name of the beast, or the number of his name."

What is this in modern terms? We're already seeing the beginning of it with a chip that can be implanted in the wrist. For instance, on May 4, 2011, the Swedish daily *Dagens Nyheter* ran a story of a regular guy having an implanted chip ("Han har ett chip under huden" by Ulrika By). It was only for opening electronic door locks.

But you don't need much imagination to see it developed into a payment chip later. And becoming obligatory "for all who want to buy and sell". The door-opening-chip guy had his chip inserted with a needle. Then it's small, indeed. This is so-called nanotechnology, engineering at the molecular level. Some say the swine flu scare in 2009 was a rehearsal for such an implant: let's say that a fatal virus is on its way, forcing people to get vaccinated; then you sneak in a nano-chip and presto, you have marked all with the Mark of the Beast. It'll be easy in Sweden where, in the swine flu scare, 60% were tricked into taking the vaccine, all in vain. Conversely, Poland's population didn't take the shot and they still live. Swedes generally got worse by it; google the terms "narcolepsy, swine flu".

However, the option of trying to get us all chipped with a buying-selling chip isn't possible anymore. People have woken up. The worst is behind us, as I intimate in this chapter. A conclusion will be given later, first some more interpretations of Revelations.

BABYLON

Now for a look at Chapter 17 of Revelations. What is depicted with its seven-pronged crown on ten heads, with a cup in its hand? Simple: the Statue of Liberty! Just look at its seven-pronged crown – and the base she's standing on that, seen from above, is a ten-pointed star. Go figure.

> *"(1) Then one of the seven angels who had the seven bowls came and talked with me, saying to me, "Come, I will show you the judgment of the great harlot who sits on many waters, (2) with whom the kings of the earth committed fornication, and the inhabitants of the earth were made drunk with the wine of her fornication." (3) So he carried me away in the Spirit into the wilderness. And I saw a woman sitting on a scarlet beast which was full of names of blasphemy, having seven heads and ten horns. (4) The woman was arrayed in purple and scarlet, and adorned with*

> *gold and precious stones and pearls, having in her hand a golden cup full of abominations and the filthiness of her fornication. (5) And on her forehead a name was written: MYSTERY, BABYLON THE GREAT, THE MOTHER OF HARLOTS AND OF THE ABOMINATIONS OF THE EARTH. (6) I saw the woman, drunk with the blood of the saints and with the blood of the martyrs of Jesus. And when I saw her, I marveled with great amazement."*
> [17:1-6]

Indeed, Babylon the Great, here and in Chapter 18, is rather much like the current USA, being enthroned over many waters, rich and dealing with the whole world... True, this may fit other countries historically; Revelations is a work of art and, as such, has an ambiguous nature. Unambiguity, for its part, belongs to allegories and this is a completely different genre. So, different interpretations are allowed to play along in prophecies like this,"it's anybody's guess". But as for Babylon the Great, you could say: the USA, symbolized in New York with the Statue of Liberty (seven horns and ten "heads"), is not a bad candidate for this title.

However, what does it all mean generally? Revelations, with all its prophecies of doom and gloom, depicts past events. That's the general view of mine. There's a lot said in this Biblical book and I haven't been into all of it. I just don't mean that this is a vision of hell awaiting man. WWI and WWII are long gone. And "the seven bad years" of Genesis 41 were the years 1996-2003, as some source meant.

The worst is behind us. The same goes for such a document as the *Poetic Edda*, telling of "the end of the world" in Voluspa. The world of Midgard sinks. But this is merely the sinking of the continent of Hyperborea, a circumpolar landmass that is no more. Voluspa then tells of the rising of Eurasia where man could live on: "The eagle flies over a waterfall hunting fish".

The current US regime may have some aspects of The Great Babylon, but its reign will come to an end, and then a new era will dawn on man, symbolized in the coming of The Heavenly City. This is to be found in Revelations, too.

Actionism is optimism and personally; judging by the intimated interpretation of Revelations and the Edda, I am an optimist. The worst is behind us. The ice age has been. So join us in the Light and let's start building Antropolis.

25. POLITICS OF THE FUTURE

Hereby some musings on the Actionist view on politics. What principles must guide tomorrow's governance, what mindset must the politician of the future have? Of this and more below. Overall it can be said: in the vein of Plato, a just society is made up of just citizens. The detail must mirror the whole and vice versa. A moral societal order can't just be established by orders and regulations. It has to be anchored by individuals having a sense of truth and justice within them. That's the Actionist take on societal matters, an esoteric attitude, stressing the inner mind of the individuals making up a society.

WORLD-VIEW

When writing political manifestos, you first have to give some sort of general overview, preferably anchored in a concept of reality as a whole. And in the book you're currently reading, *Actionism,* that structural-ontological framework was given in Chapter 1 and the chapters immediately following it. To this, an outline of history was presented in Chapter 19. In Chapters 20-21 were sketched the basics of my political creed stating (1) that I don't want NWO-style globalism and (2) that the nationalism of the future, perceived as co-nationalism, is an irreducible feature of Actionism.

In Chapter 22, it was explained that there's no risk for major war and that the worst is behind us as regards threats to our survival (for the latter aspect, see also Chapter 24). This, in all, covers international politics and to some extent domestic politics too: the future basis of governance are the peoples in their respective regions. No general, overall structures, no "meta-narratives" are to be discussed internationally before every people is safe in its "place of origin" (which applies to the Old World; in the New World current civil rights for everyone should prevail, like giving white people a right to exist alongside other peoples).

The following won't be a detailed outline as to how the governance of tomorrow shall be organized. However, from the view of Actionism some concepts have to be discussed, concepts that must guide the politics of man from now on.

SPIRITUAL

One thing the Actionist governance is not: materialistic. Thus, the moronic stressing of the current Powers That Be of "economic growth" must stop. To simply have growth is a sign of illness, of elephantiasis. An organic growth in balance with nature is something else. And this is only acquired by having the society based on spiritual principles.

Actionism is "spiritual," it acknowledges man as having a soul, an immaterial essence made up of Will, Thought and Compassion, joined with the Light. This is the crux, the irreducible foundation of all things human. The politician, as well as the voter of the future, must have this spiritual outlook. The politician, as well as the officers and functionaries running the state, and the private individual, must know the formula "I AM". This is the irreducible basis for an Actionist style governance.

I just mentioned "voter" which implies some kind of popular participation. In this respect the current, materialistic, propaganda-run kind of "democracy" the West today has, must be reformed. However, I don't support a downright elite rule. While it can be tempting to advocate a governance of elevated masters steeped in Every Possible Science, there also has also to be an element of feedback in the system. There has to be the possibility of control at regular intervals, for instance, by popular voting.

To clarify: media-drugged zombies voting for "just another NWO stooge," this is not the Actionist way. The Actionist way is informed, spiritually conscious citizens voting, choosing between reasonably esoterically apt politicians acknowledging their "I AM".

The current way of running society by way of propaganda-driven democracy has to be reformed. At the same time, to have a governance not being run "for, by and with the people," is hard to imagine, for me. There has to be feedback, popular control, a way of ousting even a "perfect, spiritual" government – because of the risk of that "perfect" government solidifying and atrophying, no longer acting for the public good.

POLITICIAN

The politician of the future has to know the meaning of I AM. He has to know Will in the spiritual sense, he has to be C_3 = calm, cool and collected in the Actionist manner. He has to know the meaning of Assuming Responsibility. The politician of the future must be a Responsible Man.

What applies to the individual, applies to the politician of the future: to assume responsibility, to have a spiritual mindset, to acknowledge that man doesn't live on bread alone. The politician of the future doesn't have to be some perfect guru, steeped in every traditional document. But he has to know of the power of Will-Thought, he has to know man's spiritual side, he has to know of responsibility and accountability, he has to show self-restraint, determination, honesty and magnanimity. This is only done by "being spiritual," by having some knowledge of meditation, of volitional mental calm, of C_3. The politician of tomorrow must know himself spiritually; he must mean what he says.

A new paradigm is about to be established. I mentioned this in the chapter on history. It's about Christ Consciousness (or some variety of it = Buddha consciousness, Krishna consciousness), the mindset of being satisfied in one's soul, of realizing one's inherent divine nature, a mindset permeating an ever larger portion of the global population day by day. The politician of the future has to adapt to this. It will no longer be possible to rule people with fear, like haunting them with the specters of scarcity, conflict and major war. The worst is behind us in this respect and we're on the threshold of a Golden Age. The leader types among us who realize this will be the politicians of the future.

BASIS

The *macrocosmic* basis of Actionist politics is the nation. As demonstrated above, in Chapter 21 when delineating the Tower of Babel simile, God inaugurated nations to safeguard man against the evils of Empire. Nations are, and will, remain the basic international units shaping man's dealings. With the concept of co-nationalism along in the equation, safeguards against chauvinism, dominance and aggression are assured.

Along with this, the *microcosmic* basis of Actionist politics is the civilized, reflective individual. This individual is a conscious person, a Will-endowed, thinking being, disposed for idealist striving and avoiding materialist ignorance. And the Actionist acronym for this microcosmic fundamental is the now well-known ASARIT = A Strong And Responsible Idealist, Taking charge. As mentioned previously in this study, the Actionist is a paragon of vigor and responsibility, embodying Schwarzkopf's dictum: "When placed in command, take charge." The person steeped in Actionism takes charge for whom, what and where he is. The Actionist way, as sketched in Chapters 1 through 7 in this book *et passim*, is the moral foundation of the governance of the future.

ACTIONISM

To use a simile employed earlier in this book: the person, having taken command of his Being and structured his life along volitional lines, putting Will before the carriage, assuming responsibility for whom he is and what he does, has performed "the personal reconquista". Several such persons can then join forces against societally prevailing nihilist materialism and perform a large-scale, overall reconquista.

The reflective individual is the base for Actionist ethics and politics, for the moral and social dimension. The next social level is the *family*. For a child to grow up with his mother and father is the thing to strive for. The nuclear family is the Actionist family ideal. Next, as intimated, the social level is the nation, the traditional ethnic groups forming states. While this pertains to the Old World (Europe, Asia) Actionism doesn't leave the New World out in the cold. All peoples shall be allowed to exist, even white people. This has got to be stated in the current aggressive agenda of "Africa for the Africans, Asia for the Asians, white countries for everybody".

EMPIRE

The antipode of everything Actionism stands for is symbolized by "the Empire," the current, materialist-nihilist regime ruling most of the world. The Empire is The Powers That Be, it's the EU, UN, USA, NATO, ASEAN, WTO etc. etc. While there might be well-meaning officers on the lower and middle-management levels, the regime symbolized by the Empire is *collectivist materialist nihilism* while Actionism is *will-driven individual-based idealism.*

It's true that the world above the level of nations may need planetary discussion forums and cooperative instances not entirely different from the UN. However, the way things are run today must be reformed. Why? Because the agenda today is nihilist materialism. The negative, atheist, irresponsible regimen ruling the world has run its course. A new way of doing things is needed – the Actionist way, a doctrine covering both the micro- and the macrocosm. A doctrine based in the reflective, conscious, Will-and-Thought acknowledging person, a strong and responsible individual, taking charge = ASARIT. A doctrine acknowledging nations as the social base for human cooperation on the international scale; God is a nationalist.

ACTIONIST IDEALS

As for Actionist concepts applicable to the role of a future politician, there are some.

I just mentioned ASARIT. In addition to this, you can mention the concept of, "a free operational spirit in a time of decay". It's true that no one is "free" within politics, since politics is "the art of the possible," the area of logrolling and more or less transparent deals. However, in a wider sense, the Actionist style politician is free because he's an idealist and not a materialist, as a person having Will and Thought to guide him; he's not enslaved by the obsession of "economic growth". He favors *organic* growth of the healthy kind, not the morbid growth of latter-day capitalism.

Thus, the Actionist politician is "a free operational spirit in a time of decay" = he's an operational esotericist, taking charge of his condition as a willful human being in a time of chaos and confusion. As I write this, we live in a time of decadence and decay, a time waiting for a new idealism to straighten things out and fix the mess mankind is in. The main feature of decadence is that no one believes in anything anymore: nihilism and materialism rules. The prevailing ideals of "democracy, freedom, diversity" are code words for elite-rule, arrogance, negativity, irony and sentimentality. For instance, the current seeming freedom of "everything being allowed", in the end results in nothing being allowed, which is nihilism. Instead, we need ideals anchored in Will, Thought and Compassion, like self-restraint, accountability, courage, determination, truth, justice, filial reverence, modesty and magnanimity.

Another Actionist idea spelling out the ideals of a new-style politician is, "to evade materialism and start building Antropolis".

ACTIONISM

Antropolis is a novel I published in 2009, as such, being about the coming Golden Age of science and spirituality, denouncing the materialist idiocy of the previous era. So the concept – "Antropolis" – is already established, now we only have to start building it, making it come real in our everyday. More on *Antropolis* in a later chapter.

HEALING

At the beginning of this chapter Plato was evoked. He spoke of just citizens engendering a just society. In the same vein you could mention Chinese thinker Confucius (or "Kon Fu Ze"), who spoke about a man having to heal himself before he can heal society.

This is the Actionist ideal of ESWY = Everything Starts With You. Now, it's true that not *everything* starts with the individual (like, in the beginning there were no individuals, there was God) – but of course, it's meant in the way that in ethics everything starts with you, you have to calm down and look inside of you, gaining mental calm before you can start to think, act and get to know the mystery of life. The individual has to search himself, he can't rely on formal systems and programs in order to find the Holy Grail.

It starts with you. Jung called this *individuation*, "how to become what you are," reaching some kind of *identity* and *self-hood* (as opposed to being a superficial egotist-materialist). A man has to go through the process of individuation before he can reach out and help others, before he can be of use on the societal level. Informed, reflective, *individuated* persons make up the Actionist society.

26. NATURE OF DECADENCE

Materialism and passivity are decadent attitudes, the mood of not acknowledging eternal values like self-restraint, accountability, courage and determination. This chapter deliberates on the sociocultural prevalence in today's Western world of decadence, the very anti-pole of Actionism.

OFFENCE

Actionism maintains that Will, Thought and Compassion were in the beginning, forming an entity choosing Light instead of Dark. This entity, God, later on created the souls of men. God took of his own Light and created soul-sparks in the form of human souls. Thus, man became a mirror of God, he was created in his image and received his nature of being endowed with Will-Thought disposed for the Light.

This is the Actionist doctrine, the idealist notion. Contrariwise, we have the creed of the dark side not acknowledging this, the power of Will and Thought heading for the Light. The dark doctrine means than man is but "a meat puppet," a material being without an eternal soul, a desire driven creature, a prey for his passions. Man lacks Will and is run by his material desires; this is the creed of materialist ignorance, of, in one word, decadence.

On a more subtle level, a materialist of this ilk can't control his thoughts. Thus, if the decadent sees something that disturbs him, he's offended, no matter if it's operationally insignificant. An Actionist, on the other hand, has control of his emotions and thoughts, every one of them. If an Actionist happens to be "offended" by something, some ordinary utterance by another free individual, he doesn't raise a lot of fuss about this, not if the event is operationally insignificant and legal in itself. The Actionist lets it pass if it's insignificant to his operation. If it *is* significant to his operation he deals with it with reasonable equanimity, seeking Rest In Action (RIA) while doing so.

In other words, to act in the everyday is a question of willpower, of assuming responsibility. The decadent, being "offended" by everything he sees, lacks responsibility for whom he is, lacking the ability to control his very being. He expects that The University Authorities, The Media, The State, The UN or whatever shall act upon his every whim and emotion. Contrariwise, the Actionist commands his own being and relegates trifles to oblivion and focuses on his current operation, which is always successful. Because he has WAP = Winning As Propensity = ingrained in his being, he knows how to posit attainable goals.

In short: the Actionist has control over his emotions, feelings and passions; the decadent has not.

SUGAR-COATED

Of course, the prevailing decadence doesn't label itself "decadence". It presents itself as "diversity, anti-colonialism, support the weak" etc.

Let's see how this is done. For instance, a modernist European might advocate massive immigration from Africa and MENA. A traditionally minded European might advocate giving them help in their local areas. In this, to label the latter as a hateful misanthrope is mere decadent rhetoric.

The modernist European might be interested in the culture of foreign, Third World countries; fair enough, but that person often couples this to a hate toward Western culture. That is, a decadent mindset.

The modernist European sees perceived weak groups (sexual and ethnic minorities) as victims, and not giving these groups massive amounts of support as a hateful attitude. However, there are already laws protecting these groups and to constantly underline their perceived weakness is decadence, an absence of acknowledging the willpower inherent in the individuals of these groups.

To encourage people of color to cherish their ethnicity and culture, but to deny Caucasian people the same right, is beyond decadence, it's injustice plain and simple.

Then we have today's academy, where the tendency is to steer the humanities away from metaphysical truth and off to social issues where everything becomes valued after its current political stature, where truth is relativized in a plebeian, horizontal striving. This is also a kind of decadence = not acknowledging any transcendent truths.

Today's polite culture often talks about "tolerance" – tolerance for what, you might ask? Tolerance for everything? But if everything is to be tolerated, nothing can be tolerated. "Tolerance is the virtue of the man without convictions," as Chesterton said.

In this way, decadence is at the core of the current regime and its *leitkultur*.

IGNORANCE

Materialist nihilism rules blind idiocy. Seemingly no one is bothered by it. The perceived absence of eternal values, of higher truths, is seen as the natural order of things. "Ya gits born, ya live and ya die and that's all there is to it."

No eternal values exist; only matter exists, and when the form has withered away nothing is left, no form, no idea – nothing. Contrariwise, Plato and Plotinus taught the existence of eternal ideas giving shape to the world of matter, an ontology compatible with Actionism and one I delineated in my 2015 book *Borderline*. Not acknowledging a soul in man or eternal values anchored in Will,

ACTIONISM

Thought and Compassion, not acknowledging eternal ideas (Greek *eidos*, plural, *eidoi*) giving form to matter: this is decadence, this is moronic materialism. It officially rules the current Western world, a world in decay and decline, a world in the grip of decadence. To not acknowledge either Will, eternal *eidoi* or eternal values is decadence, the state of being burned out, of having reached the end of the line mentally, conceptually and culturally.

To merely talk about economic growth and be blind to invisible, spiritual qualities is mindless materialism = decadence.

To be sarcastic 24/7, taking nothing seriously, is a sign of a tired, worn-out, decadent mindset.

A culture having its citizens ruled by entertainment and fear-based propaganda is a decadent culture.

A culture whose teachers engage in agenda-driven rhetoric, ignoring metaphysical truths, is a decadent culture.

A culture fighting constant wars to create fear in the citizens, and streams of refugees to challenge the ethnic integrity of the heartland, is a decadent culture.

A culture praising stories about whores and lowlifes is a decadent culture.

SIGNS

These are the signs of today's Western world. Of course everything isn't bad. It's just that you have to acknowledge the nature of things in order to get a clearer view.

Some of us, like me, are optimists. Man is on the verge of a Golden Age of art, science and spirituality. We just have to do away with ignorant materialism and start building Antropolis, acknowledging our inherent Will and Thought, the forces inside each one of us. You *can* control your feelings and emotions, you *can* live life operationally, you *can* be a constant winner in the game of life – if you only posit attainable goals.

This is the basic element of Actionism – this, and exerting volitional mental calm (C3, see Chapter 2), saying "I AM" and living in the here-and-now. The world is something of a mess right now, but it isn't impossible to create a better world, either for yourself individually or for the world at large. We won't see major war (q.v. Chapter 22), the worst is behind us. We're not afflicted by Black Death. The decadent regime we live under isn't a *1984*-style ruling with torture, it's more of a *Brave New World*-style regime ruling with propaganda and conditioning. It's true that the future Orwell envisioned in *1984* also had a central element of propaganda and "mindfuck" but today we have something the mid-20th century didn't have, we have the *internet* being able to spread the truth to the four corners of the world. The old information monopoly of The Powers That Be, executed by print media and TV, is gone. That was a one-way form of communication. With the internet we a have a system-immanent ability of feedback.

All things considered, this is a world of free information. *Mutatis mutandum*, the internet spreads the truth. Along with, this people still voluntarily read esoteric and other edifying classics, and people take meditation courses, training their willpower; overall people aren't brainwashed morons but caring people, having sincere emotional bonds to their fellow brethren and sistren. People of today have the ability to discern, to judge for themselves. The raising of the level of intelligence is a quiet, but real, phenomenon and the internet is but one tool in this.

The world of the early 21st century might seem bleak but, again, no major war will break out. And, true, mankind might be ruled by fear-based propaganda and a culture of irresponsibility and materialism; however, along with this, people can still empower themselves by mediation, studies and relations to real people. Materialism is the official agenda but, on the grass-root level, idealism is alive as never before.

ACTIONISM

IMPULSES

So what will happen with decadence and the decadent mindset? Are there still influential voices out there advocating a life in "the flesh, the passions, the impulses, the sub-conscious"? Are there still people advocating "absurdism, parody, irony" as the highest level of artistic creation? Are stories of nuclear war, an overpopulated earth, zombies and misery the mainstream of future fiction? Are "wine, women and song" the only things worth living for?

If you do advocate this, you're out of touch. You might formally be part of the mainstream but the times they are a-changing. We're heading for spiritual times – Actionist times.

And even if you don't advocate debauchery, lechery, sloth and / or gluttony, if you're some cultured figure believing in "freedom, equality, development," a latter-day sentimental materialist, then my advice is that you, instead of in *the Material*, seek the foundation of your ideals in *the Metaphysical Beyond*, in the causal sphere where all eternal ideas reside. Then you're a budding esotericist, in synch with the emerging zeitgeist.

27. SOCIETY OF THE FUTURE

You can't predict the future – but you can create it. Primarily, the Actionist, microcosmic, future is realized by being a harmonious individual, by being able to practice volitional mental calm. This can be scaled up to the macrocosmic level on the conscious individual, society at large can be built; this is the part generating the whole. This was intimated in Chapter 25, "Politics of the Future". Hereby some more musings on the society of the future, how it will be constructed, ideally and conceptually. The chapter starts with some general reflections and then moves on to a more systematic delineation of what the various parts of society should be guided by.

CRISIS

At this time of history there may still be conceptual and tangible problems to solve. "Society is in crisis," the world situation is troubled. But, in a general sense, man now has mastered nature. Overall, he has solved the problems concerning nutrition and sickness, how to feed himself and keep himself healthy; starvation and plague are not major threats anymore. This leaves us free to pursue peace – spiritual peace – for the individual and for mankind at large. And this, as delineated in this study, starts with the individual taking a deep, gentle breath. The basis of societal harmony is the individual asserting himself as a spiritual being, becoming a harmonious, "together" person.

ACTIONISM

To take a bold perspective on things ahead, you can say: when society consists of harmonious, spiritual people inside and out, then the gods may come – the famed "return of the gods" that Ernst Jünger intimated, that which was to be the defining trait of the 21st century. This he said in the 1990s, in the late diary, *Siebzig verweht*. Conversely, he meant, the 20th century was the era of Titans, of the forces of nihilism and regimentation leading man into states of "all work and no play". In contrast to the Titans, the gods that would put their stamp on this century would be gods of the Olympian type, musical, just, compassionate powers, and leading men to the water-rich valleys. But this will only come about when men have some inner nature corresponding to this, some esoteric quality of willing the good, the light and the truth. Only then will the gods return.

THE AGENDA

The Actionist agenda for the future is evident: crush materialism and eradicate passive nihilism. The direction is clear; the momentum is kept by flying the standard high. An Actionist doesn't accept the materialist, imperialist agenda. Instead, he acknowledges his Inner Light, he acknowledges his status as a civilized, adult person living his life voluntarily. Self-assertive believers, in the framework of self-conscious peoples, is the Actionist agenda.

The will of the people must be respected, there must be a possibility of feedback between ruler and ruled. "La volonté général" challenges the Empire, yesterday, today and tomorrow, through Rienzi, Napoleon and some movements in the 20th century. Rienzi is said to have challenged the Pope and the Emperor with his vision of a new empire, based on the will of the people. Then Napoleon did the same. And for the 21st century "government for, by and with the people" is a must, even though the current version of democracy with its mood of propaganda, rigged language and "mindfuck" must be reformed.

ARCHEOFUTURISM

"The secret to change is to focus all of your energy, not on fighting the old, but on building the new." Thus Socrates. And Actionism, while acknowledging Tradition, seeks to build a new, viable world on the basis of the best the past can offer.

Actionist builds the new, footed in Tradition. It's *archeofuturism*, the way of "cleansing futurism with archaism," to use the words of Guillaume Faye.

Actionist is *contra* globalism, global socialism, mondialism, imperialism, The Empire. It's against materialism, decadence, defeatism, emotionalism, negativity, superstition, sclerosis and darkness. Conversely, Actionism is *pro* the reflective individual, the family, the land, the nation, the people, freedom, art, science, life, light, awareness, responsibility, faith, Antropolis and heroism.

IDEALS

To sum up the Actionist ideals and its Imperialist counterparts, this is the shortlist.

The Actionist ideal is organic, the Imperialist is mechanic.

The Actionist ideal is will and drive; the Imperialist is defeatist nihilism.

The Actionist ideal is heroism; the Imperialist is emotionalism.

The Actionist Man is a willful esotericist; the Imperialist ideal is a desire-driven consumer.

The Actionist ideal is responsible leadership; the Imperialist ideal is faceless bureaucracy.

The Actionist ideal is the reflected individual; the Imperialist ideal is the mindless crowd.

The Actionist ideal is the small scale community; the Imperialist ideal is the Empire.

The Actionist ideal is quality of life; the Imperialist ideal is economic growth.

ACTIONISM

The Actionist ideal is archeofuturism; the Imperialist ideal is modernism.

SOCIETY

Again, the microcosmic aspects of Actionism are the person saying "I AM," the person acknowledging his Inner Light as a fragment of the Divine Light. The person being driven by willpower and compassion. Then there is the family as the next socio-political level. Then, the nation. This I've delineated above.

The defining feature of the macrocosmic dimension, that of the planetary development of man, is this: after 11/11 2011 there's no longer the possibility for major war. I've elaborated upon this in Chapter 22. You might call this "the magic zero-point" if you will. The bottom line is, after this date, major war / nuclear war / that all-encompassing violent cataclysm haunting man for a long time, is impossible. At the time of writing there may be minor wars in the east, but they are about to wind down.

This is of major importance in delineating the governance of tomorrow. The 20th century societies spent their major effort in building weapons of mass destruction. The societies of the Sat Yuga we now live in, the era of peace and cooperation won't be doing this. The preceding era was Kali Yuga: the era of death and conflict.

The shift came on 11/11 2011. That was the Magic Zero-point. Now we live in a different world. True, we have to contribute to it mentally and willfully. But even without that kind of contribution (perish the thought) , major war is impossible on this planet now.

Sat Yuga or not, we still have issues to solve, like hostile ideas of anti-European and cultural leveling being about. But the framework to deal with them is one where major war is out of the question. This also means that "major *civil* war, a breakdown of civilization by a multitude of small conflicts" is impossible. That's the nature of living beyond the Magic Zero-point.

BRANCHES

With a more peaceful sentiment enabled, how will tomorrow's national governments look, what principles will they be guided by?

In looking at the anatomy of a government you can choose *the tripartite model*. As such, this is the classical Indo-European model of "bellatores, laboratores and oratores," namely, those who fight, those who work and those who pray. In Actionist terms, this corresponds to the elements of Will, Compassion and Thought respectively. To fight and govern, make crucial decisions, takes will; to make it grow in the lands of agriculture takes compassion; and to meditate on the nature of reality takes thought.

In modern terms, this model means to structure a state along the dimensions of "executive element," "business element" and "clerical element". The first one is symbolized by the PM / President himself and the departments of state, defense and justice. The second one is symbolized by the departments of commerce, agriculture and transportation. The third is symbolized by the departments of culture and education. Primarily, this model might seem skewed since the five last mentioned departments aren't strategical in a nation's governance proper; however, for the society at large "the clerical branch" is also symbolized by the media and the academia, the modern style gurus and pundits telling us what to think. And the business branch is also symbolized by companies, factories and farms, our very means of subsistence, the producers of food, shelter and clothes etc. etc.

Now for a look at how a society might be organized, viewed through the framework of a government's different areas of responsibility. In an emerging zeitgeist of prosperity, peace and cooperation, what can – to begin with – be said of the realm of the contextual "executive element"? There will still be armies, navies and air forces in this future but they will be drastically smaller. The warmongering cabal currently ruling the world will be gone, as such dealt with in legal fashion. International relations will be solved on a basis of mutual trust, cooperation and co-nationalism. For instance, there will be no conflicts over oil since new energy sources will be used, with technology currently suppressed.

As for other sections belonging to the "executive element," every nation will still have courts of law, police and some correction system but, with the zeitgeist being more peaceful, crime statistics themselves will be reduced.

BUSINESS ELEMENT

As for the "business element" of society, "prosperity for all" will be the guiding word of tomorrow. This might sound overly naive and frivolous, but it's the truth. The current state of the world is one of artificially contrived scarcity. The world largely depends on old-school fossil fuels and a debt-based currency system. To this, men are ruled by fear (like fears of an impending war). After the Magic Zero-point, the fear-based thinking will lose ground, to be replaced by one of trust and confidence, all the more evident when the current regime of rigged markets, fiat currencies and fractional banking is gone. With currencies based on gold, and certain alleged funds ("Saint Germain Funds") being given out to all people, prosperity and safety will be the watchwords. Plagues and certain diseases now and then harassing mankind will disappear, because they're generally of the artificially, consciously spread kind, like bird and swine flu.

Overall, mankind today isn't threatened by disease as it used to be. As for the health care of tomorrow it will be focused on man as a soul-endowed organism, not a mindless machine, there to be manipulated by drugs. On a basic level, it's still true that to heal a broken leg you can and must see the human organism as a delicate machine, but in most other cases, healing must be holistic, taking into view man as a willful organism, not a soulless machine.

The same goes for the psychiatry of tomorrow. Man is a soul-endowed organism, not a machine to drug into unconsciousness. Much of the psychology of today ignores the essentially psychological aspect of man. From an etymological point of view, psychology is defined as the wisdom of man's *psyche*, which in Greek means *soul*; however, contemporary, mainstream, "school" psychology denies the existence of a soul. There's the tendency to reduce man to a biological machine, damping the utterings of psychic stress with drugs. That's a parody of psychology.

As for a last aspect of business (to which can be relegated commerce and physical and mental wellbeing) we have *communications*. Tomorrow's communications will be conducted with crystal computers and vehicles driven by crystals and magnets. Oil and its chemical derivatives will be a thing of the past. Remember the electric car? It was an engineering triumph at the beginning of the 20th century and now it's about to make a comeback, better than ever.

CLERICAL ELEMENT

The clerical, cultural, "guru-and-pundit" aspect of the society of tomorrow will, of course, be the spreading of doctrines affirming man's willful nature, his nature of being an organism endowed with a soul, a Spiritual Self. The moronic adherence to ideas of nihilist materialism will be a thing of the past. Courses in meditation and spiritual fulfillment will abound, as will the reading of books on esoteric and secret history (= history needlessly kept secret until now), and documents of ancient and more current spiritual practices, teaching man to affirm his Inner Light. This will be the new normal, instead of books dealing with crime, debauchery, lechery, lust and gluttony.

To the clerical sphere belongs *education*. In the current era, education officially aims at leveling. Still, difference in talent is tacitly acknowledged. For the coming age the watchwords in this respect will be *existential equality coupled to career-wise diversity*. This means: acknowledging that we humans have different abilities, there to be nurtured and groomed in different educational paths, it doesn't mean that a professor has existentially more worth than a plumber. Before God we're all equal, that's the existential basis. Every person has the power to affirm his "I AM".

ESOTERIC ATHLETICS

To the cultural-clerical sphere also belongs the activity of sport and athletics.

In early medieval Nordic society, the concept of "idrott" could include poetry and knowledge of runes, along with running fast and jumping long. As such, this is reminiscent of how the ancient Greek Olympic Games had competitions in poetry and song, along with the athletic contests. Thus, *athletics* in this sense approaches active esotericism while *sport*, in the modern sense, tends toward work, toil and materialism.

The athletics of tomorrow must have the above intimated spiritual element ingrained.

AGAIN

Again I say: 11/11 2011 was the Magic Zero-point. After that there's no possibility of "major war, nuclear war, major cataclysm" sending us to hell. Even if men would remain passive and negative, there's no possibility of major war erupting any longer. And if we become actively positive, embracing the essentially peaceful zeitgeist, then the Golden Age will arrive even sooner.

The Kali Yuga is over. Sat Yuga is here. An era of dominance, submission and competition is about to be succeeded by an era of cooperation, compassion and synergy. The moment Evola spoke of, that of nihilist materialism having depleted its energy whereby the Esoteric Actors can move in and take charge, is virtually here.

28. ANTROPOLIS

In 2009 I published a novel called *Antropolis*. It was published in Swedish only, in a rather limited edition. However, essentially and with time, it has gained increased meaning. Its theme of spirituality and musicality as strategic elements of tomorrow's politics has not been rendered irrelevant by the development – quite the contrary, actually. "Antropolis" is a central symbol of the Coming Golden Age.

CONCEPT

The mere concept of "Antropolis" has a symbolical quality to it. Like "Metropolis," the 1927 Fritz Lang movie, or "Heliopolis," the 1949 Jünger novel. Literary qualities aside, the title shines like a beacon: *Antropolis*.

Antropolis relates how a certain Jenro Klao restores the ruins of a city and names it *Antropolis*, dedicating it to art, science and the humanities. Crystal technology and spirituality are the key words in this new age. When the story begins, it's the year 2165 and the city is thriving on the surface, but at the same time the forces of esotericism and technology seem about to clash in this utopia. Jenro Klao then decides to leave the city to its own measures for a while, going on a trip to olden times, to Faustian cities and metropolises teeming with combustion cars and scudding clouds. When Klao returns he has the blueprint for the pacification of the Antropolitan strife, leading to a lasting spiritual way of life. Even if we're enlightened and spiritually minded, we also need a link backward as well, to past times and generations. Jenro Klao sees it as his task to revive Tradition as a cure to the threatening leveling of Antropolis' culture. It's a modern variety of "the mediator between head and hand should be heart" of *Metropolis* fame.

So much for the plot. The concept of *Antropolis* is what Guillaume Faye would call, "an idea thrown in the face of history." It doesn't have to be correct or consistent in every detail; the mere symbolic quality of the concept is sufficient to make it useful.

As intimated, the concept of *Antropolis* has a certain *Gestaltkvalität*. It's archetypal. We're currently, by default, heading for Antropolitan times. We're heading for times with innate spirituality and a renaissance for art and science. Gone are the times dominated by fear, repression and brainwashing. Antropolis shall triumph. Look around, look out your window: it's there, Antropolis, resplendent in the morning sun.

It's the emerging Antropolitan culture you're seeing. If you want to see Antropolis, look around. In Latin, that would be, "si Antropolis requiris, circumspice".

METROPOLIS HECKLERS

An interesting role in the book is played by a specific Antropolis society, "the Metropolis Hecklers". They hate the previous culture, that of Metropolis, the epitome of materialism and chauvinism, the culture they've just left. In other words, the Faustian culture. One day, Jenro Klao is invited to listen to a lecture of this society. It's held by one Bider Praxis, the Society President. He gives a broad overview of everything that's bad in our time, as the glass houses, the machine cult, the cult of movement and more, in all a critique in sync with Actionism:

> *[In this society we often heckle the 1900s and 2000s, Praxis says, standing in the pulpit, and now he intends to focus on some outstanding features of this culture. Such as the titanic machine cult.]* "Metropolis worshiped the machine, saw technology as a

synonym for machine technology. They saw man as machine: 'I Robot,' 'l'homme machine,' this was a symbol they never could free themselves from. Diseases were cured with metallic medications or surgery, while tuning in on the individual and alternative therapies were seen as aberrations. The doctor studied the human body as an object, never looked himself in the mirror and said, 'This is the answer'"... Praxis looked down at his papers and continued: "Metropolitan signs, typical idiocies in succinct form. It was also the cult of movement, uttered in competitive craze and record breaking. They even competed in eating, a desecration of the sacrament of bread if you're asking me. They spurned peace and quiet, the sight of a serene face. Metropolis's keyword was 'restless'; they worshiped restlessness, stimulated by atheism and the absence of a mental anchor, of internal security. They were attracted by any new worry: a meteor hits earth and wipes out all life, a plague breaks out, the temperature is raised one degree and drowns us all without mercy. They tried to curb this rise in temperature by various means, such as lowering home temperature a half degree, sorting the garbage and taking the stairs instead of the elevator – but this was only self-deception, a kind of crypto-religious penance for atheists. It may have been true that overall consumption and energy consumption in Metropolis was unnecessarily high, it was an untenable level of luxury – but the global rise of temperature was independent of this. It was after all a contributing factor needed to lift man into a higher vibration, the higher spiritual level that we currently find ourselves on. And cosmic collisions, we still haven't seen. I can only say: we will not see them, God won't allow it... (...) Metropolis in our hearts... It was something that kept this culture back, it seemed, some inertia of the system, some immanent syrupy heaviness – for there was actually promising features too, like crystal technology and new spirituality, complementary medicine, a surge in communication technology – but it wasn't enough, the game must be played to completion before the page turned. Some power lines must run their course after they had started." [p 55-56, this and other excerpts translated by the author]

There you have a resounding critique of civilization, of our current culture of materialism and decadence. But there's more to *Antropolis*, much more.

TRADITIONALISM

The main character in the book is Jenro Klao, a professor of history. He's the city's cultural conscience; he holds high the banner of musical powers, of zest and pizazz in a culture which is certainly better than today's materialism, but still suffers from a lack of artistic flair and style. Klao combats both factions in the city, both the new-style technocrats and the simplistic esotericists – and he does it by cultivating the traditional culture, by paying tribute to the heroes and legends of the past, cherishing the poems and songs of bygone days. With his science of *meta-history* he wants to reach a higher synthesis of poetry and life, history and science, lust and anguish.

One day Klao takes a walk in the surrounding areas. Without goal he roams over heath and woodland, marsh and fenland, until he reaches a mountain. In a cave he comes upon a certain tomb which leads to a discussion of critical science versus empathy, how tradition and emotion may be able to survive in the latter-day dry academic atmosphere:

> *"I [Klao says] came to the edge of the forest overlooking a small valley. On the opposite side sat a mountain with a cave. Aha, I thought, was this the place of the enigmatic tomb they spoke of, an old princely tomb from the Archaic Period...? I looked out over the valley, savoring the forested undulation of the landscape, the faraway mountains' bluish backdrop and the impressive image of the nearest mountain, the one with the cave. This Mount Alienor proudly arose before me, a scree lined with broken rock at the bottom and the skyline delineated by harrowing, windblown pines. – I headed for the cave, walking for a few kilometers over the usual impediments, various obstacles in the form of rubble, wetland and*

thickets. But I kept a good walking pace, I had taken a fortifying lunch – and eventually the cave stood before me, I went reverently up to it and stepped into the darkness. I had gathered a few dry sticks on the way and now I lit one of them with my lighter, giving me a decent beacon. I treaded softly over the cave floor, past the wet stones and puddles, and it wasn't long until I reached some steps leading up to a sort of platform. Up there, the floor was drier and smoother. The space widened into a hall. My light flickered dramatically on the walls. Finally I saw the sarcophagus: a rather elaborate coffin made of stone with a lid. I was visited by an acute reverence for everything. I knelt and prayed to the cave spirit, the mountain spirit, the deceased prince, the Great Spirit, everything... (...) I stood up and approached the coffin. The lid was completely smooth, bearing no inscription. So who was buried here? It wasn't known but our scholars had their theories. The leading theory was that all the talk about a prince's tomb etc. was just a myth; this was only a stone coffin in a mountain, probably a storage place for all sorts of debris. Nothing to talk about. They had examined the sarcophagus and found it empty, and this plus a customary chain of circumstantial evidence settled it. But not for me, as the meta historian I was; I held the door open for things that deserved to be true. So for me this was a hero's grave, the symbolic tomb of an Alexander, a Joan of Arc, a Napoleon or Marius. You simply need the greatness of legends – and if someone will explain away it then the projection of greatness only shifts focus. It doesn't die out. You have to have imagination, you can't just surrender to science and allow it to control your dreams. It may be that 'the modern era breaks in with its bent for criticism and restructuring,' as someone complained, that the table is cleaned 'from all the old defenseless tradition that can't put up any serious and tangible facts to defend its case'. But this indignation needs to be overcome; you have to steer around it and away to more opulent climes, to wider perspectives where your dreams can live forever. And to me, this tomb would forever be the place of greatness and mystery, a crystallization of the lust and anguish of bygone days – the epitome of history, meta history set in stone. You would always be able to come here and feel what he knew, the one came to Cyrus' tomb in Pasargade and saw the inscription: 'O man, whoever you are and wherever you've come from, I am Cyrus who gave the Persians their empire. Do not begrudge me my monument'." [p 83-85]

ANTROPOLITAN

Antropolis portrays a city in the future, a culture emerging with the impetus of science and faith, a state finding a new path in troubled times. It shows what is to come, what will dawn over the world after the materialism and mental deficiency of our times have run their course, and man turns a new page.

The novel is a profiling of some aspects of the current world – and the coming world. In a way the work is an attempt to prophesy, trying to see what the future may bring. Hereby some quotes which *in nuce* captures that attempted prophetic attitude:

> *"It was as if human culture had simply lost confidence and committed seppuku: 'see how a time, hated by itself, commits suicide'... The Metropolitan culture had run out of steam, reached the end. The Empire fell, all those venerable institutions civilization consisted of: EU, UN, US, IAEA, OAS, ASEAN..."* [p 64]

- - -

> *"And when I woke up in that temple, I realized that this was Antropolis. Or rather, this was the ruins of Metropolis on which we could build our Antropolis. Babylon the Great was fallen, now it was time for the New Jerusalem..."* [p 15]

- - -

"The memory of the time of decay time began to fade. This had, after all, been a hard-hitting crisis, a worldwide interregnum in the wake of the fall of the Empire. All order disappeared overnight and many died of sheer terror. But some had made it through, a few things had survived the devastation – and the earth as well as the human body possessed self-healing forces, there was no total destruction as some Cassandras and Jeremiahs prophesied about. Perhaps people in general forgot the misery as soon as they stopped seeing these death birds in the sky, as soon as they could sit in the sun with a ripe apple and enjoy it." [p 42]

- - -

"We all can do our bit, we all create our own Antropolis in tune with the higher powers. 'An open city, not a fortified, we're building together.' The fullness of space surrounds us, a soulful Akâsha where we can venture out as spiritual spaceships, seeking out new worlds and new life, whizzing by in an endless adventure: To seek out new worlds, to discover life, to boldly go where no man has gone before..." [p 202]

PROFILES

The novel *Antropolis* tells about many figures, distinct characters with almost archetypal function. For instance, we meet a kind of new age guru, depicted with some criticism. The drift of the portrait is that he lacks musical feeling, having no tangible rapport with the Muses, the ancient Greek goddesses of poetry, drama and history. However, this Elander Lysion character isn't wholly despicable, as this meeting in the guru's domain of Elysia shows us, with Jenro Klao as the narrator:

I sat next to a lilac hedge where some birds were singing. Otherwise, you could see an avenue of apple trees, vegetable gardens framed by holly and a pond with swimming ducks and swans. Beyond it was a small meadow where some young people dressed in white tossed a frisbee. It was idyllic – but then I also happened to be in Elysia, Elander Lysion's enclave north of the city. I sat on the patio to their restaurant and dined with the man himself, this bald, somewhat portly guru. He was dressed in an orange caftan with silver embroidery. We had just completed creamed kale with fried sheep cheese, shredded pepper and croutons. I drank of the pale green wine and said 'excellent'. Lysion nodded and said: 'Our kitchen is famous all over town.' By this, he meant their vegetarian kitchen for here they didn't even eat fish. Meat was quite rare in Antropolis; slaughterhouses there were not, and only if a person had been given permission to shoot a deer, a hare, a grouse or some other game did meat appear on our tables. [p 70]

This is a quote from Chapter 12, "Lysion". As intimated, this Elander Lysion is an important figure in the *Antropolis* story; he's a new-age guru, a rather bureaucratic bulldozer of a guru, however, advocating viable ideas such as technology having to be people-centered: meditation techniques, studying techniques, alternative medical technology – this is the definition of technology he favors, here the emphasis of human endeavor is to be. He has no sympathy for the gadget and mechanical engineering technology that Gotsis Fripp, another Antropolitanian, espouses.

FRIPP

The main story begins *in medias res*, in the middle of events, with the first chapters telling of Antropolis in 2165, a time when the once unnamed city was renovated and christened "Antropolis," as such, a burgh fairly functional after the great deluge. Then the narrator, Jenro Klao, tells about how he grew up in the countryside, a rather fine place to endure the collapse of civilization. Then he tells of how he ventured out in the world and found the ruins of this city; he settled there, in the cathedral, and eventually people gathered in the city and it seemed that a new start for man was possible. One of the people arriving was Gotsis Fripp.

The first appearance of Fripp is told of in Chapter 2. Jenro Klao, giving the background of having come to Antropolis and settled in its ancient cathedral, tells the story:

> *One day when I was sitting in one of the side chapels and read the Bhagavad-Gîtâ, I heard footsteps in the church. I got up and saw a rather gangly fellow in the aisle, slowly progressing forward and looking around in wonder. He was lean, had bushy red hair and wore a leaden-gray, seamless garment that gave a remarkable impression. This was a well-dressed man, functional variety. I came up to meet him; we were standing before the southern window with its stained glass, depicting the Savior preaching the doctrine. The man stood solemn, pointed to the glass and said: 'It's fantastic...' 'Indeed,' I said. 'Much was broken here when I arrived but this window was quite preserved. Perhaps its aura protected it.' 'Its aura? Rather it would have structural causes...' This was Gotsis Fripp, a technician and an engineer. We started walking along the aisle, looking into the sidechapels and its ancient sarcophagi, carved pillars, glass windows and more. 'The old cathedral builders knew their business,' Fripp said. 'But we too can build monuments...' In this, he might have referred to the Central Works he would build. I figured that this man could be an asset to our city.* [ibid p 17-18]

Fripp eventually becomes the city's chief engineer, a hands-on, slightly titanic machine builder, in juxtaposition to the esoteric Elander Lysion, who was told about above.

The stage is set, the drama begins: should Antropolis be a shining machine city or should it be a green new-age paradise? Or will it be something else again, something that only Jenro Klao has the plans for?

Klao indeed steers the development in his favor, coming up with a synthesis stressing the need for Musicality. Both Fripp and Elysion can contribute to the new era; overall there will be an emphasis on spirituality but technology isn't unimportant in the process. Until the synthesis and conclusion, indeed, both before and after it, the city of Antropolis is characterized by the special domains of Fripp and Lysion, respectively. After the formal inauguration of the city in 2155, these two got their enclaves in the town, on each side of the river; Lysion a temple in white corrugated steel, Fripp his Central Works tower in a dark material called smiss. Halfway between the two, in the river on an island called Sarum, settled the protagonist of the novel, the narrator Jenro Klao. Moving on to the current narrative, he tries to mediate between the two and this eventually takes him onto a multidimensional journey with stops at Leningrad, Stockholm, Paris and other historical "Metropolitan" cities, symbolic of the previous age.

Antropolis has a rich gallery of characters: the preacher Elander Lysion, the technician Gotss Fripp, the jovial mayor Gunga Surf – and the chief of police, Hadar Lacq, a veteran of the hostilities having visited the world before the advent of the new era, an era symbolized by the city of Antropolis.

Antropolis is a wreckage after this war, a relatively prosperous city in the peace that now prevails. It's a city-state without territorial enemies; an army isn't needed, so Hadar Lacq and his men form the role of police force instead. He upholds the law while dreaming of old battles – but what does he truly want, does he want to take power in the impending civil war in the city, in the struggle between Fripp and Lysion?

THE POEM

A lot could be quoted from *Antropolis* the novel. Perhaps the best way to get the specificity of it is to reproduce a certain poem – "Antropolis, the Poem," which makes up the whole of Chapter 22 and is Jenro Klao's ultimate statement about everything: his very being, history, the future of the city and all. So here it is, the musical symbol of all that Antropolis stands for. First, there's a prologue:

Antropolis, city of cities,
the city being all cities;
everywhere and nowhere,
all cities and none – Antropolis.

Then comes part one, portraying the archetypal city, the ideal city:

The shadows moving over the fronts of Antropolis,
clouds sailing in the sky;
white houses in the midday sun,
hazy mirage in the heat –
hazy mirage in the heat.

Sunset in Antropolis,
shimmering marble in the evening light;
a last glimpse of the sun,
city of marble, city of gold –
city of marble, city of gold.

Sleeping city in the moonlight,
sleeping city in the moonlight –
the houses are blue, everything is blue,
the streets are deserted.
Night in Antropolis.

Dawn in Antropolis,
façades blushing in the sun;
the day is dawning, the heat rising,
shadows fleeing, city waking –
shadows fleeing, city waking.

In part two of the poem there are more scenes of the Ideal City in vivid imagery and poignant pictures:

> *Antropolis, looming in the distance,*
> *the city within, the city that is;*
> *dreamy city, beckoning city,*
> *eternal dream, eternal city –*
> *Antropolis.*
>
> *Antropolis, the one city,*
> *city without equal, likening itself;*
> *city without reason, city without cause,*
> *city without further ado, no man's town –*
> *Antropolis.*
>
> *Antropolis, city of the world,*
> *the city a world and the world a city;*
> *world city and worlds within the city,*
> *the world of cities and the city of worlds –*
> *Antropolis.*

Part three elaborates on questions, on the dreamy nature of the city and on the eternal quality of names such as Heliopolis, Metropolis and Antropolis:

> *Antropolis, Antropolis...*
> *Why Antropolis, why this city?*
> *Therefore Antropolis.*
> *Therefore this city.*
> *Therefore this city...*
> *I want to stay with you,*
> *don't want to leave;*
> *stay with you, Antropolis –*
> *see the man becoming the man,*
> *the city of man – Antropolis.*

See the man: the human paradigm
for God's city on the hill,
the shimmering city,
the Eternal City –
is this Antropolis?

Human symbol, eternal city,
dreaming city, beckoning city:
Lycantropolis, Heliopolis,
Necropolis, Metropolis –
Antropolis.

Part four is a rather free-form exposé of Jenro Klao's travels, of his visits to the antipodes of the world. He has lived in Antropolis, is the message, in many different forms and shapes:

I have seen the shadows move
over the fronts of Antropolis.
I have walked along Unter den Linden,
Nevsky Prospekt, Folkungatan.
And Bryggaregatan, Main Street,
Lillgatan, Kungsgatan...
I was born on a street. I have
seen the gilding of the copper roofs and
the brick façades in the evening splendor,
from Babylon to Åsele,
from Thessaloniki to Torsby.
I've attended cafés from
Hastinâpura to Uppsala
and seen life passing by,
I have speculated on the agio in
Augsburg, howled under the bridges of Paris,
sung in the Moscow subway and
danced along the streets and avenues
of New York.

ACTIONISM

*I have stood at Sunset and Vine
and seen the traffic flowing past.
I have traveled "on the thumb" from coast
to coast, seen jets in a desert
with taped gills and
the "divine angle" of
Cadillac Farm – and I have
seen the temples, I have honored unknown
Gods and sacrificed everything I have to
sacrifice: my pride, my
Foolish Pride...*

*I have traveled through countries and climes –
"I went through woods, I went through
deserts" – and always ended up in the town,
the city, the burgh –
having strolled along, forging ahead,
venturing out seemingly randomly; I have
walked along avenues, meeting people,
talking to beggars and junkies,
counts and barons,
bakers and makers,
soldiers and scholars.
I have seen gray skies and blue skies,
façades at sunset and
statues in the evening light –
and I have seen Antropolis, and
I have lived in Antropolis.*

*Nocturnal city, a church bell striking –
and darkness lifting, dawn breaking –
and a jet plane flying over the city,
a con trail in the sky –
and a river roaring and street sweeping –
and everything is Antropolis,
sublime mysticism and quiet rest.*

After this, all that remains is the epilogue, same as the prologue:

> *Antropolis, city of cities,*
> *the city being all cities;*
> *everywhere and nowhere,*
> *all cities and none – Antropolis.*

This is what we have to do: create a new culture for man, symbolized in the city of Antropolis, dedicated to art, science and spirituality. So, turn away from materialism and decadence and help me start building Antropolis.

29. ACTIONIST DIARY

These are notes from the everyday of my life, mixing high and low, big and small, all presented in a predominantly "Actionist" way. The diary runs from the autumn of 2015 to the summer of 2016. The date format is day-month-year.

10/10 2015

Overcast day. Proofreading.

11/10

Judging by the starry sky at 2 AM we have a clear day ahead.

Continued proofreading. It's a word file, I call it Project 1, a book no one has ordered, a work written on speculation. Proofreading is usually a toilsome task. But this particular MS is rather interesting. However, proofreading shouldn't be too fun, then there's the risk of getting embroiled in the general feeling of the text, being swept away by the reading itself; then you might miss the typos. Ideally, proofreading should be done syllable by syllable. It's a 250-page file, I could do it in a week, however, the deadline is rather far off so there's no hurry with this one. "Deadline" means "when I will send it to a publisher for consideration," that is, January.

14/10

And another one: another proofreading project up and running. Another file, another unsolicited, uncontracted opus I felt like writing. This, then, is Project 2. The above mentioned is done, now I'm into this one, another file that has to be proofread before January = no hurry, but why not get it done right away. It won't get any more fun by having it waiting.

Proofreading will never be fun. When you have *flow* it can be moderately fun, that I admit. But normally, when having these chores, you have to make them into Actionist operations. Three Actionist concepts sprang into mind today when getting into the mood of the new file having to be proofread:

(1) MMM = the Memento Mori Mindset = if I would die now, what project would I like to have finished; conversely, what project wouldn't I like to leave behind unfinished? Answer: the file I'm now reading, this I'd like to have proofread from start to finish. Thus the act (= the proofreading) becomes one of basic necessity, of tidying up.

(2) RIA = Rest In Action = proofreading a file can be a bit stressful, you want that flow, you want to get into the mood, you can't seem to relax in doing other stuff while doing this; therefore, you should remind yourself of the phenomenon of RIA = Rest In Action = of trying to relax while performing a task. In this case, try to breathe, perform some gentle mini-meditation now and then in order to become relaxed, thus being able to read more freely while still trying to read meticulously, ironing out typos and faults.

(3) With such a relaxed-but-alert mindset any action, including proofreading, may become MAASOM = Movement As A State Of Mind.

ACTIONISM

20/10

Have been humming "Lonesome Town" all day. "Ich weiss nicht, was soll es bedeuten, dass ich so traurig bin" as Heine said.

Have been shopping. Took my bicycle and went pedaling off the usual way, about 1.5 km past houses, trees, lawns and roads, and negotiating the railroad underpass, finally approaching a big parking lot with the supermarket as a backdrop. I drove up and parked the bike, locked it, went inside, took a basket and filled it with toothpaste, rice cookies, dried plums, spaghetti, tomatoes, carrots, black radish, bananas and apples. It cost me some Swedish kronor and then I went back home, biking through the calm morning under a malvern sky. The path goes along an inlet, the picturesque Nattviken, the town proper being situated as a backdrop of this. The central city is on an island but I live on the mainland.

21/10

Woke up at 0100 AM. Went out for a walk: deserted street, nightly scene, rather mild weather, I have no thermometer but I guess it was about 6 centigrade plus. Got down to the canal and the building site, they're building a new drawbridge. It's a city street, there's a canal for small sailing boats anchoring at Nattviken, the old bridge was in need of repair, now they're getting a new one. The building / tearing down started in August, it will be done in February next year, that's the plan.

They've torn down most of the old concrete, now they're casting new concrete. In some weeks the specific bridge element will arrive by boat, the bridge is manufactured in Poland, it will be a sight to see, this shipping in of the new element and putting it in place.

After seeing this I went down to Södra sundet, "the Southern Sound": dark sky with some clouds, still water, city lights on the other side, the city island. Went back inside and took a cup of honey water and a rice cookie. Turned on the computer and surfed the net. Posted a message on a site for Jünger lovers, informing about *Ernst Jünger – A Portrait*, my Jünger bio. Then I went back to bed, slept for some two hours. At 0400 AM I got up again, cooked me some food, then sat down to write. Now time for a break again, now it's 0610.

23/10

Bright day, mild, scattered clouds, sunshine.

24/10

Have been downtown. Had to go to the library, checking a quote in a book.

The library is on the island. I live on the mainland. Usually I go by the Storgatan drawbridge, now this is to be replaced, therefore another way has to be taken. They have built (1) a main road north of the bridge building site, made by broken rock, gravel and sand, formed into the simplest kind of passage = a causeway, a solid embankment (2) a bicycle-and-walking bridge south of the building site, made of wood. This day I took my bike and crossed the canal on that narrow wooden bridge, the Western Canal. Having crossed it I was on a smaller island called Mellanholmen, a 100 m wide and 500 m long island with some apartment houses on it and on the southern tip a park. I stopped at the cape and looked out over Södra Sundet, a sound, part of the waters surrounding the Härnösand island.

From the place in question there's a fine view, habitats climbing the hilly mountain constituting the city island, and on top of the hill called Vårdkasberget there are windmills, electric power plants, something of a signature of Härnösand. A fine day this was, high thin clouds, the sun shining through, the birches were dropping their leaves, gold coins in the gutter, *quelle largessse...* The maple leaves are also falling; some maples still have some leaves on them, some green, some red, some both green and red.

I again mounted my bike, heading for the next canal bridge, a permanent pedestrian and bicycle bridge, this one crossing the Eastern Canal – and having crossed it I was on the city island proper, a 10 km square island, not many Swedish cities are situated on islands like this, only parts of Stockholm and some burgh on the west coast, maybe Marstrand.

Härnösand's city island is called Härnön, a hilly and wooded island, in the west occupied by the city with squares and rather substantial buildings. It's the residential city for the county, a small town it is but with a tangible official tradition and function. Some 20,000 inhabitants we have, not much, the cities of Umeå and Sundsvall to the north and south are much bigger.

I went up the slope to the library, finally there I stopped and admired the view, the view of a park with yellow maples and some other tree, a green tree, what species it was I don't know. I admired the statue, the bust actually, of Bertil Malmberg (1889-1958), Academy member, author of the novel *Åke and His World* (1924) which has been translated into English, otherwise Malmberg wrote of Hadean light, whirling leaves and echoes out of the abyss.

Standing outside the library entrance I also admired the dome, the cathedral, the white classical church from the early 19th century. It has round arches and green-black copper roof, this is Sweden's smallest dome. Härnösand is a diocese city, it has a bishop.

I entered the library, had the impulse to visit the depository, a walk-in depot for books not displayed in the library shelves proper. I ventured off to the label *He*, English literature and my eyes fell on Asimov, Isaac, *Foundation's Edge*, a novel from 1983, not so good as *Foundation* from 1941, this was a disappointment, still, he could write at the age of 63 and beyond, he continued to present his readers with plausible plots.

Asimov was one of my early literary favorites, also one of the first authors I read in English. For instance, I devoured the Foundation trilogy and *The Currents of Space*. I also liked *The Isaac Asimov Book of Facts*, a book presenting short paragraphs with remarkable facts in science, history, publishing, nature etc. etc. In retrospect, Asimov's books seldom seem to be *about* anything, yet they don't pretend to be anything more than what they are, glorified simulacrum that it's easy to dismiss but I personally still have some faith in Asimov. There might be more depth to novels by Heinlein, Frank Herbert, Dick and Gordon Dickson but Asimov remains a classic figure in the field, it's hard to think of SF without the presence of Asimov. The conceptual boldness of the Foundation trilogy remains a landmark, a plausible, fast-moving story of a galactic empire going through turmoil – fast-moving yet played out mostly in dialogue, not tangible action per se.

I took the elevator to floor 4, asked a librarian how to surf on the net on the library computers, and this she told me, and then I could browse the net and find a certain site. Then I went looking for the book, the thing I primarily came for – and indeed, I did find the book I was searching for, found the page, noted it, needing it for a certain study I've written. Like this: I had forgotten to note this special page number when I quoted a passage of the book, when I had lent the book some year before. It was a Ray Bradbury book. Having done what I came for I took my time to admire the view from the library's top floor, floor 4, its large windows allowing for a stupendous view of Södra Sundet, the mountains, the church and everything. Hilly terrain this is, Höga Kusten = the High Coast, rather picturesque. Specifically, I like the water flowing round this city, I'm no sailor type but conversely, to live in a city almost without any substantial river or bay or sound is questionable, like Uppsala. I lived there before, this is some stone desert, the River Fyris is insignificant and there are no lakes or such. A dry land for dry brains.

25/10

Significant message, read on a website: "Leave the light on."

- - -

Overcast, the weather of timelessness. On a bright day your view is drawn to the horizon, the place where (in Spengler's words) "space becomes time". However, under a uniformly grey sky the look is turned inward, forcing you to meditate on your being, on your I AM.

26/10

Have read poetry by Poe. Favorites: "A Dream Within a Dream," "Ulalume," "The City in the Sea," "Coliseum," "Annabel Lee". Poe has been criticized for being a bit artificial and contrived, I can see why but a bad poet he's not. He's a nihilist but that's no crime, not when you can take your nihilism into the grey area as Poe can – a grey area of "nihilism meets idealism".

27/10

I've been to Erikshjälpen Second Hand. They sell books and records, clothes and furniture. It's a charity. The books are cheap but I didn't buy any, not today. I looked at titles by Hesse, Hassel and Hamsun, nothing turned me on, I left empty-handed. Might as well, I already have a lot of unread books. Also, these books were in Swedish and German, I'm kind of into English now, that's the language I feel enthusiastic about, and "nothing is done without enthusiasm" as Emerson said.

It was a fine day, clear and a bit cold, "friskt" as we say in Norrland = fresh. I went off over the makeshift causeway, the embankment for heavy traffic. I had my bike. I crossed the Mellanholmen over its northern tip. Next I crossed the Eastern Canal and ventured over the city square, passing the palace for the county governor, an early 19th century structure in orange plaster with white corners, span roof and, as adornment, the Swedish coat of arms, the small one with the three crowns in a stately framework on top of the front façade – golden crowns on blue, the Swedish coat colors since the time of the Folkungs in the 14th century.

I was now on the city island. I just touched it. For next I went over the Nybron to the mainland, then off north along some warehouses to the second hand store in question.

I stopped by the dock. I admired the harbor, not many ships there, in fact none. But a quaint view with the 19th century houses on the opposite shore, on the island, then the rich blue of the water mirroring the clear sky; the wind blew so the water surface got a dark hue from this, still not uninviting but rather warm. In the distance, in the roads up north, the water got even darker, a common distance effect.

Härnösand is surrounded by mountains, about 100-150 m high and fairly distant, maybe some 5 km off or so, in every direction. They don't give the impression of hemming you in, on the contrary, your spirit is drawn to them and then up and away. I love this feature, this is Norrland – and I was born in this part of the land, in Åsele, situated by the Ångermanälven river mouthing some metrical miles north of Härnösand. It's the same thing in Åsele, mountains in every direction, heights with dense coniferous woods. For instance, in the States this latter feature is not always the case, like the Western US tending to have mountains with sparse forest vegetation, this is a feature I've noticed. This is never the case in Sweden, this is the taiga, here the coniferous trees grow densely. Standing in the harbor and looking south I saw a flat mountain grown with green forest, pine forest, a heartwarming sight, this is how it should look, such a sight makes me feel at home. Conversely, the above mentioned Uppsala is totally flat, Uppsala where I once lived, there's no mountains to attract the view there, to *existentially* attract the view. That's what I need mountains for, for my view to have somewhere to go, to the horizon, the place where space becomes time.

I went off to the second hand store, it was close by the harbor, I went inside, browsed the shelves, a pointless errand as such but I still cherish such an outing. Browsing things IRL is nice for a change, otherwise I tend to browse the net, I like that too, now I was in the second hand store, there's a value in looking at book spines and reading titles, deliberating on them, being given impulses on what to read and on what not to read, being reminded of titles you might already own.

For instance, when I go to that store I tend to get reminded of a graphic novel I once bought there, one by Hugo Pratt, a Corto Maltese collection. This doesn't mean that I go home and pick it up but it's a fine series and outings like these have that function, to remind you of books in that way or the other. That's why a bike ride to Erikshjälpen Second Hand is never wasted.

28/10

Poe said that the most poetic subject was "the death of a beautiful woman". I can think of other, even more poetic subjects, like "tracers in the night," "the shifting waters of the Southern Sound," "the sun shining through thin clouds" and "autumn in the mountains". That is, the four elements in all their variegated splendor.

- - -

I live in a one-room apartment. From the hall you reach an L-formed kitchen, overlooking the street. Green and white curtain. On the wall, a bar mirror with the Beefeater label.

In the hall there are wardrobes and a bookshelf, there's a door leading to the WC, there's a door leading to the living room. The living room has a curtain in green, yellow and turquoise. And a sleeping alcove formed with a bookshelf. And a working space framed by another bookshelf. On the wall, "Women on a Bridge" by Munch, a reproduction, it used to hang in my childhood home, colorful and enigmatic, three ladies looking out over a river, the fourth turned to face the spectator, "you," the one seeing the picture. She has no face, it's a form of stylization, this was often the case in early 20th century painting, this contributes to the peculiar atmosphere.

29/10

Woke up. Wrote a review of the new Telos edition of *Eumeswil*, Ernst Jünger's 1977 novel, his best. Had some pasta. Went out. Dark, early morning. The display on the Landstingshuset said 4 degrees centigrade plus, a highly mounted display, red LEDs, good to have around, I have no thermometer outside my apartment window proper.

Went the few meters down to Nattviken, surrounded by city lights, the mainland to the left, the city island to the right, rather quaint. I did a mini-meditation, reciting a mantra, "avninâshi tu tad viddhi," Bhagavad-Gîtâ 2:17 about the indestructible soul residing in the body.

I stood at my favorite spot, between two birch trees, it's a cobbled spot, I think it has been the place of a bench, now it's a very unassuming spot, very discreet, my "secret place," it's just some meters from the feeder to the Landstinget parking lot, still, it's a bit off center, a spot I like to visit at times like this, taking a breath of fresh air after some hours of writing.

The spot is close to the water; just beyond the flat there's a sloping, stone-clad bank down to the water surface proper, some two meters below. Here you can stand and take it all in, the sky, the water, the city lights. It was dark now but in spring and summer it's even more alluring, going out here in the early morning before the city has woken up, seeing the gilded clouds in the east, the rosy city on the island slope, the waters reflecting the brightness.

- - -

Have been shopping. Cold and gray, smoke on the wind, wooden smoke, a not unpleasant smell, aromatic hydrocarbons.

The fashionable winter jacket this year has horizontal calluses. It looks like a stillsuit from *Dune*, the 1984 David Lynch film.

- - -

Nietzsche reduced all metaphysics into Will, the Will to Power. He wasn't completely right in this but not completely wrong either since Will is a primeval force, as old as Thought, Light and Compassion, all in existence from the Beginning. "In the beginning was the Deed," as I said in Chapter one, echoing Nietzsche in general and Goethe's *Faust* in particular.

30/10

Places I've lived in:
- 1965-1971, Åsele, Lapland county
- 1971-1974, Enköping, Uppland county
- 1974-1985, Övik, Ångermanland county
- 1985-2010, Uppsala, Uppland county
- 2010-, Härnösand, Ångermanland county

- - -

From my kitchen window I can see the drawbridge building site, they're replacing the old bridge. Now there's no bridge element there at all, the old drawbridge is gone, a new is on its way. It's being built in Poland, it will be 15 meters long and 30 meters wide, I wonder how they will get that from the harbor and here. Having loaded it unto a trailer they can go either (1) over Nybron and Nybrogatan and across the city island or (2) over the mainland.

Maybe the trailer option isn't needed at all. The Nybron is a drawbridge too; if this can be opened and the bridge element be shipped past and into the Nattviken, then it's home free for the building site. We'll see what they choose, the bridge element is said to arrive soon.

From my window I can see the building site. A fence shuts it off from the street. You can go along the sidewalk past the end of the apartment block lining this side of the street, the four story building ending in a café; standing by the café you can see the gap where the old drawbridge was, now there's just intricate concrete structures at either end of the canal with rebar sticking up, they're casting new concrete onto this.

From my kitchen window I can see the street, usually it's rather much traffic on it, at least at rush hour. The street is Storgatan, the mainland part of it east of the E4 highway. Now Storgatan is shut off for traffic, however, cars can drive in and park, people still can visit the stores such as a pizza parlor, a café, a restaurant, a flower shop.

31/10

Dreamt I was visiting the old, closed-down armor regiment P1 outside Enköping, "Pansarregemente 1," Göta Livgarde. In my dream there were apartment houses on the premises, occupied, as if by former employees. I found this odd, then I thought: "It's a fine location near the city, that's why people still are living here." On the short end of one of the houses was a rich stone carving, rather unusual for an apartment house like this.

The houses were made of red brick. No such buildings are to be found on the actual P1 regiment I once visited, it was along with my dad in the early 70s, the time when I lived in the town in question, Enköping. Its actual barracks are spread out in the forested terrain, façades of grey plaster, two-story. However, as for the dream, I also remember visiting "the commander's house," a stand-alone one-story building of the early 18th century type, I found it rather quaint. But neither this is to be found on the actual regiment.

The whole P1 part of the dream began thus: a narrow asphalt road, going straight through a nocturnal autumn forest, a road lit by headlights from an unseen car – with myself, as the dreamer and spectator, theoretically sitting behind the wheel to get such a view. Seeing this in the dream I immediately knew, "this is P1," that was the immanent knowledge going with this view.

The dream was in a regiment but there were no soldiery elements around, no visions of serving, of duty-honor etc. So this P1 visit might represent "the regiment as a place of power, a temple area". For indeed, in my memories I often visit another regiment, the I21 regiment where I served in 1984-1985, all the barracks, the film hall, the storehouse, the garages etc. etc. having made an indelible impression on me – a place of power, symbolizing service, defense and self-sacrifice in the duty of staving off nihilist Bolshevism. A viable temple area, fondly remembered by this warrior monk.

1/11

Clear skies, mild weather. Most birch leaves down, also most of the maple leaves. However, some species still keep their leaves, for instance, on the Landstinget yard there's a rather green deciduous tree, possibly an alder.

Otherwise this is the darkest part of the year, November; it's true that the midwinter solstice around 21/12 has the least sun hours per day but then there's normally snow on the ground, now there's no snow, therefore November in Sweden is "as dark as it gets".

3/11

Have been ill. Now I'm feeling better. Maybe it was "a bout of flu," that seasonal / once a year / whatever dip.

The first symptom came on Sunday evening, that of a headache. But I have this now and then, I feel changes in atmospheric pressure. Anyway, on Monday morning I still had this headache, also, I was very tired. After honey water and the sending off of an already completed article I went back to bed, slept for a good three hours, got up, took a shower, ate, then back to bed. Skipped dinner, no real appetite, had some tea, went back to bed. Luckily I had two collections of English romantic poetry to read, poets from late 18th century through mid 19th century, authors like Byron, Shelley, Poe, Coleridge, Macpherson. The latter with his *Ossian* was an interesting experience, finally I got to read this, this prose-poetry outing without plot, this moonlit poetic lament of battles and tragic love in a Gaelic-Scottish setting. Macpherson probably wrote it himself, it wasn't ancient literature as he claimed but he may have had some original, some traditional forebears; this he conceptualized into a framework of Ossian, son of Fingal and Oscar, son of Ossian and their atmospheric, lyrical instances in a 3rd century Gaelic setting.

On Monday evening I was still very tired, in spite of all the naps I'd taken throughout the day. Headache receding by then. Went to sleep. And after nine hours of sleep I awoke this morning without headache, with regained appetite, on the road to recovery.

I probably had a fever, I don't know, I didn't measure it. But the syndrome of "headache, loss of appetite, fatigue" I know since before. In one word, flu. At worst it can erupt into vomiting. I didn't have to go through that this time. And overall, possibly the climax in the cycle of illness is passed now. However, I still feel a bit weak so I'll stay inside today.

4/11

Härnösand is a windy city – but – today, when I was off shopping, it was calm. The flags by the supermarket parking lot hung slack. Also, rather mild and bright = a fine autumn thus far.

As for the drawbridge building project it started on August 1. It's said to be completed by February. Thus, it's about half-done.

6/11

Fog, wonderful fog: as it were, the whole town is wrapped in a veil of ignorance. Wherever I go – Northern Sound, Southern Sound – I see nothing but a shore and a wide expanse of greyness, the city island completely concealed to my look. And I don't mind it, this grey weather is good to work in. I now proofread, having the second and final read-through of the word-file called Project 1.

However, the bridge building project makes itself felt. They chisel off old concrete, a pneumatic machine linked to an excavator goes knock-knock-knock all day. This was heard in September too, then by October it stopped, now they're at it again. However, I can work with it in the background, it isn't wholly invasive. And on a daily pattern it always stops at 6 PM or before. It isn't like "neighbor playing loud music" which is more of a wild card.

9/11

I'm reached by the rumor that the worlds' currencies are back on the gold standard. A rumor it is and I note it as such but if it's true it's rather epochal. No more fractional banking, no more Babylonian-style of issuing money as debt...?

- - -

Yesterday I took a morning walk. The shortest possible: down to the Cobbled Place. Finally there I looked out over the Nattviken. Cold and dark, city lights on the shores, rather still, no wind. Also, when standing there you can see rather small, distinct objects moving on the water, I guess it's the mallards drifting, they kind of do that, drifting at night, going this way and that in a sleepy haze.

10/11

Found on the net: "In the age of information, ignorance is a choice."

11/11

This day four years ago we passed the Magic Zero-point. The point beyond which the planet can't be dragged down into hell anymore.

Major war is now a thing of the past. Kali Yuga is over, Sat Yuga is here – if you want it. A new era has dawned but we also have to will the Good Times in our hearts to make this era of truth and compassion really come true. Major war can't break out – that's the basics. Then, for peace to really triumph, the peacefulness has to be anchored in our hearts. Thus, this is a transitional time.

I just took a morning walk, going down to the drawbridge building site. Lots of molds and reinforced steel waiting for the concrete to flesh it out. A new structure about to take shape, just like the World of Tomorrow, the world of peace and prosperity awaiting us.

- - -

Earlier this autumn I visited an old relative in a nearby town. Out driving in his car we passed a certain house that interested me. Telling me of the house, my acquaintance said that for a while it had been owned by a watchmaker. – Watchmaker… you don't hear that word often these days.

Where have all the watchmakers gone?

Gone to sleep to the rhythm of the star clock.

12/11

Some hipsters of today have a craze to "dress up like zombies". Why dress up as something you already are? Talk about tautology.

17/11

Actionism is an experience based ethic. It's a performance based ethic. It's not a theoretical exercise. It's an ethic of action.

18/11

The building project, the drawbridge complex: they work industriously on it, they do this and that, they make molds for concrete. They don't chisel any more, it's not exactly quiet over there at daytime but in all I'm not disturbed by any particular noise these days.

20/11

An Actionist doesn't say things like, "I wasn't made for these times." An Actionist changes the times, affects the zeitgeist with his Will and Thought.

21/11

All leaves down, sky grey, horizon clear. Icy northern wind, the snow seems about to arrive any day now.

22/11

Actionism is about reaching *operational freedom*. It's akin to the Taoist attitude of, "act is if you didn't act". It's about MAASOM = Movement As A State Of Mind.

24/11

Cold and frosty and no snow: a harsh clime indeed. It's better after the first snow has fallen, then it gets softer and brighter. Softer, because the snow cover dampens all the sounds, like that from traffic. The snow cover also reflects the light and makes the land more bright.

Actionism is a conceptual life support system.

25/11

In a sense, it's good to be controversial. The worst is to be ignored, "hanged in silence".

"You've got enemies? Good. That means that you've stood up for somebody, sometime in your life." – Churchill

26/11

Yesterday was a busy day at the building site. The men were up early, doing stuff from about 4 AM. Later in the day I saw a concrete mixer truck pass down the street, driving in reverse, heading for the canal site. So I guess it was the Big Concrete Casting day, creating the fundamentals for the drawbridge, one rampart on each side of the canal. The bridge element itself will arrive later, as I mentioned above.

PEAB is creating the fundamentals for a new drawbridge just as I, with my conceptualizations, am creating a new mental and emotional framework for a coming golden age.

1/12

Makeshift poem of the day:

"Oh my darling, see me soaring over the city, / I've left the world in ten ways so raise me a monument, / and on the stone, write: He was an adept who advocated action, / he was a scholar who fought for tradition, / he was an author who enchanted the world. / He was everyone and no one, / he was everywhere and nowhere. / He was Svensson, the man without further ado."

5/12

Snow slush, a glorified neither-or weather. The Cosmic Christmas Calm is beginning to arrive, the energy for writing is going down. This time of year favors the attitude of "unwinding, turning off the computer and reading a book".

10/12

Standing at the Cobbled Place in the early morning I could see the Nybron decorated with LED lights, a lot of miniature dots of light in a sort of veil, rather stylish. Christmas is coming.

11/12

To merely advocate "tolerance" is to advocate nihilism. Because, if everything is tolerated, nothing can be tolerated.

15/12

In two days I turn 50. In two days my physical body will have lived 50 years on this planet. The Zero Time Reference for the biological entity called "Lennart Svensson" was 12 December 1965. I thank my mother and father for having bred me; I thank God for having, prior to this, long before, created my immortal soul, a spark of Light from his Eternal Light.

It's a cold day today, no snow. We have a clear sky, rather fine weather. The air is fresh and good to breath and peace is on the land. The bridge builders keep on building, still there's wooden molds and rebar at the strategic places, still it looks very "half-done". I hear hammering, chiseling and whatnot, it's not so very disturbing. The bridge proper will be put in place after the Christmas break, in January. In February it will be completed, God willing.

17/12

Socrates advocated "the reflected life": the life worth living is one reflected upon. What happens in life becomes meaningful if conceptualized.

- - -

In Actionism Will and Thought are united into a higher amalgam, that of Will-Thought.

- - -

Today I turn 50. I highlight the event with this poem:

Jahrestag in Svenssonland,
on Storgatan in Härnösand,
50 years of peace and war,
now I'm in for 50 more –
'cos I, I wanna be, Svensson free!

Comment: the war element of my life was fighting the Cold War, doing national service in the Swedish Army 1984-1985. In this conflict we were virtually fighting, and defeating, the worst oppressor regime ever, Bolshevik Russia.

- - -

Arthur Miller (1915-2005): "An era can be said to end when its basic illusions are exhausted." This is what we see today. The decadent regime of PC-ism, coming in the shape of "tolerance, diversity," is only supported by a tiny fraction of the Westworld. No one believes in multiculturalism any more. The majority is held down by fear – fear of saying the wrong word, fear of liking the wrong post, fear of not being "diverse" enough. You can't build a regime on fear. And truly, now the game is up since the principles supporting the regime are seen for what they are, illusions.

19/12

I was expecting snow today but I got rain. However, it's not wholly unusual with Decembers devoid of snow. The real, Siberian cold sets in around January-February.

An interesting buy: *The Ring Trilogy* by Tolkien. I read a Swedish version in the 80s and loved it. Now, in a time when I'm rather much into the English language, reading the original comes in handy. I admit that I don't care very much for orcs and hobbits, it's the human drama I want, and in the case of myth something more memorable than the "talking vermin" that Moorcock saw the hobbits as. Also, the preceding volume of *The Hobbit* had more ease and playfulness, it had "jouissance". The gravity of the trilogy is a bit tedious. On every page is mentioned Evil Threatening Us From Mordor.

Nevertheless, the trilogy is a book that's good to have in the shelf. My favorite scenes are the house of Tom Bombadill, the flight to the ford, Rivendell, Lothlorien, Saruman, Minas Tirith, the dead mean of Dune Harrow and then some. Linguistically, Tolkien could be rather elaborate in some scenes but mostly he was "simple but not simplistic," letting the symbols in themselves convey the meaning. As Aldiss demonstrated in *Trillion Year Spree*, in comparison the language of Mervyn Peake was more complex, for better or worse. Peake explored every nook and cranny of language per se while Tolkien played with old words and archaisms in a mostly relatable manner, letting the symbols do the main work.

20/12

I had a vision of the bridge being completed, cars running on it. In a nocturnal haze I saw the new drawbridge bridging the cap over the canal. But it was just a dream.

21/12

Publish or perish. And now I've published a review of an Ernst Jünger book in the Swedish weekly *Nya Tider*, issue 52-53. I examine the novel *Eumeswil* which was published in English in the 1990s – and this year, 2015, it's been reissued by Telos Press. I call this a great event since *Eumeswil* summarizes the whole Jünger opus in a grand way. Novel-wise, *Eumeswil* takes in what his previous SF novels like *The Glass Bees* and *Heliopolis* said and makes it in a low-key, somewhat disenchanted but overall viable and vital way – a style devoid of embellishments, a first person narrative which is tight but loose. While not a page-turner or a leisurely read per se *Eumeswil* is Jünger's crowning achievement as a novelist and philosopher. For instance, I say this in the review (the magazine text is in Swedish, here translated by me):

> *That Eumeswil now is available in English, in this new edition, is a great event. This is "absolute Jünger" in the best form imaginable. Because, Jünger, in all his books, whether it concerns a diary, an essay collection or a novel, tends to go off topic and reflect on the*

one and the other thing. He rarely is a "straight storyteller". He's a kind of philosopher, possibly a popular philosopher, even if he's not easy to read. The thing of it is, the very form of Eumeswil (narrator in the first person singular, no linear narrative, the book being a series of thematic reports) allows Jünger to go off topic and philosophize over everything that occurs to him. The book certainly has structure, Jünger has exceptional command over what he writes; he's rather pedantic in that sense. But the reader who wants to be surprised when he reads a novel, the one who's tired of "exiting events," is advised to read Eumeswil which is something completely different. This is a collection of thoughts, whims and stories, all structured in the form of Manuel Venator's everyday reality in the city-state of Eumeswil, everything told being relevant to humanity in the early 2000s, all with a vision of the importance of spirituality and culture in an era of technocratic Titans.

- - -

Today it's the Winter Solstice on the northern hemisphere, on which I happen to live. Today, in my town, the sun rises at 9:20 in the morning and settles at 2:13 in the afternoon. That's the shortest span of daylight you get on these latitudes. From now on the days start getting longer, even though you won't notice the difference until after about a week or so. However, come January there's tangibly a different light, it's wintry and a long time to spring but the light, the very outdoor atmosphere is different. This my mother (RIP) once made me aware of.

- - -

A friend just posted this eastern wisdom on the net. It's about the use of a warrior mindset in a time of peace. These times aren't peaceful, it's a frequency war, a propaganda war, and in this it's better to be prepared for anything than being carefree. Thus:

A student said to his master: 'You teach me fighting, but you talk about peace. How do you reconcile the two?' The master replied: 'It's better to be a warrior in a garden than to be a gardener in a war'.

23/12

Some snow has fallen, enough to make it into a "Hallmark Christmas card, urban variety".

2016

1/1

2016, a new year, "a light-year," whatever, on some level there's always business as usual.

2/1

Alluding to Danish poet Michael Strunge, I'd say: It's January and I AM.

3/1

My publisher Numen Books just asked me to write a short bio of myself for their author page. Here's what I came up with:

"Lennart Svensson was born in Sweden in 1965. After a publishing career in Swedish, spawning novels, Svensson switched to writing in English. To date, he has published three book-length essays:

ACTIONISM

Ernst Jünger – a Portrait (Manticore Books 2014), Richard Wagner – A Portrait (Manticore Books 2015) and Borderline (Numen Books 2015). Svensson has a BA in Indology and has a conservative outlook on life, appreciating metaphysics, history and traditional art of all kinds. Svensson is a 'radical fighting for tradition,' striving to give the current spiritual upsurge a traditional footing. You could also say that he aims at writing serious fiction in popular form. He still lives in his native Sweden and is currently planning more essays and novels."

4/1

Some Media Channel has spoken of the possibility of partitioning Syria into smaller states. My take on this: the window of opportunity to slice up and partition Syria is long gone. As are all the other elite-club projects of creating chaos and mayhem in MENA. Essentially, the tide has turned although this remains a grey-area period, a time of transition. A.K.A. the transition from the Kali Yuga of death and decadence to the Sat Yuga of truth and light.

6/1

It's rather cold and we have a not negligible layer of snow. The snow seems to be here to stay.

The enchanting element of snow is that it's crystals. Even though you don't examine every snowflake close up the crystal presence is felt. It's different with hail, this is just frozen rain. A layer of hail on the ground doesn't speak to you in the same way as a layer of snow. Crystals are the most complex form of matter.

- - -

The catchphrase of the previous era was, "I believe". The catchphrase of this era will be, "I know".

- - -

Have just finished a book. It's an author bio, written by Per Gedin. The title is *Verner von Heidenstam – ett liv* (= in Swedish only, the title translates as "*Verner von Heidenstam – A Life*," Bonniers 2006). It's about Swedish author and Nobel prize winner Verner von Heidenstam (1859-1940).

Heidenstam's novels and poems still deserve to be read. His life, too, is rather interesting as an example. An example of what? – Of an author changing the cultural climate in a land. Heidenstam revived the nationalist spirit, making it mainstream. Before him the right-wing creed was very much about being a royalist. Now, along with the resurgent nationalism in Europe, came a more popular, "folkish" right-wing creed.

Germany was the source of power for this new nationalism. The year 1848, for example, saw efforts of German unification: the small, separate kingdoms should merge and form a unified Vaterland, the liberal insurgents meant. But all these aspirations were crushed by the forces of reaction. Only in 1871, when Prussia had become Germany's leading power, was German nationalism also embraced by the elite in question, by the current right-wing.

We saw the same here in Sweden: not until the 1870s was nationalism adopted by the pillars of society. Still, nationalism wasn't even by then a *leitkultur* in Sweden. It took some time to be more firmly anchored, to be adopted even by the artistic elite, and Heidenstam was instrumental in this. Gedin for his part describes Heidenstam's debut, *Pilgrimage and Journeyman Years* from 1888, as something of a boost to the Swedish soul. At the time the Swedish cultural scene was steeped in defeatism and "grey weather prose," 1880s literature being occupied with naturalistic depictions of urban misery. Typical book titles at this time were *Greycold* and *Poverty* (= *Gråkallt*; *Fattigdom*).

At the time this was thought to attract the audience. Realism prevailed and the poetry was harmless versifications. Now all this, with Heidenstams's example, was replaced by imagination, color and zest. Heidenstam paved the way for writers like Selma Lagerlöf, Gustaf Fröding, Erik Axel Karlfeldt and Ellen Key, and for a renewal in painting, indeed, for nationalism in general. As for literature proper Heidenstam gave the Swedish language a new poetic feeling with influences from Byron, Heine and Turgenev. By this a more freeform verse was established in Swedish.

Heidenstam quickly became No. 1, becoming the color-bearer for the new literature, Gedin says. With his debut in 1888 Heidenstam had won a clear-cut victory: he triumphed over a worn out, dilapidated literary scene. Heidenstam himself said in a letter to Ellen Key, in 1897: *"The constant painting of grey on grey in this country I killed in two years."*

These were bold words. But they were true. Heidenstam at the time of his debut was something of a force of nature, yet playful and human.

In the subject of Heidenstam I've also read *Kring Verner von Heidenstam* by Gudmund Fröberg (editor; Carlsson bokförlag, 1993). As for the person Heidenstam we find quoted on page 270 the words of John Landquist:

> *"He [= Heidenstam] had blue, kindly inquiring eyes but they also had a mysterious depth. He had a dark voice with a soft sound (...) He was genteel but without mannerisms. He sported a quiet kindness. He listened to what you said. His own speech was effortlessly improvised but then, out of the blue, there came a fitting poetic image, this being the natural movement of his thought. You felt at ease with him."*

Heidenstam had his sympathetic traits. At the same time he could, in an official context, be rather pompous. He liked playing the role of poet laurate. This backfired on him in the Strindberg feud in 1910 when Strindberg attacked Heidenstam for a few things. And the assaults found their target even though Heidenstam kept a brave face and mostly declined to answer the slights. You can say: Heidenstam in this process became a victim of the role he created for himself.

What about Heidenstam's works, then? I've read most of them and they tend to keep their allure through the ages. You could say: some Swedes like the negative nihilist Strindberg, the headstrong heckler of everything. I say nothing of this; I mean, to each his own. But many of us instead prefer the more affirmative, joyous, idealist nationalist strain of Heidenstam.

So what did he write? You could mention Hans Alienus (in Swedish only, 1892) a novel with some essential passages in verse. The overall setting is bold and compelling, mixing realism with fantasy. I'd call it a convincing example of "magical realism". Heidenstam wanted to break out of the grey-sky world of realism, otherwise dominant in his day. The hero, Hans Alienus, lives in Rome as an official to the pope. Then Alienus ventures out on a journey through the East and then under the earth, all the time experiencing a few things. It's like a Swedish version of Dante's *Inferno* and Goethe's *Faust*; Heidenstam broke some new ground with this book, "going boldly where no man has gone before". That said, maybe the book is lacking something. Heidenstam was a great poet but not so profound when it came to ontology and spiritual essence. He was like, go and meet the devil, talk to angels, then go home; there's only a semblance of depth in this book, to be sure. Its style and atmosphere are great but it doesn't really convince you on a formal level. Then again, even Dante wasn't always so profound. He brought the reader along with his style and so does Heidenstam at times. Style is personality, "*l'homme et la style, c'est la même,*" and this is a motto describing the Heidenstam project.

A figure that Alienus encounters in his cosmic journey is a haggard lady, Her Archaic Holiness (= "Den Gamla Heliga"; "Den Gamla Människan"). This, as Gedin suggests, is a Jungian "shadow," this horrifying witch embodying sorrow and misery whereas Alienus' dandy lifestyle is all about beauty and joy.

This could lead somewhere. But Heidenstam is incapable, as Jung would advocate, to integrate this shadow into his own essence. The shadows haunt Hans Alienus all the way, until the final scene in Sweden. But Alienus has no defense against this voice from the deep. The novel culminates in sentimental lines of reconciliation with the father. Heidenstam as I said was never profound as thinker; he never reached the esoteric levels that Viktor Rydberg, Per Atterbom or Stagnelius reached (or Coleridge and Eliot). But Heidenstam at least had a feeling of what existence had to offer, he understood that it's a mystery. And he could show it in his novels and poems. "*Mystery, fairytale, light of day, your depth no one can fathom*" as he wrote in the late poem "If I Were A Child".

Another Heidenstam novel is *A King and His Campaigners* (1897, in English 1902) This is a living classic, a still readable exposé of characters during the Great Northern War 1700-1718. Many of the texts are like short stories with protagonists only appearing once but we also have Charles XII appearing in fateful circumstances throughout the book.

This is no naturalistic novel. Many of the texts have a touch of theater. It's not always stories we get, sometimes we're only given static scenes. And the lines often sound a little unnatural; all speak in the same fashion, from coachmen to generals. That said, the book has power and color, motion and verve. The book's merit is the width; you become fascinated even by minor characters such as Mazeppa's ambassador, Lina Andersdotter, Måns Fransyske and others. And that is the sign of a masterpiece, how even the supporting roles are well cast.

Another prose classic is *The Tree of the Folkungs* (1905, in English 1925).

This is a romance set in the 11th century, sporting scenes from both the archaic farmer's life, the life of early medieval Swedish kings and of Vikings serving in the imperial guard in Constantinople. I here refer to the first part, Folke Filbyter; the second part, about the 13th century, is a tinge bit more ordinary, more Walter Scottish = not essential reading, however, also with some memorable scenes as such.

In Part 1 there's a lot of archaic feeling; we meet the last remnants of Asatru and we meet nature religion and shamanism. Heidenstam had a keen eye for life in the woods, for the yearning of the Swede to venture out in the forest and feel the presence of brownies, fairies and nixes. As a poet Heidenstam filled this novel with many a poetic prose passage. But it's still eminently readable as a novel, the first part that is, beginning as it does with Folke returning from a Viking raid, approaching Swedish land on the east coast and, having landed, marching off into the Ostrogothian woods in order to stake out a farm for himself. This was Heidenstam's image of the founding father of the Folkung dynasty which came to rule Sweden 1250-1319.

In *The Swedes and Their Chieftains* (1908, in English 1925) we're given many alluring stories out of Swedish history and myth, such as "Ura-Kaippa," "The Shield Maiden," "The Watchdog of the Greek King" and others from the early middle ages. They are pertinent tales about Norsemen and women, clear-cut images of a vital era, the era of Asatru, archaic moods and heroism. But also from the high and late Middle ages we get good narratives, like "Karl Knutsson and the Piper". This is almost Shakespearean: the rise and fall of a king, mirrored in the role of a beggar-cum-piper watching it all from his corner of the world.

In all this is an absolutely incomparable book about Swedish history, on the border between fact and fiction. Intended as a school book, a history reader for elementary school, it still can be read by everyone.

As for the poet Heidenstam you could mention *Nya dikter* (= New Poems, 1915)

When this was published Heidenstam was 55. He would live for another 25 years. Yet he speaks of himself as "an old man, sitting by the fire brooding". It's in "If I Were A Child," about what you would do if you were a child again. The poet sits remembering, noting that most of his friends are dead. It ends:

Mystery, fairytale, light of day,
your depth no one can fathom.

ACTIONISM

*Yet the same child am I still
and bliss is here to stay.*

This demonstrates a heartwarming, everyday piety which is always viable. This poem sports my overall aesthetic ideal: simple but not simplistic. A similar wisdom we meet in "We Human Beings". It says that we'll all die one day, it's what "we human beings" have in common. It's true that this also sounds like some kind of kitchen-sink wisdom; here you might yearn for a more spiritual outlook. Still, I like the opening lines of this poem, having etched themselves into my being:

*We, who meet for a few brief moments,
children of the same soil and the same wonder,
on the storm-ridden ness of life!*

Another poignant poem is "The Burial of Gustaf Fröding". It's written in memory of the Swedish poet colleague who lived from 1860 to 1911. The poem portrays how Fröding, while he lived, was sitting at his Bible while his hair turned white. From this the poem becomes universal in scope, "wondrously large is a human fate," but man is like a reed in the wind: "Die, die, this he constantly hears / when creating, asking, searching for truth." Then the key changes in the following lines: "All is vanity, / all things earthly die, die, / but he himself becomes the work that he fashions."

Speaking about dying Heidenstam for his own grave created this epitaph, being congenial and saying everything about *la condition humaine*: "Here lies the dust of an old man. Gratefully, he praised the incomprehensible fact that it was granted him to live a life on earth as a man." Truly majestic, simple but not simplistic.

- - -

Am listening to a collection of theme songs from TV series. The overall favorite is *Dynasty*, slow and majestic and with an unforgettable Bach piccolo trumpet. Then you could also mention highlights like these: in the genre of "hard" rock, *Miami Vice* is a standout, a raw guitar sound which is rare in theme songs; in the genre of west coast rock I'd pick *Melrose Place,* rock exuding sunshine; and as for easy listening, *Charlie's Angels,* a song expressing "easy living, holiday". Also rocking is *Baywatch Theme,* with an elemental surge of energy in the singing performance.

7/1

Polar ice cold. And project-wise I'm a bit "in between jobs" right now. Overall, situation can be summed up by: "It's a tough location but I have the essentials."

- - -

I want to live forever and die now.

8/1

Don't come to me and talk about your 3d nonsense. I'm a landlord in the astral world.

Come meet me in Antropolis, meet me in the grey area, in the Interzone, the Twilight Zone, the Borderline. Just don't come and say that your world, the everyday world, is the true reality. That's merely a contingent reality, a dependent reality, a material reduction of the deathless patterns of the astral world.

Join me in the Square of Voices in Antropolis, anytime.

10/1

I am industry. I am history. I am accountability. I am victory.

- - -

Dreamed that I was out walking with a friend. On the ground we found a folio volume with poems by nationalist Finnish poet Bertel Gripenberg. I opened the book, I read it, I can't remember now what it said but it was an appeal of "save the nation, Finland's fate is decided on the Karelian Isthmus". Deathless poetry, now gone forever in the twilight zone of the dreamworld, leaving just a memory of metallic beauty.

11/1

Yesterday minus 17 centigrade, today only minus 4. Nice.

12/1

Morning walk. Minus 4, not so excruciatingly cold. However, the wind blew and the snow fell, it was dark and rather forbidding.

Standing on my side of the canal, the western, I could see two things on the eastern side: (1) on the actual bridge rampart, a huge, ten-wheel crane lorry. The crane proper stretched some, I don't know, 20 meters into the sky (2) on a side-road, a flatbed truck loaded with the actual drawbridge. The bridge element has finally arrived, shipped here from Poland, and from Härnösand harbor most probably having been taken by this truck through the city and here. In theory, to have shipped it over Nattviken would have been difficult, the causeway in the north end of this western canal is a barrier to this. However, the details aside, the bridge renovating project proceeds according to plan. The bridge element has arrived and the crane is about to lift it in place.

Further: the winter now is firmly here. When I go out I see a landscape of snow. It has been, and will be minus centigrade for some time now. The snow is not in danger of melting from one day to another.

In this city people usually don't ride the bike in this climate. They rather walk. However, I personally like biking, even in winter. Of course, with all the snow there are parts you can't negotiate riding, you have to get off and steer the bike. However, overall the snow clearance squad keeps cycle lanes and sidewalks (and roads in general) reasonably passable so biking in winter is no big deal, I do it, I thrive doing it. Biking is in sync with my kind of rhythm.

13/1

Yesterday I was out walking at 1 PM. Then I saw a historical sight: the crane lorry had lifted the drawbridge in place. The gap was bridged.

I could confirm it on my morning walk today, in blistering cold, the building site lit by sharp, artificial white light. The bridge element was in place, the prospectively movable part of the drawbridge proper was put in place. As a side-note I could see that the crane lorry had more than ten wheels, it was sixteen actually. Built to lift a heavy load indeed. "Havator" it read on the vehicle, yellow capital letters on blue, probably not a vehicle brand name, more likely the crane service company.

According to the city hall website the bridge should be in function by February. Then Storgatan will be opened for traffic, then they can tear down the causeway, then the drawbridge shall be up and running. It'll be interesting to see them test it, having the bridge tilt up in the sky to let boats pass in the canal. That's the whole point of a drawbridge, that's the crux of this project, that's the reasonably advanced character of it.

15/1

Stock market going down, the dollar is in danger, Cassandras talk about a major crash. But this we've often heard during the last eight years. So I'd say, there won't be a crash. The world is about to change, from materialism to idealism, from Kali Yuga to Sat Yuga, and there might be some friction in the process. But there won't be starvation and such. The world will persevere. We're in the lap of the gods.

16/1

The Great Divide is looming. The separation between people that are (1) meditating and willpower-driven, predominantly Service to Others oriented (STO) and acknowledging their inner light; the other part, the (2) section of people, are those denying willpower, instead being ruled by fear and desire, uttering it in systematic irony and sarcasm, people being predominantly STS oriented. STS means "Service to Self," concept by courtesy of *The Law of One*.

This is the divide mankind is heading for. To be on the right side of the Great Divide, that's the burning question for the times we're in, the next 30-100 years or so. After them the Golden Age will be here since negative people, the STS bunch, very likely will have relocated to another plane of existence. They can't match the platform of emerging spirituality.

18/1

Have read *Bloody Beaches* by Delano Stagg. American original 1961, Swedish edition 1979. Calvin Hobbes leads a company of Marines. He's a hero receiving the Congressional Medal of Honor for his exploits on Tarawa. After the war he's aiming for a political career. As an infantry commander this prospect makes him a bit too calculating, a little too restrained. And finally, on Iwo Jima in 1945, he loses it and orders a retreat when the unit in fact has an advantage over the Japanese. Instead, platoon leader Don Avery takes command of the company.

While not utterly original in every respect I must say that *Bloody Beaches* is exemplary. The author knows what he writes about, the detail work is good, and in the 156 pages the soldiers in question have time to visit both Guadalcanal, Tarawa, Saipan, Guam, and not least Iwo Jima. This is value for money. It's much tighter and better than Norman Mailer's *The Naked and the Dead* which also takes place in the Pacific War. As a war writer you must portray the battle and this Stagg does. Mailer only gives us one measly patrol.

Patrols and commando raids, this war writers generally give us in loads. Stagg for his part has one (1) raid in his book, an amphibious raid against a radar station on an island in the Mariana Islands (Chapter 8). But this is only ten pages: tight and well-written. The rest of the fighting has level, complexity. Stagg hasn't cheated us, hasn't taken any discernible shortcuts.

A quote? Maybe from the beginning of Chapter 9, which might not be notable in itself, no stylistic class act, however, it shows two things, namely that Stagg narrates artlessly and straight and that he knows the details of the workings of the war machine. Personally, I discreetly enjoy lines like these:

> *The First Ranger Regiment was reformed to the 4th Marine Corps battalion. It became part of the 1st Provisional Marine Corps Brigade and attacked Guam in late July, 1944, after for seven weeks having been shipped around in warm troop carriers to form a floating reserve at the invasion of Saipan.* [translated from the Swedish edition, page 86]

Not everyone may be immediately enchanted by this. But what to quote then? There are no stylistic outings, no prose poetry goodies to pick here. It's just a crisp narrative and this is good enough for me. This is the book for the reader tired of the thick-as-a-brick novel with banterings and self-conscious jargon. This book is something of an unknown quantity, a gem that illustrates the old motto *Ars ist Artem Celare*: "art is about concealing your art."

An interesting sub-theme of the novel is the political ambitions of the original company commander, Calvin Hobbes. He represents *the political officer*. Not the politruk à la Soviétique but the man who, after a stint at the front, makes a career in politics, building his reputation on bravery in the field. Combat background indeed is a plus in US politics, exploited by people like John McCain, John Kerry and George H. W. Bush. Another high example is George Custer who had ties to the Democrats, hoping that Little Big Horn would catapult him to the White House. Then of course you have such as U. S. Grant, Eisenhower and Colin Powell, in one way or another making use of their service backgrounds in their political careers.

On film, there's a good picture of a political soldier in John Ford's *The Horse Soldiers* (1959). The larger attack he participates in, the higher the aspirations of this particular officer become: "Now I can run for the state legislature... the House of Representatives... the Senate... the White House!" This is a recurrent theme throughout the film.

22/1

Join me in the light. Or do whatever you want. Will is free. I can't force you.

26/1

Quote of the day, found on the net: "Faith moves mountains, but only knowledge moves them into the right place."

True that. Still, note the sequence: faith must be around first, it must move the mountain. Then faith may hire a consultant for the details, like "putting it in place".

30/1

My new book *Borderline* is now in circulation. It can be bought on relevant internet bookstores and I've received my author copy.

Mighty fine it looks with the Caspar David Friedrich painting on the cover, the image of "The Abbey in the Oakwood".

The temple of Tradition, now a ruin, is ready to be reanimated for a new era, as it were. The full title of the book is *Borderline – A Traditionalist Outlook for Modern Man*. It gives a survey of the perennial thought of Plato and Plotinos, esoteric symbolism, and how this is the fundamental for Western thought. This symbolic tradition was passed down by luminaries like Goethe and Jünger and this is also mirrored in the book, along with a critique of reductionist natural science lacking this Platonic, eidetic, "causal sphere" element. The essay also has chapters on esoteric Christianity, ethics and art, all within the framework of the Tradition intimated in the title.

On my blog I've pushed the book. The post in question is from January 14, 2016, where I for instance write:

> "*Borderline – A Traditionalist Outlook for Modern Man is an attempt at unifying Man with God, Action with Being and the East with the West. In its pages are eradicated the dualism of the thinker and the thought, the dreamer and the dreamed, the doer and the deed. At the beginning of the 21st century Man stands in a transit zone between reductionism and holism, between materialism and idealism, a glorified grey area in which only an old-new esotericism, a revived tradition of spirituality, will show the way ahead. Borderline is the main document in this respect, a clarion call for a resurgent Philosophy of Being in a time of decay.*"

Hereby some polemical quotes from the book:

> "*Scientists dream about "a theory of everything". But we'll never find the answer strictly theoretically. We must realize that we ourselves are co-creators of the Cosmos. The future is open because will is free. And once we realize that, then we might be "given access to the quiet chamber where God ponders the objects.""*(Södergran).
> [Chapter 7, Anthropic Principle]

"Ideas of the eternal quality of the essence of man, of his True Self, will come to the fore in the new era we're heading for, the Sat Yuga of truth. In all courtesy I say, acknowledge this aspect of reality, give room for it and join me in the Light." [Chapter eleven, Veda Philosophy]

"Today the Zeitgeist is in the throes of (...) chaos and confusion. A new sense of order is needed, a responsibility for the things in life that promote structure and harmony. In short, we need a more spiritual, holistic outlook." [Chapter seventeen, The Chaotic Mindset]

The format of the book is trade paperback, the number of pages is 234 and the publishing label is Numen Books.

4/2

When I took a walk at six this morning it was still dark. Temperature: minus 3 centigrade, feeling colder though, it being rather damp. I went down to the Cobbled Place and looked out over the snowy expanse of Nattviken.

Standing there I noted that the Nybro Bridge still had its decoration of LED lights, a silvery streak, a heartwarming winter symbol. On the right, on its hillock, the Härnösand cathedral sat white and classic, illuminated by its spotlights, the round arches of the towers and the plastered façade as an eternal eye catcher of this city.

I stood between two birches, leafless. The cobblestones in question weren't visible, they were covered by snow.

5/2

Yesterday I stood looking out at the Nybro Bridge. The one decorated with LED lights. This is one of the bridges connecting the city island with the mainland. Then we have the other bridge, closer by my home, situated on the street I live by, Storgatan: the Western Canal Bridge, the one being rebuilt.

As told above it was demolished in the autumn, last year, and had its bridgehead fundamentals recast before Christmas. In January the bridge element proper, the to-be movable, foldable drawbridge, was put in place. The other day I looked out the window and saw a concrete mixer truck stand by the western fundamental, pouring concrete. So now they're casting again, probably doing some additional work on the bridgehead part.

They say it will all be completed this month and maybe they succeed in this, in having the bridge open for traffic soon. Then, as I've understood, in the springtime, they will test the machinery and see if it works, if the bridge actually folds.

Thus my musings. And now, in a local monthly, *Yippie Härnösand* No 1/2016, I read some clarifying facts about the project:

- It will be completed by Week 7, the week beginning at February 15. Before the bridge is opened for traffic, a test opening will take place.
- When the bridge element arrived at the harbor after being shipped from its assembly in Poland, it came in two pieces. When in place, the two pieces of the bridge were welded together. (This confirms my suspicions; this was the only way to transport the object on lorries through town. The whole drawbridge, the foldable element, is something like 8x15 meters and that's a substantial piece, impossible to ship on one lorry, much less through a town.)
- The whole canal site will be completed by May 15, with the planting of surrounding lawns and trees, the removing of the causeway and such.

ACTIONISM

6/2

December and January are behind me. A slightly comatose feeling is always present in those months, the above intimated Cosmic Christmas Calm. Now we're moving on, now that "restful" atmosphere is slowly lifting. Leaving lethargy, heading for energy.

7/2

David Bowie died earlier this year. I've listened to his songs over the years. Here's my remarks on some of his albums, mostly 1970s works.

In short, my favorite Bowie albums are *Low*, *Heroes*, *Ziggy Stardust*, *Pin-Ups*, *Station to Station*, *Diamond Dogs* and *Aladdin Sane*.

Comments: *Low* and *Heroes*, I appreciate for the sake of the experimental strain, the soundscapes, the suggestive mood à la Tangerine Dream, Vangelis and Florian Fricke. Songs like "Warszawa," "Art Decade" and "Subterraneans" (*Low*) and "Sense of Doubt," "Moss Garden" and "Neuköln" (*Heroes*) are my favorites. Of course the title song of *Heroes* is also a stand-out (English version; when he made a version mixing German and French it wasn't so successful). Magic from the first chord about living in the enclave of Berlin, an island in the stream and a city in a dream. "Berlin isn't a place, it's a state of mind" they said in the era of the Wall and this track captures it.

Ziggy Stardust: the title song, a pop legend in nuce, Bowie celebrating his own genius by creating the Ziggy alias. It's like Jesus Christ Superstar: difficult to distinguish the man from the myth...! The songs "Moonage Daydream" and "Starman" exploit the space theme, perfect pop, happy songs. "Suffragette City" and "R & R Suicide" are a little tougher, providing a balance between light and shade.

Pin Ups: the first Bowie LP I heard. I didn't know what "covers" were back then so the Bowie versions of "Sorrow" and "See Emily

Play" were the norm for me until I heard the originals. Good covers, however, Bowie is in fine shape throughout on this record. Creatively this might have been a throw-away; if so, *beautifully* so.

Station to Station: the title song begins as a soundscape, then gradually evolves into a normal song. The more consistent sound sculpting arrived on the next album, *Low*.

Aladdin Sane: "Panic in Detroit" and "The Jean Genie" are songs that still stand. The former poppy, the latter rougher.

Diamond Dogs: the title song, "Rebel Rebel" and "1984" are noteworthy, especially the latter, sounding dramatic as it should be, the theme of "now dictatorship is behind the corner, woe and horror".

And finally, out of competition, the song "Life on Mars" from *Hunky Dory*, 1971. An epic song. As such, the text is difficult to decode, probably this is so-called "spontanistic lyrics," Bowie merely having pieced together lines sounding good, being able to be sung, lines that doesn't mean anything as a whole. Abba singer Annifrid Lyngstad did a Swedish cover of this, not so successful; however, an alluring song to take on, a crooning number, riding quite high in the pitch. The Bowie version is the only version to speak of; one of his finest moments. Finally, as for stand-out Bowie songs, we have "Space Oddity" from 1969, a drama in nuce, capturing the "step out into space" like no other opus. Maybe barring the film *2001*.

13/2

Suddenly I seem to receive less spam, less e-mails of the kind "lend easy money". Has the world's "financial elite" run out of cash? Other sources indicate that, like signs of imminent Dollar crash, the death of the petro dollar, behind-the-scenes turmoil in the US governance etc. However, in contrast to most pundits I don't see this leading to "police state, war, bloody revolution". Again, the zeitgeist is against it. Some turmoil might lie ahead us but essentially, we're "in the lap of the gods" as Queen sang.

ACTIONISM

15/2

At 0600 this morning I took a walk to the Cobbled Place. It was still dark. Nattviken was still iced-over, it being minus 6 centigrade.

As always I looked at the surroundings – to the right, on the island, the city proper and then (to the left and in front of me) the more dispersed buildings on the mainland, such as a restaurant, warehouses and such. And, in the distance to the north, the chimney of the heating plant was towering, smoke drifting from it to the south, the high structure itself adorned with two red beacons, a warning for airplanes, like a staring giant in the night.

We have long-distance heating in this town, most facilities in the town proper having their houses heated by a water-borne system, by ducts emanating from this plant. I myself am connected to the system, I have a water element, several in fact, heating elements functioning by streaming water, warm in, lukewarm out. So, to sum up, the tower I see in the distance and the facility to go with it, this I have to thank for my apartment being warm. I'm slightly impressed by the engineering ingenuity of it all, of heating the whole town with one (1) facility.

17/2

The Westworld seems to be in a state of severe angst right now. Panic is the word. If it isn't Planet Nibiru as an evil portent in the sky, it's war scare, the fear of a Dollar collapse, a "run on the banks," empty shelves in the supermarket and whatnot.

Ruling out the more cosmic chaos factors of course there could still be economic turmoil and such but overall, I'd say, tone down the panic. Panic essentially emanates from chaos people, unrestrained fellows with no order inside. It's all in the mind and some mindfulness wouldn't hurt.

More on the chaotic mindset and its remedy in *Borderline*, chapter seventeen. A passage delineating what I mean with "the chaotic mindset" is this:

A person applying the Chaotic Mindset is negative, nihilistic, ironic, materialistic, atheistic and spiritually passive, having a penchant for apathy. A man with a Chaotic Mindset is an actor having chaos inside him and projecting it to the outer world, affecting people to become passive nihilists and defeatists too. The Chaotic Mindset can engender the roles of a warmonger ("a major war will break out and we're all going to die"), a pessimist ("there's no use in trying, it has been done before, all that exists is the death of the body and the decay of matter") and a reductionist, denying the validity of the holistic paradigm, spiritualism and esotericism ("materialist science has brought us tangible affluence and welfare, spiritualism for its part is about chimaeras"). The Chaotic Mindset, prevalent in a materialist denying the Inner Realm, prevents the understanding of the concept of God being within, of the individual soul being part of the Allsoul. A man with a Chaotic Mindset conceives God as an external force – and since he can't discern God in the outer world, then he thinks he has disproven the existence of God for all time. [Borderline, p 140]

18/2

Yesterday afternoon I looked out the window. I saw this: the drawbridge in the "up" position. It folds, it works. Hurray.

It folds up, it folds down – for when I just looked outside the bridge was down again.

Not a major accomplishment from a cosmic point of view, however, it's good to see things completed.

From an information leaflet I just got I gather the following. – On Saturday there'll be a short, formal inauguration. In the summer, a more festive opening ceremony will be held. In May the canal will open for boat traffic.

20/2

I have bridged the gap. I have walked over the new Western Canal Bridge.

It's open for traffic now. That is, some fences remain and the opening ceremony will be held later today but essentially it's done, it's completed. During my morning walk I went to see it, to take a walk on it. Nice to walk Storgatan into town, to see the Dome from the proper view. Nice to stand on the bridge looking up at Mount Vårdkasberget in the south, the one with the ski slope and the wind mill.

Maybe I'm reading too much into this but it feels like a gap has been bridged, figuratively. "A bridge over the gap separating the old from the new" as I have been intimating in earlier reports. It's the same feeling of completion you get when a novel is done.

- - -

I took an afternoon walk to Erikshjälpen Second Hand. Grey sky, grey mountains in the distance. And on the quay being my goal, grey storehouses. My specific target was a cream yellow house.

As intimated, it's nice to visit a second hand bookseller even if you don't buy anything. You look at books, noting titles, deliberating, letting the thoughts wander. However, this day I did find books to buy. They were all in Swedish but corresponding English titles would be *Literary Essays of Ezra Pound* (ed. T. S. Eliot) and August Strindberg's *A Blue Book* and *The New Kingdom* plus a latter day anthology of Strindberg stories and excerpts. Strindberg could be shrill and insistent but at the same time he had energy and drive and a large vocabulary. I've just read his novel *Tschandala*, about a subhuman and his superior; details aside a vigorous, well-crafted story.

As for Pound he was a traditionalist with an attitude. I've read some of his Cantos and essays on the craft of poetry and they were worth the effort.

Headwind on my way home. General impression: still snowy, still wintry.

22/2

On esoteric websites these days you can read rumors of "disclosure," a global currency re-evaluation and a supposedly imminent restructuring of the US governance, ousting the "corporate" government having usurped it and returning it to its lawful, constitutional basis.

In short, rumors abound.

- - -

This town is surrounded by forested mountains, mountains with coniferous forest. When there's snow in the air these mountains turn grey. When the air is clear they have a more dark-green hue. Needless to say I prefer the look of these darker mountains.

23/2

Reportedly, China has stopped pegging the yuan to the dollar. Instead, the yuan will be backed by a basket of other currencies. This could affect the dollar, maybe even collapse it. Rumors, rumors.

26/2

Again I hear the rumor, from a different source than in November, that the world's currencies are back on the gold standard. Exciting times.

28/2

In minus 10 centigrade a morning walk, seeing by the theater an empty bottle of Southern Comfort: cold comfort.

Zero degree, malvern sky. Standing on the Cobbled Place the mountains at the horizon were invisible, the city ending in a rosy grey haze beyond Hernö Marina.

- - -

Grey day, wet snow falling. Weather-wise, it's not a lovely day.

5/3

Snow and more snow. Enough with snow!

- - -

The soul is constantly in a state of Being; the everyday mind is constantly in a state of Doing. Unite them and you get Action as Being, that is, to seek rest in action = RIA.

7/3

Reportedly, all the worlds' currencies are now asset backed = gold backed. It's said to have happened on 3/3, 2016. Also, since last year the US Federal Reserve is a governmental agency (and not a private one, symbolized in its web address now ending .gov and not .org). This and other rumors in the economic sphere could mean "the beginning of the end" of bankster rule and a dawn for a more honest monetary system.

The "asset backing" was finalized when the Chinese came aboard, it's said. The backing was implemented at 08:08:08:08, Beijing Time.

Which should mean, "hour, minute, second, hundredth of a second". Computers may allow for such a precision. – The number 8 is a lucky number in China. Like, they had the 2008 Summer Olympics in Beijing begin on August 8 = 08.08.08. Incidentally, as I'm writing this I'm having a snack from an octagonal plate, a "sushi style" black glass plate.

8/3

I act, therefore I am. "Ago, ergo sum," that's Action as Being, that's Actionism in nuce.

No one can abstain from acting. I act, therefore I am.

9/3

Those in the know say that "the Continental United States of America" is the legal, historical USA founded in 1783. "The corporate US," for its part, is a co-opted, illegal regime having ruled the US since 1913. There seems to be some struggle going on between these two. But as long as the current president stays in power the Corporate US remains. For instance, if the military would seize power by a coup (and hand it over to "the Continental US") it would present some legal difficulties.

As for the global re-evaluation mentioned on 7/3, this seems to mean that the Chinese yuan now is the world's reserve currency instead of the dollar.

- - -

I act, therefore I am. "Ago, ergo sum." No one can abstain from acting – not me, not you, not even a meditating recluse – no one. Even the "zazen, âsana yoga quietist" must breathe.

To breathe, and to control your breath, is to act. Thus, we all act, we all conduct operations. *Ago, ergo sum*. Affirm this and be an operational pro, always successful, always triumphant, always a winner in the game of life – winning by controlling your breath – by taking gentle breaths, not forced ones. Control your breath and control the world.

14/3

Thaw. The snow melts somewhat.

I had a bizarre dream. I was given an identification card allowing me to visit a military ship, a naval vessel. Then I got to climb a steep ladder to get aboard, an excruciatingly tough climb it was. "This is a test" I thought and finally, I made it.

Next I had to pass a guard by a table, wishing to see my ID. I had indeed been given this card but now I couldn't find it. I searched my bag but it was nowhere to be found. I unloaded a lot of stuff but the card just wasn't there, neither in my wallet. Deep angst. Then I said, "Will I be shot for this?"

"Probably" was the answer.

"Well go ahead," I said, "I don't mind it!"

So I'd say, an angst-ridden dream, the punchline however rather apt. Bushido lived by my dream self.

The dream was not about serving, it was about visiting a naval ship, however, it was about the angst associated with serving. To be a soldier or a naval sailor is about facing death – and the whole gamut of regimentation, rules, giving and receiving orders, inspections etc. is about controlling death angst, as it were. Small wonder, then, that when I in the dream had to unload my bag I found pictures of war planes in it. They were just there as a matter of course, a discreet reminder of war-as-angst. Also in this scene, I remember seeing a funny looking tracked vehicle, a model of an armored personnel carrier, rather wide and spacious though overall looking very "military". I couldn't recognize the make so I decided it was a type belonging to the current Italian army. Thus my dream reasoning. And then I woke up.

17/3

Mild and clear weather, rather windy. Spring is in the air even though there will be some setbacks, there always are in late March and April. "Spring Snow," as was the title of a Mishima novel = a symbol of transience. Change, change, it's all rearranging.

30/3

This night, a jumbled, chaotic dream; however, it was rather positive, no nightmare. It was on the theme of "let's take a balloon ride, let's go to Majorca, let's go to fantasy land, we can do it if we all intend it".

Yesterday I went to Erikshjälpen Second Hand, just another senseless outing, just a way to get around and browse the shelves. I bought Stig Dagerman's *Ormen*, a 1940s novel on angst and such, artistically rather elaborate. Tailwind when I went there, headwind on my way home, wintry cold – but the atmosphere at large these days is rather promising, spring is in the air, much of the snow has melted.

- - -

At half past six in the morning, a promenade to the Cobbled Place. The spot as such was bare, the cobbles could be seen. The flanking birches: still leafless. The sound of Nattviken: still covered by ice. The expanse at large and the shores beyond: covered by fog. The temperature rather mild, well above zero centigrade.

1/4

Recently I published the book *Borderline*. See the entry for 30/1. Now the Finnish website Sarastus has published a review of the book. The author of the piece, Markku Siira, sent me an English translation of the text which I then published on my blog Svenssongalaxen on 10/3. In it, Siira noted the prevalent pessimism in national-radical and traditionalist circles. They see only Kali Yuga, not the end of it. Then Siira has this:

> "Apparently one needs to be born Swedish to achieve a particular mixture of bright optimism and traditionalism, as is the case with Lennart Svensson. Svensson, who was born in 1965, is a writer who in addition to his Swedish works has previously written English portraits on Ernst Jünger and the composer Richard Wagner. Svensson lives in Northern Sweden, and has a degree in Indology; in the course of these studies, Svensson became convinced of the truth inherent in the Traditionalist school of thought. In 2015, Numen Books published Svensson's latest book Borderline: A Traditionalist Outlook for Modern Man. I purchased this book after reading Svensson's blog and after having followed his Facebook updates, which interested me, but also irritated me somewhat because of his lavish future optimism and excessive esoteric syncretism. However, it is at times broadening to step beyond one's own stubborn trains of thought, and read something different."

Siira next, among other things, notes the broad perspective of the book, encompassing art, philosophy, science and morality as well as depicting a cavalcade of artistic and philosophical "borderline cases" like Goethe, Carl Jung, Swedenborg, T. S Eliot and Edith Södergran. Then, in view of this, the pay-off:

> "Despite this breathtaking character cavalcade, Svensson's work is held together by a clear red thread of perennial philosophy. This thread bridges together the holy writings of the Indian Bhagavad Gita, Christian mysticism, as well as Western arts and sciences. Svensson has also read his Julius Evola, and encourages readers to give him a chance, even in the midst of our seeming chaos and nihilism, for a world-view based on order and balance, as well as for the meditative "I AM"-way of life. As is always the case in human spiritual development, everything starts with oneself; this is

how the Evolian spirit of nobility can be excavated from under the internal indolence through esoteric knowledge and active action."

2/4

My brother Robert is dead. I was notified of this on Wednesday, March 30. He died in sleep of a stroke, apparently. He was two years older than me. He had experienced milder strokes before. His grandfather died in the same way.

Robert was an artist. About 50-100 of his oil paintings and aquarelles of Norrland motifs are hanging in Swedish homes.

3/4

List without comment: authors I've met IRL and exchanged a few words with. – Bertil Mårtensson, Erik Granström, Sam J. Lundwall, Sten Andersson, David Brin, Alf Yngve, Katarina Bjällerstedt Mickos, Erik Andersson, David Nessle, Maths Claesson, Johan Frick, Peter Englund.

5/4

Yesterday I spent drawing a map. It's for a fantasy I've written; manuscript done, now the map is done too. The map came out fine but I'm glad that I don't have to sit down for projects like this every day, doing fine lettering and inking etc., making sense of a cosmic vision on an A3 sheet. – Made up names for this world that I'm proud of, they sound kind of apt: Frockory, Ninoltaya, Dorylaon, Nustara, Telladan, Stricaria, Ditteli, Rinsehamn (these were place names; now for personal names): Torarin, Atyescha, Bigelon, Herstal, Sacrovir, Eofor, Andradion, Lobring.

- - -

List without comment: authors I've seen IRL (figures I've merely seen, not spoken to): Brian Aldiss, Jon Courtenay Grimwood, William Kennedy, Paul Davies, James Gleick, Ola Larsmo.

6/4

On the Manticore Press site there was recently a review of *Borderline*. In it, N.M. Phoenix praises the book's synthesis of holism, anti-reductionism and mysticism. The survey of perennially minded, traditionally inclined authors treated in the book is also appreciated:

> "The ending chapters cover Nietzsche and a few profound poets whom portray Tradition and holistic thought. It is difficult for me to reiterate his chapter on Nietzsche, which also discusses Evola in depth, but it is certainly one of the best chapters. It ties in much of what was recently mentioned and its relevance to the teachings of both Evola and Nietzsche. Following this chapter is a discussion on Södergran, T.S. Eliot, Freidrich, Swedenborg, and Jünger respectively. These were no less enjoyable chapters, and I have personally fell in love with Södergran whom I was unaware of until this work."

As a coda of the review Phoenix has this:

> "Borderline by Svensson is worth reading, contemplating, and applying in practice. Even weeks later I recall parts and allows me to shift how one thinks about things. It is an excellent survey of Perennialism, and is filled aplenty with writers and philosophers to further study. Think of it as a college course, or lecture, and contemplate the content. It is well worth the time and effort."

- - -

The ultimate way to pursue a hobby is to be "armchair active". Example: instead of building a model railroad you read books and magazines about it. This has many upsides. (1) Low cost; you only buy the odd book and magazine, no actual objects and gadgets. (2) Storage; most hobbies tend to have storage problems but to store a few books is easy. (3) You don't need to show off your hobby as you otherwise get the urge to do with your collection of X, your railroad layout or whatever.

To be armchair active in this way is a *conceptual* way to pursue a hobby, a way to do it by constant planning, imagination and dreaming. It's subtle, it's ideal in the Platonic sense.

Personally I was active casting, painting and collecting, even sculpting tin soldiers in my late teens. Nowadays, I'm satisfied reading books on the subject. In the process I've even increased my appreciation for plastic soldiers, once seen as a degeneration of the model soldier, however, figures like Herald and Britains Deetail were exquisitely well sculpted and painted. Overall, miniature soldiers have the upside of being easily stored.

7/4

Standing by Nattviken earlier this morning I saw a clear horizon and scattered clouds. A nice change from a week of fog and rain.

- - -

My brother Robert Svensson was born in May, 1963, and he died in March, 2016. He was 52 when he died. He was an artist, a painter in aquarelle and oil on canvas and privately active as a draughtsman (pencil, ink). He was educated at the art department of Wik Folkhögskola for two separate years (1984-1985; 1986-87). In the 1990s he had exhibitions at Galleri Dombron, Uppsala, at Café Mannaminne, Nordingrå and at his own Galleri Söråsele, Åsele, to mention the most important exhibitions.

He was an artist at heart, a born creator of pictures. It's true that he also was a rather fine writer; for instance, when studying at

Uppsala University in the late 1980s and 1990s writing essays and papers came easy to him. However, I'd say: writing was a game to him but pictorial shaping was serious. He lived and breathed all the aspects of painting and drawing, pondering nuances and coloring, the color of the sky, the color of shadows etc. etc.– as well as different styles of drawing comics, of composing frames in movies et cetera. For instance, maybe he told me or I told him that David Lynch's TV series *Twin Peaks* was filmed in studios with ceilings, inner roofs, making the scenes more homely, a feature absent in all the other TV dramas and comedies since way back.

Such a feature, watching TV and noting how the scenography was composed, this could occupy him endlessly. He was something of a glorified loiterer and drifter, having a hard time to get going with some projects. "I'll get into it, next day, I promise" he could say. And yet he did deliver, like the covers he drew for my Swedish novels *Antropolis* and *Till Smaragdeburg.* I envisioned the layout and he implemented it, doing fine lettering and adding drawings.

He had his lazy traits but he also was a go-getter, taking charge. Like leading his rock band the Neurones in the 80s and 90s. They performed live here and there and did some demos and recordings, like having a song on a Spanish anthology album. When googling it now I can't find it. However, the point is that when leading his band he could take charge and be a musical inspirer and leader at the same time. He played guitar and sang and career-wise this didn't lead that long but the demos (I still have copies of them, some 10-15 songs) had a lot of flair and pizazz. He was a musical man, a man led by the Muses, the Greek gods of poetry, song and art.

He also liked to read (Tolkien, the odd sf tale, fairy tales, books on art, comics) but his main interest along with art was *music*. With a basis in new wave rock and pop he also cherished jazz, ambient and whatnot, even the odd Swedish *dansband* song and heavy metal song. Subsisting on his paper route work he could "waste" away his days by playing records, drinking coffee, drawing...

As for me and Rob (as he was called) we were rather close from our early childhood and until about the year 2000. When we were young we played with cowboys and Indians and toy cars, we drew and played games, we assembled plastic models, all of it having some aesthetic quality, that of appreciating the very layout and feel of the game, or, that of building dioramas and giving an illusion of reality, a constant art project going on for ever – like, I'm personally still at it, writing novels that are some sort of conceptual dioramas. – We lived in Övik, Ångermanland where we went to school, and then in the late 80s we reconvened in Uppsala where we both studied and had our respective student bedsits. The meetings we had during these years could be rather far apart, however, in some ways they were essential, we bonded, we inspired each other with that odd line or fact. Then, after the millennium, we kind of drifted apart. Not that I criticize him but at the end he became rather lethargic, like not answering letters.

He died of a stroke and he experienced a slight stroke last year too, this could be an indication of his general state. I wouldn't say he faded away, he did work with his paper route to the end, distributing morning papers to homes with his bike and for this you need some condition. However, he became a bit aloof, a bit "dormant" at the end.

I still think of him every day, as I've almost always have. But we'll meet again, that's the logic of reincarnation, "no meeting is the first, no goodbye is the last" as Dénis Lindbohm said. The soul is energy and energy can't be destroyed, only transformed into another physical state.

8/4

I don't remember what I dreamed last night. Jumbled dreams, over and over. I have some way to go before I'm in the "willpower-controlled dream" state.

- - -

Worldly memes useful for the esotericist: curb your enthusiasm – be cool – prepare to die and follow me.

- - -

"What you can create you can control." And I've created the Svensson persona, now I will control it in the conceptual lands ahead. Like, if I recite "tat satyam, så âtmâ, tat tvam asi" and envision something, then I become that vision.

9/4

A Facebook friend today shares this quote: "I drank the silence of God from a spring in the woods." (Georg Trakl)

10/4

When creating an art work you should strive for perfection. However, total perfection can never be attained since only God is perfect.

Art is never about "depicting it as it is". Art is always about interpretation, reduction and profiling, plus adding something of your own. Take, for instance, a statue, a bronze casted depiction of a man. They are never strictly humanely proportioned. Either they are elongated or a bit compressed in their proportions. There is no one, singular way of doing it. There has always got to be some interpretation and stylization. On the other hand, if you can depict perfectly "as it is," you must be God.

When posting this on the net a friend supplied this line, from author Torbjörn Säfve writing about artist Iván Augeli: "denature in order to accentuate". That sums it up rather well, how an artist has to stylize and give an interpretation of the motif.

11/4

Actionism is a holistic creed, a moral creed footed in ontology. The ontology of Actionism says that the essential reality is invisible, consisting of patterns copied in the material, tangible world. I mentioned this in chapter seven, "Metaphysical Action". More on the subject, of how Actionism is footed in perennial ontology, ontology and idealism, is given in my essay *Borderline* (2015). This text for instance says that we have to see the Whole first; conversely, like Descartes to try to prove God by deduction is dishonest.

Moreover, in the biological realm, the Gestalt of the whole, given by the Platonic idea, shapes the organism, not the DNA molecule. The DNA of a cell is reportedly the same in a leg cell and an arm cell so DNA can't give us the shape of the whole organism.

Symbols and Gestalts are representations of the Idea, of *das Urbild*. The Ideas rest in the causal sphere, from there projecting order and reality into the everyday world.

Essential Reality consists of these kind of ideas and patterns. No one can put himself above this Reality, this *Sein*. We're all beings in this reality, in German, *Seiendes im Sein*. You can't exclude the *Sein* of yourself when examining the *Sein* of the universe. This is pointed out by German philosopher Hugo Fischer who is a recurring figure of the book, as is the Platonic philosopher Plotinus as well as Goethe and Ernst Jünger. They all embraced the ontology of idealism, of invisible patterns governing nature and man.

You can't, as modern science tends to do, reduce everything into something else. This is impossible. Gödel's theorem forbids it. An organism can't be reduced to a machine. An organism functions holistically, a machine functions serially.

You can't understand the human mind by dissecting the brain. In the same vein, you can't understand the phenomenon of radio transmitting by taking a radio apart. You have to know about radio waves.

- - -

Some more memories of my brother...

He liked westerns, the Wild West myth as an iconographic phenomenon; to us being born in the 60s westerns were a staple diet in comics, films and TV series. A favorite comic of his was Lucky Luke, a French western comic series. And soon, when I inherit Robert's Britains Deetail figures, 54 mm cowboy figures, I will think of him. They will be constant reminders of his being, a kind of memorial statuettes.

When building plastic models his favorite was planes, WWII planes. He had an *aerial* trait – for in addition to this, he wrote his Bachelor of Art degree paper about the bird paintings of Swedish artists Lars Jonsson and Gunnar Brusewitz. And my father said that, in his last phone conversation with him on March 26, Robert said that he would go out later and look at the birds. In spring the migratory birds return to Sweden, the snow-free and drying, soon-to-sprout lands, having some wealth of bird life.

He's standing in the Uppsala plain, looking at the birds... a worthy image of the man he was. "I'm far, far away, with my head up in the clouds..."

- - -

A non-event in my non-life.

I go out. Then I do some errands. Then I go home. Halfway home I notice I have no gloves. Now where did I lose them? No matter where, I haven't got the energy to go back and search for them. Here today, gone tomorrow; that's my strategic decision, standing downtown in this state. Then I go home. Then I see the gloves lying on the hat rack.

You could say that this is a story with the moral, "sometimes laziness wins" – like, I didn't go back to diverse places making a fool of myself asking for lost gloves that weren't there. No gloves lost, no fool made.

12/4

More memories of my brother...

His favorite pop band was Echo and the Bunnymen.

His favorite Swedish comics artist was Jan Lööf.

He liked the memoir books by Swedish artist Peter Dahl. Robert wasn't so much into Dahl's art per se but he liked the way he told of his artistic career in autobiographical books (*Kanske konstnär* etc.). Specifically, he appreciated Dahl's lifelong project of creating a fantasy land with tin soldiers, toy cars, a model railroad and model houses, the land "Caribanien," a virtual masterpiece of conceptual art.

Robert was a blond, Nordic guy, about 178 centimeters tall, of a somewhat compact build. He was a man of the "pyknic, athletic" type, not the "leptosome, slim" type like me. We indeed looked akin but we were of different somatic models.

I mention his overall look because in my novel *Antropolis* (2009) I have a chapter where the main character meets up with the artist Tim Parill. Parill's specific look is made up, he's a fiction as such, but his behavior as a distracted artist receiving a guest in his studio is very much based on Robert:

> *"In one of the segment houses lived Parill. Once up on the fourth floor, I entered a bright, lofty atelier, a real studio unlike my own that was just the upstairs floor in my house. A smell of turpentine and oil struck me. I found the master himself seated at a table reading Antropolis News. I bowed slightly and sat down, Parill nodded and stood up. (...) He offered wine, toasted me and asked if I would buy anything – but when I said no, he continued to read his paper. I took the opportunity and looked around in the studio, a spacious room with a ceiling height of three meters. A window only to the north; thus it must be for a painter, this I knew, because the light from the north was smoother than the saturated, flowing, over-the-whole-day-shifting southern light. Everywhere sat canvases; they were both landscapes and abstractions and some individual portraits, all of it unmistakably Parill. There was*

colorism and rich layers of paint, there was the play of forms, there were power lines meeting and parting, there were foaming streams, dark jungles and psychedelic meadows."

The following I say of the studio as such, again not a living portrait but the mix of odd objects is important in giving this artistic portrait:

"In Parill's studio there was much to see. For instance, on a shelf sat a fragment of a Mediterranean pot, certainly with ancient origins; the heartwarming color was light brown, terra di Siena, overlaid by time and having become timeless. The next item was a brass statuette of a dancing Shiva, four-armed and surrounded by a wreath of flames: prabha-mandala as we all know it. Then there was an enamel tea caddy in white and crimson, a tin soldier with faded paint, a miniature horse in green glass and a harlequin doll. Magical things all of them, not directly there to be depicted, rather to be seen as "lightning rods for the invisible, collectors of magical powers"... They helped to create atmosphere, mood, ambiance in the room. They were talismans for the magician he was."

Lastly we have this image of the artist, "very Robert" if I may say so:

"Parill sat and stared into the air. Dust particles danced around in a sunbeam. Then he suddenly got up and went to his easel. From a hanger he picked up a painter coat, black and full of color patches in quaint randomness. He wiped his fingers on it while he painted. I glanced at the canvas, a landscape with a few houses next to a lake and a sun over some mountains on the other side. (...) You could see yellow fields and shady houses, a copper green lake and a blueberry sky. From a tube Parill pressed out some paint onto the palette and seemed to have forgotten my presence. He picked up a brush, approached the canvas and started working at the shadows cast by the houses. He put on green and blue, crossing the brush strokes and having the colors blend. "Shadows are never black," he said. I agreed to this wisdom, bowed and headed for the door."
[Chapter sixteen, "The Artist"]

- - -

People look down on me for being a grey area figure. To them, I only want to say: I'm no faceless titan, spewing out law clauses and figures. I'm a man depicting what he sees and part of this means living in the grey area, the twilight zone, the borderline between art and science, life and thought, power and spirit.

- - -

In the wintertime snow falls. When the snow clearance squad has cleared the streets, the sidewalks and the cycle paths they sprinkle sand over them, as an anti-slip measure. Then, in the springtime when the snow has thawed away, they have to sweep up the sand. Then they filter it from debris and then they can use it again.

Anyway, they sweep up the sand and these are the times, from mid-April and on when there's no snow to talk about, when it has thawed away and the anti-slip sand has no function. They have to be on the safe side, there can be snowfall even in April but from, say, late March and on we have this view of bike lanes which is symbolic: sand on the asphalt, useless sand and grit that tend to cut holes in the bike tires, and then there's the process of sweeping up the sand, it's like sweeping your room, a tidying process, it looks nice when it's done and then there's also some sand left, this is no issue, this is rather quaint, it's the testimony of "winter's gone, spring is here," one of many such along with the blossoming of coltsfoot and scilla, the smell of horse manure spread on the fields and the longer days, the increasing amount of sunshine.

13/4

List without comment; pop groups and rock acts I've seen live: Wilmer X, Sator, The Leather Nun, Imperiet, Neurones, The Shamen, Indochine, Style Council, The Cure, Kajsa och Malena.

ACTIONISM

14/4

I began this diary in October. I did it by saying that I was reading a proof, searching for typos and misspellings in a word-file. I also said that the file – called Project 1 – was a work written on speculation, no one had ordered it by then, no had contracted me for writing it. I just felt like writing it, this study on 20th century science fiction and fantasy, conceived from a conservative point of view. How do writers like Heinlein, Tolkien, Lovecraft, Dick, Ballard etc. etc. look at eternal values like duty, honor, courage, faith, responsibility and self-restraint? That was my angle and in this I was able to deliberate on writers on the fantastic like the above, writers I've been interested in since the early 80s.

Now then. The work, when sent to a certain publisher in January, was appreciated and they offered to publish it. Also, they got going pretty quick in producing it. For instance, by early March I was sent a PDF of the book which I proofread; I didn't mention this in this diary, proofreading isn't much to write about, you just do it. And then there was even more work done by the publisher (like doing the cover, a very fine one) and now, at long last, the book is out. I was notified of it yesterday and I can now look forward to a writer's copy, the reception of which is the "coda, end product and final outcome" of a book project as far as I'm concerned.

This is graduation day, "the day when your kid leaves home". You still have contact with the book (like promoting it) but in essence it's done when it's out and can be bought. You can conceptually-creatively put it behind you. – *Mutatis mutandum*, this is what I put up as a blog entry on Svenssongalaxen yesterday, promoting the book.

- - -

Science Fiction Seen from the Right is now to be bought from an internet bookstore near you. This study examines 20th century SF and fantasy, focusing on works having some discernible relation to

eternal values such as faith, responsibility, duty, honor and courage. The Chapters depict American and European authors like Heinlein, Herbert, Lewis, Tolkien, Jünger, Boye, Howard, Lovecraft, Borges, Pournelle, Dick, Bradbury et cetera. In addition, there are chapters delineating the development of the genre and a look at comics, films and specific themes such as nihilism, history and war.
Some product details:

> Paperback: 378 pages
> Publisher: Manticore Press (March 24, 2016)
> Language: English

Some quotes from the book could come in handy. For instance, this I say about Ray Bradbury:

> *"We all know that Ray Bradbury (1920-2012) was a man longing for years gone by, for the American 1920s with T-Fords, striped cotton suits and icecream sundaes. But this kind of sentimentality can't be tolerated in a study like this. Tradition isn't about being sentimental, it's about acknowledging Eternal Values, values that still can lift us, inspire us and guide us, offering an alternative to the current materialism and nihilism. For in essence, sentimentality is a form of nihilism. Therefore it takes some time to sort out the Bradbury stories having to say something to us even today, stories about Faith, Musicality, Awareness and Courage."* [p 299]

And about H. P. Lovecraft I, for instance, say the following:

> *"Lovecraft had read Oswald Spengler's Decline of the West (1918-1922), an outline saying that the Westworld is doomed, having its best days behind it. Decadence rules and this Lovecraft for instance conceptualized in his New York stories (He, Cool Air, The Horror at Red Hook). He cherished the Colonial times when white anglo-saxons ruled America and he resented the large-scale, 20th century-style immigration; q.v. the short story "The Street," catching in nuce the sociological development of America. Lovecraft was*

ACTIONISM

pretty much against the modern lifestyle and embraced old-school and archaic attitudes aplenty." [p 235]

The following is another take on the subject of nihilism in science fiction:

"[N]ovels like Gene Wolfe's The Book of the New Sun (1980-1983), Sam J. Lundwall's No Time for Heroes (1971) and Harry Harrison's Bill, the Galactic Hero (1965) are all rather enjoyable, the first for its accomplished style, the latter two for their drive and wit. -- That said, to have an executioner as main character (Wolfe) overall leads out into nothingness, as does the banterings of the other two, I figure. A hero is led by Will, Truth and Compassion; an antihero is a symbol of the opposite, of decadence, whose core concept is nihilism. If you accept that, then these books can be estimated at their true value. Just don't come and say that they're some kind of all time, essential classics pointing the way ahead. For this some embracing of ideals is needed, some spiritual elevation." [p 332]

The following I say about Jerry Pournelle's classic of Military SF, *The Prince* (2001):

"Duty, honor and mayhem, portraying "the muddy, bloody business of fighting on the ground". This is one for the grunts, basking in "the everlasting glory of the infantry". This is serving, this is loyalty, this is bonds of friendship, tied in blood; a gust of wind from the archaic, staged in the future. Thus, we again have the archeofuturist strain that often seems to accompany right-wing SF." [p 293]

A portal figure of the book is Robert A. Heinlein. In Chapter one I for instance say this regarding his topical fiction:

"The ideals of olden times are still viable. Self-restraint, self-reliance, responsibility and nobility of character must be remembered and imparted, again and again. And in his 1950s novels Heinlein did

just that. Maybe his later books strayed off into "strange lands" for a right-winger but we must remember that Heinlein remained an anti-communist all his life, bent on opposing the most nihilistic and murderous regime there ever was, this in a time when the mainstream intellectual embraced socialism and collectivism." [p 16]

In other words, this is what you get in *Science Fiction Seen From the Right* – a venturing out into the vistas of wonder and glory, right-wing style.

- - -

That was the blog post. As for this diary, at the beginning I also said that I proofread another file, "Project 2," but this one is still living in the never-never land of "development". Another non-event in my non-life. But I shouldn't complain; for its part, to have the SF book out is a rather fine achievement. I don't need a gold medal for it but indeed, as intimated it was 30 years of reading SF and fantasy and deliberating on it that ended up between its covers.

15/4

Dear diary: I AM.

16/4

List without comment, my diverse likes. Favorite classical composers, Wagner and Bach – Favorite food, vegetarian casserole of the exquisite kind (the kind I cook) – The years when rock and pop music was the most interesting, 1967-1987 – The two best Swedish esoteric writers, Swedenborg and Stagnelius – The five best books by Jünger, *The Adventurous Heart, Eumeswil, WWII Diary, Heliopolis, On the Marble Cliffs* – Best film of the 21st century, *Into the Wild* by Sean Penn.

17/4

I've found a magic moment in my life – any moment, experienced as such in gentle tranquility. Using willpower to calm down, and then I've arrived – in the Sea of Tranquility.

19/4

Cold, grey morning. It was nicer yesterday when I saw this from the Cobbled Place: the sun risen over the island, sun shining over the dome right onto me, then the expanse of Nattviken free from ice, a clear blue mirror, then the buildings on the other shore in transparent lucidity.

- - -

The Universe is female, space is round.

25/4

You don't need a hobby. Merely "staying alive" is hobby enough.

2/5

On April 28 the burial ceremony for my brother was held. It was at Kärlekens kapell by Arnäs kyrka, Ångermanland county, Sweden. It was a dignified ceremony with only family present, where among me.

The white coffin was adorned by wreaths from relatives and friends. For instance, the members of his old band The Neurones had sent a wreath with a poem on the theme of "we rested under a tree, always under a tree," very heartfelt and apt. One of the music pieces played during the ceremony was Freddie Wadling's "Nu lyfter vi från marken," a secular psalm, if you will.

It was a grey day but halfway into the ceremony the sun shone in. That was no coincidence, I say as the estoericist I am.

10/5

Last week I went to Uppsala. We had to clean out Robert's apartment. He was single and his lease has been terminated, his lodging on Tunabackars gård 10 had to be evacuated. We did it in three days, taking every single item and giving away some to charity, taking some for ourselves and throwing away some. Due to "operational security" (q.v. the end of chapter eighteen in this book) I won't give all the details but this was indeed a logistical challenge. We had to coordinate the X number of factors in time and space and work hard.

It was an operation. So given the actionist penchant for operations, what are the lessons? I admit that I dreaded the task. So much had to work, so many elements had to be synchronized. However, I mustered my Will and had a silent pep talk with myself the days before I traveled south. I envisioned that the whole thing would run smoothly. I wanted it to go well and it did.

In any operation you must have alternative options and "plan B's" and this we had. But we didn't look pessimistically on it. It was a case of "get up and go, let's do this thing" and this mentality carried the day. As such, it was an example of "Action as Being".

So indeed, we went operationally ahead. But what of the mourning and the piety? We were in fact dealing with a dead man's estate. To this I'd say, there was reverence around. That said, this event was 90% about getting the job done. It was "now" or never".

Thus, we threw this and that item away, like diverse junk Rob had collected over the years. As an artist he gathered stuff to use in his dioramas and installations and all this had to go to the container marked "combustible". So this cleaning out operation was a mostly unsentimental act. Not entirely though. Personally I didn't feel depressed by the mere occasion of going to the apartment and looking around. It was the first time I visited it although he got it already in 2012. It was a fine habitat, a one-room apartment with green wallpaper. In the living room proper there were also green blinds which created a serene atmosphere. Also, the house and the whole area was built in the 40s, a solid craftsmanship and not some prefab notion. It was brick houses with saffron yellow plastering, the rows forming quaint yards and neighborhoods. Aesthetics influenced everything Robert did and he pondered carefully where to live before selecting this apartment.

Everything in the apartment had to go and it was implicit that I could lay my hands on anything I wanted. For instance, I got some comic books by creators like Carl Barks, Hergé and Edgar P. Jacobs, comics I once had read and now will see again. Among the books I treasured there were Heidenstam's *The Tree of the Folkungs* and *Hans Alienus*, an omnibus volume of Oscar Wilde's works, books by Nietzsche and an assorted stack of science fiction. Also, some model soldiers and cowboys were mine for the taking. For instance, he had some fine looking medieval knights and some unpainted WWII soldiers of the Airfix and Matchbox kind. These objects I took a closer look at yesterday, here at home, taking a day off and painting some. Great fun and a way of winding down after this major haul.

So in all, I'm grateful to my brother for bequeathing all these things to me. To me he isn't dead, he's ever present and getting all this stuff underlines it. He's ever "gentle on my mind".

- - -

More reflections on the cleaning out of my brother's apartment...

Robert had a talent for carpentry. And in his apartment there were many custom built bookcases, all of them with a makeshift look yet fully functional. It was a system of one or two stable, ready-made, purchased bookcases to which he added his own constructs. To this there were ingeniously incorporated vitrines housing the best art objects, there were shelves for CDs and vinyls, and the walls as such were decorated with nationalistic paintings and prints, all of them framed. He never put up a poster without a frame. He had idol portraits too and even these had frames, like pictures of Slade, Elvis and Zarah Leander.

He had style, he had ideas of home decoration. To this came a certain collecting mania. He didn't know where to stop. The wardrobes were full of additional comic books, diverse paper bundles and compendium, fine-but-unused clothes, junk of all kinds. It might be the case that if you have space no one can stop you from filling it but for the record it must be said that he did amass a lot of useless things.

For instance, he owned six bikes, four of them functional. The latter were given away and / or sold and the two dysfunctional ones were thrown into the "scrap metal" container at the recycling central. Now, I shouldn't judge and complain but there were times when we asked ourselves what he thought when he amassed all these things.

We salvaged things. And we threw away some, having first sorted them according to the recycling station pattern of "combustibles," "wooden furniture," "metal," "plaster, glass and mirrors," "tyres," "chemicals," "porcelain" and "paper". The recycling station also had a container for "usable stuff" and there we put things like books, tabletop games and toys. He bought many things cheaply at second hand stores, some of it I now could salvage (like Crescent toys medieval knights, tin soldiers, Matchbox "cars of yesteryear" and a Märklin HO scale steam engine) and the rest were handed over in the "usable" compartment. Thus, theoretically, this may now gladden some people; when this usable stuff has been transported to the municipal second hand store "Återbruket" some other persons may look at them and found them quaint, a bargain, "a thing they don't need for a price they can't resist".

To transport the stuff from the apartment to the recycling station we hired a van, a Renault Trafic. I rented it and drove it. It was the smallest available van and I wanted it thus; as long as it could house a bed it was alright, we didn't need the larger type of van they offered, the Renault Master. That's a fine vehicle too and I've driven it once but if I can choose I pick the Trafic, the smaller the better, if you aren't a driver by trade then you're glad if the vehicle is a handy as possible. This Trafic was a fine specimen as such, top modern as rental cars tend to be. It did fine service for two days and I liked that but I was even gladder when I could return it on midday at day three.

More could be said about this operation. I tend not to mention a lot of people in this diary and that's for the sake of "operational security". However, the X number of people helped in doing this and they were all thanked by me IRL – and, for what it's worth, I now thank them again. I had a lot of help in this, like my sister who, in mere work intensity counted since April, ended up doing "more than half" since she lived closer by the actual site. In this May Event I had promised to help her and now I did this and I thank God that I was able to be there for her. It was a family affair that simply Had to Be Done and God helped us – because we helped ourselves.

I conceived of the "hire a van and haul the stuff to the recycling station part," I reconnoitered the site and made it work during the actual event. Not that I need a gold medal for this but I did contribute with this crucial part, a Responsible Man living the spirit of Action as Being.

The fact of knowing this, of knowing that I did help with plans and execution and that it all went reasonable smoothly prompts the feeling of "having participated in a military operation and then having been demobbed". That's the mood of these days. True, as an Actionist I know that the road goes ever on, that There Is Only Here and Now and we all have to operate 24/7. To be is to act and to act is to be. However, there are times of more intense operations and periods of less intense operations and these days, after the May Event, is a time of less intense operational activity.

As for having been demobbed etc. I half-jokingly said this during the event, that this is like a military exercise and then normal laws of rest and food has to be suspended. Also, I did sleep over in the actual apartment – and night two, when the bed had been thrown away, I only had a thin mattress on the floor to sleep on. But as I said to my companions, it's like a military exercise, you have to be prepared for things like these. And the mattress night camp was more than OK, I slept about as well on it as I do in my bed at home.

The whole event lasted slightly more than 3 days and nights, some 80 hours. I left Härnösand by train at 9 AM on Wednesday and was back home on Saturday at 7 PM, going off the train with two suitcases packed with books and other goodies bequeathed to me.

11/5

The project with the drawbridge continues. Now they're cleaning up and doing detail work, like putting up railings and restoring the adjacent lawns. The bridge for pedestrians and cyclists is removed, at least the wooden part of it, left remaining are two steel beams, maybe they need a special crane lorry to lift them.

The causeway is gone, the virtual barrier to the north, the embankment over which the heavy traffic was led when the bridge was built. That whole detour is gone, the gravel that made up the road is removed and topsoil is spread out and leveled, I guess they have sown grass seeds in it, that's how they restore the lawns.

- - -

To be a Responsible Man, performing Action as Being in an eternal Here and Now. That's what I do.

13/5

Today it rains. However, until now May has been warm and bright. When I visited the Cobbled Place yesterday the sun shone and the water and air had that warm blue color. The grass was green and the birches flanking the place had tender green leaves. I was surrounded by "the darling buds of May," as it were.

14/5

Dreamt I was in Joensuu.

- - -

An exquisite Actionist wisdom *in nuce* is this, found on the net: to complain without coming up with a solution is called whining.

19/5

I'm an intellectual advocating action, a rebel fighting for tradition.

22/5

Wordsworth defines poetry as "emotion recollected in tranquility". Rather apt.

Three songs with an Actionist theme that are topical to me right now:

- "Now I'm Here" by Queen. It's about living in the here-and-now. TIOHAN = There Is Only Here And Now. Have been reminded of this song because of inheriting a CD from Robert with the best of Queen.
- "Survivor" by Destiny's Child, the chorus. It's about not giving

up and instead trying harder, an affirmation about "making it" and surviving. Before going south to clean out Robert's room earlier this month I had this as a spirit-raising mantra – not as a statement of "having survived my brother" but as a way of "surviving this logistic challenge".

- "Rocket Man" by Elton John. Again, the chorus part is to be focused on, where, in this case, the title simply is underlined: I'm a Rocket Man. Because, the verses utter some kind of complaint about having to leave earth and travel to space. But the chorus is triumphant: Rocket Maaan... I'm a Rocket Man. In Actionist terms this is about Movement As A State Of Mind, doing stuff and triumphing: Winning As Propensity. Another song that came to me via the inheritance from Robert's estate.

Above, on February 7, I mentioned Bowie's "Space Oddity" as a serious masterpiece capturing the essence of "going to space". "Rocket Man," for its part, was issued about the same time but it's in a different style, it has serious strains but is also vaguely ironic, like mentioning that you can't raise your kids on Mars. And, to this, the triumphant mood mentioned above; Bowie's song had nothing of that. I only want to say that John's song has been played more than once this month on my CD.

As an artist I'm a Rocket Man, flaming triumphantly in the sky, a David Bowman of *2001* going Beyond the Beyond and Within the Within. Fire and movement!

24/5

I don't drug myself into oblivion. I don't want to "forget myself". I want to *remind* myself of my spiritual self. And this I do by constantly meditating on the "I AM".

27/5

After a long period of grey weather, finally, some sun.

- - -

Dear diary: result of my soul searching after my brother's death: I AM.

2/6

Rather warm to be early summer: 20 degrees centigrade in the shade.

3/6

Summery warmth, fragrant smells, verdant trees. Paradisaical. I also sit and work these days, doing cleaning up in files, proofreading and whatnot. The schedule isn't so tight, deadlines are far off so I can take time for hobbies if I want to, like painting model soldiers, doing collages and montages of photos and pictures or writing down song lyrics and learning them by heart.

As for the last hobby, learning lyrics, I've just done that with "Rocket Man". Great song, ironic and serious at the same time. It fits my mood right now, a cultural / artistic statement and then some. It's more than just a story of an astronaut and of being "a star in the sky" – for, like any great artwork it's got a "third meaning" as Roland Barthes said, beyond mere information and symbolism. Rocket Man!

8/6

List without comment, the history of 50s nostalgia: Sha Na Na, various "Golden Oldies" radio stations, *Grease* the musical,

American Graffiti, Happy Days, Grease the movie.

9/6

I inherited a nice batch of comic books, books and CDs from my brother's estate. I don't need any more books and records. Still, the pull to go to Erikshjälpen Second Hand and check it out is strong. It's that urge of, "venturing out to Ye Olde Curiosity Shoppe, browsing the shelves, making a bargain, buying something you don't need for a prize you can't resist".

- - -

In your life there's the things you "should" do, and then there's music permeating everything, the very soundtrack of your life. "Life is what happens to you while you're busy making other plans."

10/6

It's raining.

- - -

Am reading a selection of William Blake poetry, prophecy etc. He's like a poetically gifted Swedenborg. He even refers to this "Buddha of the North" in one line, defending him: "*O Swedenborg! Strongest of men, the Samson shorn by the Churches*". ("Milton," Book the First)

11/6

Yesterday I visited the Cobbled Place.

Standing there I was surrounded by greenery. The flanking birches had dense foliage. The one on the right almost blocked out the entire view of the city island. Only through the leaves the dome could be discerned, for example.

The sky was grey. From the north, straight at me standing there, a cold wind blew, making small waves on the Nattviken. And personally, looking due north, I saw this beyond the Nattviken proper: the habitats on the mainland and in the distance a green hill, covered by coniferous trees and the odd hardwood tree.

Next, looking in a more north-easterly direction, beyond the Nybron I saw another hill, one also covered by wood but of a more blue-green hue. The farther away the bluer the green gets.

15/6

Interesting relationship: I'm currently reading a collection of William Blake poems inherited from my brother Robert. Blake also had a brother named Robert, one who died at 24 in 1787.

Blake's brother was younger than him while my brother was older than me, true, but they both had the role of inspirers. As for Blake's brother inspiring him the following poem is taken as an example of that:

> *Piping down the valleys wild,*
> *Piping songs of pleasant glee,*
> *On a cloud I saw a child,*
> *And he laughing said to me:*
>
> *"Pipe a song about a lamb:"*
> *So I piped with merry cheer.*
> *"Piper, pipe that song again:"*
> *So I piped: he wept to hear.*
>
> *"Drop thy pipe, thy happy pipe,*

Sing thy songs of happy cheer!"
So I sang the same again,
While he wept with joy to hear.

"Piper, sit thee down and write
In a book, that all may read –"
So he vanished from my sight;
And I plucked a hollow reed,

And I made a rural pen,
And I stained the water clear,
And I wrote my happy songs
Every child may joy to hear.

- - -

Morning walk on Kullen, "the Hill," a part of town on the mainland north of the E4 highway and west of the railroad. The abundant raining at the end of May has made the lawns emerald green. Lilacs blossoming. Sunshine. I was the only one out except for the odd car and lorry.

- - -

Challenge everything, spiritualize everything, conceptualize everything.

21/6

We all live in the grey area now. Some of us know it, some don't.

22/6

ACTIONISM

Sunrise, sunset. Another day in Maya of Illusion.

27/6

Nietzsche speaks of, "how to philosophize with a hammer". In Actionist terms, this could be a symbol of: to combine Thought with Will. Nietzsche deserves kudos for stressing Will in the process.

28/6

On my morning walk: 15 centigrade plus, warm and comfy. On the Cobbled Place: surrounded by greenery, a blue ridge ahead, rather calm water surface, mallards swimming placidly about. Blue sky, no clouds.

30/6

I live alone but I'm not "alone". God is my co-pilot. Loneliness is an invention by atheists, as Nietzsche so aptly says in *Der Fröhliche Wissenschaft*.

1/7

The herring gulls fly around like crazy these days. I guess they're protecting their newly hatched young. When I go out in my backyard these gulls fly around crying and even shitting on you – so I get the message, I shouldn't take my walk in that direction, toward the park and the canal. Instead I can go downtown, early in the morning no one's out, that's fine for this walker. The other day I went up and around the cathedral, a white classical building from the mid 19th century, stately with columns and all, situated in a park. And partly surrounded by wooden houses from the same era, rather quaint.

3/7

These days are spent with proofreading. A rather fine occupation when you're "in between jobs," when you don't really know what to write.

6/7

Proofreading. A way to get into the mood is saying: "I AM the proofreading."

7/7

Summer in the city, green lawns, green trees. The road outside my window is newly asphalted, they did it at night, thus they didn't have to close down the road. It's the Storgatan, one of the two main roads connecting the island with the mainland. I live on the mainland.

PART III

Sat Yuga Suggestions

30. THE COMING GOLDEN AGE

The first part of this book focused on the person, "the small world". The second part focused on society, "the big world". In this part the study returns to elements discussed above, aiming at making some sort of synthesis, on the whole envisioning a grand future for us all. The coming era will be a new golden age for man. Currently the planet is ruled by a nihilist-materialist regime. To radically reform it might take some time. But after that the sun will again shine on us.

THE FESTIVAL

Picture a plateau overlooking a city, bounded by a river. On the far side of the plateau, on a hillock, is a temple with a gilded dome and red sandstone walls, catching the evening sun.

Standing on the plateau you can see the temple, the river, the city with its harmonious structures and buildings and surrounding fields and copses. The plateau forms the city square; here is found an assembly of tables adorned with flowers, the surrounding houses having walls decorated with garlands and colored lamps. People are sitting down at the tables, eating, drinking and enjoying themselves. There is music and laughter. In a nearby park flowers are blossoming, the verdure of trees shining in emerald splendor.

All this is a symbol of the Coming Golden Age for man, a time of peace and festivity, of glorifying ourselves and our Inner Light.

ACTIONISM

The age we've just left, the Kali Yuga era, was characterized by strife, domination, competition, violence, darkness and despair. The coming age, the Sat Yuga of peace, will be characterized by harmony, cooperation, abundance and mental elevation. At the time I am writing this, earth still suffers under a materialist, nihilist regime denying the rights of people to live and thrive in their respective countries, but this regime will be defeated. With time, a governance of Justice, Truth, Freedom and Peace will be realized. The governance of tomorrow is one of Free Will, of shared prosperity, of human rights and responsibility and justice and freedom of expression for all. The scene of the city with the temple, the river and the feast being prepared is a symbol of all this, the Coming Golden Age, of Sat Yuga being realized.

But don't just wait for it. You must Will it, in the Actionist way. Free Will is the seed of the Coming Golden Age – *your* Will. Muster your Will and let's start building the Antropolis era. Don't sit around waiting for someone else to do all the work.

PEACE PROCESS

We stand before a celebration of peace. The development essentially calls for peace, not peace as in capitulation. Instead, from a position of spiritual and worldly strength the New Era will be implemented. This is a *Casus Pacis* = a Reason for Peace. Actionism is part of a peaceful evolution. This is a peace process. This is a curing of the ills of our personal beings and of the world at large.

This is a strategy to implement a peaceful evolution in the micro- and macrocosm, in our personal beings and in the world. To change the macrocosm we have to start in the microcosm. The individual has to work with himself. ESWY = Everything Starts With You.

After cleaning out the materialist nihilism, the defeatism and idiocy, all the evils of our civilization, the coming age will be a celebration of inspiration and creativity, harmony and compassion, abundance, peace and awareness, a mental elevation occasioned by everybody's united Will-Thought.

LENNART SVENSSON

NEW SUN

A seemingly new sun will shine over humanity. It will be a sunshine zeitgeist. The world will become a virtual Sunshine State.

And in this new era a coming guru might say: "I am the light of the world; I am the New Improved Sun."

BEYOND DUALITY

The emerging human society is going beyond duality and conflict, heading for a new level of mental awareness. In all this, every nation will be secure in its place of origin. This is no multicultural rhetoric, hiding ulterior motives. It's Actionism, founded on co-nationalism and human biodiversity.

The emerging human society will be one of assuming responsibility – by individuals and by politicians alike. No longer will our leaders be stooges of a secret elite, an alleged shadow government. In the emerging society transparency will prevail, not secrecy and agreements in smoke-free rooms. In the Actionist creed the individual is responsible for his moral decisions – and since Actionism is a Doctrine About Everything the same principle of responsibility can be applied on the macro level, in all instances of political governance.

The governmental concept of Actionism is driven by authority from above and confidence from below, in a positive, affirmative two-way flow.

POEM

In the beginning of this Chapter I described a city on a plateau, surrounded by a resplendent landscape and with a festival in progress in the city square. It's the Conceptual City of the Future – a further development of the Antropolis I told about in Chapter

28. In such a city there would be certain institutions, like a House of Remembrance, a House of Birthing and a House of Healing, all of them dedicated to holistic intuitions embracing the workings of the human subtle bodies. It's about affirming the Light – through history, in the act of giving birth, biologically and conceptually, and about healing wounds, somatically and mentally.

Specifically, a House of Remembrance is a house dedicated to history, to man's past, to the viable, fruitful traits of it, like the outline of history given in this book, that of history being about man's spiritual self-realization. A House of Birthing is a place where new philosophic concepts can be born in an atmosphere of creativity and peace, as well as a place for new babies to be born, incarnations on this plane of Elevated Masters; the only ones wishing to incarnate here in the future will be specially disposed beings of the exquisite kind, accepting to have another turn in a physical body to raise his brethren.

A House of Healing in such a city is a hospital of a human-friendly atmosphere, a place affirming that man is an organism, not a machine. It takes into account the subtle bodies of man, especially the Etheric Body. It's also a place for mental healing, in this respect, also intent on treating man as a living being, not as a biological machine being able to be manipulated with drugs.

SUBTLE BODIES

Some deliberations on the just mentioned "subtle bodies" might be needed. Essentially, man isn't matter, he's energy. By way of his spirit, he has an energetic element enabling him to access higher mental levels.

Man's being consists of five bodies or levels: Physical Body, Etheric Body, Emotional Body, Mental Body and Spiritual Self. And generally, realizing, acknowledging and nurturing the latter element, the Self, this Âtman of Hindu fame, is done by receiving the higher, subtle energies currently bombarding earth. Reportedly, there's a massive download of subtle energy going on right now. Acknowledge this and raise yourself mentally and spiritually.

We are energy, color and light. Our spiritual energy unites us with the cosmos. We have to nurture and take care of both our physical bodies and our subtle bodies. In Actionist terms this is rendered as, "the ignored body screams, the ignored soul is silenced". This means: signals from a neglected body are louder than those from a neglected soul; however, both body and soul must be cared for. From Latin, we have the saying, "mens sana in corpore sana" = a healthy mind in a healthy body.

SPIRITUAL SELF

As intimated, man's subtle bodies are five in number. First, we have the Physical Body which is made of matter. The next level, the Etheric Body, is called Ka in ancient Egyptian; in Sanskrit, it's called Prâna and in Chinese, Chi. Reportedly, this serves as a blueprint or a hologram for the physical body, embracing it and enclosing it as a glorified life support system. The next level, the third, the Emotional Body, is the source of an individual's feelings and emotions; it's "the soul". The Mental Body, for its part, is the abode of thoughts and values. The higher spiritual consciousness is housed in the Spiritual Self, level 5.

These five levels together constitute the whole person. Individual varieties exist at each level, but to have these five levels is common to all men.

The levels, especially the etheric body, can be strengthened by letting cosmic energy flow into them. This is done by meditation and affirmation, as is the cleansing of the soul and mind (emotional and mental body) of negative thoughts. Also, taking brisk walks in natural surroundings strengthens your being on all levels. Allow energy, light and prâna (= the cosmic energy of life) to heal you on all levels. This is covered in the Actionist concept of OYTO = Opening Yourself To Opportunity = allowing your being to embrace the energies needed for change.

ACTIONISM

CHANGE

Can you feel the change in the earth, the wind and the rain...? The time of this writing – the mid 2010s – is a transitional phase – for you, for the world. Overall, major war is now an impossibility. In Chapter 22 I deliberated on this, giving circumstantial evidence. A more spiritual way of putting it is this: a higher energy signature of planet earth now makes war impossible. Major War is history, but The Powers That Be try every trick by way of propaganda through mainstream media. We can counter this by re-establishing our connection with the Divine Light. What we do, as persons, is important in the Psych War now raging.

The meaning of existence, now even more than before, is to defend, nurture and affirm Light and Life. It's about transforming your body into a living library of wisdom, making every cell of your body into a body of light. It's about awakening to a new awareness, a state allowing man to realize his divine Inner Light.

GENERAL PERSONAL ADVICE

As for the times ahead, I've already given some advice on what the individual can do. Like in the chapter on history (Chapter19) where I mentioned that you, who want change from the current regimen of ignorant materialism into spiritual idealism, you must *want* the change, you must realize it with Thought and Will, you must stop being negative and start embracing the Light. A shortlist of general advice for the individual might be this:

- Free yourself of old energies, of the usual "controlling matrix" of fear and scarcity, doom and gloom. Instead, without surrendering your own being, open your mind to new possibilities; at least, try this as an experiment.
- Change is in the air, in the earth and water; feel it. Feel it...! A closed mind doesn't realize this, it only sees doom and

destruction. Conversely, an open mind acknowledges the hardships ahead in defeating materialism, but it also sees possibilities.
- Get onboard in the liberation work. It isn't done by sitting around watching things happen; essentially, it's done by your cooperation.
- If you have questions, seek within yourself for the answer. Because "individuum est ineffabile" = the individual is indescribable = there are unseen depths within you, giving you energy and guidance.

PERSONAL ACTIVITIES

As for more tangible advice in the everyday, here are some:

- Eat lighter, less heavy food.
- Exercise gently, like choosing power walk before running.
- Take a deep breath.
- Laugh, if you can.
- Dream big, remembering the advice of Jünger: "We're not defeated because of our dreams but because we haven't dreamed intensely enough." This was said in the novel *Eumeswil*, written in 1977 and currently available in English.
- Stay in your heart, acknowledging Compassion along with Will and Truth. Get in sync with the heartbeats of the universe.

THE CITY

In the Conceptual City outlined in this chapter there's a quiet joy, there's expectancy in the air. A festival is in progress in the city square, as intimated at the beginning; there's music and laughter, a celebration is about to take place, a feast of joy and light, a New Era for man and the cosmos – for what takes place on earth matters to the whole galaxy and the whole universe, just as, conversely, when earth was dragged down into materialist idiocy this also affected the surrounding spaces.

There's music and *festivitas*, there's a party and everyone with a reasonably positive and affirmative mindset is welcome. And you could surmise that a poem performed at the occasion was the following:

> *I'm in love with her and I feel fine –*
> *living in this Midsummer Century –*
> *praying at the Water Place of Good Peace –*
> *under the New Improved Sun.*

31. ACTIONIST MUSINGS

As already stated, Actionism is a total way of knowledge, a moral doctrine both for the individual and society at large. Actionism teaches you to launch your personal *reconquista*, as the necessary first step for a second, overall *reconquista* liberating society from the prevailing materialist idiocy. Actionism gives you the whole gamut, an ethical guidepost for both the microcosm and the macrocosm, for both the individual and the whole society. The societal, meta-narrative aspects were more or less confined to the middle section of this book and in this last section the perspective is, more or less, again focused on the person. At least in this very chapter, the subject is to straighten out some issues for Actionism as a personal moral.

GET A GRIP

You might have gotten the hang of it now, you might have figured out the gist of the Actionist philosophy: that of getting a grip on yourself, of stopping being an ironic dandy and instead summing up your Will, getting a haircut, starting living in the reflected here-and-now, saying "I AM" and acknowledging your Inner Light, in the process having some knowledge of volitional mental calm, of C3, as the Actionist concept is called.

ACTIONISM

You have all this, you have learned your lessons, and still you might not be "happy," you might feel more uptight than ever, waiting for that "triumphant feeling," waiting for the personal Golden Age to arrive.

If so, you've read it all wrong, maybe getting hooked on the chauvinist, mock-heroic aspects of it all. I admit that this might be a pitfall, that of superficially being hooked to concepts like "Action," "Operations," "Willpower" etc. and expecting life to be an adventure right away.

Then I can only say: the goal of Actionism is still to live a successful, willpower-driven life acknowledging Light. Everything I've said above, especially in Chapters 1 through 7, still holds; this is the way to a better life. However, for the subject at hand, that of not becoming an uptight, "victory"-fixated parody of a rigorist, a fake-Nietzschean armchair chauvinist, you have to remember this concept: WAP. That is, "Winning As Propensity" which has been mentioned previously. This propensity for winning, for being successful in everything you do, means: to posit attainable goals. The basic goal of this kind is: taking a breath, being able to take an unstrained, deep-but-gentle breath. Being able to perform this "operation" successfully is the basis of Actionism, this is Winning As Propensity.

So then, the imagined reader I have in mind, the "having learned the basics of Actionism but feeling more uptight than ever"-person sketched at the beginning of this Chapter, having now taken that breath and realized that this is the fundamental operation to perform; this person has now, hopefully, calmed down. And if he hasn't, he can remember the concept of RIR = Rest In Rest = the usual way of resting, doing "nothing". Conversely, the Actionist concept of RIA = Rest In Action, isn't the only way to rest. It's true that action, per se, can serve as a form of glorified rest. But this common-style action is not the only way to find rest. You can also lie down on the bed and calm down your breathing. This is an aspect of RIR = Rest In Rest, as opposed to the RIA = Rest In Action, the way of feeling leisure when performing a tangible, hands-on operation.

Thus, the imagined, overwrought neophyte might now have calmed down. And he might now be ready to hear some more musings on the personal meaning of Actionism, some, as intimated at the beginning of this chapter, a tying up of loose ends and comments on things that might not be clear yet.

DISCLAIMERS

At the end of this book is a Disclaimer. It reads:

"Central to the doctrine of Actionism is responsibility. – Therefore, I, Lennart Svensson, as the author of this book and creator of the creed of Actionism, am *conceptually* responsible for the ideas, views and narratives presented in this volume. And you, as the reader, are *existentially* responsible for your reaction to it. You are responsible for the way you personally choose to relate to the ideas, views and narratives presented in this book."

You get the drift: you, as a person endowed with Will-Thought, are responsible for your every thought and action, including how you react to what you read in this book. My hope is that you learn better from it, finding the way to a smarter, more energy-efficient life. But I have no illusions as to how people might misunderstand it; there's always the risk that people might and if so, the above disclaimer stands as a safeguard against whatever may come.

You willingly choose to read this book; then, for better or worse, you take the consequences. You have a free will. You are free to read this book; you are free to ignore it.

As for disclaimers and reservations, what more do I have? Do I have to conceive of every conceivable misunderstanding and say "This is not Actionism"? Of course not. However, one general such disclaimer, already intimated in the Chapter Operations 1 (Chapter 14) is this: in speaking of military style operations, don't take it too literally and evolve into some "army of one" running amok with a fiery eye. The trait of discussing military operations is done by way of simile and metaphor, helping the peaceful individual to operate more efficiently in his everyday. Castaneda, for instance, has the warrior simile all over his books without it ever relating to modern war, chaos and destruction. His teacher, Don Juan, makes that reflection once. Being "a warrior" in Castaneda's context is about raising yourself mentally, finding that "moral equivalent of war", giving you a kind of heightened awareness, leading to feats of spiritual-volitional prowess. In speaking of military operations as I do, I tread the same grey area, as does also the document Bhagavad-Gîtâ where Krishna tells Arjuna to fight and fight well. Most gurus tend to play down this warlike element of Bhagavad-Gîtâ; not so Julius Evola, though, the man whose thought was delineated in Chapter 12. In *Metaphysics of War*, the Chapter "The Aryan Doctrine of Combat and Victory," he stresses that the warrior element in Bhagavad-Gîtâ (as in verses 2:37 and 2:38) is the defining trait of this spiritual document. The verses in question read:

hato vâ prâpsyasi svargam jitvâ vâ bhokshyase mahîm
tasmâd uttishta kaunteya yuddhâya krita-nishcayah

Either you are killed and you reach heaven, or you win and will enjoy the world. Therefore rise, Arjuna, and fight with determination.

sukha-duhkhe same kritvâ lâbhâlâbhau jayâjayau
tato yuddhâya yujuasva naivam pâpam avâpsyasi

Having become equal to luck and misfortune, gain and loss, victory and defeat. Get ready for the battle, thus you won't be entangled in materialism.

PERFECTIONIST FALLACY

It's true that an Actionist strives for perfection. To be "a better man" is always the goal. However, this striving must never sink into a dualist division of "perfect and "non-perfect". Like: "to exercise every day in the hardest possible way is the only way; to merely take a walk thrice a week is useless" – or, "to know every Actionist acronym and concept by heart is the goal, everything else is useless". This is the perfectionist fallacy. Conversely, any kind of physical exercise is better than none. And having just taken *one* Actionist wisdom to heart is better than trying to know it all in a flash.

The Actionist should strive for some kind of "perfection," to better himself morally. The person not in tune with this kind of endeavor should not be an Actionist. However, this process of "becoming better," "becoming someone else – yourself" isn't done by rigid programs, although Actionism has its fair share of concepts and guidelines. The Actionist is foremost guided by intuition, not a rigid set of rules. This is expressed in the sentence, "ethical perfection attained through intuition, not in programs". This means: as a thinking, feeling actor you do what has to be done, not by relying on formal programs. Instead you're being guided by intuition. C.f. Matthew 5:48, "*Be perfect, therefore, as your heavenly Father is perfect*". This kind of aphoristic guidance is what the Active Idealist needs, not rigid programs.

Be perfect = strive for perfection. But don't succumb to "the perfectionist fallacy," myopically examining every situation from the viewpoint of perfection. If you compare yourself with others, you may become dejected. In that case, you must remember WAP = Winning As Propensity = you're on your own path of striving; being able to take a deep, gentle breath is the ultimate operation, a thing we all can be successful in. The right kind of perspective makes you into an energy-efficient operator in every instance.

The Actionist is "becoming someone else – himself". It's about ABY = Affirmatively Being Yourself. It's about choosing to be the one you are, realizing the limitless possibilities of your personal being. Compare Nietzsche's *"wie man wird, was man ist"*.

Avoid the perfectionist fallacy, that of seeing "only one path". You have to find your own path. This means: that given that there is an objective, transcendent reality, the way to realize this can be different for different people. There's no "one size fits all" in ethics.

ACTIONISM

EVOLVED GURU SYNDROME

In the realm of "perfectionism and its pitfalls" there's also this, what we may call "The Evolved Guru Syndrome".

Let's say that you've developed mentally and spiritually over the years. You have learned the force of Will; you have learned to take command of your thoughts and emotions. You've learned to reign in anger, envy and lust. You've read every traditional, spiritual document you once wanted to read, you've learned your lessons, both academic and IRL. You have become, not perfect, but "more perfect" than you were. Then, there's the risk of loosening your Will powered command over your feelings and desires, you might think that such an enlightened guru is allowed some pride, some outing in debauchery, some indulgence.

This is a danger to acknowledge. Because, even the developed mind must keep living the reflected life, keep having Willpower at the fore, keep employing volitional mental calm, keep living according to Eternal Values like modesty, self-restraint and accountability. Even an evolved master is allowed some fun but fun can be had in many ways, only not in ways hurtful to others, nor in ways lowering the level of idealism that defines him as a master.

There's no permission for an "evolved master" to go out and be embroiled in materialist nihilism now and then, to indulge in "sin", because he conceptually, as a teacher and an esotericist, has "climbed every mountain and stormed every fortress". We come here to learn and learning is an ever ongoing process, even to the more evolved. The more evolved you are, the higher the demands become. *"From everyone who has been given much, much will be demanded."* (Luke 12:48)

It's true that life gets easier when Will-Thought governs your being, but as intimated, there's no permission to indulge in "sin," not even in pride, only because you're an elevated teacher figure. Now, you needn't be 100% perfect (= don't fall for the perfectionist fallacy) so "a spate of irony" is no deadly sin, to give but one example. As long as you're at least 51% positively disposed, at least 51% STO = Service

To Others disposed, then you're on the safe side. But, make sure you constantly scrutinize your own being, as regards your moral stature. No one else will do it for you. Willpower, responsibility and being able to calm down to reassess any situation, is the Actionist way.

32. VARIATIONS ON A THEME BY POE

Actionism is a doctrine for a reflective, active, willpower-driven person, a positively disposed esotericist acknowledging his Inner Light. The Actionist can meditate, he can be alone. Conversely, there are people who can't be alone, who can't meditate. Their mindset is alien to the Actionist creed.

THE MAN OF THE CROWD

In Edgar Allan Poe's short story, "The Man of the Crowd", the narrator is in London; he sits at a café studying the crowd and various types you can discern in it. Then he spots a sinister looking man, a restless person who only seems to walk around. The narrator starts to follow him around and the man just saunters, he drifts in the crowd. Specifically, he seems to seek energy from crowds.

This the narrator more or less concludes. At the end, he confronts the man and puts himself in front of him. The man shows no reaction. He just stares and then goes off, off to gain some further fleeting energy from other drifting people, from the eddying crowd. "He refuses to be alone. He's *the man of the crowd.*"

Details aside, this figure might be a symbol of the current media-drugged zombie, the person unable to lie down and seek volitional mental calm. The person who constantly has to seek stimuli from the internet, from TV, from computer games. Then, overwhelmed by fatigue, he may fall asleep. Or maybe not. Maybe he, like the man in Poe's story, just keeps going – the story guy drifting in the city, the media-drugged zombie playing another round, seeing another show, surfing into another website he just has to check.

RESTLESS

The Man of the Crowd was an active person, he might have gotten some exercise from his drifting, but strikingly, he was restless in all this. What a difference from an Actionist who can seek Rest In Action = RIA, gaining a sublime mental calm by doing stuff, tapping into energy stores of a subtle kind, going along as if supra-conducted. An Actionist drifter of the city, a conscious, reflecting *flaneur*, gains energy from his outings in the cityscape, looking at things and going haphazardly in this or that direction. A decadent, on the other hand, gets depleted of energy by his drifting. Why? Because he has no order inside. Everything starts inside, everything is decided within = "I'm innern ist's getan," as Goethe said.

TRADITION

The unreflective flaneur is a materialist-nihilist dandy. The *reflecting* flaneur is an Actionist, living according to mottos like, "avoid materialism and defeatism, embrace tradition and self-reliance". This means to stop being an ironic dandy, start being an assertive agent footed in Tradition. So you see, an Actionist may have a past of being a dejected materialist but it's never too late to change your ways – never too late to take the Actionist path, the subtly energetic path, the path of seeking Rest In Action.

An Actionist gets energy from subtle dimensions, from sources unseen, sources beyond food and drink. An Actionist seeks a different empowerment – he seeks "empowerment through strength out of the absolute". An Actionist draws energy from higher, divine realms. This is what sustains you in the long run, not mere food and drink.

ACTIONISM

An Actionist is an active idealist, positively shaping his existence. His modus operandi can be described by the acronym ANOTTBOTSOTT = Act Not On The Thing, But On The Soul Of The Thing. This is a way to ennoble every act, turning away from its immediately material purpose and making action into an l'art-pour-l'art. For example, when going shopping, act not with the single purpose of "buying proteins to keep your body alive"; act on the soul of going shopping and enjoy the ride as such, say hello to people you meet, thereby exemplifying the archetype of The Good Neighbor.

AVOID THE BAD

Actionism stresses the positive and fruitful aspects of life. But it doesn't ignore the negative sides, the ones you have to deal with to reach perfection. In order to list some concepts dealing with negative aspects in the personal, ethical realm, here are some.

- Being unable to choose is hell = conversely, to be free is the human condition, even though this freedom can cause existential angst. However, this angst is preferable to not being able to choose at all, which equals slavery and imprisonment.
- Waste of mental energy = like, hanging out with negative people, thinking defeatist thoughts, reading books that bore you. Find out what enriches you mentally and what drains you. God is energy; save mental energy, don't waste it.
- All things are lawful but not all are beneficial = self-restraint in the vein of St. Paul = use your free will with discernment.
- Having a circle of positive people = conversely, to get rid of acquaintances draining you of energy.
- Stopping the eternal revolt against yourself = make peace with yourself = acknowledge that You Are You = "Loving oneself is the beginning of a life-long love affair" (Oscar Wilde).
- See No Evil (Hear No Evil, Speak No Evil) = the Buddhist concept of Shaping Existence Positively (q.v. SEP). It's about

letting Will govern your mind (= speak no evil) and senses (hear no evil, see no evil). Indeed, evil has to be confronted, but to indignantly focus on the ravages of evil leads nowhere, instead Will must lead you to greener pastures.

SHINE

The above section listed concepts more or less dealing with the negative. Hereby some concepts of the genuinely positive kind, still concerning the personal life: how to strive and get better, gain energy, shine.

This survey begins with ESWY = Everything Starts With You = realizing that a calm mind is the basis of everything = always calm down, always be C3, whether you're about to "act" or to "contemplate". Conversely, you can't rely on abstractions, on "meta-narratives" and mirages, like "science" and "democracy," the "development" and "progress" of which shall bring us peace and prosperity just like that, like manna from heaven. The Actionist creed is a total way of knowledge, a way of liberating people and society, but in doing this it has to start with the individual affirming his Willpower and Inner Light.

It starts with the person, the individual being able to think and act volitionally. That person is prone to this wisdom: "Life isn't about finding yourself, life is about creating yourself". This is a saying by George Bernard Shaw, a motto incorporating the Actionist attitude of esotericism (the truth is within, Greek *eso*), of using Will-Thought to sound out your inner, creative possibilities. It can also remind you of Nietzsche's dictum "wie man wird, was man ist" = "how to become what you are". It's true that both Nietzsche and Shaw were atheists; they, and thinkers like Simone de Beauvoir and J. P. Sartre, stressed this "creating yourself" in a non-esoteric way. Actionism doesn't take that path, Actionism is an idealist, divinely orientated doctrine saying that your Inner Light is a mirror of the divine Light, the individual Will a mirror of the divine Will. Having said that,

Shaw was somewhat right in saying that we create ourselves; we are co-creators of our being, along with God, both our personal being and being at large.

The creative, shaping element is present in another acronym, this one: SEP = Shaping Existence Positively = to make your life into a project, an artwork = affirmatively "doing what you can with what you have where you are".

Three more personal, positive concepts are these, viable conceptualizations of the holistic creed that is Actionism, a creed where the part is mirrored in the whole and vice versa:

- Love your neighbor as thyself. The words to note here are, "as thyself". Because everything starts in "self-love," in affirming and acknowledging that you're an individual, an ideo-ethical operation depending on the I AM-impulse to be embraced as a matter of course.
- The ignored body screams, the ignored soul is silenced = signals from a neglected body are louder than those from a neglected soul. However, both body and soul must be cared for. In Latin this is captured as, "mens sana in corpore sana" = a healthy mind in a healthy body.
- The more you give, the more you get = "cast your bread upon the waters, for you will find it after many days" (Ecc. 11:1) = the value of magnanimity and generosity.

DIVINE CONCEPTS

Man is divine. Man is shaped after God by (1) having an immortal soul, a fragment of his Eternal Light, and by (2) having the proportions of his body made after a divine blueprint.

Man is divinely shaped and divinely led. As mentioned earlier in this chapter, the Actionist moves along, seeking Rest In Action, gaining energy from invisible, divine realms. You could say: Poe's "Man of the Crowd" didn't have this divine perspective, nor even

Poe himself or Nietzsche, G. B. Shaw, Evola or Don Juan of the Castaneda books. Personally I'm not explicitly opposed to atheistic approaches, I tolerate atheists as persons and I understand that not everyone can conceptualize reality as I do. However, as regards the Actionist creed, it doesn't shy away from using concepts like "God, divine, the Absolute," it doesn't shy away from conceiving the highest reality as both a person and an abstract ever-presence, both called "God". As for aphorisms conceptualizing the role of the divine in the Actionist everyday, as well as this divine element we have the following:

- Making your person a bridgehead of the divine = realize the unity between your spirit and God = acknowledge your Inner Light.
- The one we move in, exist through, and live in = a Biblical definition of the Logos, the Divine Word of "I Am" through which everything Is What It Is.
- *Tat Tvam Asi* = It is you = unity between the Individual and the Absolute. A Sanskrit saying in the Upanishads, an ancient Indian anthology profiling the affinity between the human Self and the Godhead in a multitude of ways, a collection of rather unsystematic documents having since been systemized into Vedânta Sûtras. As they stand, however, the Upanishads are a rare instance of suggestive passages and alluring renderings on the theme of man and God, a spiritual artwork in the region of The Gospel of John, Swedenborg's *Dream Diary* and Philip K. Dick's *VALIS* and *Exegesis*.
- I Am That Which Is = the ultimate reality is something that merely Is, that can't be questioned. Ontologically, something has to be acknowledged without constant reflection, discussion and debate. That which simply is, is holy; it's Real beyond everyday reality. And That Which Is, is divine, it's God. Conversely, everyday reality is subordinate to change, it's the "Maya of Illusion," something less real.
- Unifying Will-Thought and Light equals God = in the beginning

Will chose to merge with Thought, then Will-Thought chose Light instead of dark and became God resplendent. When an Actionist acknowledges this, he gets connected with supreme reality, with the beginning, with everything: all in one and one in all.
- Clarity in things, clarity in yourself = God is in everything and everyone: in the objects as ideas, in men as Inner Light. He who sees this, observing the world gives him a sense of belonging.
- FIA = Faith In Action = faith, God-realization, can never be a theoretical exercise. It has to be integrated into your daily life. Why? Because we all have to act.

METAPHYSICAL APHORISMS

Since I've now been talking about God, the highest ontological reality, we'll continue on that track – the metaphysical track, the nature of being at large. These concepts give you the Actionist wisdom *in nuce*:

- As we are, so we see = truth is within, truth is an esoteric phenomenon. A sad person sees sadness around him; an energetic person sees energy around him.
- Holism is the goal and the starting point = the Actionist ontology is about seeing wholes, the Big Picture = analysis and dissection are mere instruments for understanding the holistically working micro- and macrocosm. In the same manner, the Actionist ethic is about seeing wholes, about embracing things in a holistic matter and not always dissecting them.
- Materialism is friction and imbalance; idealism is harmony and balance. The Actionist way doesn't need to talk of "sin" in the overwrought, usual way, as if it's something damning you, putting you in need of being "forgiven by God". Because, to avoid materialism is only a question of direction in life, a question of striving for harmony and balance.
- See life in form, spirit in matter = a summary of the Actionist metaphysics, seeing matter as formed by inherent ideas =

Platonic Idealism.
- TIOHAN = There Is Only Here And Now! Are you having a grudge against a relative, a friend, a neighbor for some irrelevant thing? Forget it, forgive him; there is only here and now. Are you feeling proud of some achievement, do you want to tell the world of it in the hope of receiving a gold medal, praise and a celebration? Forget it, there is only here and now! Are you having a birthday, are you feeling sentimental over the years passing by? Rejoice, by all means, but don't take yourself too seriously. For there is only here and now. To quote the poet:

Yesterday is history,
tomorrow a mystery,
today is a gift,
that's why it's called the Present.

POE

This Chapter began by discussing a story by Edgar Allan Poe. The story was about a man not capable of being alone, the urban figure of the Man of the Crowd. Poe himself was a grey area figure sometimes advocating nihilism, sometimes hinting at eternal instances. One poem of his earnestly asks the question of there being more than we see without external senses: "Is all that we see or seem / but a dream within a dream?"

The Actionist answer is: no, life isn't merely a dream. It's guided by invisible forces, eternal ideas, eternal values anchored in the divine Will, there to exist until the end of time. The individual can reach them by going off from the flurry of everyday existence, going off from being occupied with Maya of Illusion, and instead trying to see eternity by way of introspection. In being alone, in meditating in splendid isolation, the person might reach That Which Is = the above mentioned reality beyond everyday reality, that which exists without it being ontologically questioned.

Eternal truths are reached in solitude. And the funny thing is, Poe did appreciate the state of being alone, of solitude. In the essay "The Island of the Fay" (1841) he deliberates on the activity of going out in nature, alone, and meditating upon the beauty of the sky, the verdure, the water in the form of a brook.

Poe acknowledged the power of solitude. And he warned against being merely "a man of the crowd". A current aspect of that figure, the crowd-seeking everyman, is that of the "anonymous internet commentator": the man spewing bile with chance remarks, the man dragging everything down with negativity, a latter-day "Debbie Downer" acting in the protection of internet anonymity. While I acknowledge that internet anonymity is a protection against the all-seeing eye of the Empire, it has also to be mentioned that an Actionist isn't an anonymous poster of this kind. An Actionist assumes responsibility for whom and what he is. If this stops him from posting anonymous comments, it's probably for the common good, and probably, all things considered, for his own best.

You don't answer mail from anonymous persons, do you? You don't speak with people IRL that do not introduce themselves, do you? You don't speak with people going around with a paper bag over their heads, do you? Again, for instances of operational security, anonymity may be acknowledged, but overall, the Actionist way is that of having an open visor, stating your purpose clearly.

The lonely person, speaking with God, can't be anonymous. So, as a valedictory piece of advice for this chapter, I'd say: take time to be alone, speak to God and state your purpose. Like, "I Am That Which Is" = unity between the individual and the Absolute.

Take time to be alone, speak to God and say, "I have an Inner Light, I acknowledge the divine origin of this light, thank you, God, for letting me live a life on earth as a human being."

An Actionist doesn't ask God for "forgiveness for his sins" or some other exoteric, passive nonsense. An Actionist thanks God that he's able to operate, that he, as a person, is able to see his own Inner Light as an aspect of the cosmic, all-encompassing Divine Light.

33. WILL AND THOUGHT, FIRE AND MOVEMENT...

Some time ago I found this on the internet: "If things don't seem to arrive, then arise." In a general sense, the meaning was, and is, this: if the Empire of Evil doesn't actually fall and crumble, if it goes on ruling in sublime idiocy, don't sit and despair. Instead, realize your empowerment and change yourself as a first step, becoming a more will-driven, harmonious person. This is the only way to guide yourself and others to a more informed, reflected everyday, an everyday based on self-determination of individuals and peoples, with mutual respect based on co-nationalism. In order to overthrow the rule of materialism we first must will it on a personal level, acknowledging idealism and Light in our personal beings.

STRONG

Just as the Western world seems to have forgotten the word "Will" and its fundamental, positive connotations, it looks down on the word "strong". The usual cosmopolitan attitude to power and strength, even legitimate power and strength, is antipathy and detestation. If a policeman uses force in taking a violent criminal into custody, people call it "use of excessive force". If a police force breaks up a violent demonstration, the same people call it "fascism, the end of popular rule, the end of everything".

Instead, these "bleeding heart" people should listen to an icon sometimes lauded by Polite Society: Mahâtma Gandhi (1869-1948), the man who advocated non-violent resistance. Overall, Gandhi was no feeble man, no person advocating weakness although his mindset was rather peaceful. He said this on the importance of being strong: a weak person has no freedom of action: "The weak can never forgive. Forgiveness is the attribute of the strong."

A general wisdom by Gandhi was this one: "Even if you're a minority of one, the truth is the truth." That's why Actionism says ESWY = Everything Starts With You = esoterically gained truths of Will and Thought are the basis of ethics and politics.

In order to quote some viable wisdom from seemingly "hugged to death" icons of today, you might also think of Nelson Mandela (1918-2013). The following lines by him are a kind of Actionist wisdom. The first is about fear, a veritable deadly sin:

"I learned that courage was not the absence of fear, but the triumph over it. The brave man is not he who does not feel afraid, but he who conquers that fear."

An Actionist avoids "the perfectionist fallacy," an Actionist is in a constant process of "try, fail, try again, fail better," of RAWALTAFA = Rather Act Wrongly And Fail Than Abstaining From Action, and on this Mandela says: "The greatest glory in living lies not in never falling, but in rising every time we fall."

Two general wisdoms by Mandela are these:

- "There is no passion to be found playing small – in settling for a life that is less than the one you are capable of living."
- "It always seems impossible until it's done."

ABSOLUTE ACTION

Will and Thought, Fire and Movement, Action as Being: that's the Actionist creed.

Actionism is about Absolute Action, Radical Action, the beauty of the reflected action.

In the mind, Will may command Thought, but Thought also influences Action. Thus, it's justified to speak of "Will-Thought". Thus, Actionism is Will-Thought, it's Will to Action.

Being equals thinking; Being equals Action. "Life" and "Thought" relate to each other as "Will" and "Thought," that is, as more or less inseparable features. In the same vein, you have to live your creed.

Live your creed, live your life, and don't demand to be as good as your brother, for if so, you might also have to be as bad as your brother. Focus on your own qualities before wishing to have someone else's.

WILL

The West has forgotten the meaning of "Will". In ancient times it was called *thelema*. As in, "genthêto to thelema sou" = thy will be done = the will of God. True Will is always akin to divine Will. To Will is to will the good.

This, man knew, back in the day. Again, I quote the Gospel of Philip, verse 64: "Will doesn't make them into sinners, but lack of will does".

Will is will to the good; lack of will is desire, bound for the dark.

In modern times, Nietzsche rediscovered Will. He may have been anti-esoterically disposed but he was on to something when he glorified Will, when he reduced all of ethics and metaphysics into Will, the Will To Power Over Yourself = WTPOY, in Actionist terms.

The West has forgotten Will, it has ethically forgotten the meaning of being strong. However, Actionism knows Will and moral strength. An Actionist is ASARIT = A Strong And Responsible Idealist, Taking charge. An Actionist doesn't sit down and wait for things to happen, he makes things happen, if only by taking charge of his own being. That's the moral foundation, now and always: ESWY = Everything Starts With You. To be sure, there are objective instances like Will,

Thought, Compassion and Light, the metaphysical reality came before man and the individual Souls, but in ethics any endeavor has to start with the individual asserting his moral existence by saying I AM, taking charge of his being and relaxing his body by taking a deep and gentle breath, thus unifying mind with body.

BASICS

Man's soul is a dyad of Will and Thought, wrapped in Compassion and embracing the Light. This is the basis of everything, not merely Actionism; you can't deny the fundamentals of existence. You can't expect that decadent materialism, feebly marketed as "tolerance, freedom to choose 48 labels of toothpaste, self-hate" is the way ahead. Decadence is to embrace darkness and despair.

If you so choose, go on, be a decadent. Just don't come and say that you have the answers to the challenges man faces at the beginning of the 21st century. The future belongs to individuals asserting their I AM-nature, to persons acknowledging their Spiritual Self, their willpower and drive, their Fire and Movement, persons affirming Action as Being.

The Actionist lives by Action as Being = to be is to act, to act is to be. In this way he proceeds until movement becomes a state, eventually ending up in a timeless here, an eternal now. Anchored in higher dimensions, he gains access to a *multidimensional operating system*, as it were.

YOU AND THE WORLD

You might like to hear affirmative, strengthening lessons on how great it is to have Willpower and drive. That's the Actionist hymn and Actionism will always continue to praise Will whenever it's proper. However, in the overall scheme of the Actionist stressing of the Self, of starting to work on yourself, on ESWY = Everything Starts With You, you have to think like this:

"There's nothing wrong with the world; everything is my fault!" This means: of course there are problems to be solved in the world. These problems have been highlighted in this study, like materialist nihilism being the official ideology in the world today. But when looking at yourself and your being, you can't blame The Society, The Man, The System. If you're feeling uneasy, "not so funny on the inside," then it's *your* responsibility to fix this. The first step is to take a deep, gentle breath. The second is to start practicing volitional, mental calm = C_3, q.v. Chapter 2. Along with this, you have to consciously affirm Will, you have to acknowledge your being as a Willful creature, able to see the affinity between your Inner Light and the Divine Light.

Everything starts with you. Only by having a harmonious microcosm can you build a harmonious macrocosm?

COLD, DARK, GREY

If your everyday seems "cold, dark, grey," what to do? Affirm your Inner Light. By acknowledging that you have a soul, a Spiritual Self that is a fragment of the Divine Light, then the dark is conquered. It takes Willpower to do this, Willpower to think in these ways. Sometimes you have to force yourself to see the Light.

THE ANSWER

People come to me and ask for guidance. Then I say: seek the answer within you. We're all created in God's image. Our individual, spiritual Light is a fragment of the Divine Light.

The answer is within, in the soul. "Im Innern ist's getan," Goethe said, "It's decided within". In this, I can only give you guidance to seek the inner truth. I can give you a sense of direction, presenting to you a basic attitude = the esoteric attitude, that of seeking the answers within your eternal being, your Spiritual Self.

Relax, take a deep, gentle breath, and say "I AM". That's the beginning of the Actionist way – a way of healing, of becoming both strong and compassionate.

It's that simple. But the simple is difficult.

Acknowledge your divine nature, your Inner Light. Acknowledge the power of Will, Will to do good, Will to Light. Will is by definition something good. There's no "evil will," a truth pointed out by French philosopher Alain.

Specifically, read Chapters 1 through 7 in this study if you need answers to the basic questions of "what to do, how to act". To realize âtman, the divine nature of our beings, is the Eternal Natural Way. To realize the divine nature of our inner being, the affinity between individual soul and all-soul, is the way.

MEMENTO MORI

To repeat: when plagued by the dark, think Light = I have an Inner Light, a fragment of the Divine Light.

Further, in the realm of "everyday bouts of angst," thinking of "Memento Mori" might help. When beset by everyday boredom, everyday lack of energy, everyday lack of direction, the thought of "Memento Mori" = my physical body has a limited lifespan, might be a sobering thought. For me personally, from the mid-1990s and for some years, the MMM = Memento Mori Mindset, especially ingrained by Castaneda's *A Separate Reality*, helped me get through in moments of meaninglessness.

Thinking "Memento Mori" made me sober up, enabling me to keep going. I didn't get "ready for the grave," instead, MMM, as intimated, makes you reboot the system, gives you everyday energy for everyday purposes = operational zest = the energy to do your everyday chores and then rest = Rest In Rest.

Even atheist existentialists like J. P. Sartre and Simone de Beauvoir gained sobriety and energy by thinking "Memento Mori". This is an honest, heartfelt tip for the person lacking drive in his everyday.

True, the thought of "Memento Mori" isn't fun to get acquainted with, at first it might drag you down a bit, but in the long run it lifts you, elevating you above common death angst, letting the idea of death (= the death of your physical body) invigorate you mentally and spiritually instead. Having defeated death angst, your mind is freed to deliberate on more fruitful subjects.

COMPASSION

Some lines on compassion. Actionism highlights compassion as a fundamental value. Then some of you might have this problem, that you acknowledge and show compassion in your everyday without getting anything back, no one being compassionate toward you. To this I say: true, it's a hard world. But you'll have to forgive your fellow brethren in this respect. "Forgive them, for they know not what they do." Then, summon your Willpower and live on. Don't stop embracing compassion though; just don't expect that it's a barter where you get it back at once.

Compassion remains a fundamental character of the cosmos. It's an ideal to acknowledge and embrace, now and always. But, don't fall for the "perfectionist fallacy" in this respect. Like: "JC was perfectly compassionate in every moment and if I'm not as good as he was I'm a bad person." To this I say: Jesus was indeed a loving person but he didn't for that matter go around hugging everybody. Compassion is an ideal to strive for. However, if you're not "100% compassionate," don't feel lost.

Strive for perfection, but don't fall down in dejection if you're not perfect in every detail during that operation. This applies to "being compassionate" along with everything else. Not realizing this is succumbing to "the perfectionist fallacy".

Being compassionate has to show in tangible acts. It can't remain a theoretical example. But again, it begins with embracing it in your mind. To be at least 51% STO = Service To Others oriented, is the crux. This is the ideal mindset. If all mankind has it, then we're in paradise. On the road to this state, don't feel dejected if not everyone around you is as kind as you. This is a process. Life is hard. Summon your Will and live life with all that it entails. Acknowledge Will, Thought and Compassion, as parts of the Whole that makes us human.

In your everyday, "too much compassion" can make you paralyzed. To balance it, muster Will and live more fully integrated. Just as reason must be balanced by intuition, sympathy must be balanced by courage.

DEVOTION

Actionism is an esoterically founded doctrine. Its God image is esoteric = inner = the divine nature is within us. We aren't "God", hands down, but we all have a divine nature, waiting to be realized and acknowledged by our Will-Thought.

Thus, an Actionist doesn't specifically "praise God," he's not in for the devotional attitude, even though the act of "praising God" might be beneficial per se (because it's better to "praise God, ask God for mercy, long for heaven" etc. than to be a dejected decadent). However, in essence, the esotericist mode of being is directed at "affirming one's Inner Light, saying I AM, realizing the luminescent nature of being a Will-endowed being".

It takes time to get used to the *esoteric* paradigm after having been brought up within an *exoteric* paradigm. The usual Western way of seeing God is that of an external force. So again, if the striving disciple feels lost, then old-school ways of gaining spiritual strength: "God help me" etc., are allowed. Such postures may give the same burst of spiritual energy as saying "I AM, I have an Inner Light". However, now man has to learn the *esotericist* way. The exoteric way is one of the past.

When the esotericist paradigm is established, the atheist will have a hard time explaining away God. These days it's still done in straw-man fashion, like: "where's your God, I don't see him sitting on a cloud". In the near future, believers will have the esoteric God concept as default mode, and then the atheist will be left out in the cold. Because, merely by looking at yourself in the mirror you will see God, that spark in the eye, that "soul spark," "das Vünklein der Seele" that Meister Eckart spoke about.

WILL AND THOUGHT

To merely know isn't enough. To merely gather wisdom from a book isn't enough. We have to understand by living; life and thought are inseparable, as the Existentialist school taught. Again, this illustrates the essential unity of Will and Thought, the Actionist way of being.

EVERYTHING

Everything exists. If you want harmony, then harmony is real. If you want peace, then peace is real. If you want freedom, then freedom is real.

FORGIVENESS

The Actionist is driven by Will. This includes the Will to forgive.

This means: on a macro level the Actionist is against The Powers That Be, the agents of societal decadence and materialism. But in seeing these operators, these "Robot Radicals, PC pod people, Social Justice Warriors", as individuals, the Actionist has the power to forgive them. "Forgive them, Father, for they know not what they do."

The Actionist fights the injustice of the Empire, the regimentation, the anti-white instances, the decadence, the banality. However, when facing the individuals belonging to this other side, he forgives them in his heart, as persons. The Actionist strives for a better world, but he won't "let the sun settle over his anger". On a personal plane he has the will to forgive, the ability to abstain from judging every person. Thus, he gains peace of mind, thus, he can operate as a complete human being: on the macro plane being against The Empire, but on the microplane being able to forgive Individual NN, serving the selfsame Empire.

PERSONAL ACTIONISM

To summarize the personal, microcosmic side of Actionism, you could have these key words:

I Am – willpower – raise yourself spiritually – one life, one breath – take responsibility – holism – an Aristocrat of the soul – Antropolis – vita activa, vita contemplativa – shaping life positively.

INDIAN WISDOM

On the net I found this, some Native American Wisdom in the form of "The Ten Indian Commandments". They have some affinity to the Actionist creed. Along with Castaneda's wisdom (q.v. Chapter 10), another shamanic instance, this is in sync with Actionism:

- "Remain close to the Great Spirit."
- "Do what you know to be right."
- "Look after the wellbeing of mind and body."
- "Take full responsibility for your actions."

ACTION

Actionism means action, to act, if only to breathe. We all have to act, we all have to breathe = to be is to act, to act is to be.

Actionism is about the Will-endowed, reflecting person mirroring his Divine Origin, enabling a society governed by the principles of Will, Truth and Compassion.

Actionism has the answers to morals and politics, to ethics and societal ideologies, to the principles of the micro- and the macrocosm. Actionism acknowledges man, family, nation and the entire planet as viable organisms, in opposition to the current ignorance seeing man and society as mere machines, possible to manipulate with science and technology. The current prevailing creed is a dead creed, a creed of death advocated to dead men. Actionism is life advocated to the living.

Actionism is in sync with the emerging world peace, growing after the passing of the Magic Zero-point. The prevailing decadent creed is a creed of yesterday, ready for the dump of history.

34. DELIBERATIONS

For better or worse, we now live in spiritual times, times mentally and immaterially focused, in contrast to materially. Also, we have a modicum of affluence, no one has to starve. But people are lost and spiritually insecure.

We need a new Awakening = to awake to the meaning of Idealism = to aim for Higher Values and combat materialist ignorance.

We need a Revival = an outreach program to bring people to acknowledge their Inner Light.

PASSIVE IDEALISM

God is the Primeval Light, and we, as individuals, are sparks of that Light. You will only have to look at yourself in the mirror, seeing that spark in your eye, to be convinced of God's existence. "God loves himself through us," as Simone Weil (1910-1943) said.

Reading the essays of C. S. Lewis (like *The Screwtape Letters* and *Mere Christianity*) you get the feeling that Lewis, for one, missed out on this esoteric aspect of Christianity. God is an external force, to Lewis, we have to reach out to it, God must hear us, etc. That's why Lewis will never be a central guru to Actionism.

Lewis, God bless him, was something of a "passive idealist". But, now's the time to focus on the *active idealist*, affirming his Inner Light, living his life in volitional spree. Lewis is worth reading, but he lacks Willpower as a driving force in his spiritual outfit. His was a

Paulinian mindset, a follower of St. Paul: only by grace, faith alone... Once, this was needed to counter Orthodoxy, but now to disregard Will and Action completely in your faith is odd indeed. These are volitional times – so get in sync with the times, affirm your Will = see that it harmonizes with God's Will = God helps the one who helps himself.

The trait of "faith in action," of action also being morally relevant, is a centerpiece of Actionism in the concept of Active Idealism. I dedicated all of Chapter 5 to this concept. In short, Active Idealism is to act in accordance with Being, to affirm the affinity of Will and Light. Again, it's about acknowledging the dictum, "God helps the one who helps himself." Conversely, to merely wait for divine grace is passive idealism.

JOY

I personally have my moody days, too. But I also, inexplicably and unconditionally, can know joy.

I know inspiration, dedication, joy. The unconditioned, spontaneous joy. Joy that isn't contingent upon something, dependent upon something.

Lying down on the bed at the end of the day, getting overcome by mirth: such is the unconditional joy.

In order to experience it, the advice is: allow it to happen. Relax. Calm brings clarity of mind. A lucid, resilient mind makes it easier to receive the joy and feeling that is immanent in the cosmos.

Christians often speak about joy, the glorified feeling they're experiencing. Personally, I once stood outside of all that, rather often feeling hatred and cynicism. And the joy I felt was conditional: now is the weekend, now I'm happy... now I'm at the pub, so much fun... but when I go home, I'm depressed...

Admittedly, as a creative person, I could experience "spontaneous joy," which is different from joy derived by performing a certain act. To create = to write is indeed an act, but in the trance of inspiration there's something truly unconditional.

The religious joy is called *bhakti* by Hindus. *Bhakti Mârga* is the path of devotion, of selfless love of the divine. Then, there are the Jnâna Mârga and Dhyâna Mârga also, the ways of knowledge and meditation, respectively. The former is the road of philosophy and deliberation, the latter the road of what we usually call *yoga*. So if you have a hard time acknowledging this divine joy, this bhakti, then try walking these other paths, Jnâna Mârga and / or Dhyâna Mârga. For in the end, all roads meet. It's called "Integral Yoga".

The Jnâna Mârga is the philosophy and ontology road, the Dhyâna Mârga is the meditation road, what we in the West usually call "yoga".

"Praise him, ye heavens of heavens, praise him with tambourine and cymbal"... "Come let's adore him"... "Hark, the herald angels sing, glory to the newborn king"... I'm an esotericist, having God within me, so I don't usually adore anything outside of me. But, of course, I like this traditional Biblical bhakti feeling too, like in some of the last numbers of the Book of Psalms and other spirituals.

TOWARD AN UNDERSTANDING

As intimated, in the past, I was somewhat adverse to the Christian concept of joy. And now I understand it. I now understand what Christians preach when they preach joy. Religious joy is unconditional joy. However, I would stress that I've never experienced any turn-around, any "defining moment" in this respect, like a bolt out of the blue, changing me in an instant or whatever. To me, the whole process was more discreet. But I did change. Over time the basic chord of cynicism was replaced by one of affirmation. This kind of Light-affirming transformation may differ from person to person.

However, once the change occurs, there must be no half measures when you've become a believer, an esotericist. Sure, you still can have doubts and ponder, but this 'to be religious' (of Lat. *re-ligare*, "reforge") is, like Kierkegaard said, a total experience, subjugation under a universal force. This is no novelty store where you haphazardly put together the world-view that fits you. Even though, for that matter, I'm a sort of syncretist, too. What I mean is that holism rules, the big picture.

Well. There is joy. And now I hum the spiritual "Just A Closer Walk With Thee," perfectly portraying that unconditional joy. A quiet joy.

LIFE

There is joy in seeing the sun in the sky, as the police officer Crews does in the series *Life*, in the opening scene of the first episode of this series. It was aired at the beginning of the century; in Sweden, in 2008. Damian Lewis played the lead as a Buddhist police officer in Los Angeles. The figure of Charlie Crews, the role that Damian Lewis plays, to me is unique in terms of TV cops. That is, he's not a cynic like Jim Caruso in *CSI Miami*, no self-righteous technician like Wolfgang Petersen of *CSI*, no emotional manipulator like Vincent d'Ononfrio in the first run of *Law and Order*. Crews is a Zen policeman, cool without being cynical, and with a life-affirming naivety that his colleagues shake their head at. For instance, they think he's crazy when he offers people fruit; he often eats fruit, healthy and fine, fitting for a man newly turned Buddhist.

He has a basic joy in what he does. But he also has a hard core. His eyes are far-seeing and penetrating at the same time. Imagine a Steve McQueen with an esoteric sounding board, there you have Damian Lewis in *Life*.

- - -

Episode 1 of *Life* had some fine details. Like the beginning, with Crews looking at the sun, bewildered. He's free of prison, he's a policeman falsely accused for murder, but now he's out and he can live again.

The idiosyncrasies of Crews were successively demonstrated while he and his colleague solved a murder. He had become a little twisted while doing time for a murder he didn't commit, talking to himself and thinking out loud, but overall he was sustained while in prison by reading a book on Zen Buddhism. Once in this episode, restored to his former job as a policeman, he was visiting a prison and was harassed by two guards (he allegedly killed a guard when he was in jail, not popular among the guard corps). Thus, he was severely tried, but he kept his calm and just said:

"Anger has no target, anger is unproductive. What you're angry at, you find important. I don't think you're important..."

And then he walked away.

It was also fun when he drove the car he had bought with the compensation money, a black Buick Regal Turbo. In a Buddhist spirit, he said while he was driving:

"I'm not attached to this car. I'm not attached to this car. OK, I'm a little attached to this car..."

The episode ended with a firefight against a suspect in a shabby house. The suspect was armed and opened fire, but in the end he was downed by Crews' counter-fire. Crews reached him before he died, took hold of his hand and said quietly: "Just go back to sleep..."

Our life down here is but an illusion, a dream. In heaven, however, we have our true being.

- - -

A fine episode, one of the last of Season One, began with Crews spying on a conversation in a park, doing this while sitting in his car, listening to a Buddhist tape to while away the time: a perfectly selected reading voice echoing words of wisdom.

You hear that voice as a voiceover to the scene. It said things like: "My exhalation is someone else's inhalation – we all walk the earth, good and evil alike – therefore, I'm the friend of my friend – therefore, I'm the friend of my enemy."

There followed a murder mystery, which was solved in the end. Meanwhile, Crews had become suspect of the murder of a former police officer, a figure appearing in the opening scene. The episode ended with the funeral of the police, a uniformed police officer's funeral that Crews hadn't been invited to because he was the suspect of the murder, and had been put under internal investigation. But Crews was at the cemetery to attend the funeral of the other victim of the episode. There, he was greeted by two women who knew this other victim. In the background could, again, be heard the voiceover of the Buddhist tape: "My exhalation is someone else's inhalation – we walk all the earth, good and evil alike – therefore, I'm the friend of my friend – therefore, I'm the friend of my enemy."

TV crime series don't get any better than this.

MOOT

Crews was the friend of his friend, the friend of his enemy. Love thy neighbor. Do I personally do this? This rule is abused today. For instance, in the land of Sweden of 2016 we are forced to accept mass immigration on humanitarian grounds. Here we have MENA immigrants, let them become Swedish citizens = help thy brother. But I don't accept this interpretation, this take on reality. The waves of immigration are created artificially. Blindly accepting such a colonization of your land isn't compassion, its slavery.

Love thy neighbor, love each other as brothers, are ideals I acknowledge. But defending the ethnic, social, historic and political independence and integrity of my native land, in countering mass immigration, doesn't nullify my embracing of this principle per se.

PEACE

I hereby declare universal peace. I nurture the spiritual development of everyone; I welcome the raising of everyone's consciousness. Once this elevation has started it's contagious, we're many in this world having risen beyond the condition of resentment and complaint – so you do the same, get ready for a new era, a coming Golden Age.

You're a miracle and you're blessed.

READ

Read on the net: "When people stop believing in God, they don't believe in nothing – they believe in anything!" People of today may be confused and high strung, the atheist-nihilist faction is seemingly strong, but this is just a symptom of the spiritual revival coming. People aren't indifferent, people have strong opinions, and this a sign of the mental elevation, as such a confused mental state at this point of development, but things will sort themselves out with time. There's no way for people to deny their Inner Light. People do have eyes to see with, an ability to spot that Spark in the Eyes. This is the divine element in man; people will acknowledge it, every one, worldwide, sooner or later.

LIGHT

As French thinker Alain said, there is no "problem of free will". Will by definition is free. The opposite, to be bound, is called desire. Desire is about indulging in materialism, which is of the dark. Will is about acknowledging Light.

We evolve spiritually and mentally by interacting with Light. That's where true joy is experienced. Conversely, darkness, per se, doesn't evolve us. Darkness is the absence of Light, but Light isn't mere absence of dark. For instance, there are light particles called photons but there are no darkness particles, as far as I know. Light is a carrier of information, darkness is absence of information.

Light isn't defined by darkness or anything. Light simply is.

Thus, evolve from the duality of dark-and-light to unity, to an affirming of the Light. That's where the essence of man's development lies. To intuitively acknowledge Light evolves us, not negativity, darkness and suffering per se.

FORM

"The Best form to see God is in every form." – Neem Karoli Baba

DEVELOPMENT

The world is developing into a realm of Light, harmony and beauty. It's true that there still are problems around, the current regime is materialist to the bone, decadence *in nuce*, but eventually a Golden Age is about to be inaugurated. So realize this and *match the platform* by being reasonably positive and affirmative, starting with acknowledging your Inner Light. ESWY = Everything Starts With You.

HARMONY

Mutatis mutandum, the project of Actionism acknowledges the doctrines of Plato, Plotinus, Krishna, Jesus Christ, Meister Eckart, Goethe and Ernst Jünger. An Actionist acknowledges his Inner Light, he stands for the Light, I AM the Light, a being in sync with God and the heartbeat of the universe.

An Actionist acknowledges Will, Truth, Compassion and Light, he praises inspiration and optimism, he praises the spirits of adventure and exploration, he praises the peaceful coexistence of people in their respective places of origin, he acknowledges the Rule of Law, academic freedom, freedom of speech and artistic freedom.

So be it.

ACTIONISM

NO IRONY

In peace, as in battle, there's no irony. They are both conditions where you draw power from the invisible, from *akâsha*, space, the fifth element.

EVERYDAY

The everyday reality is the dependent reality, the conditioned, Maya of Illusion, the changing world, *die Seiendes*. The unconditioned reality is the true reality = the eternal = Being = *Sein*. More on this in *Borderline*.

FEAR

"The cave you fear to enter holds the treasure you seek." – Joseph Campbell. Reflection: you have to deal with your inner demons. To do stuff you are afraid of, within reasonable limits.

ART

Anonymous quote: "When thy hand has drawn a perfect line, the cherubim descend to delight themselves in it as a mirror." This could make you think of Orpheus, whose music entranced even the gods. Devas do create and inspire art, but the praise for earthly artworks should mainly go to the person creating it, the human artist. Influenced by what he has seen in the astral world, he conveys his vision to the physical world, adding something of his own to it. That's why we have to acknowledge the artist. You can't, as a passive idealist is wont to do, merely say that God is to thank for all art. While there is a divine element in every artwork, there is also something there being the result of the artist per se.

HAMLET

Hamlet, that play: there's no mystery to it operationally. Hamlet is asked by the ghost of his father to avenge his murder. In order not to pose an obvious threat to the murderer, Hamlet plays the fool. He isn't mad, this is just a ruse, and this is clear to us having read Saxo Grammaticus's original version of the Amledus story.

You could say: Hamlet might "be" this or that, the play and the figure might be open for interpretations, but the heading-for-revenge-and-playing-the-fool-so-as-not-to-seem-a-viable-threat
is an interpretation making sense, both in view of the Saxo source and on its own terms. Hamlet is conducting Operation Revenge and playing the fool is simply part of the modus operandi. This is clear to those of us who haven't just been sitting behind a desk reading books all our lives.

MANTRAS

An Actionist mantra: "I'm action, not dejection. I'm action, I'm satisfaction." An Actionist shapes his life actively. Because, it isn't enough to say, "I believe". You must also be able to say, "I act".

Another mantra: "I'm Victory, I'm Willpower. I'm the Active Tradition giving life to a new era. I'm action, I'm tradition, the active tradition of self-reliance, accountability and vigilance."

Everything is action. In the beginning was the deed, as Faust said. In the beginning Will united with Thought. Then Will-Thought chose Light and the union brought forth God, a shining entity of infinite splendor, saying I AM to seal the deal. In itself, this "I AM" was a performative statement, much like the way Actionist philosophy is done. By saying it, it's done. Like a ritual.

Mantra: "I'm Action, not dejection. I'm Will united with Thought, a Will-Thought merged with the Light. I acknowledge my Inner Light and bring hope to the dejected, strength to the weak, pointing out a road ahead for mankind."

ACTIONISM

Mantra: "I'm Will to Action, Will to Light, Will to Will the future into a distinct symbol of Faith, Hope and Charity."
Actionism is Faith telling everyone to keep the faith. No man is "down and out" unless he thinks himself down and out. No one can beat a man having faith in himself and his mission.

C3

Fear rules the man who doesn't meditate. Desire rules the man lacking Willpower. The basic demand for calling yourself an Actionist is that you have calm, inner calm, volitional mental calm. C3 = being calm, cool and collected is the Actionist fundamental.

HOMO AGENS

An Actionist is Homo Agens = the man who acts. His creed is Actionism = ATF = Active Thought Framework.

An Actionist is positively disposed = at least 51% positively disposed.

Actionist mantra: "I'm the Power of Thought. I'm the power of meditation. I'm the Power of the Word; my statements are performative = saying it is doing it, making it become real. I'm a glorified affirmation. I'm Here-and-Now. I'm Holism. I Am."

CREED

Everything is a challenge, everything is a work of art, everything is an operation. Walk the talk. *On s'engage et puis on verra*. Being mentally elevated, having a "crisis mentality," being ready to deal with any situation, any time. This is the glorified *heightened awareness*. To be anchored in Sein, not in everyday trifles: "*The average man is hooked to his fellow men, while the warrior is hooked only to infinity*." [Tales of Power, p 7]

Mantra: "I'm Differentiated Man, an Aristocrat of the Soul. I'm Responsible Man, Action Man – Acting Man – Operational Agent – Absolute Man."

"I'm Traditional Man. I'm an Active Esotericist, taking charge. I'm matter transformed into energy. I'm a narrative style directly involved in the events."

"I'm avoiding excessive emotionalism. I let Will govern Thought."

"I state my purpose clearly, saying it out loud. I acknowledge the power of performative statements = saying it is doing it, like a ritual. This is the power of affirmations, like: 'I Am That I Am in action here, now and forever,' as Shanta Gabriel said."

WILL

Mantra: "I'm the impossible overcoming the possible. I'm freedom vanquishing necessity."

"I'm a guide, pointing the way ahead. I'm the rebirth of divine inspiration. I stand in a glorified grey area, preaching new life to a confused culture. I preach life to the living, not death to the dead."

"I'm a free and active idealist, stating my point of view. I'm an operational esotericist leading the way to a new era – an era of Responsible Men acknowledging their Inner Light, taking charge of their condition as thinking, reflecting beings."

"I'm the acknowledged Light, going beyond materialism. I bring fire and movement to a solidified age, bogged down in chaos and confusion."

I AM ACTION

Mantra: "I am Victory, I am Willpower, I am Action."

"I'm a free man in a modern democracy."

"I'm a creative Self in an ever-present Now. I go Beyond the Beyond and Within the Within."

"I'm pure Will, pure Action; I'm the Victory of Victories. I'm Will choosing Light, Will willing itself, Will willing God, the Self thus becoming What It Is – free and responsible at the same time. "

"I'm standing at the edge, living in a glorified grey area. I'm standing in the Borderline between two epochs – between the Faustian Era on the one hand and the Antropolitan Era on the other, between Kali Yuga and Sat Yuga, between Dark and Light, Death and Life. In this respect, you who preach war belong to the past. We who declare responsible peace are happening now; tomorrow belongs to us."

"You who prophesy war are out of time, out of your depth. You should all do us a favor: enter your fancy underground shelters, close the door and stop disturbing the rest – that is, We, the Living."

"War mongers belong to the past. War prophets, your time is up. The relation between pessimism and optimism, war-mongering and peace projection, dark and Light, is captured by George Bernard Shaw: 'People who say it cannot be done should not interrupt those who are doing it.'"

QUESTIONS

You might ask yourself: "Does life have a meaning? Why is life difficult?" Then I say: Life is hard, therefore meaningful. We come here to learn. Life is a school.

TOTALITY

Get ready for the Total Tradition.
Get ready for Radical Holism.
Get ready for Integral Esotericism.
Get ready for Radical Aristocratism – Active Thought – Antropolis – Archeofuturism.
Get ready for life beyond the Magic Zero-point: war is over, now realize peace.

Get ready for Radical Spiritualism – Willful Esotericism – Active Idealism, the contemplative ethic of action in a coming Golden Age.
Get ready for Action as Being.
Get ready for I AM.

Get ready for life beyond Maya of Illusion – life beyond Metropolis – life in Active Thought – life in Antropolis.

35. ABOUT GOD

We all know the saying, "I AM". This is an Actionist fundamental, a performative saying acknowledging existence, the reflected life and the divine connection. If you expand the saying into, "I Am That Which Is," it gets even more interesting. This means: the ultimate reality is something that merely Is, that can't be questioned. Ontologically, something has to be acknowledged without constant reflection, discussion and debate. That which simply is, is holy; it's Real beyond everyday reality. Conversely, everyday reality is subordinate to change, it's the "maya of illusion," something less real. That Which Is, in this respect, can be seen as God. God is holy; God exists, beyond deliberations and wordplay. The following Chapter is about God.

SO INDEED

So indeed, God is, God can't be questioned? True: from an ontological point of view, "God Is," period. That's the God concept Actionism supports. As such, it's a help in order to conceive of God, to understand what God means.

How can you talk about God? Words aren't enough. Or maybe they are, in the hands of a poet:

> "*God is a resting-place on which we lie reclining in the Whole /*
> *pure as angels, with saintly blue eyes answering the hail of the*

stars; (...) god is the fecund seed of nothingness and the ashes of the burned-down worlds; god is the myriads of insects and the ecstasy of roses; / god is a prison for all the free spirits; / god is a harp for the hand of the strongest wrath; god is what longing can induce to descend to earth!"

This is how Swedish-Finnish poet Edith Södergran (1892-1923) conceived her God. She was a free-thinker so she spelled "god" with a lowercase letter. Still, she had the strains of a mystic, and in this poem she captured the essence of the omnipresent God, and, in addition to that, she captured just what I mentioned myself, the difficulty of even talking about God in human language.

IN THE BEGINNING

In the beginning was God. Or rather, as I showed in Chapter 1, there were forces like Will and Thought, and even before that there was the silent Compassion of the unmanifested cosmos. These forces, then, having united with each other and Light, developed into God: "I AM" he said, the statement itself being the performative act confirming the event.

God, a being of Light, Will, Thought and Compassion, then created human beings, human souls. Individuals have the Divine Light within. In each of them is a spark of the divine. The mystic Eckart (1260-1328) called it *scintilla animae* = the soul spark. Look at yourself in the mirror and you might detect it. Live life and detect it, in discreet instances of unconditional joy.

The soul is in God, God is in the soul. The Hindus call this "the affinity of Âtman with Brahman". The invisible God, the omnipresent God, "it is you" = *tat tvam asi*, as it reads in *Chândogya Upanishad*. And, in the Gospel of John, we find the same idea of divine omnipresence, of man's soul mirroring God: "you are in me and I am in you" (17:21).

The individual human being has a soul spark, an Inner Light, a Divine Light. This is what makes him human. The divine presence in every creature is well captured in this quote of Shri Aurobindu (1872-1950), about how God took of his own Light to create man and how God thus divided himself to experience division, experience himself even more thoroughly, a divine *gnôthi seavtón,* as it were: "Existence that multiplied itself for sheer delight of being, plunged into trillions of forms so that it might find itself innumerably."

UPANISHADS

I just quoted one of the Upanishads, a mystical document in a theological-artistic grey area. These Upanishads say a lot about God's presence in man. Like *Shvetâshvatâra Upanishad* VI.11: "Eko devah, sarvabhûteshu gûdhah" = "there is one God, hidden within all beings". Being present in all creatures, God is everywhere and nowhere, seemingly, because he's invisible, he has no body; he's "ashariram sharîresu," "the disembodied in the bodies" (Katha Upanishad II.22). Further, he's "the undivided in the divided," "avibhaktam vibhaktesu" (Bhagavad-Gîtâ XVIII.20).

God is the essential soul of everyone. He sees everything, experiences everything. God is Being, Knowledge, Eternity: "satyam jnânam anantam Brahma" (*Taittirîya Upanishad* II.1). In the soul of everyone God is "the unseen seer, the unheard hearer, the unthought thinker, the unconceived conceiver" = "adrishto drashtâ, ashrutah shrotâ, amato mantâ, avijnâto vijnatâ" (*Brihadâranyaka Upanishad* III.7.23).

ACRONYMS

God is in everything and everyone: in objects as ideas, in men as Inner Light. For he who sees this, observing the world gives him a sense of belonging. This, in the Actionist mode, is expressed as, "clarity in things, clarity in yourself".

Another viable concept is this one, one whose essence was the starting point of this Chapter. It reads: I Am That Which Is. So again, to explain this fundamental truth: the ultimate reality is something that merely Is, that can't be questioned. Ontologically, something has to be acknowledged without constant reflection, discussion and debate. That which simply is, is holy; it's Real beyond everyday reality. Conversely, everyday reality is subordinate to change, it's the "Maya of Illusion," something less real.

I've talked about the Beginning, in Chapter 1 and this chapter. And, if you need a concept for the Actionist, look at this instance for how God came to be, it would be: "unifying Will-Thought and Light equals God". That is, in the beginning Will chose to merge with Thought, then Will-Thought chose Light instead of dark and became God resplendent.

WALSCH

An interesting aspect of God in the 21st century is brought to us by American Neale Donald Walsch (1943-). He wrote *Conversations with God* in 1995. Allegedly he knows God; he has talked with him. Details aside, Walsch's books convey a viable esotericist theism, a conversation with a traditionally footed, albeit syncretistic, God.

For instance, people often try to contact God through prayer. So, what is a prayer? Is it an asking for something? Walsch, for his part, has a different approach. He maintains that the person praying should be convinced that he's already heard. Therefore, the prayer becomes more of a thanksgiving than an "asking for," a mere request.

This kind of wisdom is what makes Walsch worth paying attention to.

As for this approach to prayer, it isn't new. It's a known fact that God can only give what's in his kingdom, what's in his power to give. He can give you "more light" = more of the divine light of which you're created, of which you consist = the light you already have within = therefore, prayer should be a thanksgiving and not a request.

This is esotericism; this is divine thought in sync with Actionism. The rest of this chapter makes an Actionist reading of the Walsch

ACTIONISM

creed. So this is no carbon copy of Walsch's thought, it's a profiling and conceptualization of it, as was also the case when I treated Castaneda and Evola in Chapters 10 and 12.

LIVE THE CREED

Swedenborg seems to have meant that action is more important than faith alone. You have to put your faith in movement, in action; the Pauline "faith alone" isn't enough as a viable creed. I admit Swedenborg's wisdom in this. The "faith alone" idea may have arisen to counter the far-reaching adherence to Old Testament laws, the orthodoxy of the Holy Land around the year zero, but this doesn't mean that a man's actions are unimportant for his spiritual development. Actionism, for its part, is about raising yourself mentally with selfless action. And, as for the more moral side of beneficial action, Walsch (in *Conversations with God, Book Three*) brings up the question: of what benefit are great insights and knowledge in a society if we don't integrate them into societal practices? For our modern society may be advanced, but it's technology, natural science and engineering which are advanced while in the sphere of ideas we are a primitive society where only the material counts. The death of the body and the decomposition of matter is the official creed.

Decline, death and decay: this is the materialist nihilism taught in TV, academics and mass media. But traditional doctrines are still studied by a select few, Perennial Thought teaching about Will, Truth and Compassion. And in books like Walsch's, the essentially same idealist creed is advocated, conjuring up a different world. He channels someone he calls "God," offering us esotericism, wholesale and retail, clear-cut aphorisms:

- Time is not a movement but a field through which you move. (*Conversations with God, Book Two*)
- The soul creates, the brain reacts. (Ibid)

- Serve life first. This will be the new creed of spirituality. (*Tomorrow's God*)
- You can never run out of loneliness in your life until you run out of the loneliness within you. (Ibid)
- In life you don't need to do anything. It's entirely a matter of what you choose to be. (*Conversations with God, Book Three*)
- If I don't go within me, I go without me. (*Conversations with God, Book One*)

COURSE

The Walsch opus is a journey through matters simple and advanced, from a basic course in esotericism through a premium. Personally, I read these books somewhat cursorily, much of the content coming through as rather familiar to a man having already read the Gita, Plotinus, Goethe, Meister Eckart and Ernst Jünger, but for those who want a primer in spirituality, *Conversations With God* (book one) is highly recommended. Like some latter-day Philip K. Dick, Walsch is sitting around and suddenly finds himself communicating with God through writing. And when he asks, "How do I know that you are you? That it's not fake," then it's just like in Dick's notes on his theophanic experience, the *Exegesis* and the novel *VALIS*.

ESSENCE

In *Tomorrow's God* we get this charming thought: "Think of God in a way that's good for you". This is like the Hindu concept of *ishta-deva*, of choosing the form of God that fits you. If you want to worship the elephant god, you do that; if you want to worship Vishnu, you do that. For you in the Christian realm, you can choose to see God as the Wise Old Man or an abstract ever-presence, a light being or however else you want. The essence of what you acknowledge is still the same. God is real, God is one; we only conceive of him differently.

ACTIONISM

In Actionism per se, this is expressed as, "finding your own path". This means: given that there is an objective, transcendent reality, the way to realize this can be different for different people. There's no "one size fits all" in esoteric practice.

Of course, here I also remember Râmakrishna who said: "All gods are god – but don't worship the tiger god! All water is water – but don't drink dirty water!"

RECURRING

A recurring theme in the *Conversations With God* series is that everything has happened, you know everything you need to know, but you don't know that you know. Thus, we're eternal Light Beings, eternal spirits, referred to the incarnation here on Earth, but in our spiritual stature we're gods. The memory is not in the brain, it's a field of information we have access to through the brain.

We have access to eternity and therefore have infinite possibilities. We can get everything we want; it's said in the Walsch books. It can make you think of the old US Army motto: "Be all that you can be."

In *Tomorrow's God*, Walsch's God further deliberates on this theme. The following is what Jesus reportedly might have said if he had lived today: I am the life, the way and the truth. Live your life the way I lived my life, walk the same path I have walked. That is, follow me and you will experience God. Believe in me and you will believe in yourself, and vice versa. This is the truth that I came to you to reveal.

In *Conversations with God* (book one) something similar is expressed: you know that there's a God, but you don't know that you know it. Perhaps you're waiting for the experience of God; nevertheless, you have it already...

This is the heart of esotericism: we know everything we need to know if we just look inside ourselves. *Gnôthi seavtón* = know thyself.

Also, keep in mind what the pragmatic Dr. Johnson said: "We don't want to be informed, we want to be reminded." Such *anamnesis*, nonforgetfulness or remembrance, was also central in Plato's doctrine. We have the light within, we must only acknowledge it.

CIRCULAR

The Walsch books can be quite sophisticated. They can present metaphysics and ontology of the highest kind, albeit in popular form. Like: a person exists, he IS (just as God is: I AM THAT I AM, as it says in the Old Testament). We exist, and we can't choose *not* exist. You may choose not to know yourself, but then you miss out on much of what you've received as a gift.

All true ontology ultimately becomes circular. Walsch notes in *Conversations With God* (book one), that his informant returns to the same things all the time. To this, God retorts: "this is just like life," and then Walsch has to surrender. Elsewhere, God says in the same book that you should affirm the circular reasoning by becoming the circle, not only moving in the circle. Indeed, an elegant holistic payoff; it's like Aeon Flux saying that she *is* the edge after being accused of "skating the edge".

Some more goodies from these books, slightly edited by me:

- To put yourself in hell to avoid having to get there is like committing suicide for fear of death.
- An ascetic lives not meagerly; he forsakes mere egotism, not the divine joy.
- God's ideal is to be realized through us, "God loves himself through us". (Simone Weil)
- Freedom is to lower your expectations. The goal is to live selflessly in the moment. (This is reminiscent of WAP = winning as propensity.)

EVER-PRESENCE

God is in everything, we learn in the Walsch books, God is the yin and the yang, the Alpha and the Omega, the beginning and the end. He's both good and bad, and yet beyond it all: *Jenseits von Gut und Böse*.

A certain Dénis Lindbohm (Swedish author, 1927-2005) was of the same opinion: God is both black and white, good and evil. The evil is needed to get to know the good. You shouldn't, for that reason, be completely relativist or worship Satan; the true God is beyond the everyday good, he stands for the good in a greater sense, as Plotinus said. To acknowledge this God must be the goal, without denying the earthly existence with all its nuances.

Moreover, these books have their funny passages. Walsch objects: "You're joking with me," to which God counters with: "So what, it was I who invented humour"... This may be the kind of thing that made them into the bestsellers they are.

ARTIST

The words "God" and "life" can be said to be synonymous. This, a Swedish musician once discovered when he was at a certain treatment center for alcoholics. Apparently, it was a Christian institution, too, because at some point he was sitting there with a priest who suggested that they pray. "But I can't pray, I don't believe in God," the musician said. "Then pray to life," the priest said, and this did the trick. The musician had an elevating, clarifying experience, he was "redeemed". Not that Actionism ever means that we're doomed, for, we can always affirm our Inner Light, which it might be said was happening here. And then the musician went off to write a song about building a temple.

The trait of connecting God with life is also encountered in the Walsch opus. In *Conversations With God* (book three), the channeled God says that he's not the result of a process; he *is* the very process. He is the creator and he is the process through which he's created.

And in *Tomorrow's God* it's stated that life is a process of change. The words "God" and "change" are synonymous. God is change inasmuch as life is an ongoing process, a self-rolling wheel, a rotating galaxy. Worship life and you worship God. Along with this we, of course, also have eternal forms, the eternal *eidoi* in the causal sphere. And the elements of Will, Truth and Light aren't, in themselves, subject to change.

However, speaking of change, you may think of Nietzsche: "*Nur wer sich wandelt, bleibt mit mir verwandt.*" This pun essentially means: "only the one who transforms himself is akin to me."

WISDOMS

The Walsch series has a lot of wisdoms. Like: there are those who see things as they are and say "Why?", and there are those who dream of things that never were and say "Why not?"

This is a fitting paean to creators and pathfinders. It can make you think of a sign I once saw at the home of an acquaintance, saying: "There are three kinds of people: Those who *make* things happen, those who *watch* things happen, and those who *wonder* what happened."

GOD

A consistent teaching of the Walsch books is that God doesn't care about us. This may sound paradoxical, but what it means is that you shouldn't worship God in order to "calm his anger" or some other misconceptions that are still around. For instance, St. Paul reportedly meant that Jesus was crucified to atone for the wrath of God toward man, which is a totally insane, primitive idea, having no support anywhere. Instead, the New Testament (Gospel of John) says that Jesus was sent to the world because God loved the people, he wanted to lead them onto better paths, nothing else.

In the beginning God gave us free Will, this'll never change. We're beings of Will and Thought, remember. Therefore, "God doesn't care about us" because he doesn't steer every step we take, he isn't fretting about the possibility that man now would choose to turn his back on him. He's God, the origin of everything, as demonstrated in Chapter 1 of *Actionism*, and no Homerian god with human characteristics. God, for that matter, isn't indifferent; if we recognize his light within us, then probably some kind of joy resounds in the invisible. "This is my ideal: that I should be realized by you," it's said in *Conversations with God*. This again reminds me of Simone Weil's idea that God wants to know himself through us. He wants to see his Light within each of us, and he wants us, as bearers of that light, to recognize it in order to amplify it.

If we, by our free Will acknowledge that we're children of the Light, if we choose to be a part of God, well then, a lot is gained. In harmony with what I said in Chapter 1, this could possibly be said to be God's plan: that we use our free Will to return to the source of Light. We were given free Will to use as we wanted, venture out everywhere, even to "the dark," and if we would choose to return to the fold then the father would welcome us. "Behold, the prodigal son has returned, let's have a feast..."

36. THE DANE

In the previous chapter I spoke about God. Now for some more in the same vein. Specifically, the topic is Danish philosopher Sören Kierkegaard (1813-1855) who conceptualized man's condition in this way: it's in relation to God that man becomes what he is, free and responsible at the same time. Hereby some Actionist notes on Kierkegaard, a man like Castaneda (q.v. Chapter 10) stressing the need for existential responsibility.

SUMMARY

Why has Kierkegaard remained a topical philosopher ever since the late 19th century? Maybe because of the following.

For instance, Kierkegaard says: subjectivity is truth. This doesn't mean that you ignore natural laws or verifiable historical facts. It's a moral statement, meaning: you can't live life objectively, like some academic philosopher having the formal answers to everything, "dreaming of systems so perfect that no one will need to be good" (Eliot, "Choruses from The Rock", 1934). Subjectivity is the personal reality of life. In this respect, *anxiety* is coupled to freedom as an opportunity, not a punishment. To be able to choose might be scary but this fear has to be met head on. This Kierkegaard meant in the study, *The Concept of Anxiety*, 1844.

ACTIONISM

You have to be true to yourself and others. And – again – it's before God that man becomes what he is, free and responsible at the same time. To really understand God and reality is impossible, therefore *faith* is needed, and a tolerance toward some of the paradoxes of everyday life. This Kierkegaard meant in *Fear and Trembling*, 1843.

In *Either / Or* (1843) Kierkegaard attacked materialist nihilism. You have to bypass the state where you simply indulge in entertainment and art, instead, a man worthy of his name must head for a more authentic life, a life confronting the eternal questions, the reflected life in the Socratic sense. Look inside and affirm the Inner Light, as an Actionist would say.

Kierkegaard believed in God. But he also influenced atheist thinkers, like Nietzsche and Sartre. And of course, it's better being an atheist existentialist than an ironic dandy, a melancholy romantic or an indignant intellectual; all this is essentially to be found in *Either / Or*. The existentialist has at least begun to think, to question the alleged objectivity of the daily opinion and placed himself in the middle of the problem. To see yourself in the mirror and realize that *this*, the reflecting person, is the philosophical basis = ESWY = everything starts with you. The dandy, the romantic and the intellectual for their part, to Kierkegaard, seem to be beyond all hope: the dandy just wants to have fun, the romantic just wants to die in style and the intellectual only has his indignation.

LEAP OF FAITH

As for Kierkegaard's view on "the paradoxical," "the leap of faith," this could be said: A person reading documents of religion may be beset by objections and doubts, such as "did Jesus really exist?" or, "was Arjuna really lectured by Krishna on the field of Kurukshetra?" Questions of conditioned plausibility and factuality tend to cloud the essential questions, those of existence and being. Not all questions can be solved intellectually. You have to embrace the mere situation of living with all your soul. You can't analyze every problem like a jigsaw puzzle, you can't expect to reach every solution by way of an equation, completely and definitely. Instead, spirituality is a holistic phenomenon that man puts himself in. You can't study it from the outside.

Therefore, you must refine your everyday reason to the levels of intuition, grasping the sense of the ineffable. Then you take that leap which Kierkegaard spoke of, the "leap of faith," after which you may live a whole life, a passionate life. Then you have accepted the core of spiritual thought, also realizing that there can be paradoxes and contradictions but that these opposites belong to the whole. You have to let intuition and feeling inside. You can't, however, as Ernst Jünger sometimes had the urge to do, always have a "spiritual pioneering force" venturing ahead and building bridges to the invisible. Then you've misunderstood what life means, what "coming here to learn" means.

The reflecting man has to solve his problems by himself. You must essentially help yourself, you can't rely on automatic salvation through membership in a congregation, or rely on systems à la Hegel, systematically solving all the problems once and for all and leaving no room for the essentials, namely, the Will-Thought of the individual, which is a mirror of the divine.

ANXIETY

As intimated, Kierkegaard also analyzed the concept of *anxiety* = angst, the enduring fear of existence. The animals have no fear, he said, man on the other hand has it, and it's because we men have the freedom to choose, while the animals live instinctively. So having anxiety, and doubting the existence of God, for example, is quite normal. *C'est la condition humaine*, as it were.

Just believing directly, naively like a child, may be good. But the question is: how many today really can do this? Apparently, doubt is the contemporary way to relate to the major, ontological questions. We all wrestle with God until sunrise; some give up while others just go away confused, convinced that God is an illusion. And some discover their Inner Light as a personal mirror of the divine. Kierkegaard, for one, wasn't exactly that kind of *esotericist* but he was way ahead of his *exoteric* time, the 19th century, where congregational Christianity was the norm and the rest was a budding passive nihilism.

- - -

Freedom begets anxiety. But at the same time (said the Dane in his inimitable jargon) you realize, "that anxiety is the reality of freedom as the opportunity to opportunity"... to stand before the apparent futility, facing the void, this begets anxiety. As indicated, the animals don't have this; they head unknowingly toward the fullness of God. We human beings, on the other hand, we must look into the emptiness and accept that everything we see in the material world is only illusion and deception. When we have done this, having seen the clouds scudding over a desolate world, perhaps we become insane. Or blessed.

INDEED

Indeed, do you become insane or blessed when facing the Nothingness? The answer depends on how esoterically inclined you are; if you can embrace the idea that the true nature of existence is invisible and that the things we see are but expressions of ideas. The object is there for the idea to present itself in to our senses. This, again, is the Platonic idealism which is the ontological foundation of Actionism, idealism as such being treated in *Borderline*.

SUBJECTIVITY

"Subjectivity is truth," Kierkegaard meant. This put him in opposition to both Hegel and High-Church Christianity, with moral systems and systematic creeds ignoring the Will-Thought of the individual. Instead, Kierkegaard meant, you should go out in the quiet desert where you meet yourself. "Subjectivity is the personal reality of life," he called it. This is the starting point. This is Actionism = ESWY = Everything Starts With You.

Having in this way discovered Essential Reality in your own being, you may go on to experience the truth of objective values, reaching them through personal trial and error – by living. There we have existentialism and Actionism in a nutshell: the heart of the creed is not to preside in the academy and pontificate about various problems without facing any personal difficulties, without having to put your personal being into the equation. Instead, you must expose yourself to reality and "tear your nails bloody on the wall of everyday" (Södergran).

Objectifying the issues (such as school philosophy does), is merely explaining them away. Instead, you must come to grips with them; realize the adventure inherent in them. You have to go out into the world as a personal actor and live the volitional, Willpowered life.

Objectivity, for its part, is required in disciplines such as physics, mathematics and logic. But the things that affect human existence, like morality and ethics, can't be solved step-by-step and formally, because, for these, *subjectivity* must be the starting point. We live subjectively, but this doesn't mean "accidentally" or "haphazardly," it means to live honestly. In Kierkegaard's words, "come to existence" is to be in your element, "in your esse". *Esse* is Latin for Being. As in Actionism, this an ethic footed in ontology. You reach the essence of reality and thereby the essence of yourself. You reach the basis of reality when you become real to yourself and others.

This is what "finding yourself" means. This isn't merely some impulse to do this and that. It's about basing your being in essential reality, in tuning in to the cosmos, in reaching volitional mental calm – C_3 – footed in your own being.

To find oneself is the most important thing in life. It's like finding the Holy Grail. And this isn't so easy to find. What's needed is cutting yourself off from the outside world, meditating and tuning into the stillness, shutting off your sense of pride and your desires. It's about cutting down your expectations to a minimum and enjoying existence as such.

TO BE ALIVE

To simply be: such a cliché. But the truth is simple. "It's better to exist than not to exist," Leibniz said. "Ain't it good to be alive"...

Finding joy in nothing, in peacefulness, in existence itself, this can be likened to "the starry moment when one chooses himself," as Kierkegaard says. You don't have much to choose from really; you are who you are, you can't become someone else. The choice is actually already done. And now you probably realize the joy of living the life you live, in being who you are. You have "found yourself".

37. DER PULVERKOPF

Ernst Jünger called Nietzsche "der Pulverkopf" = "Gunpowder head". In this he highlighted the fierce nature of Friedrich Nietzsche (1844-1900). Nietzsche might have been an antispiritual atheist, but he was on to something in his volitional creed. Nietzsche rediscovered Will and gave it the central role it deserves in ethics.

DRIVE

Actionism stresses the unity between Will, Thought and Compassion, in society and man, in the cosmos at large, even in God. Friedrich Nietzsche, for his part, was wrong in striking out the last element of the three, Compassion. Because, Compassion is a central ethical element. He was wrong when he said, "War and courage have done more great things than charity" [*Thus Spake Zarathustra*, Chapter 10, this and other quotes taken from the online version on Project Gutenberg http://www.gutenberg.org/files/1998/1998-h/1998-h.htm#link2H_4_0015]

This is rigorism and brutalism, eventually leading into sterility and banality. Nietzsche went to great lengths in trying to "de-conceptualize" compassion, without success.

Still, Nietzsche's Willpower driven creed, the elemental power exuding from his thought, symbolized in *Thus Spake Zarathustra*, is something that will always inspire Actionist thought and attitude. Therefore this chapter.

Nietzsche rediscovered Will. As intimated earlier in this study, Will in the form of *thelema* is known in Christianity ("thy will be done" = "genêthêto to thelêma sou"). The Gospel of Philip talks about "lack of will" making people into sinners. Conceptually, Christianity knows of the elemental force of Will, its divine, light-related nature. But in the West in the 18th and 19th centuries, Will seemed to have been forgotten. The pious man of the times was only a passive instance, there to receive the light by the grace of God. This "by faith alone"-creed had old roots (St. Paul) and, by the time Nietzsche arrived, had caused the Christian doctrine to degenerate into passive idealism along with ritualism and banality.

Long story short, Nietzsche rediscovered Will. He may have taken it too far. His overall creed threw out all esotericism, all metaphysics. Still, Will is an elemental force. It's the "fixed point by which you can move the world," as it were.

Will is needed to overcome hardships, to make the possible out of and therefore triumph over the impossible. Will can move mountains. Conversely, if a person doesn't have Will he'll never be more than a "meat puppet," a vegetating animal.

Will isn't everything. There's got to be Thought and Compassion in a person's mindset, too. However, conversely, to ignore Will is impossible for a viable ethic.

WILL TO POWER

For better and worse, Nietzsche has a way of expressing himself with flair and verve. This creates a leeway to interpret his volitional creed in this way and that. However, Actionism interprets Nietzsche's talk of "Will to power" as WTPOY = Will To Power Over Yourself. The following passages in *Thus Spake Zarathustra* are the fundamentals of a viable volitional creed, one that isn't prone to be reduced into some searing rigorism or banality, of chauvinism or other "power" related nonsense. This is the spiritualist, Actionist, reading of the doctrine in question. It starts with discovering Will inside you:

> "Yea, something invulnerable, unburiable is with me, something that would rend rocks asunder: it is called MY WILL. Silently doth it proceed, and unchanged throughout the years. Its course will it go upon my feet, mine old Will; hard of heart is its nature and invulnerable. Invulnerable am I only in my heel. Ever livest thou there, and art like thyself, thou most patient one! Ever hast thou burst all shackles of the tomb! In thee still liveth also the unrealisedness of my youth; and as life and youth sittest thou here hopeful on the yellow ruins of graves. Yea, thou art still for me the demolisher of all graves: Hail to thee, my Will! And only where there are graves are there resurrections."

That was Chapter 33 of *Zarathustra*, "The Grave-Song". And in the next chapter there's a further deliberation on the power of Will:

> "That is your entire will, ye wisest ones, as a Will to Power; and even when ye speak of good and evil, and of estimates of value. Ye would still create a world before which ye can bow the knee: such is your ultimate hope and ecstasy. The ignorant, to be sure, the people – they are like a river on which a boat floateth along: and in the boat sit the estimates of value, solemn and disguised. Your will and your valuations have ye put on the river of becoming; it betrayeth unto me an old Will to Power, what is believed by the people as good and evil."

Before this, in Chapter 31, Zarathustra speaks of light, spiritual indeed:

> "Light am I: ah, that I were night! But it is my lonesomeness to be begirt with light! Ah, that I were dark and nightly! How would I suck at the breasts of light! And you yourselves would I bless, ye twinkling starlets and glow-worms aloft! And would rejoice in the gifts of your light. But I live in mine own light, I drink again into myself the flames that break forth from me."

ACTIONISM

You get the drift. Nietzsche affirmed Will and Light, a spiritual lodestar in a miasma of mediocrity and passivity.

THE FLOOD

Nietzsche's Zarathustra is the spring flood breaking all barriers. In Chapter 56 ("Old and New Tables") this very metaphor, that of the spring flood, is employed, as such, very captivatingly, symbolizing, as it were, Will breaking its bonds of frozen conceptions of weakness and passivity:

> "When the water hath planks, when gangways and railings o'erspan the stream, verily, he is not believed who then saith: "All is in flux." But even the simpletons contradict him. "What?" say the simpletons, "all in flux? Planks and railings are still OVER the stream! OVER the stream all is stable, all the values of things, the bridges and bearings, all 'good' and 'evil': these are all STABLE!" Cometh, however, the hard winter, the stream-tamer, then learn even the wittiest distrust, and verily, not only the simpletons then say: "Should not everything – STAND STILL?" "Fundamentally standeth everything still" – that is an appropriate winter doctrine, good cheer for an unproductive period, a great comfort for winter-sleepers and fireside-loungers. "Fundamentally standeth everything still" –: but CONTRARY thereto, preacheth the thawing wind! The thawing wind, a bullock, which is no ploughing bullock—a furious bullock, a destroyer, which with angry horns breaketh the ice! The ice however—BREAKETH GANGWAYS! O my brethren, is not everything AT PRESENT IN FLUX? Have not all railings and gangways fallen into the water? Who would still HOLD ON to "good" and "evil"? "Woe to us! Hail to us! The thawing wind bloweth!" Thus preach, my brethren, through all the streets!"

This style as such may be captivating. It's very unusual for a philosopher. However, to render a critique of the above passage on conceptual grounds, this can be said: to philosophically state that everything is in flux, everything changes, is to be led astray by Maya of Illusion. Essentially the nature of reality is governed by eternal ideas, *eidoi*, resting forever in the mind of God.

To be like Nietzsche, to dethrone God and instead worship "change, life, evolution," leads nowhere. Instead you have to seek unity within, unity between your individual soul and the all-soul. The reality of God, in this sense, is the true "beyond good and evil": beyond everyday good and evil.

ETERNITY

He may have been an atheist, however, Nietzsche still sang praise and joy to higher realms. "For I love thee, O Eternity", q.v. *Zarathustra*, Chapter 60. He was into divine attitudes in saying "I tremble with divine desires" (Chapter 48) and in his conceptualizations of Dionysus. As I've shown in Chapter 19 of *Borderline*, Nietzsche was crypto-religious, a closet spiritualist.

Also, Nietzsche virtually discovered the "I AM" impulse by himself, without being inspired by Christ, whom he despised or, at best, ignored. When Nietzsche in Chapter 4 of *Thus Spake Zarathustra* mentions the following, it's a discovery of the power of the unconditioned Self:

> *""Ego," sayest thou, and art proud of that word. But the greater thing – in which thou art unwilling to believe—is thy body with its big sagacity; it saith not "ego," but doeth it."*

And, if the reader has a hard time understanding the archaic style, then the last line can be rendered as "that which does not say "I," but *is* I." Details aside, here Nietzsche was on to the elemental nature of having a Spiritual Self.

Nietzsche inhabits a grey area of philosophy, spiritualism and nihilism that's active and brimming with energy. The backbone of the creed is the volitional element. Nietzsche discovered Will and moved the world.

The Zarathustra book has many brilliant moments and passages, even anthem-like poems, quotable in themselves. I'll restrict myself to one further quote, from the end. In Chapter 80, "The Sign," Zarathustra is back where it all began, in his cave on a mountain. To be a preacher on a mountain is stylish, compare, for example, Jesus during the "Sermon on the Mount". The ever bright, ever inspiring phrases of Nietzsche in this case read like this:

> *"In the morning, however, after this night, Zarathustra jumped up from his couch, and, having girded his loins, he came out of his cave glowing and strong, like a morning sun coming out of gloomy mountains. "Thou great star," spake he, as he had spoken once before, "thou deep eye of happiness, what would be all thy happiness if thou hadst not THOSE for whom thou shinest! (...) Well! The lion hath come, my children are nigh, Zarathustra hath grown ripe, mine hour hath come: This is MY morning, MY day beginneth: ARISE NOW, ARISE, THOU GREAT NOONTIDE!" Thus spake Zarathustra and left his cave, glowing and strong, like a morning sun coming out of gloomy mountains."*

38. SPIRIT OF ACTIONISM

I will, I am, I think: that's the spirit of Actionism. "I am that I am the rebirth of divine inspiration": that's the spirit of Actionism.

SHAKESPEARE

In Shakespeare's plays there are many a good Actionist instance. Like this, from *Hamlet*, Act 4, Scene 4 (as for the word, "fust" it means "to rot"):
What is a man,

If his chief good and market of his time
Be but to sleep and feed? A beast, no more.
Sure, he that made us with such large discourse,
Looking before and after, gave us not
That capability and god-like reason
To fust in us unused.

That's the Actionist spirit. This is fire and movement, get going, action as being, operational esotericism.

In another Shakespeare play, *Julius Caesar*, we read lines like: "I'm the brother of danger... I am like the northern star. I am not afraid to tell gray-beards the truth...!" That's the Actionist spirit.

ACTIONISM

As for a third Actionist quote of Shakespeare, we, of course, have *Richard III:* "Victory rides on our helmets!"

I WANT

I want the strong to be just and the weak to discover their will, so that they can also be strong.

Men shall be strong and gentle. Women shall be sweet and warm.

We now live beyond 11/11 2011. We live beyond the Magic Zero-point. There's no risk for major war now. We no longer have to live in ruins. Yet people behave as if they do. So I say: beware of those who only have ruins inside them.

Prepare for peace. The current situation is one of emerging peace. What I see around me are reasons for peace, "Casus Pacis," as it were. But many people can't conceive of peace. They have war and destruction inside. Thus, make peace with yourself first, then get ready for peace. Today, there are social, economic and political issues to solve in the world. And The Powers That Be are bent on creating chaos and war. In all this, try to stand firm as a free, reflecting citizen, demand your right as a man, but don't go around peddling visions of a war that won't come.

We're building a new world with Active Idealism, the nuclear family and co-nationalism, all with a positive shaping. That's the Actionist spirit.

FREE

In the chapter on Kierkegaard (Chapter 36) I mentioned his idea on freedom: it's in the relation to God that man becomes what he essentially is, free and responsible at the same time. I interpret this as: by discovering our Inner Light, two things happen: we become free and are given a feeling of being elevated, of being something more than mere animals. In realizing our divine nature we feel the ability to live free, talk free, do whatever a man can, "being all that you can be," and at the same time get a sense of responsibility, a responsibility to nurture this character. Because a light has to be kindled or it will die out.

Nietzsche was also into the problem of freedom. He didn't reach as far as Kierkegaard in this respect, but he did indeed ponder the problem. He took a look at the opposite of freedom, slavery, and realized that not all men want to be free:

> *"Free, dost thou call thyself? Thy ruling thought would I hear of, and not that thou hast escaped from a yoke. Art thou one ENTITLED to escape from a yoke? Many a one hath cast away his final worth when he hath cast away his servitude. Free from what? What doth that matter to Zarathustra! Clearly, however, shall thine eye show unto me: free FOR WHAT?"*

Thus, we read in Chapter 17 of *Thus Spake Zarathustra*. This could remind you of Don Juan, Castaneda's teacher, who once said this about "cutting our chains of self-reflection," of stopping our internal monologue. Doing this "... is marvelous, but also very undesirable, for nobody wants to be free." [Castaneda 1991 p 89]

ASSORTED

Having chanced into Castaneda again, that Actionist regular, hereby some assorted quotes of his that lie close to the Actionist sentiment:

- "To like people or to be liked by people is not all one can do as a man." [1990 II p 94]
- "[T]hose who think they are above animals live worse than animals." [Ibid p 69]
- "To assume the responsibility of one's decisions means that one is ready to die for them." [1990 III p 59]
- "We either make ourselves miserable, or we make ourselves strong. The amount of work is the same." [1990 III p 198]

- "Seek and see the marvels all around you. You will get tired of looking at yourself alone, and that fatigue will make you deaf and blind to everything else." [1990 I p 52]

In short: that's the Actionist creed.

THE OPPOSITE

There's an Actionist spirit and there's a mindset rather opposed to it. Actionism doesn't shut anyone out; it welcomes anyone being ready to change, to acknowledge Will and Thought, affirming his Inner Light. Having said that, there are many attitudes that are anti-actionist in intent: like "being offended" by everything coming in your way, even trifles, like being overly concerned of what to do and not to do in social situations, the constant subject of today's comedy; like treating reality as a theoretical example and not putting yourself into the matrix; like not acknowledging your Inner Light, not acknowledging the role of Willpower in order to get things done, be it take a walk, pass an exam or climb a mountain; like flaunting every feeling, reacting on trigger words, resorting to name-calling and being a defeatist; like lacking self-restraint, honor and a sense of duty; like having a desert inside and projecting it to the world.

Actionism invites every person to stop being a decadent materialist and start acknowledging Will, Thought and Light. Having said that, from an operational point of view an Actionist has to avoid these kinds of persons, these "vexations to the spirit," those "disturbing the doers by saying it can't be done".

SPIRIT

This chapter is about the Actionist spirit. One author coming close to it was Hunter S. Thompson (1937-2005). In *Hell's Angels* (1966) he wrote about the essence of riding a bike, that of being close to the edge: *"The Edge... There is no honest way to explain it because the only people who really know where it is are the ones who have gone over."* [quoted from https://en.wikiquote.org/wiki/Hunter_S._Thompson]

He's on to something there. To live on the edge and not go over is the crux. How to do it then, not "go over"? It's done by willpower. If you live on the edge and feel like you're losing it, say to yourself: "I don't want to go over the edge, I want to remain on the edge."

That's the essence of using life on the edge as a mental elevator. It's the Actionist concept of raising yourself mentally by living on the edge. As the reader should know by now, it's conceptualized in ARYM = Action Raising You Mentally, as such, one of the ten basic acronyms of Actionism.

So then, does an Actionist live constantly on the edge, in a figurative sense being "constantly edgy"? No. An Actionist also rests (RIR = Rest In Rest), he mediates, he sleeps, he reads books and listens to music for pleasure.

But he's also capable of RIA = Rest In Action. And that means living on the edge fairly constantly, without "going over, going beyond, losing it". Instead, it means gaining energy from being in such an acting trance.

It's a difficult feat but it's a reality nonetheless, an instance being a mental reality, a psychological state to explore if you have the daring. That of experiencing MAASOM = Movement As A State Of Mind, of doing serious, operational stuff and feeling relaxed by it, day in/day out, year in/year out, all your life. The details of this were fairly well explained in the Operations Chapters (Chapters 14 - 18).

In short: Movement As A State Of Mind, Rest In Action and Action Raising You Mentally are the Actionist spirit *in nuce*.

> *"The Edge... There is no honest way to explain it because the only people who really know where it is are the ones who have gone over. The others – the living – are those who pushed their luck as far as they felt they could handle it, and then pulled back, or slowed down, or did whatever they had to when it came time to choose between Now and Later. But the edge is still Out there. Or maybe it's In."* [Thompson ibid]

There we have it: the Edge as a mental, inner phenomenon. It is you. Again, remember Aeon Flux, who when she was accused of "skating the edge" simply said, "I *am* the edge".

39. ACTIONIST POEMS

Once there was a man called Frank Herbert, the author of the *Dune* epic. Among other things, he succinctly conceptualized Willpower in his "Litany of Fear" (q.v. end of Chapter 23). In the same vein I will now try to conceptualize Actionism in the following poetic attempts.

THE HERO

The Hero faced the task:
move these bronze bulls, laid out
in cross-shape, and the shield will
be given you. And the Hero got going
and moved all the bulls at once,
symbolizing that in life you need both the
Cup of Sympathy and the Pentacle of
Valor, both the Sword of Reason and the
Wand of Intuition. Too much sympathy
makes you paralyzed, too much valor makes
you inhuman; too much reason makes you blind,
too much intuition makes you dissolute.

The Hero found a spear and a shield, he defeated
the Fire Dragon and the Beast. He told

ACTIONISM

*the Hovering City of Hell to move, letting the
sun shine in once again. He conquered
the Land of Decadence and planted the Heron
Banner on the hill, displacing the Snake Banner.*

*The Hero had inner calm, he meditated
on the I AM, he affirmed his Inner Light.
He let the Unicorn run free, cleansing
the lakes poisoned by the Fire Dragon;
he let the Eagle fly free, enabling a world of
heroic freedom, borne on the wings of eagles:
on the wings of eagles, we're heading for a Golden Age;
on the wings of eagles, preparing for another stage.*

SERGEANT F.

*Sergeant F. was ready to die,
having Memento Mori ingrained
in his being. He demanded of his
men what he demanded of himself:
to be ready to die.*

*There was no duty, honor, country.
There was only combat, only battle.
Only this was real, only this remained.*

*He was Movement As A State, Winning As
Propensity, Rest In Action. He said
to himself: I AM the battle, I move
with the battle. I AM.*

LENNART SVENSSON

MELINA STARR

Melina Starr, free at last,
walking through a park,
buying an ice-cream, hugging
children, enjoying a day off,
realized that she hated all this
R&R nonsense. What she actually
wanted was another mission, living
the operational life 24/7,
seeking rest in action.

RESPONSIBLE MAN

He wrote the rules for
the Game of Life: how to
always win, always be successful,
Winning As Propensity taught to
the people, to all and sundry, to you
and me, my sister and my brother,
my uncle and my cousin and the village oaf.

He conceptualized military history
into ten basic tenets, condensing
History of Man into a powder, just add
water, drink it and be reanimated.

He taught man I AM, willpower and
affirming of the Inner Light, thus enabling a
liberation movement freeing earth from
alien influence. He was the first Responsible
Man, he was the rebirth of God in Man, the
founder of the First Human Civilization,
taking man to interstellar realms and establishing

ACTIONISM

*contacts with positive aliens, the race of gods, raising
man to their level, creating the ultimate apotheosis.*

CLOUDY DAY

*Don't say it's rosy when it isn't.
We also need the cloudy, overcast day –
"a blue day, when life is hung out to dry."*

*We need contrasts to see wholes. We need
winter, however short. A clime of constant
sun can dry you, suck the life out of you.*

*When "a neutral mood" occupies you it
may have to run its course. However, you
must never be negative. Endemic fear and loathing have
no reality. Systematic negativity and indulging in
suffering lead nowhere.*

*Come grey sky, use it for a reboot,
a neutral pause. 51% percent
positively disposed is the Actionist way.*

FIGHT FOR FREEDOM

*Fight for freedom, fight for the planet,
fight for peace. Willpower is drafted and
sent to the front. It's a psychic war, a war
of nerves and I will win it. My energy
isn't spent, my armor isn't destroyed.*

*Will is the leader, Thought is the planner –
and somewhere in the van, along with parade
gear we have Sympathy, the readiness to*

*forgive your enemies. "Forgive us – if you can" –
they might say when we've defeated them and liberated
the poor and wretched from their dens of torture.
Seeing the victims of decadence, seeing their wounds, seeing
their corpses, we must look at the perps and pose this
question: can we forgive these criminals for their heinous
crimes?*

*We must be prepared to forgive them, entertain the
idea of forgiveness. There must be no "cry havoc,"
no drumhead court-martials; forgiveness
must come to the fore, however, executed from
a position of strength. Therefore, the war is still going on,
the battle still rages – the battle for Planetary Freedom, for
a future of co-nationalism, spirituality and safety for all,
for art, science and creativity, for Willpower and Light –
because, to will is to will the Light.*

ONTOLOGICAL LANDS

*Do you know where I am?
Seek me in the Ontological Lands,
you can find me there...*

IF NOT

*If not now, when?
If not me, who?
If not here, where?*

ACTIONISM

PILGRIM

*I'm a weary pilgrim coming
to a church, laying down
by the altar to sleep.*

*The sleep lasts an eternity –
and at the end of eternity
I wake, walking out into a
world transformed.*

GOLDEN CHILD

*I'm a flower of society,
a golden child,
come rule the golden age with me.*

*I've got gold in my bloodstream,
I'm a living, walking,
talking Fort Knox.*

*I see gold on the spire,
gold in the sunset, gold on
the sandstone, gold on the pine trunk –*

*gold medal, golden crown,
golden shoes, golden helmet,
golden fleecing – come share*

*the riches, come enter the
Golden Age, come see the gold
shining in the sun. You are gold.*

LENNART SVENSSON

WILLPOWER

Willpower wills itself,
wills the Light, wills
every action into a
reward in itself. I AM
is the formula, nullifying
every dualist delusion.

MYSTICAL WORLD

The Mystical World is the world where everything is of God,
where everything is animated,
where the essence of all is spiritual.
God flows through everything in the world,
in The Mystical World, a world where I live –

but I have to convince me of it every day,
each day having to meditate on the cosmic energy,
the energy that flows through the world,
the energy that is within me, that comes from God,

that is God.

ICH HATTE EINE KAMERADEN

Ich hatte eine Kameraden...
  I once had my comrades,
  I once had a little friend,
  I once had I life –
  I figure...

ACTIONISM

Now I meditate on
the I AM, seeing
the Inner Light, a mirror
of Lux Aeterna –
I live again, I live
here and now,
ain't it good to be alive...

This I say to you,
comrades and friends,
absent and present,
near or far, dead or alive.

SING THE ROAD

I sing the road as I walk,
I realize the road,
I singalize the road.

My singing is my walking,
my walking is my singing.

The road goes ever on,
the road is ever new
and still the same,
the goal is here
and the time is now:

THE POWER OF NOW.

LENNART SVENSSON

WINNER

*The winner drinking wine
from the golden chalice,
having completed his private crusade,
having fought the demons of his mind,
defeating them with Will and Thought.*

*The winner sauntering over the lawn, the
winner preparing for the victory banquet
in the palace – the winner thinking back
on his Days in Hell, waking with a cold
sweat every day, having to fight the demons,
having to live in a world of rain, stain, black ink –
remembering discovering Will, taking control
of his being, the remedy being "take a deep breath,
relax, calm down, let Will guide the Thought,
let them merge into Will-Thought and become
a high-grade alloy of determination, faith and courage."*

*The winner going to the Palace, the winner enjoying
the moment, the winner treasuring the Power of Now –
to thrive in the instant, to thrive in eternity, to live
forever and die now.*

WHY PREACH

*Why preach to people
with a heart of stone?
I'd rather sing to the birds,
the mountains, the trees.
I sing to the sky, humming
a mantra to the divine inside,
the soul-spark, the mirror of*

ACTIONISM

the godhead.
I AM that light,
ever shining light,
shining through the day,
shining through the night,
shining forever.

MYSTERIUM

Walking from room to room
in my condominium
in the glory of Byzantium,
my virtual aquarium.

Standing in the quiet of the Soul Room
not feeling gloom
for I live in post-calvarium,
the time after Christum
and his death on Golgathum.

Going from room to room
in this living aquarium
in the glory of Byzantium
and pondering a mysterium,
the riddle of universum.

CAMOUFLAGE

Going off to war with Camouflage?
Then settle your account with life.
Acknowledge death, prepare to die.

Camouflage draws a line in the sand

and says: "He who is afraid to die
can go to Hell. The rest of you, follow me."

Hard words from a hard man. But
not empty words. They are true
words, words from a real human being.

Camouflage is human. He has
seen everything, knows everything.
And yet these dreamer's eyes...

A dreamer and a realist, a genius, a madman,
a demigod. And the twinkle in the eye, shrapnel
in the ditch and gunfire in the distance.

Going off to war with Camouflage?
Can you endure his look? – Write
your will, sum up the gumption,

grab the rifle. Platoon right face,
forward march. "Goal: enemy army.
Direction: eternity." Death or Life,

win or lose, everything is equal
when you go to war with Camouflage.
You live here and now, you're the master

of the moment. You have the dream
in the eye, the bullet in the pocket
and the wind in the ears. That's your life,

your world, your breath. So onward
through the night, destination combat
zone, Hals und Beinbruch.

40. HYMN TO THE ACTIVE LIFE

We all have to act. Then, making a virtue of necessity, let's praise it, praise willpower and drive in the form of a "Hymn to the Active Life".

I AM FORMULA

Is there an answer to the riddle of "life, universe and everything?" British author Douglas Adams gave the answer in the form of a number: "42". But that was just satire. My personal, earnest, viable Answer to Everything, the basic Actionist formula, is this: "I AM".

FREEDOM

Freedom is to realize your limitations.

IDEALIST AVANTGARDE

I say: we must crush ignorance. It's time to eradicate materialism from the face of the earth. This is the rallying cry of Actionism.
 I mean, who, in his right frame of mind, can acknowledge materialism as an idea? It's the very absence of an idea, it's darkness

and despair. The same goes for defeatism. How can you be passionate about an approach leading to failure? Defeatism has got nothing to do with philosophy, it's a case of psychopathology.

We, the idealist avant garde, have to clean out the brothel of materialism the world has turned into.

CLEARLY

I don't use irony; there's no time for that any longer. I state my Actionist case, clearly and without reservation. It's time to inaugurate a new era of order, beauty and harmony, ending the reign of materialist nihilism.

PEACE

Actionism is a peaceful evolution. This is a peace process. This is a curing of the ills of our personal beings and of the world at large.
Actionism is a *Casus Pacis* = a reason for peace.
Actionism is a strategy to implement a peaceful evolution in the micro- and macrocosm, in our personal beings and in the world. To change the macrocosm we have to start in the microcosm. The individual has to work with himself. ESWY = Everything Starts With You.
The governance of tomorrow is one of Free Will, of shared prosperity, of human rights and responsibility, and justice and freedom of expression for all.
Reportedly, a fundamental of politics is this: "The secret of freedom is to educate people, the secret of tyranny is to keep them ignorant." Ergo, today tyranny is impossible since the truth always comes out on the internet, sooner or later.

ACTIONISM

POWER

Power is that which the rulers say they don't have.

DO YOU FEEL LUCKY?

I've got a question for you. Overall, in your life as a whole, do you experience joy, ecstasy and passion? Or do you experience sorrow, dejection and fear? Do you wake up saying, Hallelujah? Or do you wake with a curse on your lips?

TEACHER

I'm a teacher telling Western Man to summon his Will and create a new world. I'm a teacher saying to Western Man: leave your mindset of dejection, decadence and fear, and start building instead of destroying. Build yourself up, don't systematically castigate yourself, don't drag yourself down with "perfectionist programs" that you can't meet. Instead, learn WAP = Winning As Propensity, posit attainable goals and become ever successful in the game of life.

Posit the goal, "to take a deep, gentle breath = victory". Then take that breath. Then you're a winner.

Gentle breathing, gentle thinking. Apply the pattern of: attainable goals = successfully completed missions = victory upon victory. Rinse and repeat, how hard can it be?

NOW

We live in the Now, whether we like it or not. Essentially, past and future are illusions. Therefore, reinterpret your *everyday now* into an *eternal now* – and live forever.

DIVIDE

To be on the ascending side of the great divide… What I call "the great divide" is, on the one hand, people having some sort of spiritual, immaterial guiding light in their lives, and, on the other, people being materialist nihilists. The latter can indeed be guided by some fine values but, since these values aren't anchored in the ontological aspect of reality, they are essentially decadents, and as such, people rather impossible to reform, impossible to teach a spiritual outlook. Some can be reformed, but not all. Most of the materialist camp is on the not-ascending side of the great divide.

That's the condition of mankind right now. Not all of humanity will ascend. The not-ascending part will, according to esoteric theory, be relayed to a dimension with seemingly continued dualistic concepts. The rest will ascend, be elevated to the astral world and beyond.

That would be an explanation of "being on the ascending side of the great divide".

SYMBOLS AND EMBLEMS

A symbol Actionism could use would, for instance, be the Chalice. Here we ,for example, have The Holy Grail, a symbol of the Divine Energy, standing for everything that's noble, elevated and spiritual, in man and beyond. Adjectives describing this strain would be: Chalicism, Chalistic, Chalician, Chalisco. The Chalice as symbol of the female, in a time of increasing female energies. Other fine symbols are the Tree of Life and the Rising Sun, the Book of Life and the Tree of Knowledge.

Symbol: the Sagittarius arrow.

Symbol: the sunburst sign.

LIES

To allude to Newton's law of reaction you could say: every lie produces an equal and opposite counter-lie.

TIME

If time is measured movement, and movement is a state, then time doesn't exist because you can't measure a state.

CLOWNING

When watching clowning you may be forced to take on a fake nose, for in the clown's tent the Law of the Clown applies.

PROOF

On page 60 in *Borderline* we gather the wisdom of, "absence of proof isn't proof of absence". This can be seen as a critique of "argumentum ex silentio" = "argument from silence," indeed taking the absence of evidence to be evidence of absence. The paradigmatic, reductionist science of today often tends to the attitude that "there's no proof for phenomenon X, therefore it's proven that phenomenon X doesn't exist". But this is invalid since "absence of proof isn't proof of absence".

GOOD

"The only thing necessary for the triumph of evil is for good men to do nothing."

THOMPSON

Hunter S. Thompson said, that "when the going gets weird, the weird turn pro". In the same vein, you could say "when the going gets weird, get weirder".

JACKIE

Jackie Kennedy used to say, "I am here and yet I am not here". The Zen of being a party hostess...?

FIGHTING

Fighting is easy, living is hard.

HERE AND NOW

There is only the here and now: an endless here, an eternal now.

THOUGHTS

The brain creates no thoughts , but the thought creates the brain. More on this in *Borderline*.

DEATH

When you die some say that it gets dark, others say you meet a Being of Light. For some it brightens, for others it darkens.

INDIFFERENCE

Carl Sagan: "The universe seems neither benign nor hostile, merely indifferent." Don Juan of the Castaneda books also says something like that. Therefore, seek meaning in the Inner Light and project it to the outer world. As we are, so we see. What we ourselves think about the universe, matters. Like: I acknowledge my Inner Light as a fragment of the Divine Light, a light also manifested in the stars and the galaxies. With this in mind, the starry sky doesn't seem so indifferent.

NO PRISON

The Gnostic metaphor of existence as an "iron prison" essentially leads wrong, since as humans we always have our free Will. Essentially, the prison metaphor was invented by a weak person hating life, not an Active Esotericist taking charge of who he is.

EMBODYING THE CREED

Stanley came to Africa as an atheist, but after meeting Dr. Livingstone he was converted to Christianity. Stanley later recalled: "It was not Livingstone's preaching that converted me, it was Livingstone's living." Again, Life and Thought are inseparable, Will and Thought often being a single phenomenon.

BREATHE

You're never in such a hurry that you don't have time to catch your breath. One life, one breath.

STORY

Anyone can have an opinion about something. But not anyone can tell a funny story.

ARTISTIC FREEDOM

In art, "breaking every law" is easy if you don't know they exist. This is the strength of naivest art.

NIETZSCHE

"Life is a choice between suffering and boredom." Nietzsche, allegedly, said this. An Actionist would oppose this dejected attitude (an Actionist finds meaning in Will-Thought), however, it says something of the condition of modern man.

PLUS AND MINUS

To explain why some of us are optimists, some pessimists, you could use the terminology of, "negatively programmed – positively programmed". Our disposition goes beyond Will and Thought, often we simply "are" this way or that. Again, this is an example of "the Great Divide" spoken of previously in this chapter.

POUND

The need for action instead of sitting around waiting for someone else to act: "A slave is someone who waits for someone to come and free him." – Ezra Pound

ACTIONISM

HEIDENSTAM

Swedish poet, Verner von Heidenstam said: "He has faith, to whom much is holy." And, "miracles only happen to the faithful". In this respect the following wisdom comes in handy: "Build a temple and the gods will come."

ART

Created freely within a structure, the ideal artwork is tight but loose. More on this in *Borderline*.

NATURE OF THE QUOTE

The quotable element in prose is the poetic; the quotable element in poetry is the prosaic.

OPERATIONAL WISDOM

You're not defeated until you acknowledge yourself as defeated.

FORD

Henry Ford II used to say: "Never explain, never complain." This is an aristocratic attitude, elevated and equanimous, like Jünger's *désinvolture*.

LIFE TO THE LIVING

I preach life to the living, not death to the dying. The sun's still shining in the land of the living.

As an Actionist I'm a Teacher of Will, a Teacher of Power. I revive Will as a concept, I teach people to summon their Will and create a new world.

DECADENCE

To the dying defeatist strain within philosophy: take your reductionism, your utilism and behaviorism, get out of Antropolis, lock yourself up in your Deep Underground Military Bunkers = DUMB, and never bother us again.

DEDICATION

Dedication is a central element of the Actionist action. Dedication so strong that it propels a human being beyond his natural limitations, making him a bridgehead for the divine.

I don't compromise with materialism, not per se. I mean, I forgive the materialist ignorants, the defeatist madmen for spreading a false doctrine, but against the materialist doctrine as such, Actionism is ruthless. To establish Actionism, we must affirm the Light, the Inner Light. The materialist enemy must feel that a Tsunami of Idealism, a Hurricane of Reality is about to roll in, destroying the basis for the materialist creed forever. We must keep our dedication alive and fan it to an incandescent fountain of joy and celebration. The victory of idealism is assured only if we want it if we're dedicated to the cause of Will, Thought and Light.

Dedication is the central element of Actionist action. This is Operation Dedication.

PLANETARY

The current planetary struggle is about idealism versus materialism. When are you going to join forces with idealism, join the Light? You have to take sides. Not deciding to take sides is collaboration with the dark.

Make a decision...! Everyone has to do it. ESWY = Everything Starts With You.

If not you, who? If not now, when?

THE GLORY

The glory of meditation: to make your body into a temple and your heart into an altar.

Again, a fine mantra to meditate on is "I Am That Which Is", the Actionist concept expressing essential reality.

CREED

To sum up the Actionist creed in a couple of lines, you could say: no irony, no excuses. Never explain, never complain. State your case, clearly and without reservations.

State your case, live the creed – the creed of – There is only here and now – Take responsibility – Seek rest in action – Do what feels right – One life, one breath – Nothing exists, and everything – Everything connects and still doesn't.

ACTION TIME

This is Actionism. It's Action Time – time to liberate earth from materialism, and time to inaugurate an era of peace, harmony and inspiration.

41. ACTIONIST SUMMARY

Hereby a summary of Actionism in the form of various lists. They summarize concepts, acronyms, basic tenets and then some.

ACTIONIST CONCEPTS

If I begin with a list of "actionist concepts", I get the following – a list of terms like "action as being," "active idealism," "frequency war" and "magic zero-point".

- - -

- Action as Being – we all have to act. To be is to act, to act is to be. I act, therefore I am = *ago, ergo sum*.
- Active Esotericism – see "Active Idealism".
- Active Idealism – to act in accordance with Being, to affirm the affinity of Will and Light. To acknowledge the dictum, "God helps the one who helps himself." Conversely, to merely wait for divine grace is passive idealism. (A virtual synonym to Active Idealism is "Active Esotericism".)
- Active Thought Framework – a synonym for Actionism, stressing the merging of Will and Thought.
- Aristocrat of the Soul – a learned man, a man governed by

ACTIONISM

Tradition and Eternal Values, having knowledge of literature, art and Perennial philosophy.
- Assuming Responsibility – responsibility is one of the prime expressions of Will. To take charge of your life, to be accountable for your actions; conversely, not to blame others; this is the Actionist concept of responsibility. It's about living in the here and now and facing life head on.
- *Casus Pacis* = a Reason for Peace (as opposed to the old concept of "casus belli" = a reason for war). Actionism is part of a peaceful evolution. Essentially, this is a peace process, a curing of the ills of our personal beings and of the world at large.
- Esotericist Paradigm – Actionism has an esoteric, inner, God concept. Conceiving of God as an inner force, seeing man's Inner Light as an aspect of the Eternal Divine Light, is the basic element of the Esotericist Paradigm. Conversely, up until now the Westworld has employed an exoteric, outer concept of God, making man strive for something exterior when turning away from materialism and starting to live a more spiritual life. But now the search has got to be directed inward, to the realization of a person's Inner Light being a fragment of the Divine Light; this is employing the Esotericist Paradigm.
- Frequency War – Western Mainstream Media is bent on lowering people's mental frequency, making them sad and pessimistic. Instead, a mind being optimistic and positive vibrates higher. To counter the MSM shenanigans, primarily by ignoring them, is step one to win the Frequency War. Step two is to meditate on the I AM, summon your willpower and shape your life positively. No one can defeat a Will-endowed individual affirming his spiritual Self. More on Frequency War in Chapter 23.
- Integral Esotericism – in ancient India the way to God was delineated in four separate ways, mârgas. The way of knowledge, the way of meditation, the way of dedication, the way of actions – respectively, jnâna, dhyâna, bhakti and karma mârga. But they are not mutually exclusive, in fact, the latter-day idea of *integral yoga* unites them all. The Responsible Man can meet God and

express his creed both by knowledge, mediation, devotion and acts. Another aspect of this kind of Integral Esotericism is to acknowledge Plotinus' dictum of "everything is harmony, formed of opposites".
- Magic Zero-point – 11/11 2011 was a portal to a new spiritual era. After this date, the Magic Zero-point, there's not any longer the possibility of a major war. More on this in Chapter 22.
- Midsummer Century – we're heading for the Midsummer Century, the Coming Golden Age.
- Responsible Man – the Responsible Man takes charge of himself, both his physical and spiritual being. He assumes responsibility for his every breath, every thought, every action. As such, he's the man of tomorrow, the building block of a spiritual society. The Responsible Man is a knowing esotericist taking charge for whom, what and where he is. He isn't "thrown out into the world" in the Heidegger sense of "*geworfen*," neither can he see himself as "condemned to freedom" as Sartre saw man's condition. For more on Responsible Man, see the Coda following right after this chapter.
- Supra-conscious – trance-like, as if in a state of trance.
- Will-Thought – the combined element of Will and Thought. Example: a person decides to become a more harmonious person. Is the origin of this "a Thought" or is it mere Will exerting its force? Since it's hard to decide which, it's convenient to call this an instance of "Will-Thought impelling him to become a more harmonious person".

ACRONYMS

The reader is by now familiar with the Actionist acronyms. These abbreviations might be of some use. The acronym, used with some restraint, is a fine way of conceptualizing the world. As for a memorable acronym, I come to think of Heinlein's TANSTAAFL = "there ain't no such thing as a free lunch," symbolizing the no-

nonsense Responsible Men making up the Moon colony of the novel *The Moon Is a Harsh Mistress* from 1966.

The Actionist Acronyms are meant as a support for the mind in remembering the various ideas and concepts of the creed. They are not meant to be memorized as such, making the Actionist into some robot rattling off incomprehensible sounds, speaking in code.

However, for the person wishing to memorize some acronyms, see the list "The Ten Basic Tenets of Actionism" later in this chapter. In all, the acronyms listed below are eighteen (18) in number.

A musical spirit, an attitude of being guided by the Muses, as such, a sense of playfulness and ease, is integral to the Actionist mindset; conversely, the Actionist mind is not a Titanic mind, guided by rigid systems. Therefore the list of Acronyms is to be taken as a guide, not a program to follow slavishly. There is some method to the various sections of acronyms below (ethics, metaphysics, operations). However, since Actionism is a total way of knowledge it's hard to separate the essence of some acronyms, some of them having a bearing on more than one field. Such multi-purpose acronyms are ESWY (Everything Starts With You), FIA (Faith In Action) and OYTO (Opening Yourself To Opportunity), to name but a few. However, they, and other grey-area acronyms, aren't placed in several departments, they only occur once.

ETHICS

- ABY = Affirmatively Being Yourself = choosing to be the one you are, realizing the limitless possibilities of your personal being. Cf. Nietzsche's "wie man wird, was man ist" and someone else's "become someone different – yourself".
- ANOTT-BOTSOTT = Act Not On The Thing, But On The Soul Of The Thing". This is a way to ennoble every act, turning away from its immediately material purpose and making action into a l'art-pour-l'art. For example, when going shopping, act not with the single purpose of "buying proteins to keep my body alive";

act on the soul of going shopping and enjoy the ride as such, say hello to people you meet, thereby exemplifying the archetype of the Good Neighbor.
- ESWY = Everything Starts With You = realizing that a calm mind is the basis of everything = always calm down, always be C3, whether you're about to "act" or to "contemplate".
- FIA = Faith In Action = faith, God-realization, can never be a theoretical exercise = it has to be integrated into your daily life = because we all have to act.
- MMM = Memento Mori Mindset = to be aware of your mortality = to know that you're going to die = knowledge of the limited lifespan of your physical body, this knowledge ultimately giving you mental calm. "Memento mori" is Latin for, "know that you are mortal".
- OYTO = Opening Yourself To Opportunity = allowing your being to embrace the energies needed for change.
- RAWALTAFA = Rather Acting Wrongly And Learning Than Abstaining From Action = we all have to act = the trial and error of life.
- RIR = Rest In Rest = seeking rest in rest, peace in peace, silence in silence. The usual way of relaxing; you don't always have to "get going" in order to relax (q.v. RIA = Rest in Action).
- SEP = Shaping Existence Positively = to make your life into a project, an artwork = affirmatively "doing what you can with what you have where you are".
- WTPOY = Will To Power Over Yourself = an Actionist interpretation of Nietzscheanism, making the individual the focus of the volitional life.

METAPHYSICS

- TIOHAN = There Is Only Here And Now!

OPERATIONS

- ASARIT = A Strong And Responsible Idealist, Taking charge = the Actionist is a paragon of vigor and responsibility, embodying Schwarzkopf's dictum: "When placed in command, take charge."
- ARYM = Action Raising You Mentally = get going and have your inner mind become more lucid, the action clarifying your thoughts *en passant*. ARYM is about "raising yourself mentally by living on the edge" = operational activity as an intelligence tool, clarifying and structuring your mind en passant. It's about living on the edge as mental elevator. As such, it's a phenomenon akin to the Actionist concept of NAMO (q.v.) and to Cyril Fall's concept of "readiness to fight for information". Some things aren't understood, realized or acknowledged unless you get going; you sound out your inner mind by becoming active, having the thoughts clarifying themselves while you're engaged in any kind of action. It's also akin to Nietzsche's idea of "only those thoughts that come by walking have value," that is, thoughts having clarified themselves while you were out walking.
- COTAK = Conducting Operations To Attain Knowledge = making education into an intelligence operation = the recon patrol as a symbol of getting smarter, getting a wider outlook, becoming more informed.
- MAASOM = Movement As A State of Mind = the trance-like phenomenon when you experience movement not as measurable but as something static, yet free and fluid, something like "an eternal here, an ever-present now," going nowhere and everywhere, being no one and everybody at the same time.
- NAMO = Napoleonic Modus Operandi, expressed in Napoleon's own words as, "on s'engage et puis on verra" = "get going, then take a look around" = get going operationally in order to clarify the situation. Some situations can't be grasped by merely sitting and watching, you have to become engaged in them to fully fathom them. This Napoleonic "activism" is akin to the wisdom of Colin Powell, the advice to the subaltern / platoon leader

being, "Don't just stand there, do something!"
- RIA = Rest In Action = to rest while doing something. It's the Tao of acting: "act as if you didn't act". This is Zen-style relaxing-while-acting, being 100% concentrated and 100% at peace. In the novel *Savrola*, Winston Churchill told about a hero with this trait, a man of action shaping his life actively, seeking *rest in action*, the ability to experience movement as a state.
- WAP = Winning As Propensity = learning to win = to constantly posit attainable goals in your personal operation and, having reached them, acknowledge them as the victories they are.

THE TEN BASIC TENETS OF ACTIONISM

If I should summarize the Actionist creed in ten acronyms, it would be the following.

- - -

1. C3 – Calm, Cool and Collected
2. WTPOY – Will To Power Over Yourself
3. MMM – Memento Mori Mindset
4. ARYM – Action Raising You Mentally
5. MAASOM – Movement As A State Of Mind
6. WAP – Winning As Propensity
7. RIA – Rest In Action
8. RIR – Rest in Rest
9. TIOHAN – There Is Only Here And Now
10. ESWY – Everything Starts With You

THE FIVE CENTRAL CONCEPTS OF ACTIONISM

The reader might ask: "Above was listed the central Actionist tenets in acronym form, however, where is that formula being 'the answer to life, the universe and everything,' the statement unifying man with God, action with being, ethics with ontology – I AM?" That's a viable question. Therefore I will below list "The Five Central Concepts Of Actionism," wisdoms not suited to make acronyms of as such, and the list is indeed topped by I AM.

- - -

1. I Am
2. Active Idealism
3. Responsible Man
4. Action as Being
5. Midsummer Century

ACTIONISM IN 36 WORDS

When writing novels you're advised to write a synopsis at the beginning of the file containing the manuscript. This should also be done for nonfiction books and essays. And in that spirit, here's a 36 word summary of what Actionism is.

- - -

Actionism is about summoning your Will to lead your Thought, merging the two to Will-Thought and affirming the Inner Light, a spark of the Divine Light. To all this, saying "I AM" is the performative confirmation.

CODA: RESPONSIBLE MAN

The key figure of Actionism is the Responsible Man. The human archetype for Actionism is the Responsible Man. Responsible Man is Willpower embodied. Responsible Man takes responsibility for his every breath, every thought, every action. Responsible Man takes charge of who he is, as a spiritual being and a private citizen, and as such, he's the building block of the future governance because politics are all about assuming responsibility.

Responsible Man takes charge of everything he encounters. When noting that he's a soul, he takes charge of this, meditating on his metaphysical essence, his "I AM". When noting that he's an *embodied* soul he takes charge of this, nurturing and taking care of his body. When noting that he's a societal individual he takes charge of this, giving everyone their due according to Will, Truth and Compassion.

- - -

Responsible Man is the man of tomorrow. The time is up for dandies, degenerates, materialists, defeatists, relativists, dolts, wine-bibblers and blockheads. The time is up for drugged zombies of all kinds: zombies drugged on excessive food, zombies drugged on wine and liquor, zombies drugged on psychotropic stimulants, zombies drugged on media, zombies drugged on their sense of helplessness.

The time is up for all these degenerates. The time is here for a man taking charge. The time is here for Responsible Man.

ACTIONISM

- - -

Responsible Man takes control of his thought and his breath. He has Willpower to the fore in his being. This microcosmic control is the basis for a macrocosmic control. By controlling his breath, Responsible Man controls the world.

Show me a man who controls his breath, and I'll show you a man who controls the world.

Responsible Man controls his breath and thus controls the world, the micro- and the macrocosm. Responsible Man is Willpower embodied. Responsible Man acts as if he doesn't act, seeking rest in action. Responsible Man defines "victory" as "being able to take a deep, gentle breath" and so becomes ever victorious in the game of life.

Responsible Man lives in an eternal here, an ever-present now.

Responsible Man is free because he knows that he's responsible for everything he does.

Responsible Man says, "I AM", and so he's ready for anything.

DISCLAIMER

Central to the doctrine of Actionism is responsibility. Therefore, I, Lennart Svensson, as the author of this book and creator of the creed of Actionism, am *conceptually* responsible for the ideas, views and narratives presented in this volume. And you, as the reader, are *existentially* responsible for your reaction to it. You are responsible for the way you personally choose to relate to the ideas, views and narratives presented in this book.

SOURCES

Abelar, Taisha: *The Sorcerer's Crossing*. New York: Viking Books, 1992

Agerskov, Michael: *Vandra mot ljuset* (Danish original, Vandrer mod lyset, 1916). Stockholm: Amelins förlag 1995

Atkinson, David M.: *Leadership – By the Book*. Camarillo: Xulon Press, 2007

Bolling, Anders in Dagens Nyheter 6/9 2012: *Minskande krigstrend bröts*

Castaneda, Carlos: *The Teachings of Don Juan* (1968). London: Arkana, 1990 I

   – *A Separate Reality* (1971). London: Arkana, 1990 II

   – *Journey to Ixtlan* (1972). London: Arkana, 1990 III

   – *Tales of Power*. New York: Simon & Shuster, 1974

   – *The Second Ring of Power*. London: Hodder and Stoughton, 1977

   – *The Fire From Within* (1984). London: Black Swan, 1985

   – *The Power of Silence* (1987). New York: Pocket Books, 1991

Combüchen, Sigrid: *Om en dag man vaknar*. Stockholm: Norstedts, 1995

d'Annunzio, Gabriele: *Elden* (Il fuoco, 1900). Stockholm: N&K, 1946

d'Este, Carlo: *Patton – A Genius for War*. New York: HarperCollins, 1995

Evola, Julius: *Meditations on the Peaks – Mountain Climbing as Metaphor for the Spiritual Quest* (1974). Rochester: Inner Traditions, 1998

- *Metaphysics of War*. London: Arktos 2011

- *The Mystery of the Grail* (1938). Rochester: Inner Traditions, 1997

- *Path of Cinnabar* (1963). London: Integral Tradition Publishing, 2009

- *Revolt Against the Modern World* (1934). Rochester: Inner Traditions, 1995

- *Ride the Tiger* (1961). Rochester: Inner Traditions, 2003

- *The Yoga of Power* (1968). Rochester: Inner Traditions, 1992

Grip, Göran: *Allting finns*. Stockholm: Forum, 1994

Guénon, René: *The Crisis of the Modern World* (1927). Hillsdale, NY: Sophia Perennis, 2001

Hansen, H. T.: Foreword to Evola, Julius, *Men Among the Ruins*. Rochester: Inner Traditions, 2002.

Hayes, Stephen K.: *Ninja – Spirit of the Shadow Warrior*. Burbank: Ohara Publications, 1980

- *Warrior Ways of Enlightenment*. Burbank: Ohara Publications, 1981

Janos, Leo, and Yeager, Charles: *Yeager: An Autobiography*. Toronto: Bantam, 1985

Jünger, Ernst: *Der Kampf als inneres Erlebnis*. Berlin: Mittler, 1922

- *Über die Linie*. Frankfurt: Klostermann, 1950

- *Eumeswil*. Stuttgart: Ernst Klett Verlag, 1977

Melchizedek, Drunvalo: *The Ancient Secret of the Flower of Life*. Sine Loco, 1998

Random, Michel: *Japan – Strategy of the Unseen*. Wellingborough (GB): Crucible, 1987

Skott, Staffan: *Det nya Ryssland och arvet efter Sovjet*. Stockholm: Hjalmarsson & Högberg, 2009

Spengler, Oswald: *Västerlandets undergång – konturer till en morfologi om världshistorien*. 1. Gestalt och verklighet 2. Världshistoriska perspektiv (1918-1922). Stockholm: Atlantis, 1996

Stagg, Delano: *Blodig strand* (*Bloody Beaches*, 1961). Stockholm: B. Wahlströms Bokförlag, 1979

Svensson, Lennart: *Borderline – A Traditionalist Outlook for Modern Man*. Melbourne: Numen Books, 2015

- *Eld och rörelse*. Uppsala: Etherion, 2007

- *Antropolis*. Uppsala: Etherion, 2009

Walsch, Neale Donald: *Conversations With God*. London: Penguin, 1995

- *Friendship With God*. London: Penguin, 1997

- *Communion With God*. London: Penguin, 2000

- *The New Revelations*. London: Penguin, 2002

- *Tomorrow's God*. London: Penguin, 2004

Wilgus, Neal: *The Illuminoids*. London: New English Library, 1980

ABOUT THE AUTHOR

Lennart Svensson (1965-) is a Swede, still living in the Kingdom of Sweden although he mostly writes in English these days. He's known for his biography of Ernst Jünger and the conceptual essay *Borderline – A Traditionalist Outlook for Modern Man* (2015). In Swedish he has also published novels and he's currently preparing more essays and novels. In his spare time he enjoys art and music and the collecting of model soldiers.

INDEX

Action as Being 24, 29, 32-35, 51, 311-312, 332, 335, 336, 371-373, 392, 418, 446, 453
Akhenaten 194, 196
Anti-white 210, 378
Antropolis 6, 37-38, 166, 181, 217, 228, 234-235, 239, 244, 250-251, 253, 255-264, 296, 319, 324, 347-348, 379, 393-394, 444, 458
ARYM (Action Raising You Mentally) 30, 31, 33, 39, 52, 115, 132, 147, 150, 158, 161, 422, 449, 452
Bacon, Sir Francis 197
Bacon, Roger 197
C3 (Calm, Cool, and Collected) 21-25, 28-29, 35, 39, 52, 54, 115, 149, 219, 221, 231, 238, 354, 364, 374, 389, 391, 410, 448, 452
Caesar, Julius 40, 147, 223, 418
Campbell, Josef 389
Casanova, Giaccomo 179
Castaneda, Carlos 8, 24, 28-29, 30, 32, 40, 43, 60, 66, 68, 70-76, 90, 108, 201, 355, 364, 375, 379, 397, 406, 420, 439, 456
Co-nationalism 207-211, 215, 229, 232, 246, 348, 370, 419, 428
CPPCG 210-211
d'Annunzio, Gabriele 39, 90-108, 456
Economic growth 203, 229-230, 234, 239
Engdahl, Per 207
Escoffier, Charles Auguste 159
ESWY (Everything Starts With You) 52, 148, 235, 347, 364, 371-372, 388, 407, 411, 436, 445, 449, 450, 452
Evola, Julius 10, 41, 43, 45, 71, 79, 87-90, 108-126, 150-151, 195, 197, 201, 249, 315, 317, 357, 366, 399, 456
Falls, Cyril 32, 43
Goethe, Johann Wolfgang von 10, 13, 61, 185, 201, 275, 292, 302, 315, 322, 362, 374, 388, 400
Hillary, Richard 35, 40
ICERD 210-211
Individuation 85, 235
Jung, Carl 292
Jünger, Ernst 10, 39, 43-44, 53, 64, 77, 99-100, 110, 113, 169, 179, 201, 217, 243, 250, 268, 274, 286-287, 289, 302, 315, 317, 322, 328, 330, 352, 388, 400, 408, 412, 443, 457, 459

Kali Yuga 38, 110, 215, 245, 249, 280, 289, 299, 315, 347, 393
Kennedy, John F. 198-200, 220, 317, 440
Kierkegaard, Sören 67, 84, 201, 383, 406-410, 419, 420
Lawrence of Arabia 127-129
MAASOM (Movement As A State Of Mind) 52, 148, 158, 165, 188, 266, 281, 422, 451-452
Magic Zero-point 245-246, 249, 279, 380, 393, 418, 446, 448
Mahâtma Gandhi 371
McCandless, Christopher 34, 40, 162-164
Melchizedek, Drunvalo 193-196, 457
MMM (Memento Mori Mindset) 16, 28, 30, 39, 52-54, 83, 115, 139, 152, 266, 375, 450, 452
Moltke, Helmuth von 141, 159
Napoleon 27-28, 43, 105, 142, 146-147, 153, 223, 243, 254, 451
Nationalism 203-206, 207
Nietzsche, Friedrich 31, 37-40, 48, 50, 61, 99-100, 109-110, 115, 118, 121, 123, 215, 275, 317, 333, 343, 358, 364, 366, 372, 404, 407, 412-413, 415-417, 420, 442, 449, 451
Operations 5-6, 27, 29, 32, 43-45, 52, 55, 98, 133, 137, 139-141, 154-155, 162, 166, 176, 180, 183-185, 187-188, 266, 312, 332, 335, 355-357, 422, 449, 451
Patton, George S. 54-55, 456
Perfectionist fallacy 150, 357, 358, 359, 371, 376
Poe, Edgar Allan 271, 273
Politics 6, 8-10, 12, 85, 101, 108, 114, 123, 125, 127, 198-199, 203-204, 229-230, 232-234, 242, 250, 301, 371, 380, 436, 454
Remarque, Erich Maria 151
Responsible Man 20, 38, 40, 45, 53, 231, 335, 336, 392, 426, 448, 453, 454, 455
RIA (Rest In Action) 26, 52, 147, 158, 163, 237, 266, 311, 355, 362-363, 422, 451-452
RIR (Rest In Rest) 26, 52, 57, 355, 397, 422, 450
Roosevelt, Theodore 198
Sat Yuga 38, 43, 215-17, 245, 249, 280, 289, 299, 303, 345, 346, 392
Schwarzkopf, Norman 19, 33, 41, 53, 70, 139, 233, 451
Shaw, G. B., 48, 364-366, 393
Skott, Staffan 173
Steiner, Rudolf 19, 90, 121, 196
Södergran, Edith 43, 49, 62, 99, 182, 302, 315, 317, 397, 410
Taylor, A. J. P. 173
Thoth 193-195, 197
TIOHAN (There Is Only Here And Now) 52, 57, 337, 368, 450, 452
Wallensteen, Peter 213-214, 217
WAP (Winning As Propensity) 29, 42, 53, 115, 177, 237, 355, 358, 402, 437, 452
Weil, Simone 381, 402, 405
Wilcock, David 201-202, 219-221
Wilson, Woodrow 198
WTPOY (Will To Power Over Yourself) 17, 39, 42, 53, 138-139, 372, 413, 450, 452
Yeager, Charles 54-55, 457

www.ingramcontent.com/pod-product-compliance
Lightning Source LLC
Chambersburg PA
CBHW080722230426
43665CB00020B/2581